MANUAL FOR EMERGING ARCHITECTS

wonderland

MANUAL FOR EMERGING ARCHITECTS

Edited by
wonderland platform for european architecture
Silvia Forlati and Anne Isopp
with Astrid Piber

2nd, revised edition

Birkhäuser
Basel

This manual is a collection of expert contributions, firsthand accounts from practices, and a series of five poll-based surveys on how to conceive, establish, develop and run an architectural practice today. Since 2006, when we started to work on these issues, the conditions for architect practices have changed, also because of economic crises and of an evolving attitude about Europe. It is clear that the situation will continue to evolve in directions we cannot yet foresee. This manual does not, and cannot, offer definitive answers for now or for the future. Instead, our intention is to provide the specific information needed to get a picture of the situation that we find ourselves in. We hope that this will help emerging architects to find their own way into the realm of planning and building and to make informed career decisions; also, we hope this manual will encourage new questions and finding new answers about the possible role of architects in the coming future.

Silvia Forlati and Anne Isopp

prologue

wonderland started as an exhibition for and by eleven young Austrian architects in 2002. It has since developed into a European platform for emerging architectural practices that supports collaborative projects such as collective exhibitions and project spaces. Its first transnational project was the **wonderland** Europe Tour, which, between 2004 and 2006, connected 99 practices from nine European countries.

"... can hardly wait for the change to happen!"

Silvia Forlati and *Anne Isopp,* co-initiators and co-editors of this **wonderland** volume, met *Tina Gregorič* and *Michael Obrist*, who took part in the **wonderland** tour with their practices *dekleva gregorič arhitekti* and *feld72.* Both currently work as professors of architecture at the Vienna University of Technology. We sat down to discuss what has changed in the industry over the past ten years and what challenges architectural practice is faced with today.

wonderland: Since our beginnings in 2002, we have been following and analyzing how the profession evolves and what challenges it faces. The two of you were just starting your practice in the early days of wonderland. What challenges were you confronted with at the time, and what is different for emerging young architects today?

Michael Obrist: The big difference is that, back then, there were still open competitions. And nobody needed a portfolio to get in. There were two ways of acquiring projects. One was to become initiative as providers of the concept or the process and then to go out and find allies who would help you realize the project. This worked well under certain conditions. The other possibility was to take part in competitions. A lot of what we developed in public space at the time is now a regular part of the university syllabus.

Tina Gregorič: Each young office at the time had a different starting point. The only common ground was the enormous amount of open competitions where you could submit proposals without any prior references. And this was an opportunity to get bigger commissions. It was of course important that, as a young office, we could take part in any competition. Nowadays, no young office in Slovenia or anywhere else in Europe has the same conditions we had at the beginning of the 21st century.

My partner Aljoša Dekleva and I spent almost two years at the Architectural Association in London researching the radical approach of mass customization in collective housing. When we came back to Ljubljana, we wanted to prove, based on our research at the AA, that it was actually possible to build new socially aware neighbourhoods. We had to start with the smallest possible commission, a 43 square-meter house. It was in the residential domain that we were allowed to challenge the obvious, but we also had to take on a three-year-long fight with building-regulation authorities. This first project was proof that it takes fighting at all levels, from detailing to administration, to achieve the standard of architecture we believe in. Now, 15 years later, I still believe it was an extremely formative experience for our practice. What it taught us is that we will not achieve anything without heart and fight.

wonderland: There are still young architects today who want to start their own offices. What advice would you want to give them?

6

Tina Gregorič: Challenge authorities and call for a competition system similar to that in Switzerland, where both established and young offices with no prior references in that particular field are invited to compete. Fight for this way to organize competitions and get commissions.

wonderland: Changing the rules of the game is surely important, but could we, just for the moment, go back to the opportunities and challenges you see for offices that are starting now? Those younger offices, where are they heading? And how should they do it?

Michael Obrist: Speaking of young architects, I don't think we need to worry much about ideas. Every generation produces an enormous amount of ideas and is full of hungry young people who take up architecture. I think, it's about how we can bring creativity together with a chance of earning a livelihood. There are certain jobs for which will earn you a huge amount of money, but if you put the label of "architecture" on it, it's over. And that's completely absurd. It destroys offices, it destroys possibilities, particularly for beginners in the industry.

wonderland: Do you think young architects can only survive in certain countries?

Tina Gregorič: There is no universal answer to this. Not in any single country nor in the European Union or anywhere else. It's actually about rules and legislations linked with extremely localized conditions. It is those systems that define your opportunities. Take Denmark, for example. Why is there so much progress in certain typologies in terms of public education and public health in this particular country? And why is architecture there on a completely different level than in most other European countries? It's because of the particular systems and backgrounds and rules by which the Danish offices operate. The rules they put in place years ago based on a sixty-year tradition of high-class design now allow all the young or non-young offices to try out new things and benefit from them. They do transform their own social reality and environment at a one-to-one scale. I think that young offices can hardly wait for the change to happen. It's our moral obligation to define the environment in which the young offices will be able to participate and help create the future.

wonderland: Do you think that it used to be possible to get a foot in the door plug and receive commissions and then pursue your own agenda in the competitions system while today getting a foot in has become way more difficult and you need to adjust your projects accordingly?

Michael Obrist: Not necessarily. You already find yourself in an environment of change if you consider what people want. It is completely different from when we started. Architecture was a very unique act somewhere in the open landscape or in the city. But right now, clients are much more open. We have a very informed society as well as highly informed young offices. You don't have to be highly educated, you just have to be informed. And you can be the game changer who brings certain new ideas to certain new places and does interesting things.

Tina Gregorič: As a young architect, you have different opportunities to participate in this proliferated version of the profession of architect. When it comes to competitions, there's one huge problem: all the systems put in place in Europe in the last 15 years require established references and bank guarantees even before you can even throw your hat in the ring. It's a game that only established firms can afford to play. So all the creative young architects are driven more towards the artistic, research, the abstract, writing, without even thinking that they could ever design and build something in real life. And this is the biggest fear I have, as a professor and an observer, about how these creative minds are dealing with the system: that there might not be enough great minds left to actually build and create the real-life built environment. I advise all my diploma students to realize their projects in their respective hometowns, to present their projects to local authorities. This way they could start something which could become a reality in various different ways in the community they come from.

wonderland: It is very interesting that you should teach your students how to deal with the system. What are the skills that training or education needs to provide? How broad should the range be? Should it include the construction process, participative planning, dealing with society? Where are the opportunities?

Michael Obrist: They are everywhere. If you move to the country, you are not just the architect moving to the country, but a highly educated person poised to change that world. This has already transformed what used to be called "the province" into something else and pushed it in different directions.

Tina Gregorič: Officially, studying architecture is a design training with the goal of enabling you to construct houses or parts of a city, but it also allows you to do, and become, something completely different, because the least you will learn during those five years is that the only way to solve problems is creative thinking. But assuming that we are still going to have some architects left, they must be able to conceive, and execute, design and building projects large or small, "from the spoon to the town," as proclaimed by Ernesto Rogers. They have to understand that there are standards – too many of them, to be sure – which they have to address early enough in their projects in order to challenge them or find ways around them if they want to do something that is relevant and not conformist. If you just meet all the standards, you won't be able to make any headway. Speaking of skills needed, we should actually be able to address the wider contexts in which architecture operates.

Michael Obrist: As a student of architecture, you go from analysis to synthesis. And if you are not able to achieve the synthesis within yourself, you can achieve it through the larger entity of the office. The office is made up of different people who are able to react to a problem. You don't have all the control. The office can react as a whole to certain kinds of things. And I think this is precisely the advantage of our profession, that we are able to shape something as a result of all this combined knowledge and thinking.

wonderland: Why are students more interested in doing artwork or participation rather than taking on real construction tasks?

Tina Gregorič: If you venture to start a practice or studio, on your own or in a collective, conditions are great for those kinds of projects, and sometimes you will remain in this field. There are more and more international platforms glorifying this direction to the point that it is actually becoming the other side of reality. Yes,

I think it's an escape from reality. We should also start changing the system so that smart young architectural studios may stand a real chance of getting their hands on some actual construction, given that we as a society will not stop building any time soon.

wonderland: When we started wonderland, we were under the impression that in Slovenia there were a lot of opportunities to build really big projects. Here in Austria, a lot of teams started out doing an art project here and a participation project there. What should young people in the profession do if all they can land in the beginning is art projects?

Michael Obrist: First of all, we didn't call them art projects. And nobody could survive by just doing participatory stuff. We started this because we believed in real-life projects. But we didn't want to wait until the big opportunity came along. We wanted to get hold of reality. Sometimes, reality was much more radical than all those ideas of how our society could be shaped, and we tried to take that as a starting point. So, it was not that we wanted to do an art project. The interesting thing for us is a practice that brings the two things together. One reason we get invited so much these days is precisely because we are able to combine them in many of our projects. Architecture is a profession of many, so university has to lay the groundwork for the mainstream. The mainstream is absolutely relevant for our city, although it has super-fantastic architects as well. We need both, and professional education should be based on a general knowledge of the field.

Tina Gregorič: We have to acknowledge that local conditions define progress. Also, it's wrong to think that Slovenia was a fairyland for architects in the late 1990s, early 2000s. It's true, we were able to take part in all those open competitions, but we still had to fight, and we still had to raise and spend money because we were up against 20, 30 or 40 other studios. But it was a new country, we were well-educated, we had all this spirit, and we wanted to help build the new identity. When we came back from London, we wanted to prove that we were among the best. Five years later, opportunities still were the same, but the new young offices did not want to go the same way we did. We had taken out a loan to set up our practice. And we sustained the practice on borrowed money while doing art and design research projects that could not actually keep us afloat. On the other hand, of course, when we became part of the wonderland, we indeed wondered, "Why the hell can't we apply to a foundation to actually do a project like Million Donkey Hotel instead of entering a competition for a 200.000 square-meter development?" Our frustration came from the other side. But this need to fight animated us as individuals. For many students, the setting today is just too comfortable to fight: Why should you be fighting for a better future when it is already here?

Michael Obrist: But if we say that the better future is already here, this has to do with our total amnesia. It is a disastrous landscape that we have constructed for ourselves, and we should be ashamed of ourselves for what we built in the last 50 years. But instead, we are getting used to it. We get used to anything. Unfortunately.

Tina Gregorič: We should be critical about the immediate environment in which we drive, walk or which we experience in any way, because it has become a huge disaster. We can't just stick to the rules and standards and actually take them for granted.

wonderland: You are referring to local conditions here. We are from a generation that has come to discover Europe as a frame of reference. Will this framework be still here for the next generation? Is it possible to be local and European at the same time? How would you describe the relationship between those two?

Tina Gregorič: Europe is something we all belong to. And yet, each country still strives to remain independent at many levels. Competitions in countries like Norway and Slovenia are held in weird languages that no one else from the European Union understands. You cannot enter them if you do not have someone in your team who speaks the language. But language is just the first step. The second step is local regulations and standards. The fundamental idea of Europe as a unified single market in reality encompasses so many super-localized specifics that are deliberately forged within individual countries in order to provide work for local offices. This is still our reality, I think.

Michael Obrist: I have no idea how the young generation feels about Europe. Because I don't feel that they are fighting for it. We were educated in the dark eighties. Fear was one of the dominant forces. I was afraid of nuclear disaster, and I was afraid of the Russians. And then we found this new world – Europe – and it was amazing. The young generation takes it for granted now, but it's such a fragile system in every sense.

Tina Gregorič: Everything is super-fast while architecture remains extremely slow. Everything that is in our smartphones is more or less superficial, but architecture is supposed to be super-profound. So, you might say that we are on the wrong side of how things are going, but we are still able to shape this planet where all those virtual-reality users walk the streets with their phones held up before their eyes.

Michael Obrist: We have been shaping the planet for hundreds of years. But today, building an app gets more attention than building a city. If we talk about sustainability, we talk about sustainable office buildings. And then you look at how the Medici built their offices five hundred years ago in the Uffizi, which are still in use as one of the major exhibition spaces of the world. That's what I call sustainability. Show me one app that is still in use after three years.

Tina Gregorič: Precisely. We should be crucial in that we create the better "real" space for all the virtual things to happen.

getting started

where to go

what to do

how to keep up

Follow the white rabbit ...

#1

POPULATION PER REGISTERED ARCHITECT

If one had to decide where to set up office on the basis of this index, Bulgaria would be the logical choice. Here, with one architect for every 3,577 inhabitants, one would find the lowest density in Europe. Italy should be avoided in any case: with one architect in every 386 inhabitants, it is the European country with the highest density of architects, worldwide only second to Japan. EU-wide, the ratio has been estimated to be one architect for every 1,567 inhabitants, with a total of 597,100 licensed architects.
Population source: Eurostat January 2016
Architects source: Architects' Council of Europe (ACE) 2017
(www.ace-cae.eu)

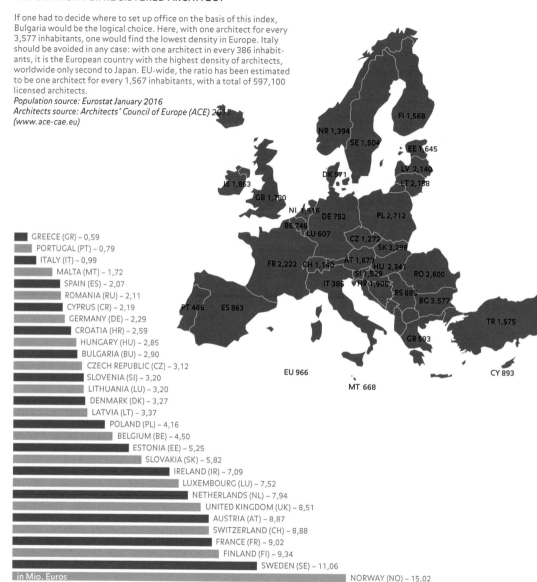

- GREECE (GR) – 0,59
- PORTUGAL (PT) – 0,79
- ITALY (IT) – 0,99
- MALTA (MT) – 1,72
- SPAIN (ES) – 2,07
- ROMANIA (RU) – 2,11
- CYPRUS (CR) – 2,19
- GERMANY (DE) – 2,29
- CROATIA (HR) – 2,59
- HUNGARY (HU) – 2,85
- BULGARIA (BU) – 2,90
- CZECH REPUBLIC (CZ) – 3,12
- SLOVENIA (SI) – 3,20
- LITHUANIA (LU) – 3,20
- DENMARK (DK) – 3,27
- LATVIA (LT) – 3,37
- POLAND (PL) – 4,16
- BELGIUM (BE) – 4,50
- ESTONIA (EE) – 5,25
- SLOVAKIA (SK) – 5,82
- IRELAND (IR) – 7,09
- LUXEMBOURG (LU) – 7,52
- NETHERLANDS (NL) – 7,94
- UNITED KINGDOM (UK) – 8,51
- AUSTRIA (AT) – 8,87
- SWITZERLAND (CH) – 8,88
- FRANCE (FR) – 9,02
- FINLAND (FI) – 9,34
- SWEDEN (SE) – 11,06
- NORWAY (NO) – 15,02

in Mio. Euros

(THEORETICAL) ANNUAL VOLUME OF BUILDING PROJECTS PER ARCHITECT

Next to the density of architects, a second way of estimating potential clients per country is to look at the annual turnover of building projects and divide this by the number of registered architects. According to this index, Norway and Sweden have the highest volume of projects per registered architect and should be the place to go in Europe, while Greece and Portugal should be avoided. But be careful: things can change. In the last five years in half of the European countries, estimated turnover sank by approximately 20%, while other countries like Germany, Malta, or Denmark saw an increase.
Annual building volume source: Eurostat November 2017

getting started

Follow the white rabbit …

Where and how can you set up office as an architect? 'Getting Started' indicates possible answers and solutions in three sections. We start with the question 'Where to go', and survey and discuss legal and registration differences between the EU countries, the advantages of setting up business in the country, in a big city, or in more than one place, and the difficulties involved in moving office.

In the second section 'What to do', you will find a mix of experiences and individual strategies, and the third and last part ideals with the field of tension of money, quality, and time. 'How to keep up' shows that a good marketing strategy can help to achieve the desired media presence – but is no guarantee of economic success. ◼

THE AVERAGE PRACTICE

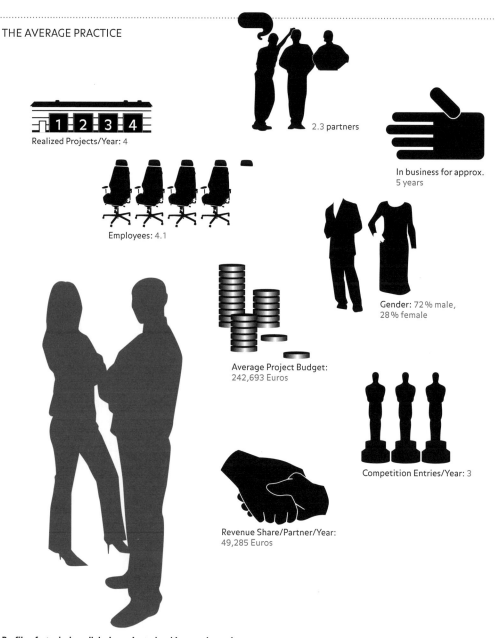

Realized Projects/Year: 4

2.3 partners

In business for approx.
5 years

Employees: 4.1

Gender: 72 % male,
28 % female

Average Project Budget:
242,693 Euros

Competition Entries/Year: 3

Revenue Share/Partner/Year:
49,285 Euros

Profile of a typical small design-oriented architectural practice

According to our survey, the average architectural practice is teamwork. The partners set up office together after an average of 6.9 years of study and 2.7 years of work for other practices. Their initial investment, during the first year, is less than 10,000 Euros. Most commissions result from personal contacts. Every second practice engages in other fields than architectural design. Taking part in international competitions, having projects abroad, and being based in more than one country is common.

Half of the projects started eventually do not materialize. The practices regularly work unpaid extra time, at least on selected projects, and in half of the cases they work whatever hours it takes to produce the best possible design.

See reality check #1 / page 44

Source: Wonderland #1 Survey – by SHARE architects, 2005

where to go

One thing is certain: the choice of location for a new architectural practice is about finding adequate office space at an affordable price and deciding on where this place might be. The current generation of architects starting up a practice can in fact fully benefit from a professional title recognized throughout the EU and from the growing globalization of both education and job market.

Each location brings with it a set of specific conditions that will determine the opportunities and stumbling blocks involved in starting a practice.

Even if a common regulation applies throughout the EU, licensing requirements for architects widely vary among the different countries.

AT: In Austria, the professional title of 'Architekt' is protected but not the function of architect. Registration with the regional branch of the national professional association, the Bundeskammer der Architekten und Ingenieurkonsulenten (BAIK), is compulsory. For architects from EU countries, no notification of the chamber is required for temporary and occasional cross-border services, but architects are obliged to supply the client with the relevant information. Architects from EU countries applying for title recognition need to provide a valid diploma, professional qualification, and authorization to practice in their home Member State. www.arching.at

BE: In Belgium, the professional title of 'Architecte' is protected, as is the function of architect. To work as an architect you have to be registered with the national chamber, the Conseil national de l'Orde des Architectes (CNOA). www.ordredesarchitectes.be

BG: In Bulgaria, both the professional title of 'Архитект' and the function of architect are protected. To work as an architect, you have to be registered with the national chamber, Chamber of Architects in Bulgaria (CAB). European architects who want to practice in Bulgaria must have a diploma (master's degree) in architecture recognized by the Chamber of Architects in Bulgaria and must register with the Chamber of Architects. https://kab.bg

CH: The Schweizer Ingenieur- und Architektenverein (SIA) is a private organization, registration is voluntary. Admission requirements to practice as an architect in Switzerland differ from canton to canton. In only six of 26 cantons, regulations of the architectural profession are in place. Thanks to bilateral agreements for free trade and mutual recognition within the EU, European architects can provides services in Switzerland but registration is compulsory. www.sia.ch

CY: In Cyprus, registration with the national professional association, the Cyprus Architects Association (CAA), is mandatory. www.architecture.org.cy

CZ: In the Czech Republic, the professional title of 'Architekt' as well as the function of the architect is protected. To work as an architect, you have to register with the national chamber. There are two ways of practicing as a foreign architect in the Czech Republic: as a visiting or resident person. Either way, you have to register with the Czech Chamber of Architects (CCA). A temporary license is valid for one year. www.cka.cz

DE: In Germany, the professional title of 'Architekt' is protected, but each German state has its own regulation. The function of architect is not regulated. Registration with the regional branch of the national chamber, the Bundesarchitektenkammer (BAK), is compulsory. www.bak.de

DK: In Denmark, neither professional title nor the right to practice is legally protected. There is no compulsory registration with any professional association. However, to obtain the internationally recognized title of 'Architect MAA', membership of the Danish Architects Association (DAA) is required. www.arkitektforeningen.dk

EE: In Estonia, the professional title of 'Arhitekti' is protected. Registration with the national chamber, the Estonian Association of Architects (EAA), is compulsory. www.arhliit.ee

ES: In Spain, the professional title of 'Arquitecto' and the function of architect are protected. Registration with the national chamber, Consejo Superior de Colegios de Arquitectos de España (CSCAE) is compulsory. www.cscae.com

FI: The architectural profession is not regulated in Finland. The official job title is 'Arkkitehti'. There is no compulsory registration, but over 70 percent of Finnish architects are members of the voluntary professional association Suomen Arkkitehtiliitto – Finlands Arkitektförbund ry (SAFA), the Finnish Association of Architects. www.safa.fi

FR: In France, the professional title of 'Architecte' is protected, as is the function of architect. Registration with a regional chapter of the Conseil national de l'Ordre des Architectes is compulsory. www.architectes.org

GB: In the United Kingdom, the professional title of 'Architect' is protected by law but not the function of architect. Registration with the Architects Registration Board (ARB) is compulsory. Non-EU nationals and those not covered by the scope of the European Directive need to comply with UK training and registration rules. Their application is examined on a case-by-case basis. If individuals do not hold qualifications listed under the Directive, their qualifications may be assessed for equivalence. www.arb.org.uk

GR: In Greece, the professional title of 'Architect' or 'αρχιτέκτονα' is protected but not the function of architect. To work as an architect, you have to register with the Technical Chamber of Greece (TEE-TCG). www.tee.gr

HR: In Croatia, both the professional title and the function of architect are protected. Registration with the Croatian Chamber of Architects (CCA) is compulsory. www.uha.hr

HU: In Hungary the professional title of 'Epítészmérnök' is protected along with the function of architect. Registration with the Chamber of Hungarian Architects (MEK) is compulsory. If European architects want to practice in Hungary, they need to have a one-time permit for the project that will be valid for a year, on top of an EU-accredited diploma and a license to practice in their own county. If architects want to become members of the Chamber of Hungarian Architects, they must have a valid diploma and meet the same requirements as Hungarian architects. www.meszorg.hu

IE: In Ireland, the professional title of 'Architect' is protected, though the function of architect is not. Registration with the Royal Institute of the Architects of Ireland (RIAI) is compulsory for those who wish to use the title architect. To register, an entrance examination is required. www.riai.ie

IT: In Italy, the professional title of 'Architetto' is protected, as is the function of architect. Registration with the local chapter of the national chamber at the place of residence or work is compulsory. The name of the national chamber is Consiglio Nazionale degli Architetti, Pianificatori, Paesaggisti e Conservatori (CNAPPC). www.awn.it

LT: In Lithuania, both the professional title of 'Architektas' and the function of architect are protected. There is no obligation to register with the Architects' Chamber of Lithuania (ACL). www.am.lt

LU: In Luxemburg, the professional title of 'Architecte' is protected; the same goes for the function of architect. Registration with the national chamber, Ordre des Architectes et des Ingénieurs Conseils du Grand-Duché de Luxembourg (OAI), is compulsory. To practice as an European architect in Luxemburg, you have to have a recognized diploma, a residence permit (autorisation d'établissement), and need to be registered with the OAI. www.oai.lu

LV: In Latvia, the professional title of 'Arhitektiem' is protected, as is the function of architect. Registration with the national chamber, the Latvian Association of Architects (LAA), is compulsory. www.latarh.lv

MT: In Malta, the professional title for architects, 'Periti', is protected but not the function of architect. Registration with the national chamber, Kamra tal-Periti (KTP), is compulsory. www.ktpmalta.org

NL: In the Netherlands, the professional title of 'Architect' is protected but not the function. Registration with the national Bureau Architectenregister (BA) is needed to use the title, though not to practice the profession. Architects who are registered with the BA can, if they so wish, become members of the Bond van Nederlandse Architecten (BNA), the only professional association of architects in the Netherlands. www.architectenregister.nl; www.bna.nl

PL: In Poland, the professional title of 'Architekt' is not protected, but the function is. Registration with the national chamber, the Polish Chamber of Architects (IARP), is compulsory. www.sarp.org.pl; www.izbaarchitektow.pl

PT: In Portugal, the professional title of 'Arquitecto' is protected, as is the function of architect. Registration with the national chamber, Ordem dos Arquitectos (OA), is compulsory. www.oasrs.org

RO: The professional title of 'Arhitect' is protected in Romania. Registration with the national professional association, the Architects' Chamber of Romania (OAR), is compulsory. www.oar.org.ro

SE: In Sweden the architectural profession is not regulated. But to bear the professional title of 'Arkitekt SAR/MSA', membership of the professional organization for architects, interior architects, landscape architects and spatial planners, Sveriges Arkitekter (SA), is prerequisite. To qualify, a valid degree and two years of working experience from an EU country are needed. www.arkitekt.se

SI: In Slovenia, the professional title of 'Arhitekt' is protected but not the function. Registration with the national professional association, the Chamber of Architecture and Spatial Planning of Slovenia (ZAPS), is compulsory. www.zaps.si

SK: In Slovakia, both the professional title and the function of 'Architekt' are protected. Registration with the national professional association, the Slovak Chamber of Architects (SKA), is compulsory. www.komarch.sk

General sources: www.ace-cae.eu/architects-in-europe
Compiled by Astrid Piber, updated by Anne Isopp, November 2017
For additional information also see the European Commission's Regulated Profession Database:
http://ec.europa.eu/growth/tools-databases/regprof/index.cfm?action=homepage

19

Setting up office

Big city or small town? Back home or somewhere else? Architects who want to set up their own practice will have to deal with the question of location. Six teams of architects report on the advantages of their particular choice of location.

Compiled by Anne Isopp

SMALL PLACE //

ü.NN Founded in 2004 by Oliver Rüsche and Tobias Willers in Attendorn, Germany – a small town with a population of 25,000 –, and with a small branch in Bremen, a port city of just over half a million people.

Their first project provided the impetus for Oliver Rüsche and Tobias Willers to set up their practice ü.NN in the little town of Attendorn. As Attendorn is Rüsche's birthplace, he had good contacts there. "This makes it far easier to acquire projects, compared to the situation in Bremen, where I am only an incomer", says Tobias Willers. Before and after the founding of ü.NN Rüsche and Willers organised several interdisciplinary architecture and art events, using unusual spaces in the region. The goal of these events was always to identify mostly unused potential of existing spaces and transform these into a new understanding of cultural, artistic and architectural use. During their first five years they have realised over 20 regional projects spanning the area between Attendorn, Dortmund and Frankfurt. The office, in the former company kitchen and dining area of a local steel factory (Hoesch) is nowadays a lively and experimental space for concerts, theatre and private functions. In 2006 ü.NN has furthermore initiated and financed the Attendorner Kulturstipendium (an annual international art competition and exhibition) which gives young artists the chance for a 2 month long creative spell in the spaces around the office. www.uenn.de

spado architects Founded 1999 by Helmut Rainer-Marinello and Harald Weber, now led by Harald Weber & Hannes Schienegger. Based in Klagenfurt, Austria – a town with a population of 100,000.

In 1999, Helmut Rainer-Marinello and Harald Weber set up their practice named spado in St. Veit an der Glan, a small town in Carinthia with a population of 13,000. As both of them come from this southernmost Austrian province, they moved back to Carinthia to live and work here after completing their studies in Graz and Vienna. There were two main reasons to set up office here: the possibility of realizing some projects and the changing circumstances of working in the province. The Alpine-Adriatic Region (Slovenia, Friuli, Carinthia, Croatia) is gradually growing together, and there are new communications which redefine the relationship between city and province. "Another advantage is that there are not too many committed architects in Carinthia, which makes it relatively easy to get involved in exhibitions or to give lectures", says Harald Weber. In 2005 they moved their practice twenty kilometers to the regional capital Klagenfurt. But as they stayed in the same province this move made little difference to the way they run their projects. www.spado.at

BIG PLACE //

EXYZT Founded 2002 by Gil Burban, Nicolas Henninger, Philippe Rizzotti, Pier Schneider and François Wunschel. The practice was based in Paris, France – a capital city with a population of 2.2 million. In 2014, the collaboration came to an end.

The five team members of EXYZT have known each other since they were students at the La Villette School of Architecture in Paris. Following a successful joint venture in Parc de la Villette, the student friends set up their own practice in 2002. "Paris is a good place for us to start this", says Nicolas Henninger and names some of the advantages of working in a big city: the dynamic urban life, the cultural diversity, and good travel connections. The five members of EXYZT worked not only in France but also internationally, with projects going on in Barcelona and Latvia and a one-month installation at the Berlin Palast der Republik. They made international contacts through travelling or by taking part in workshops and seminars. In the end, they did not succeed as a team, and they shut down the company in 2014. Still, they all have benefited from the international experiences and contacts, like for example Nicolas Henninger, who lives, works and teaches in London today. www.exyzt.org

4A architekti Founded 1997 by Leigh D'Agostino (GB), Ludvik Seko (CZ), Jan Schindler (A), Peter Hudak (SK). Based in Prague, Czech Republic – a capital city with a population of 1.3 million.

4A architekti – as the name suggests – are four architects who have known each other since they were students in Prague and who later set up practice together. The unusual thing about them is they are not only all members of the Czech Chamber of Architects but also individually with their national institutes, British, German and Slovak. "Being members of our respective architectural authorities broadens our knowledge base and adds recognition to our achievements, which in turn helps us get new clients and new jobs", explains Leigh D'Agostino. "For example, a British client can communicate in his native tongue, fully expressing his aspirations for the project. We can make clear project comparisons between the Czech and British systems for both parties to understand. We know how it works here. It helps communication and, most importantly, it builds trust." www.architekti4a.cz

MORE THAN ONE PLACE //

elastik Founded 2004 by Igor Kebel and Mika Cimolini. Based in Amsterdam, Netherlands (population 810,000) and Ljubljana, Slovenia (population 287,000).

Igor Kebel and Mika Cimolini, who studied together at the Berlage Institut in Holland, have worked together on projects since 2002. In 2004, they officially set up their joint practice named elastik which stands for converting constraints into design opportunities. They are based in Ljubljana and in Amsterdam. "So far, we have had projects in many different countries", says Igor Kebel, who runs the Amsterdam office together with Freek Dech. Working together across such distances has its advantages and disadvantages. "One disadvantage that is an advantage at the same time is that communication must be much more precise and thorough. This is a bit exhausting, for sure, but never superficial. The advantage is that you work internationally. You have the flexibility and also the broadness of approach." They meet up once a month, either in Amsterdam or in Ljubljana – the rest of the time they communicate by Internet. Naturally, projects in Slovenia are handled in Ljubljana and Dutch projects in Amsterdam; international projects are divided between them. www.elastik.net

osa Founded 1994 by Sebastian Appl, Ulrich Beckefeld, Britta Eiermann, Karsten Huneck, Oliver Langbein, Anja Ohliger, Anke Strittmatter and Bernd Trümpler. Based in Frankfurt, Darmstadt, München and Hamburg, Germany; Vienna and Graz, Austria; London, United Kingdom.

The eight team members of osa got together in their student days at the Darmstadt University of Technology. None of them would have expected that this working partnership would still be operative today, especially since following their graduation they all went to different cities. But they still get together in new project groups. "Someone brings up an idea or a competition, and a team is formed around it. Then we communicate a great deal by phone or Internet, and from time to time we meet. What follows is a short phase of intense collaboration", says Ulrich Beckefeld, who is based in Vienna. The advantages: "The different locations bring different approaches and cultural influences together – simply through the way the teams function." The disadvantage: "You always have to find new modes of discussion; ideas are quickly pooled, but making decisions can be very difficult." www.osa-online.net

FRANCESCO MATUCCI ARCHITECTURE Founded 2002 by Francesco Matucci. Based in Florence, Italy.

"Let's say: My office follows me", says Francesco Matucci, who has been working on his own since 2002. Before that, he lived in Copenhagen most of the time, but, coming from Florence and with part of his family living in Madrid, he didn't confine himself to working in Denmark. He took part in competitions in all three countries and cultivates contacts there. "A very important thing about living and working in different places is the continuous on-the-job training in translating cultural models and habits, different ways of living and working." He does not see any disadvantage in working at different locations – apart perhaps from the fact that you can only be in one place at a time. Since 2009, he has based his office in Florence, developing projects, taking part in competitions and benefiting from his international experiences. www.francescomatucci.com

Max. duration of education
Duration of compulsory internship after completion of studies

Compulsory examination
Compulsory registration yes (Y) / no (N)

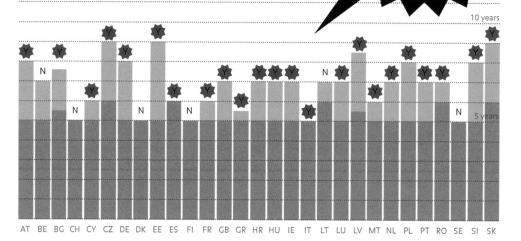

10 years

5 years

AT BE BG CH CY CZ DE DK EE ES FI FR GB GR HR HU IE IT LT LU LV MT NL PL PT RO SE SI SK

Compiled by Astrid Piber and Anne Isopp

STEP BY STEP OR JUMP-START

2.7 years is the average working experience obtained by the architects surveyed before starting their own practice. Only 22 % jumped into independent practice immediately after completing their studies.

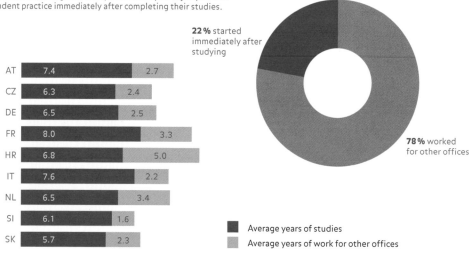

22 % started immediately after studying

78 % worked for other offices

	Average years of studies	Average years of work for other offices
AT	7.4	2.7
CZ	6.3	2.4
DE	6.5	2.5
FR	8.0	3.3
HR	6.8	5.0
IT	7.6	2.2
NL	6.5	3.4
SI	6.1	1.6
SK	5.7	2.3

Average years of studies
Average years of work for other offices

Source: Wonderland #1 Survey – by SHARE architects, 2005

CROSSING BORDERS
Recognition of Professional Qualifications in the European Union

Text by Bert Bielefeld, Dortmund, Germany

If architects want to work in another country, the first step is to learn about the conditions of admission that apply in the respective country. Many states, such as China or the U.S., prevent or complicate access of foreign architects to their domestic markets by specific laws or sophisticated admission procedures.

In the EU, a number of fundamental steps were taken to implement free provision of services and freedom of establishment also in the area of qualified professions such as architects.

Free provision of services and freedom of establishment inside the European Single Market

With regard to cross-border professional activity, the European Union has defined a number of fundamental principles that apply in all EU member states. First and foremost, these are the so-called market freedoms in the European Single Market:

- Free movement of goods (art. 23–38 EC)
- Free movement of workers (art. 39 EC)
- Freedom of establishment, (art. 43ff. EC)
- Freedom to provide services (art. 49f. EC)
- Capital and payment freedoms (art. 56ff. EC).

These rights have direct effect in each EU state and on every EU citizen. Beyond that, there are directives in place that have no direct effect and need to be transposed into national law within a specified period, which may lead to different interpretations of their contents at a national level. The EU Services Directive 2006/123/EC (the Bolkestein Directive) provides the general legal framework for the provision of services in the European Union. The directive applies to both the permanent establishment of service providers outside their home country state and to cross-border provision of services.

Aside from the free movement of services and the right of establishment, the right to practice in the respective destination country is most important for architects and civil engineers. The Architects Directive regulated the professional recognition of architects within the EC (now EU) from 1985 to 2005 when it was replaced by Directive 2005/36/EC on the recognition of professional qualifications. This directive summarizes various directives on regulated professions and thus also supersedes the previous Architectural Directive 85/384/EEC of 10 June 1985.

The professional training level of architects

The Architects Directive was drawn up in order to achieve a standardized quality of professional training in architecture and and to make it easier for architects and civil engineers to practice their profession Europe-wide.

The old and new directives list national educational institutions and organizations (universities, universities of applied sciences engineering colleges, art academies, academies, polytechnic schools, etc.), whose graduates are automatically qualified to work as architects in all EU Member States. The revision of the Directive and the EU-wide introduction of the BA and MA curricula initiated far-reaching reforms of academic education in the existing and new EU Member States.

Foundations of professional recognition

Excluded from the general freedom of services are, because of the qualifications necessary, a handful of regulated professions like architects or civil engineers. The fundamental principle of mutual recognition/admission is that *if applicants are entitled to practice their profession in their country of origin on the basis of their national qualification, they are entitled to practice in the host country as well.* This may also apply in cases where a diploma is not required in the country of origin (for example in Sweden) while the host country does require a national diploma. The only prerequisite is a full practice license issued in the home country. If applicants come under the professional recognition directive by virtue of their diploma or qualification, they can practice their profession anywhere in the EU.

Unlike professional practice, recognition of an academic title obtained in one Member State by universities of another EU Member State is usually regulated by national legislation. As EU law does not apply here directly, national authorities decide about the recognition of a job title like architect or civil engineer: *the profession of architect or civil engineer may be practiced in all EU states, but the respective job titles will not be automatically recognized in each country.*

Registration procedures

According to the Directive, in order to start working in another EU Member State, proof must be furnished that the qualification obtained is covered by the Directive. The host state can for example request that the applicants:

... provide an affidavit proving that they did not go bankrupt in their country of origin

... have the necessary funding for providing the intended services

... are covered by the professional indemnity insurance required in the host state and provide a certificate from an insurer in their home country covering the insurance guarantees required in the host country (this is usually a mere formality in all cases, except for France).

The complete list of possible requirements can be found in Directive 2005/36/EC, Annex VII. In the case of temporary work abroad (freedom to provide services), the host state may, in order to warrant the applicability of a local disciplinary regime, require a temporary, automatic registration or pro forma membership in a professional association, provided that the provision of services is not unduly delayed or impeded. As a rule, this pro forma membership cannot be denied to anyone, so no special "exam" is necessary.

If an architect wishes to work abroad permanently by setting up office there, a certificate of reliability may be required by the host state, for example, a criminal records certificate. Other than that, the same national, work-related formalities such as membership in a professional association or chamber and compulsory insurance must be provided for a permanent establishment.

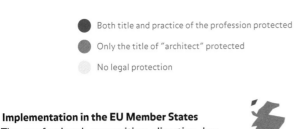

- Both title and practice of the profession protected
- Only the title of "architect" protected
- No legal protection

Implementation in the EU Member States

The professional recognition directive has been implemented into national law in all EU member states. In the "younger" EU member states, the directive provided for swift approximation of legislation to EU standards. Whether the professional practice, job title, or the authorization to present building documents are protected by law depends in almost all states on how the existing regulatory framework has evolved (see figure).

In contrast to the fields of public tender and compensation, where there has been a tendency towards liberalization, there is clearly a trend towards more regulation with respect to protected professions in Europe. Not only have some of the new EU Member States introduced registration systems in addition to powerful professional associations; Ireland, too, has followed the example of Great Britain and set up a registration office analogous to the British ARB (Architects Registration Board) to regulate job titles or professional practice. This affects not only domestic planners, but also architects from other European countries in particular.

In Northern European countries such as Sweden, access to the profession is easy because there is no state regulation or protection of the profession. This function is taken over by the membership in the SAR (Svenska Arkitekters Riksförbund). In federal states with a professional chamber system such as in Belgium, Germany, Austria or Italy, registration paths are clearly defined but even there additional requests for certified copies, translations and other documents may occasionally cause pro-forma memberships to be delayed, which in turn may lead to schedulingproblems in specific construction projects already under way.

Eastern European EU Member States frequently seek to coerce foreign architects into entering joint ventures with local planners. Sometimes, a new protectionism is put in place, which virtually prevents professional access in countries like Poland. Even though the legal situation is clear, foreign architects in almost all states meet with hidden protectionism and all sorts of obstacles, against which legal action may of course be taken but which in professional practice nevertheless often entail an odyssey of nerve-racking red tape.

Even if professional chambers, institutions or registration authorities keep trying to erect barriers, knowledge of the European requirements should enable architects to enforce their right to work in another EU member state.

Useful Links

Eurowide awards: http://ted.europa.eu
Download EU directives: https://eur-lex.europa.eu

Any architect with the wish to work in another EU member state would be well-advised
to study the Professional Qualifications Directive and its national equivalents.

The Directive is downloadable at
http://eur-lex.europa.eu/LexUriServ/LexUriServ.do?uri=OJ:L:2005:255:0022:0142:EN:PDF

Database of the University of Siegen:
www.architektur.uni-siegen.de/ipb/laenderdatenbank.html (in German)

A useful overview of national conditions for service-exporting architects
and engineers can be found on the website of the University of Siegen at
www.architektur.uni-siegen.de/ipb/laenderdatenbank.html?lang=d.

Network for Architecture Exchange: www.architekturexport.de

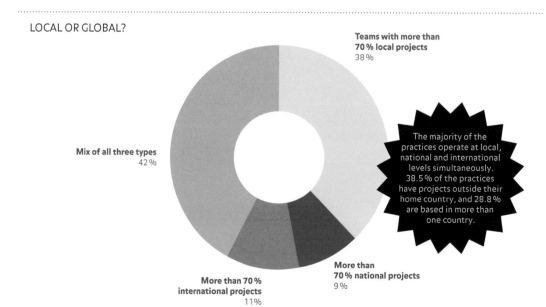

LOCAL OR GLOBAL?

**Teams with more than
70 % local projects**
38 %

Mix of all three types
42 %

**More than 70 %
international projects**
11%

**More than
70 % national projects**
9 %

The majority of the
practices operate at local,
national and international
levels simultaneously.
38.5 % of the practices
have projects outside their
home country, and 28.8 %
are based in more than
one country.

Source: Wonderland #1 Survey – by SHARE architects, 2005

CROSSING BORDERS
Moving to a foreign country

Text by Anne Isopp

Studying architecture abroad is one thing, but setting up practice as an architect in a foreign country is quite another. The latter generally involves more serious hurdles to be cleared. We talked to six architects about their motives for making this move.

Birgitte Louise Hansen (1)
Born in Denmark / Moved from Copenhagen to Rotterdam
Founded Birgitte Louise Hansen in Rotterdam in 1999

Birgitte Louise Hansen had several starting points. She started practicing as an architect while still studying architecture in Denmark. Between 1990 and 1996, she realized several projects under her own name with clients from art and cultural organizations ranging from small to large scale, from installation art, site-specific performance art to indoor and outdoor exhibitions. 1997 she decided to move to Holland. "I wanted space to breathe, to get new inspiration and meet new people." There is no specific reason why she chose Holland. After working for several architectural firms, she started her own office 1999 in Rotterdam. Besides working as a designer, she also engages in a number of other activities, most importantly teaching architecture analysis and research, reflective writing and speaking. To set up an independent practice in the Netherlands you need to have at least three clients. The majority of her clients have been Danish. "When I came to Holland, I had done a lot of work for people from the art sector and I continued doing so for several years. My work was therefore often (mis)understood as art, which made it difficult for me to market myself as an architect", says Birgitte Louise Hansen. After defending her doctoral dissertation (PhD) in 'Architectural Thinking in Pratice' at the Technical University in Delft, Department of Architecture, in 2018, she hopes that her written work will travel across borders and bring her more international projects.

Dana Čupková (2)
Born in Bratislava, Slovakia / Moved to Pittsburgh, USA
Founded DCm STUDIO in New York City in 2000 and co-founded EPIPHYTE Lab in Ithaca, New York in 2009

"I'm not tied to one location", says Slovak Dana Čupková and recounts her previous stops: from Bratislava, where she studied architecture, she moved to Malaysia to practice and learn about bio-climatic principles of design from Ken Yeang. Then she relocated to Los Angeles, where she completed her Master of Architecture at UCLA, and from there to New York City. In New York, she worked for various firms, first full-time, later part-time, in order to have sufficient time left for her own projects. There she founded her first office DCm STUDIO, a practice which focused on smaller scale, but versatile projects. To set up a practice in the USA, registration and exams are compulsory. "But with a smaller scale practice you can manage without registration for a short while", she says. In 2006 Dana moved to Ithaca, New York, to pursue a more academic career. She is a Visiting Assistant Professor at Cornell University. While teaching architectural design she co-founded an architectural design and research collaborative: EPIPHYTE Lab. The work of EPIPHYTE Lab combines researched-based knowledge on computation and ecological adaptation with real world experiments and fabrication related projects. Cupková currently lives and works in Pittsburgh, pursuing an academic career at Carnegie Mellon University. She teaches architectural design at the CMU's School of Architecture and heads a MS program in Sustainable Design, while still running her own design-research practice, which was one of the winners of the 2017 American Architecture Prize for a small renovation project. www.epiphyte-lab.com

Yukiko Nezu (3)
Born in Japan / Moved from Tokyo to Amsterdam
Founded urbanberry in Amsterdam in 2001

Tokyo is the biggest metropolitan area in the world, but still insular in spirit. These were the reasons that motivated Yukiko Nezu to go abroad. She wanted to live on the continent and to experience multi-cultural life. She chose the Berlage Institute in the Netherlands to study. "I like the different way of working", says Yukiko Nezu. "In the Netherlands, I see that everyone is equal. In Japan, you have a top-down system. This kind of hierarchy does not suit me." She wanted to stay, and in order to get a visa, she had to open her own practice. This was the beginning of urbanberry. In the beginning she had to submit at least three new projects every year with the Aliens Police Department to furnish proof that her business is still in operation. Meanwhile, she has got a permanent visa. Today, she develops architectural designs and master plans for local projects. Sometimes she also works for Japanese clients in the Netherlands.

www.urbanberry.com

Roisin Heneghan + Shih-Fu Peng (4)
Born in Ireland & New York + Raised in Ireland, United States and Asia / Moved from New York to Dublin
Founded Heneghan Peng in New York in 1999

Roisin Heneghan and Shih-Fu Peng founded their joint practice Heneghan Peng in 1999 in New York. Aside from working with SOM and Michael Graves, they prepared occasional competition entries together at weekends or during the holidays. They won their first international competition in 2001 – a civic office complex in the Irish county town of Kildare. After this they moved to Ireland. "It wasn't very complicated. We had to get a license from the Royal Institute of the Architects of Ireland (RIAI) and go through a series of interviews", says Peng. The office complex is now completed, and they continue to find most of their work through competitions. "It's very hard. The chances are very slim – less than one percent", says Peng, who together with his partner is very successful in this area.

They attracted particular attention in 2003 when they won the competition for the Egyptian Museum in Cairo as one out of 1557 entries from 83 different countries (see #5 making competitions – Experience reports). The practice is now based in Dublin and Berlin, and a significant part of the work is in other countries. In 2016, they won a competition for the Canadian Canoe Museum and were pleased to be working in North America again. www.hparc.com

Tom van Malderen (5)
Born in Belgium / Moved from Brussels to Valletta (Malta) where he works in an architect's practice

Tom van Malderen has lived and worked on Malta since March 2001. He is employed there in the island's biggest architecture firm (45 people). He met a Maltese architect at a summer workshop in Stockholm who offered him this job a few years later. "For someone of my age, this was a very tempting offer, so I went", says van Malderen. His particular qualification was that, in contrast to most young Maltese architects, he already had experience working on large projects. What he particularly likes about Malta is the latent holiday atmosphere and the foreign culture. "Architectural education in Malta is more focused on the engineering aspect, and design aspects tend to be marginalized", says Tom van Malderen. "This gives you a great advantage on the design level, but it also means that every now and then you have to overcome some reservations regarding the feasibility of one's designs." To be allowed to work in Malta, a work permit is required. If you want to open your own practice, things are far more complicated. You need a 'local warrant', and additional university courses must be passed to obtain the professional title of 'Perit', the official title of an architect on Malta. His role within the office shifted from concept design for larger-scale projects to scenography and exhibition design. He also established personal connections with a number of visual artists and organizations that have resulted in some exciting exhibition design projects outside Malta. www.ap.com.mt

Ton Matton (6)
Born in the Netherlands / Moved from Rotterdam to Wendorf, Germany
Has a virtual branch office in Rotterdam and the headquarters in Wendorf, Mecklenburg, Germany

Ton Matton is a suburb-refugee. As an urban planner, he came to a point in 2001 when he had enough of Dutch housing policy with its ever-same suburbia developments based on arguments of being urban and rural at the same time. He looked around for a house that would suit his ideas. In the East German community of Wendorf in between Hamburg and Berlin, he found what he was looking for, an old school which he, together with his wife, sociologist and writer Ellie Smolenaars, turned into a heterotopia named Werkstatt Wendorf. As former squatters, they moved in as it was, changing the atmosphere by adding functional installations such as a jungle shower, a free range kitchen, chicken coop and several climate control devices. They welcome guests who come to work in full concentration for a while; writers, painters, photographers, musicians, philosophers and, since the sports hall became a green screen studio, also filmmakers belong to the core visitors. "There is an unbelievable amount of natural free space here, which opens up your mind for new ideas. I do research in hypermodernity, finding interesting ways of rural living in history and trying to connect it to contemporary urban lifestyles", says Ton Matton, who grows his own firewood. The electricity is produced with solar panels, as is hot water. Since he has lived in Wendorf, he has had more commissions than ever before: "When I moved here I became international and thus more interesting." In Germany, he was Visiting Professor at the Hamburg Academy of Fine Arts from 2003 to 2005, and has also taught at the Wismar University of Technology, Business and Design, from 2009 to 2012. Since 2014, he has been a professor for Space & Design strategies in Linz, Austria. Lately, he started a project series of 'Potemkin villages' in Almere (NL): temporary structures set up in villages threatened by emigration and decline create the image of a better future and suggest alternatives to the current sad situation. "The fact that I live in Wendorf doesn't mean that I can't be reached. I live in Central Europe. I have satellite Internet, a Lada Niva four-wheel drive, and a mobile phone, like everyone else in the Global Village." www.mattonoffice.org

what to do

Defining the What of an architectural practice provides the basis of one's identity and will have an influence on everything that follows. Many choices need to be made: small big details like choosing a name, and tricky details such as whether to make it a one (wo)man show or build a team.

In order to decide on a type of organization that will match the work produced, you will need to find out what kind of product you are interested in delivering, and if you are able to do so. You will have to face the big question of what your field of action will be. Will you be a purist? An all-rounder? A cross-breeder?

Text by Eva Boudewijn, Amersfoort, Netherlands

Mind Your Design!

A characterization of different types of architecture firms

As an architecture student, your primary and perhaps only focus is the craft or art of architecture. Your dream is to make a job out of your passion, so you start your own architecture firm. But starting a successful business takes more than talent, knowledge and passion. Too often, young architects forget that organization design is equally important. Setting up office entails implicit choices about, for example, the business structure, working method, and type of clients. But are these choices the right ones? Do they fit to your strengths, talents and ambitions as an architect, as an entrepreneur, and as a person? And do they combine well?

	STUDIO	OFFICE	BUSINESS
Basic Principle	My idea	Our client	The product
Core Quality	Innovation and creativity	Relation and risk management	Technical and functional expertise
Characteristic Way of Working	Improvization	Project management	Standardized routines

The Architecture Studio

Distinctive to this type of architecture firm is its strong leader or 'guru', who leaves a distinct signature on each and every project. To them, projects are just a means to an end to make their precious and often most creative and innovative ideas materialize. Clients are just considered stakeholders in the process of realizing the ultimate idea.

The Architecture Office

Offices are focused on providing service, experience, and reliability. In projects, offices try to keep a balance between pleasing the client with a design that complies with the client's wishes and reaching an acceptable aesthetic quality. Offices make sure that the project can proceed as planned and risks are minimized. The relationship that the architect maintains with his clients is often viewed as the most important factor for the continuity of the office. The office is by far the most common of the three types of architecture firms.

The Architecture Business

In the architecture business, technical expertise and quality of the product are essential. Businesses are like well-lubricated architectural machines. Functional and technical feasibility, legal requirements, and a devotion to efficiency are important from the very start of a project. Businesses can deliver good technical quality at a relatively low cost. This makes them reliable contractors, who are able to make architecture a profitable business.

Personal skills and talents of the architect

When you start your own architecture firm, solo or as a partnership with kindred spirits, the entire operation depends on your talents and skills. Your education has provided you with knowledge and skills concerning aesthetics, design techniques, a certain technical expertise, etc. This is an essential starting point, but in itself not enough to be successful as an architect. Other skills have to be developed as your architecture firm evolves. Every type of architecture firm requires different skills to be successful.

> When you start your own architecture firm, solo or as a partnership with kindred spirits, the entire operation depends on your talents and skills.

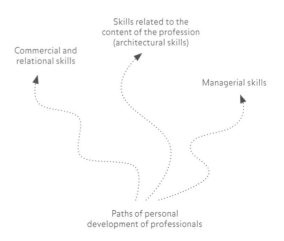

Skills related to the
content of the profession
(architectural skills)

Commercial and
relational skills

Managerial skills

Paths of personal
development of professionals

Skills and type

	STUDIO	OFFICE	BUSINESS
Architectural Skills	The studio is primarily valued for this skill.	The lack in innovation is compensated with relational and project managerial skills. Creativity is required to meet the client's wishes.	Architectural skills need to be expanded to a vast technical expertise to assure quality and a smooth building process.
Commercial & Relational Skills	Commercial activities are focussed on 'brand awareness'. An established distinctive signature can compensate for a lack of relational skills.	Accordingly to its basic principle, offices are primarily valued for their outstanding relational skills.	Since the building process and final result is standardized, the co-operation with the client is less intensive. Therefore relational skills are less important.
Managerial Skills	Studios are infamous for bad project management. Basic project management skills are required, but studios do not need to excel in this area.	In order to serve the client, project management skills need to be well-developed, to minimize risks and to control the project budget and planning.	Businesses are primarily valued for their project management skills and therefore need to excel in this area.

> To be successful, the structure of the organization should support the identity of the architectural firm.

The structure of the organization

The outward appearance of an organization is (and should be) a reflection of its character. In practice, organizational structures develop organically over time. The unconscious choices that are made along the way can result in a poor match between firm type and organizational structure. At worst, this could lead to inconsistent self-presentation of the firm to prospect clients, underdeveloped talents and skills, and unproductive and frustrated employees. To be successful, the structure of the organization should support the identity of the architectural firm.

In a studio the 'guru'/dominant architect is in the center of the organization, surrounded by the employees (designers, architects). This structure hardly knows any formal or formalized lines of communication.

In an office, the architect concentrates on the aesthetic aspects of a project, while the office manager or 'chef de bureau' takes care of the managerial side of the projects and the firm.

The structure of an architecture business is the most elaborate one of the three types. This type often comprises several professionally organized units in the form of separate firms or design or project departments, which operate independently within the architecture business. The board of directors does not necessarily consist of architects.

Image and distinguishing features for clients and employees

Consciously or unconsciously, clients, prospects and potential employees also distinguish between types of architecture firms. Which clients are attracted to which type of architecture firm? And which company characteristics are attractive for which type of employees?

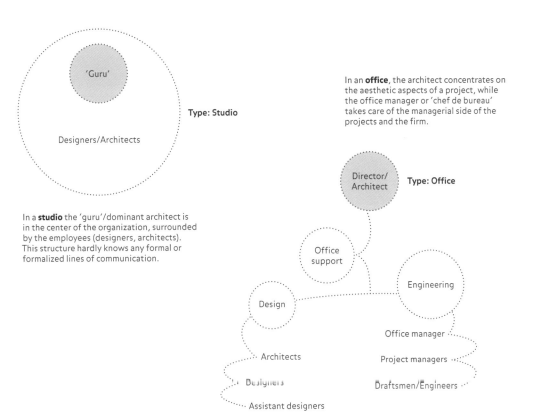

'Guru'

Type: Studio

Designers/Architects

In an **office**, the architect concentrates on the aesthetic aspects of a project, while the office manager or 'chef de bureau' takes care of the managerial side of the projects and the firm.

Director/Architect   Type: Office

In a **studio** the 'guru'/dominant architect is in the center of the organization, surrounded by the employees (designers, architects). This structure hardly knows any formal or formalized lines of communication.

Office support

Engineering

Design

Office manager

Project managers

Architects

Designers

Draftsmen/Engineers

Assistant designers

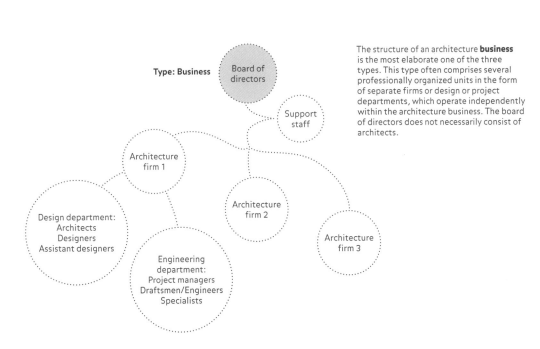

Type: Business   Board of directors

Support staff

The structure of an architecture **business** is the most elaborate one of the three types. This type often comprises several professionally organized units in the form of separate firms or design or project departments, which operate independently within the architecture business. The board of directors does not necessarily consist of architects.

Architecture firm 1

Architecture firm 2

Architecture firm 3

Design department:
Architects
Designers
Assistant designers

Engineering department:
Project managers
Draftsmen/Engineers
Specialists

Working method characteristics

	STUDIO	OFFICE	BUSINESS
Characteristic Working Method	to get started right away without a clear definition of the design task a lot of artistic freedom the design, innovation and creativity have priority over the clients' wishes working methods are not fixed teamwork originates organically	the project starts after an extensive intake with the client the client is informed/involved every step of the way the proven method of project management is used to phase the project teamwork is based on a division of tasks	the project starts after signing the contract final results are determined at the start of the project time and energy is invested in controlling the planning, the budget and technical requirements designing and building is a routine activity using formalized standards and procedures teamwork is based on specialization
Pitfalls	difficulties in finishing off the design due to the everlasting search for the ultimate design lapsing into amateurism (ignoring the client) not paying enough attention to the technical feasibility of the design	difficulties in finishing off stages in the project in an attempt to meet the client's wishes insufficient coordination between design and engineering	disturbing the healthy balance between design and engineering by over-rationalization/standardization of the creative process becoming inflexible to meet the needs and wishes of the client getting stuck in too much bureaucracy and paperwork
Challenge/ Opportunity for Growth	not to 'lose' the client in the process, but to involve the client	to keep the desire to please the client within reasonable limits	giving room to creativity

The client who chooses to contract a studio likes to be surprised: he knows that hiring a 'guru' will make the final result somewhat unpredictable. From his point of view, the budget for building his dream is more or less secondary to the statement he wants to make through his building.

The office-client's choice is based on his relationship with the architect-director; he knows that his wish is the office's command. An important criterion in the selection process is the office's experience with similar projects. For the client, this specialization assures minimization of risks.

The architects of the office aim for effectiveness and client satisfaction. After all, a strong relationship with clients is vital for the continuity of the office.

The architecture business is contracted by clients for its reliability, efficiency, low price and technical know-how. The client's choice is based on the qualities of the firm, not on those of a specific architect. The business then provides the expertise that is required in these specific stages of a project. Because of their size, vast expertise and structured working methods, businesses can handle large, complex projects.

Employees and type of architecture firm: what is the attraction?
The studio attracts young, promising designers from all over the world. Most of these designers have the aspiration to leave the studio one day to become a 'guru' themselves.

The architecture office attracts designers who are willing to commit themselves for the long run. Becoming a partner and even taking over the firm is a viable option. The attraction of the office is also determined by its clientele and specialization. Potential employees want to realize projects in close cooperation with the client. They are prepared to start low and work their way up the corporate ladder.

The architecture business attracts designers that appreciate technically complex designs and want to optimize the building process. Designers that value a technically reliable result and like working in professional project structures will feel right at home at the architecture business.

Type awareness as an instrument

Even if architects, clients and employees each may have their own preferences, none of the types described can generally be said to be superior to any other. Each type can be successful, provided that choices are made deliberately and implemented consistently. As is the case with every theoretical model, these types of architecture firms hardly ever occur in their pure form in real life.

The strategy of choosing

Success depends on consistently living the choices you make. Have you established what your identity and talents are? Then be bold and choose to exploit your own strength! Translate your identity into the genes of your firm. But be prepared, that sometimes to choose means to lose.

Strategies to upgrade your architecture firm

Strategies to enable an architecture firm to serve different types of clients are: cooperation with complementary types, collaboration in a professional network, and outsourcing. The other option is to create hybrid (project) teams or a hybrid type architecture firm. When creating an architecture firm that keeps two types under the same roof, separating the two types into two autonomous organizational units is recommended, so that each type can cultivate its own talents and ambitions. No matter what choices you make, it is all about aligning your talents and ambitions with the structure, working method and skills of your architecture firm. So mind your design, live your choices and be successful! 🐾

The theory of types of architecture firms is deducted from a model of self-knowledge: achievement of goals, whether personal or organizational, completely depends on the strategy chosen. Parallel to this model of self-knowledge, organizational consciousness springs from:

- **Imagination:**
  dare to dream of the future – what do you want to be and where do you want to go?
- **Conscience:**
  what values stimulate or obstruct the realization of your dream?
- **Freedom of choice:**
  make the choices that serve your dream

It is all about aligning your talents and ambitions with the structure, working method and skills of your architecture firm.

About POACHING!

"Maybe, architecture doesn't have to be stupid after all. Liberated from the obligation to construct, it can become a way of thinking about anything – a discipline that represents relationships, proportions, connections, effects, the diagram of everything."

Rem Koolhaas, Content, 2004

Text by Paul Rajakovics, transparadiso, Vienna, Austria

Poaching is a hedonistic principle. It combines cunning, freedom, the wilderness and the lure of what is forbidden. The poacher tracks foreign prey. Yet poaching is also a practice of everyday life, a strategy for survival. Michel de Certeau described this notion in *The Practice of Everyday Life* as an intellectual exercise performed by reading, "The reader produces gardens that miniaturize and collate a world, like a Robinson Crusoe discovering an island; but he, too, is 'possessed' by his own fooling and jesting that introduces plurality and difference into the written system of a society and a text. He is thus a novelist. He deterritorializes himself, oscillating in a nowhere between what he invents and what changes him. Sometimes, in fact, like a hunter in the forest, he spots the written quarry, follows a trail, laughs, plays tricks, or else like a gambler, lets himself be taken in by it. Sometimes he loses the fictive securities of reality when he reads: his escapades exile him from the assurances that give the self its location on the social checkerboard."

A change in the image of the profession

Changes in socio-economic conditions hardly allow any possibility of retaining the classic image of the professional architect. Almost imperceptibly, economic neo-liberalism has, under the pretext of reduced aesthetics, made its entry into the field of architecture. To overstate the case: any intellectual approach means a danger for returns on capital and computer-optimized building transactions. At any rate, there will soon be no more demand even for technicians in the process of implementation, despite much-repeated claims to the contrary, but rather for lawyers, who are able to play a game of contractual penalties in order to squeeze out what is presumed to be the best price for the client. And so optimal architectural details will be retrieved from computer archives and legally confirmed by ISO-standards, whereas actual payment for the construction work can be organized through 'protected companies' by way of premiums. Design and the project submission processes could be reduced to a minimum through the use of archived solutions in the form of simple combinations of tasks for almost any field, like in the planning of prefabricated housing. In customized architecture, for example, this has already become a reality today. Bemoaning long-gone professional ethics is no help here; all that can be done is to confront the question of how

creative potential might be introduced again into architecture and urban planning.

In response to neo-liberal economic structures, OMA has entered into an intellectual liaison with them. Creative potential is no longer seen in architecture or classical urban planning, but rather in reprogramming them. In this way, this potential is channeled as a creative force onto the terrain of local authorities and developers. However, OMA has even gone one step further: with the foundation of AMO, a think-tank for programs and counter-programs has been established in which architects can work consistently on selected subjects that are independent of architecture. Here, employees focus on marketing questions in just the same way in which they examine aspects of the worldwide connections of globalization in relation to a variety of subjects and occasions. Yet at the same time, this level of the independent think-tank has in turn become an economic factor for OMA. As a result of this, global players such as Prada, Volkswagen, and Ikea are now among AMO's prestigious customers. The architecture can immediately be supplied by OMA – where it makes sense to do so. The advantage of the work of AMO lies quite simply in the playful handling of these fields and subjects, where a more open approach is likely to open up new potential (in foreign territory), which could not be detected by a consultant strictly working along the guidelines of his professional expertise.

So why are there so few successful imitators of OMA/AMO? At present, the system only works due to the unique role that OMA/AMO has been able to adopt for itself. Their self-presentation as global players in the media and the authority of a professorship at Harvard provide them with a unique image amongst companies. Yet OMA's secret also lies in its traditionally anachronistic approach to the formulation of tasks that is ultimately based on a founding structure that was quite unusual for its time: a Dutch architect, who was actually a playwright and journalist (Rem Koolhaas), an artist (Madelon Vriesendorp) and two Greek architects (Elia and Zoe Zenghelis). The know-how drawn from various professions and cultural backgrounds helped to put given tasks in a wider perspective. Today, OMA/AMO certainly works very differently: Rem Koolhaas is at the zenith of his career, but also at the top of a pyramid of many young architects who are ready to work and/or poach a lot for (very) little money.

The image of the profession has undergone great changes, both in terms of its social status and in the eyes of architects themselves. Architecture has always presented itself as a profession for generalists. That may be the reason why some architects still claim that architecture is the 'supreme discipline' – the all-embracing art. At the same time, the pressure on an individual to be able to do it all by him or herself is, in reality, normally far too great. That is why, for some time, specialization has become common in architecture. In many cases, specialists have even set up their own offices, each of which focuses on one specific area, such as planning applications, construction and detail planning. For everything beyond this, experts from the other disciplines are called in. On the other hand, in the big architectural offices, architects from all fields work together.

The 'designer architect' likes to see himself at the top, not only as far as the process of implementing a building contract is concerned, but also in terms of his own personal importance. The media then present the architecture as noble profession, which is defined solely in terms of design. Even in the mid-twentieth century, the image of the profession promoted by Le Corbusier, for example, resembled that of an ingenious superman: "I wish that architects would become the elite of society, intellectually the wealthiest of human beings, that they would be open to everything. Architecture is an attitude of mind and not a profession. I see further: the architect should be the most sensitive person, the most well-informed of all the connoisseurs of art. He should be able to judge sculptural and aesthetic productions even better than his technical calculations."

The team versus lone warriors

On examining Europe-wide networks such as Wonderland from outside, it becomes obvious that the architects involved are mostly teams and not individuals. Teamwork as a brand label, but also in the sense of the division of labor, is one of the most significant outward signs of the changes in the image of the architectural profession. Yet they still exist, those lone warriors, the 'model geniuses', the frustrated owners of architectural offices who feel that they have not been given due recognition, who – like Corbusier – still see architecture as the 'supreme discipline'. However, it is becoming increasingly evident that they represent what is, in all probability, a discontinued model. Moreover, teamwork has gained new significance in an (architectural) world determined by increasingly narrow economic parameters. Flexibility and adaptability to changing conditions give a better chance to a small but well-rehearsed team than to a large architectural firm with many highly specialized employees. Teamwork is also a result of the impossibility of keeping an overview of the architect's vast field of work. Teamwork thus may take two directions: on the one hand, it is a form of internal cooperation on a peer basis with different roles and skills which are then communicated to the outside as a single entity, and on the other hand, it can take the form of cooperation of the team with other collaborators from related areas or even with local government, investors, developers and administrative authorities.

Teamwork, however, must be conceptualized in order to be successful: it requires much social intelligence and frequent restraint of one's ego in decision-making processes. In many cases, the corset may become rather tight in the process, conveying a feeling of being caught in a partnership of convenience. In the best-case scenario, a team also provides emotional and social support and helps to cope with the extreme demands of the profession's reality. Often, it is an economic necessity for one or more team members to work for other office practices or institutions, or alternatively, to teach at a university in order to ensure economic survival. How else could one financially survive the protracted period between competition tender and start construction? Today teams are emerging not only out of necessity, but rather because the added value of teamwork has finally been recognized as the only way of meeting the current complex demands made on the architectural profession. This means that many different skills must be brought together in order to be able to do canvassing, planning, and execution in parallel. In return for the reduced appearance of the ego, each team member is equally involved in the success of a project and in the symbolic capital connected with it.

However, no less importantly, teamwork provides the best basis for poaching in other fields without having to completely abandon the field of architecture itself.

Working field versus interdisciplinarity

From cartoonist to writer of children's books, from curator to artist, from writer on economics to rock musician, trained architects are found in many other fields. Sven Nordquist, author of the famous *Petterson and Findus* series of children's books, is a trained architect, as was the former director of the Jewish Documentation Centre, Simon Wiesental, as well as the legendary mountaineer Luis Trenker. The list of architects who turned their back on architecture and were successful in other fields, especially in the visual arts, can be extended almost infinitely. Who would still think of Marjetica Potrc (artist) or Peter Pakesch (curator and museum director), as trained architects?

On the other hand, there are also many examples of successful architects who never studied architecture: Tadao Ando (boxer), Viktor Grün (stand-up comedian), Peter Zumthor (carpenter) or Vito Acconci, who moved on from being a superstar of performance and concept art and became an international architect. Moreover, increasing complexity in all specialist areas make clear-cut boundaries between disciplines ever more obsolete. Demand for transdisciplinary positions grew as traditional disciplines splintered into ever smaller specialized segments. Today, for instance, lawyers with an additional technology or engineering degree are certainly among the most keenly sought-after job candidates. Meanwhile, project-oriented data have been introduced where previously extensive and time-consuming interdisciplinary exchange was necessary. It is not that we no longer need the expert opinions, but rather that information often has to be incorporated into a project very quickly, in order to keep up with competitors. A quick look at the Internet provides a first insight into the foreign territory, which then becomes decisive for further decision-making. A common working field opens up the possibility of new role distribution in the approach to architecture. In the process, hiding behind the barriers of one's own discipline is certainly not a possibility; rather, it is facing the task at hand together. The field of work does not enquire about the origin of an idea, but follows tactical and strategic considerations.

Old pop and new topicality

The Royal College of Art in London organized a series of lectures with panel discussions which took a stance against "ego-oriented cliché of the fountainhead architect" and in which groups of British architects such as Archigram, NATO, muf, UFO or G4 (Alsop, Agents of Change, Branson Coates, and FAT) discussed their approach to, and mode of, teamwork. The interesting aspect about G4 is that this group, which is actually comprised of several teams, regards itself as a collective – spanning several generations of architects. Together, they want to establish themselves above and beyond project partnerships reviving the long tradition the idea of the collective has accumulated by now.

Particularly in the 1960s and '70s, significant groups of architects were formed with pop music as a model. The group became a new strategy of self-presentation that derived from the youth culture of that time and opposes the classical image of the architectural profession. Impersonal group names indicated the primacy of the collective over the individual ego. The groups established pursued a wide variety of utopias: Archigram, for instance, cherished a boundless belief in technology and infrastructure. They combined colorful collage-like representations as a new kind of aesthetics in the presentation of architecture with the lavish use of material technology and an unbridled belief in technological innovation. A quite different, though also montage-based, approach was demonstrated by the Italian group Superstudio, which communicated the abysmal nature of structure and technology, yet without abandoning the ambivalence between political pessimism and criticism of consumerism on the one hand, and utopian concepts on the other. Their criticism of Modernism was manifested in the way they rejected it. Today, almost all these approaches can be seen in the context of the events of 1968, even where it is only a matter of formal criticism or deconstruction, as in the case of Coop Himmelblau, where 'Coop' again is short for 'cooperative' in the sense of a manifesto for the collective. What all these groups had in common was that they sought to herald a new beginning and that their manifesto-like character was more easily communicable through the art and university scene than through building projects. These groups did not focus on architecture alone, but rather propagated a collective and holistic lifestyle based on the rejection of traditional social models. The Californian Ant Farm group also proclaimed the rebirth of architecture, based on their experience of the hippie movement. Speed and technological hedonism were coupled with the mobility of the American lifestyle. Thus many of their projects include cars, though not without an element of critique. As with the literature of the Beat Generation at that time, it was hedonism, the moment, and the abyss that expanded the architectural horizons of Ant Farm. The abrupt end of Ant Farm was related to the fate of their office, which burned down. Their whole work was destroyed and their manifesto-like House of the Century in Texas was flooded with mud. This almost symbolic end of the group in 1978 is symptomatic of the (first) failed attempt to expand the image of the profession. Almost all the groups of this epoch broke up in the late 1970s, when social consensus had it that 1968 had failed as a movement in the face of reality. The claims of utopianism were simply too much. However, the secret wish of many architects to transfer the aesthetics to a holistic lifestyle remained.

The Situationists around Guy Debord, who had partly helped to organize the revolution of 1968, had also developed a wide variety of methods to include the instant and/or the situation in the design process. Here, urbanism was presented as a new overriding discipline using improved psycho-geographies, and a new subversive view of architecture and urban development became possible. While urban development no longer inspired manifestos about planning, but rather about the construction of situations, Constant, and to some extent also Aldo van Eyck, began to explore dynamic architecture the view of which is manifested through a situation or a moment. An extended notion of urbanism developed: "Unitary Urbanism", a theory of the overall application of artistic and technical means that combine in the total construction of a milieu dynamically connected to behavioral experiments, is regarded as the basis for the designer's intervention in the everyday space or the sphere of action. However, this became manifest rather in the rejection of a society hungry for the spectacular than in the manipulation of individual freedom. Détournement (misappropriation) or dérives (drifting), for example, were developed as urban methods. Naturally, this is a largely unused field of possibilities for urbanists (even though much has been written about it, a broader practice has not gained ground yet).

However, it is not surprising that in the late 1970s or around 1980, the exponents of the dystopian punk movement in London encouraged a revival of Situationist ideas. The group NATO (Catrin Beevor, Nigel Coates, Robert Mull, Christina Norton, Mark Prizeman, Carlos Villanueva-Brandt and Melanie Sainsbury), who at that time were part of a scene that included Sid Vicious, Johnny Rotten, Jamie Reed and Vivienne Westwood, attemp-

ted to introduce punk culture into everyday life through trash architecture.

More important today is the influence of Robert Mull and Carlos Villanueva-Brandt & Co, who were active as teachers at the Architectural Association and other schools of architecture, and still are today. Their expanded notion of architecture influenced many young architecture groups in the London of the 1990s.

Groups of the 1990s

In the 1990s, FAT (Fashion, Architecture, Taste) or muf architecture/art, established a new type of architectural office in the midst of the booming creative scene in London. Although these two groups, which are still active today, are very different, they share an almost programmatic light-heartedness – even in the group names. Art or fashion, taste or art – their expanded notion of architecture applies easily. Whereas FAT were given building opportunities early on in their career, the Museum Pavilion in St. Albans was the first remarkable building by muf. muf (Liza Fior, Katherina Clarke (artists) and Melanie Dodd (architect)), which was originally conceived as a purely female group, have focussed their work on the different notions of space: public space, architectural space and the research in space: "Since 1996 muf has established a reputation for pioneering and innovative projects that address the social, spatial and economic infrastructures of the public realm. The practice philosophy is driven by an ambition to realize the potential pleasures that exist at the intersection between the lived and the built." muf works extensively in the field of art and culture, as well as in the area of exhibitions and urban interventions. As a consequence, the extended muf group also includes other artists and an urban planning theorist. Their purview is a distinct working field that is defined by the backgrounds of the individual partners.

Around 1993, the group K-architectures was founded in Montpellier, France. Here too, the different backgrounds of the individual members define an interesting interdisciplinary working field. In 1996, Thierry Verdier (art historian and architect), Karin Herman (graphic artist), together with Jerôme Sigwalt (architect) won a sensational Europan competition in Aubervilliers. Radical urban development and socially ambitious initiatives in the banlieue were transformed into Photoshop representations for the first time. Perhaps it was these representations that helped the Photoshop image-editing program to establish itself as a medium of architectural communication before it became the rather overused general tool that it is today. (K-architectures have also been part of Wonderland). One could also name many other groups established in the 1990s that work on a more open field: Propeller Z (Austria; architecture/industrial design/graphic design), Stalker (Italy; art/architecture), The Poor Boys Enterprise (Austria; architecture), Crimson (Holland; architecture and research).

New potentials and Wonderland

All in all, it is legitimate to speak of the phenomenon of architecture 'pop groups' as a Europe-wide movement in the 1990s. However, in recent years, Wonderland's way of looking at areas of work has been dominated more and more by the increasingly difficult economic situation. Long project lead-times, together with cuts in the cultural budgets that used to support an expanded notion of architecture have led to changes in production conditions. With Wonderland a new, heterogeneous generation of architects has presented itself to the general public, a generation that covers a broad spectrum extending from provider of services to a responsible co-designer of society, and one which explores foreign territory not only within the cultural field.

The gulf between academia and practice continues to widen. Creative thinking today means continual reinventing of one's job and the professional field, so as to be able to operate in the market and to build, and pursue, parallel strategies.

In fact, the poacher is someone who is pursued, who is always on his guard for fear of being

caught. Yet, this also means staying always one step ahead of one's pursuers, even ahead of capital "as the sole power capable of bestowing bliss". Young architects are increasingly focusing on other creative fields of activity, such as web and graphic design, event design or cultural projects in general. The search for new urban development solutions, such as to the problem of shrinking cities, also brings up issues that involve the (practically infinite) extension of the purview of the profession – architects and urbanists are being consulted for their advice on almost insoluble social and structural questions. However, at the same time, in Germany – and above all in Berlin, the center of current architectural developments – unemployment among architects is becoming a serious topic. In this situation, some of the Wonderland teams also go 'poaching' in other cultural fields, for example EXYZT (Paris) with their 'Berg' at the Berlin Palace of the Republic, or Peanutz, with their spectacular exhibition designs. Yet, more homogeneous teams do better in terms of a more goal-oriented and effective style of poaching. Recently, I met 'star' (all of them former AMO collaborators): this young team from Rotterdam today earns a living on making statistics and producing visual statistical renderings. This niche guarantees their survival, while they are still waiting for building commissions. For young architects today, the large-scale and demanding architectural commission becomes the much-hunted prey. Some of these poachers would very much like to bag something in their own territory, for a change …

Alternatively

Poaching can also mean remaining an amateur, entering foreign territory and looking around with curious eyes, perhaps in order tap some (foreign) potential. Yet those who poach should also accept that others will go poaching in their territory … ▪

REALITY CHECK #1: GETTING STARTED

A survey about getting started in architecture across Europe

The Wonderland network provided the basis for this survey, getting us in contact with 99 practices from 9 different EU countries (Slovakia, Czech Republik, Croatia, Slovenia, Austria, Germany, Netherlands, France and Italy).

The survey included a total of 37 questions taking approximately 45 minutes to fill in. Sent out in early November 2005, it received 58 responses. Each country is represented by a minimum of 5 practices; what they have in common is that they are small (less than 7 people on average).

Given the number of participants, it obviously is a very relative measure. We nevertheless consider it an indication of the prospects that small practices are faced with in their first years.

We received both positive and negative feedback. Some doubted the relevance of the issues raised. For others, the questions were helpful to create greater awareness of their own strategy, after adding up, for example, for the first time ever the real number of working hours that went into a project.

In addition to the quantitative data, the practices were asked to write about their own story and strategy. A selection of these stories offer another, maybe more qualitative, kind of reality check of what it is like to start working as an architect in Europe today.

GROUP IDENTITY OR ONE-(WO)MAN SHOWS

2.3 partners is the average size for the Wonderland-type of practice. The majority of the practices are run by 2 to 3 partners, 21% are one-(wo)man shows, 10% have more than 3 partners.

More than 3 partners
10%

Single practice
21%

2 or 3 partners
69%

FEMALE FACTOR

Women are still a minority: of 135 total architects surveyed, only 38 (28%) were women.

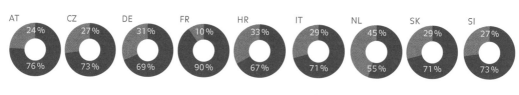

AT	CZ	DE	FR	HR	IT	NL	SK	SI
24%	27%	31%	10%	33%	29%	45%	29%	27%
76%	73%	69%	90%	67%	71%	55%	71%	73%

● Percentage of male partners   ● Percentage of female partners

Source: Wonderland #1 Survey – by SHARE architects, 2005

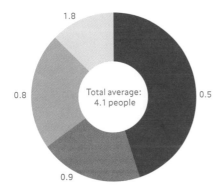

1.8

0.8

Total average:
4.1 people

0.5

0.9

Number of employees/collaborators
(not including the partners)

8 years

The Czech teams appear to be the most successful in business terms. They realized the highest number of projects (with, for example, an average of 14 built projects in their 4th year). They have an average of 9.6 employees and their average annual revenues are at least more than twice as much as everybody else's. One additional detail may be worth noting: they have at least one person employed in administration. A secretary.

getting started

- ● Administration
- ● Trainees
- ● Part time architects, technologists
- ○ Full time architects, technologists

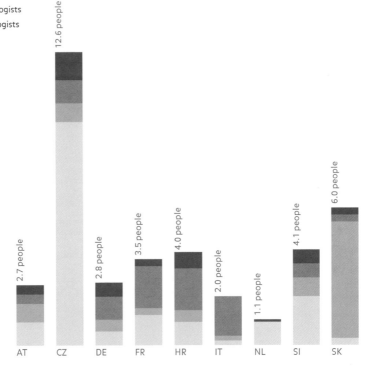

12.6 people

2.7 people

2.8 people

3.5 people

4.0 people

2.0 people

1.1 people

4.1 people

6.0 people

AT   CZ   DE   FR   HR   IT   NL   SI   SK

Source: Wonderland #1 Survey – by SHARE architects, 2005

Field of action

Asking young architects about their field of work, you will receive a wide variety of answers. This makes it clear that universal definitions of what an architect does have gone out of date. Below we introduce five teams and their highly personal self-definitions.

Text by Anne Isopp

/// PURISTS 100% architecture ////////////////////////////////////

ATMOSFERA Founded 2002 by Bernarda and Davor Silov. Based in Zagreb, Croatia

"No one who has ideas will sit around and wait for clients to come along" – this is the strategy of ATMOSFERA, a practice engaged in strategy, architecture and design. The two architects behind this name do have any number of ideas. In fact, they have many, many projects in stock, half of them concrete commissions or competition entries, the other half unsolicited projects. Davor Silov and his wife Bernarda who set up ATMOSFERA in 2002 want to convince clients of unusual building solutions: "We want to take a step ahead in form and shape." Both of them reject the term 'utopian', which is commonly used to label them, notably so in connection with their 'Diving club' project. They say: "We keep fighting against the notion of utopia, because we don't see that it reflects what we do. To us, all our projects are realistic, and we think it is only a matter of time until they will materialize." The 'Diving club', one of their first projects, is a water-filled sphere of stratified glass for people to dive inside while watching the birds and clouds outside. They consider visionary, experimental and conceptual design to be a necessary prerequisite for the architectures of the future. Davor Silov would not want to busy himself with run-of-the-mill architecture: "Making architecture for someone who just wants a cube with a roof on it? I don't have interest and time to do that." In the future he wants to work on a few nice projects every year – "in a peaceful way". In this way, ATMOSPHERA produces, apart from their realized architectural output, many purely exploratory designs intended for nonspecific sites and clients. Their motto is: "30% design, 40% freedom and 30% work". www.atmosfera.hr

MAP STUDIO Founded 2004 by Francesco Magnani and Traudy Pelzel. Based in Venice, Italy

"The common thread throughout all different scales is the focus on architectural design." Francesco Magnani and Traudy Pelzel both got their degree in Venice but also studied in Portugal and Sweden. Their portfolio includes projects involving refurbishment of existing buildings, such as the Torre di Porta Nuova in the Venetian Arsenale, new constructions, residential interiors, and exhibition designs. One of the main challenges they face is how to keep in control of the design throughout all project stages. This is important in order to guarantee the necessary quality of the final result. Especially in Italy, this also has an impact on the size of the practice, given that because of the limited market for architectural services larger offices have difficulties focusing exclusively on architectural design. "There is a fine balance between the size of the practice, the quality of the projects and the number of the projects needed to guarantee the survival of the practice itself." In Map's view, the building approval process in Italy is of particular importance and calls for specific planning and strategic approaches to further the realization of the project. All in all, Map is proud of their portfolio of realized projects today, particularly so considering the deep Italian crisis of recent years and the persistent lack of dynamism of the Italian context. www.map-studio.it

/// CROSS-BREEDERS Interdisciplinary approach, hybrid projects /////////////

no w here Founded 1999 by Karl Amann and Henning Volpp. Based in Stuttgart, Germany

In the beginning, no w here was merely a practice for participation in competitions. Until 2005, Karl Amann and Henning Volpp held teaching posts at the university in Stuttgart. It was their success in the 2001 competition for the Domsingschule (Cathedral School) in Stuttgart that brought them a large amount of work. Now the two spend

one-hundred percent of their time in their office. From the very start, they sought collaboration with other special-ists. Together with fellow-architect Sibylle Heeg, they established the Gesellschaft für Soziales Planen (GSP, Society for Social Planning) in 2003. In the meantime they have completed a number of nursing homes and related facilities. "We realized that our profile as architects is not much help in approaching people who commission nursing homes", says Karl Amann, who, like his partner, divides his time between their architecture practice, no w here, and GSP. It is important for him to always have projects at different levels. Success in one area can be an advantage in another: "In the Domsingschule project, the client was the Catholic Church. We showed them our GSP work and were promptly invited to take part in a competition for a hospice. As no w here architects, we would never have been invited." According to Amann, working in so very different areas helps you keep your freedom of thinking.
www.nowherearchitekten.de, www.sozialesplanen.de

ALL-ROUNDERS Situation-dependent forays from an architectural basis

Encore Heureux Founded 2001 by Julien Choppin and Nicola Delon. Based in Paris, France
Julien Choppin and Nicola Delon are all-rounders. Even before completing their studies, they set up their own prac-tice as a collective named *Encore Hereux*, as they wanted to further develop their graduation project, *Wagons-Scènes* – a train that is convertible into a concert hall. To be able to afford their independence – "the first three years we worked in our kitchen, but now we have something that resembles an office" – they also worked as graphic designers, 3-D modelers and web designers. "By now we can do so many things – we want to experience as many things as possible," says Nicola Delon. After 11 years of practice without a built project, they delivered their first building, Petit Bain, a cultural venue floating on the Seine at the foot of the Bibliothèque nationale de France in Paris. Now an office employing about 20 people, architects and non-architects, they develop their activities around four main pillars: buildings, new or to be renovated; scenography, temporary or permanent; reuse as a research field but also a daily practice; and more experimental, artistic or research focused projects such as books or movies. Moreover, they still want to experiment on diverse scales, programs and types of commissions (public or private). Their work ranges from the reorganization of the international headquarters of the Michelin industrial group in Clermont-Ferrand to an art installation underneath a Paris ring road, aimed at redefining and easing the relationship between local residents and sellers at an informal flea market held on weekends. Julien Choppin: "This is the kind of project we want to do more often: There is a problem, and we find a solution." http://encoreheureux.org

Artgineering Founded 2001 by Stefan Bendiks and Aglaée Degros. Based in Brussels, Belgium
"From the name Artgineering, one might assume that we are an artists' collective. However, we research and publish on urban planning and mobility, and currently, we are realizing several public space projects mostly in Belgium: squares, parks, bicycle highways, etc." Stefan Bendiks and Aglaée Degros work at the interface between urban planning and mobility. The unresolved relationship between urban development and infrastructure has come to be one of their main themes. "Just as the motorway and the city are strictly separated from one another, so are urban planning and traffic engineering. This is precisely where our projects begin." They address this issue in research projects and artistic interventions, but also through commissions to actually build public spaces. Today, Stefan Bendiks is an internationally renowned consultant for active mobility, and Aglaée Degros is a professor for urbanism at the Graz University of Technology (TU). Stefan Bendiks: "Over the years, we have adopted a particular line when confronted with the question of what Artgineering actually does. It is good for potential clients if they can put us into one category or another." If this results in concrete design tasks, such as the Park Belle-Vue in Leuven, this is very much what Artgineering is out for: "We have always been looking for the most effective way of changing things." This may equally take the form of a planning contract or an art project. In the beginning, they still dealt with architectural commissions in a classical sense: "But we quickly found that this was not what really interested us. There are many practices that see what we do exclusively as a prelude to the construction of buildings. But for us, and this is an important point, this is not so. For us, it is simply the most effective way of changing reality." www.artgineering.eu

FIELD OF ACTION

Purist, All-Rounder or Cross-Breeder?

For more than half of the practices surveyed, a substantial part of the work (more than one third of the working time) lies outside of the field of architecture.
Apart from the services provided to other companies, their portfolio includes teaching (60.4 % of the practices), graphic and webpage design, journalism, and event management (41.5%).
While operating in an expanded field of action may help to generate more commissions, it does not offer higher income margins than architecture. See page 58.

The **Cross-Breeders** interact with and draw from other professions, create hybrids.

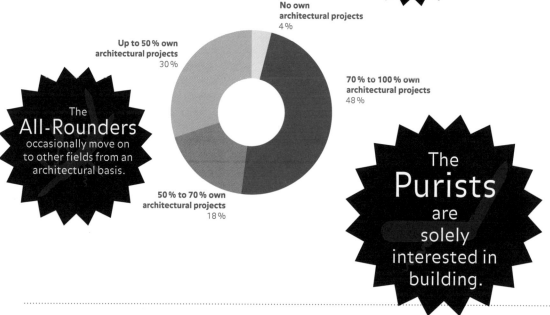

No own architectural projects
4 %

Up to 50 % own architectural projects
30 %

70 % to 100 % own architectural projects
48 %

The **All-Rounders** occasionally move on to other fields from an architectural basis.

50 % to 70 % own architectural projects
18 %

The **Purists** are solely interested in building.

Other fields

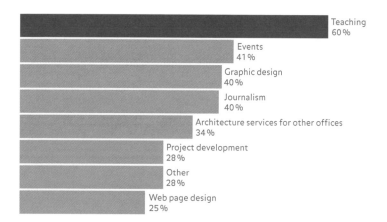

Teaching 60 %
Events 41 %
Graphic design 40 %
Journalism 40 %
Architecture services for other offices 34 %
Project development 28 %
Other 28 %
Web page design 25 %

Source: Wonderland #1 Survey – by SHARE architects, 2005

how to keep up

No other profession requires more skill to strike a reasonable balance of time invested, quality achieved, and money gained. Of the 58 practices surveyed, 95% admit to offering part of their work for free. At the same time, working hours add up to an average of 51 per week, and the project survival rate is estimated as being less than 50% on an average. Clients are difficult to find and easy to lose. Media success is no guarantee of business success.

What counts, and needs to be learnt in time, is the ability to run a business, negotiation skills, trust-building capacities, time management and marketing in all its forms.

Negotiation between aesthetics and client demands

Interview with Eva Boudewijn

Interview by Astrid Piber

I n the beginnings of every architectural practice, the essential thing is winning clients. First client contacts and first projects are then hoped to lead to follow-up commissions. Client relations are vital for growing a portfolio and a business. But what is the position that the client/user has in a start-up practice, and how client-oriented are you willing to design? Traditionally, architectural education is focused on aesthetic and creative aspects. The business knowledge of running an office has to be acquired on the job – learning by doing. Eva Boudewijn worked for many years as a business consultant and trainer.

wonderland: *What do you think young start-up architects should consider first?*

Eva Boudewijn: It all begins with your own identity: knowing who you are and believing in what you want to be and knowing your aspirations, so that you can translate that into a form or type of organization. So soul searching should be the first move to know what kind of architect you want to be.

Isn't there a natural conflict between the creative side of architecture and running an architectural business?

Conflict will always be there. If you want to avoid it, maybe you should keep architecture as a hobby. If you want to make it a business, you will always have to deal with clients and keep your organization running. Maybe you can join up with a partner who focuses on the commercial and business aspect. It is one option of not having to do that all yourself. But, I guess, not many start-ups can afford that luxury.

Why do you think that architects and designers need business consultants?

Architects, especially beginners in the profession, are preoccupied with architectural content. But when you start a business, then there is more to it than just architectural content. You have to keep in mind this formula: 'effect = quality × acceptance' – that you have to be able to sell your content or your talent and make that attractive for a client. Besides architectural content, the commercial side or networking and the managing of your business are essential.

How does an architect find his/her client?

There are several strategies, and they are related to what type of architect you are. I would say that a studio needs to develop some sort of brand awareness and invest a lot in publishing and public relations. The other strategy is networking, making sure you know a lot of people to whom you can

$E = Q \times A$
(Effect = Quality × Acceptance)

Architectural talent and skills alone are not enough to be successful. Success depends on your ability to get acceptance for your design or vision. This requires excellent communication skills. It starts with establishing an authentic relationship, being able to explain and convince and overcome conflicts and irritations.

present yourself and produce good work, because this gives you word-of-mouth to get new assignments.

Does cold acquisition work for architects?
Cold acquisition is a strategy in which you skip the stage of building a relationship and go for the contract right away. To some extent it could work for a studio-type firm. After all, a successful studio should have established some brand awareness, which means that they have a name that means something to people. In generally, I would say cold acquisition does not work, because you need the client's trust, and that takes time and effort and networking.

But many architects are afraid of becoming like vacuum-cleaner salesmen ...
I think it is a prejudice. First, you have to find the people to get in contact with. The rule is quite simple: you have to make contact first, and then you can do business. It never works the other way around. That is the big difference to being a vacuum-cleaner salesman:

You have to make contact first, and then you can do business. It never works the other way around.

you don't have a standardized product; you are offering a service. Services are sold because you have a name, or the prospect client trusts you and your qualities, and you can prove that you are a reliable creative partner.

There will always be someone who offers a cheaper, faster design. How do you bridge the difference in approach and quality awareness between architect and client?
Clients' project calculations usually are very tight. They are not based on real hours, real activities. In other industries, it is common to estimate how many hours it will take, multiply that with your hour rates, and make a price. In architecture, this is different; that is a disadvantage. You should not sell yourself short. I know that – especially when starting out – you will be eager to accept an assignment for a very low fee. That's okay, as long as you make a conscious choice that this is your investment you make in order to get other projects, to make a name for yourself as an architect. But you should try to calculate beforehand how much you are willing to invest, how many unpaid hours are acceptable for you.

If one has successfully made contact (or has established a relationship), how does one take the step to a contract?
Well, at a certain point, the relationship is evolving, the prospect is interested in your ideas, your designs, and he'll give you what I would call 'buying signals', and these you have to be alert to. Don't be afraid to say "This is now the fifth time that we are talking about this project; when are we going to do business?" That may be difficult, but it helps when you know what you want to accomplish. Don't be too pushy, because this may have an opposite effect.

So, how does one maintain a good client relationship?
That does not happen by itself. Even if you had a good client relationship before the assignment, you still have to work on it. It means involving the client and communicating what you are doing, and being explicit about what the client has, or is expected, to contribute.

Do architects have to be afraid that clients become 'king' in the process?

No, I don't think so, it is more of a partnership between the client and the architect. Both provide input, have responsibility, and both have decisions to make. If you want to design without client interference, do it for yourself as a hobby. When the client pays the bill in the end, he has to get a service or building that he is content with. You have to consider the wishes of a client, and see it as a challenge, see it as an input and inspiration and try to find creative solutions.

How do you find a client whose interest matches with the ambitions of the architect?

As an architect, you have to be aware that everybody involved in a project has different ambitions. If the client wants to have something very fast, it will probably be more expensive, and maybe the quality will have to be lower. This is the field you have to negotiate. Don't be tempted to make decisions for the client, but present the decisions that the client has to make and make him aware of the consequences of his choices.

> **If you want to design without client interference, do it for yourself as a hobby.**

But sometimes your client does not know what he/she wants. Can you as an architect influence him?

Yes, I think it is worthwhile to invest time, and money, too, to get a clear picture of your client's requirements and wishes before you start designing. So you could use workshops, exchange ideas to help your client form a picture in his head. This is not very common for architects, who often want to start designing right away.

A client is coming back to you for a new project; does that mean you delivered a good design?

Yes, but it also might be – since designing is only one part of the service – that the client is very satisfied about the process or the way you have cooperated. I think that it is a good sign in any case, and I think it would be worthwhile to ask the client why he's coming back to you, what qualities he really likes in your work or the way you work, so that you can use that to readjust and confirm your own strategy. ❦

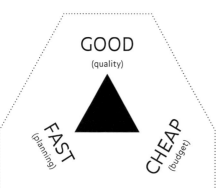

GOOD
(quality)

FAST
(planning)

CHEAP
(budget)

In every project there is a tension between quality, budget and planning. Better quality often is more expensive and takes longer to realize. The challenge of every project is to balance these three aspects. This can be complicated when the designer and the client have different ambitions. When it comes to making decisions, explore the consequences for the quality, budget and planning together, so that each party can make their decision.

START-UP INVESTMENT

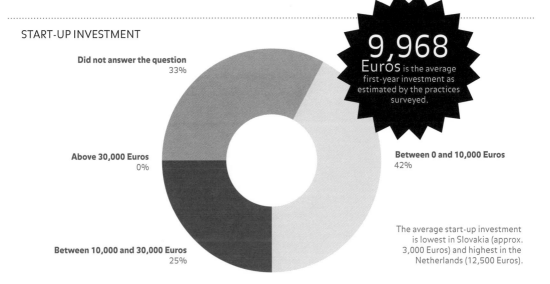

Did not answer the question
33%

Above 30,000 Euros
0%

Between 10,000 and 30,000 Euros
25%

Between 0 and 10,000 Euros
42%

9,968 Euros is the average first-year investment as estimated by the practices surveyed.

The average start-up investment is lowest in Slovakia (approx. 3,000 Euros) and highest in the Netherlands (12,500 Euros).

GETTING CLIENTS

Reason for acquisition

Previous work 45%
Other 32%
Study 19%
Competition 15%
Social contact 8%

First project

Renovation 33%
Competition 31%
Self initiated 30%
Single-family house 27%
EUROPAN competition 4%
Commission through previous office 2%

Connection to first client

Social contact 68%
Previous working relations 25%
Competition 23%
Family 23%
Other 23%

Paradox: to get your first project you actually need to have a previous project to show for. Getting clients and projects through competitions is possible: 31% of the practices got their first commission this way, and 49% name this as one way of getting clients now.

Clients now on the basis of ...

Social contact 89%
Projects built 57%
Competitions 50%
Other 28%

Source: Wonderland #1 Survey – by SHARE architects, 2005

Getting started

DANCE OF THE MARKETING MIX

There is no little 'vade mecum' of marketing taught in schools today – in contrast to microbiology and nuclear physics. The following article presents a little ABC of marketing from an architect's point of view.

Text by Tore Dobberstein, complizen Planungsbüro, Halle and Berlin, Germany

What is it about the m-word? In intelligentsia circles, we often complain about the advertising overflow on television, in our virtual and real mailboxes and in our favorite lifestyle magazines. Are we now supposed to start doing it, too? Using manipulation? Using brainwashing? Offering bargains in the art of building?

The experience of young architects indicates the way that things are going: for most design and planning offices, it is not easy to get, or keep, a foothold in the market. The building sector is subject to its own economic cycles, which means that every crisis will come to an end – but also that no boom will go on forever.

The fact is that there are many suppliers of planning services, but little demand for their work. This is probably the main reason why the interest in marketing is increasing among architects. Still, is there anything that we can learn from the world of marketing? Doesn't architecture have a quite different pace than ordinary consumer-oriented businesses? After all, everyone knows clients who do not have the slightest idea of what is really good ...

Decades of research have hitherto not produced a uniform marketing doctrine. Theorists distinguish between marketing for consumer goods, marketing for investments and even marketing for services. The services that we

as architects have to offer are located somewhere in the overlap zone of these three fields:

In relation to market competition, we need the image of a 'must have' fashion label.

Considering the financial risk taken by our clients, we do clearly need the reliability of a mechanical engineer or building contractor.

And finally, the fact that client satisfaction is largely dependent on the extent of our compliance with their wishes would suggest the kind of service-mindedness you tend to find in a massage studio.

That sounds like renouncing all our values and ideals in favor of reckless commercialization. And this cannot be the solution. What is more, we all know that personal values and ideals are precisely the factors that have made successful colleagues leap into the limelight.

Thorough architectural marketing should begin with some basic strategic questions:
What do I stand for? Where do I want to go? The answer is: positioning. Many Wonderland teams have a comprehensible philosophy or mission. We can learn from the marketing world that, once found, this positioning does not last forever, but rather is dynamic in character. For example, the image of a young practice definitely has an expiry date.

Moreover, it is important that we present a uniform and coherent self-image to potential clients; with coherent referring to all interfaces of our practice – working material, the office itself, portfolios, visiting cards,

lectures, web presence, articles in journals etc. To do so is less a matter of brainwashing than of acknowledging the fact that the brain cannot endlessly distinguish logos, names and colors. In creative professions in particular, people are always re-inventing themselves: "Have you seen our new logo?" Not a good idea! Only with one definite identity will we be adequately perceived. A so-called corporate image is the basis to make sure that the character of our office – i. e. what we are – does not become blurred.

Once we have created such an identity, we can begin the marketing work. Here we can go by the classic tenets of marketing, those 4 P's that are common knowledge in the business world: Product, Price, Place and Promotion.

We have to check whether our market positioning, our image, and the services that we offer (Product) form a comprehensible unity. In addition, our pricing policy (Price), distribution policy (Place), and our communication (Promotion) need to be harmonized and tailor-made for us.

What is the product that we are offering? Extending the range of activities is a trend currently found in many architectural practices. Teams such as blauraum Architekten (Germany) or fabrica (Slovakia), for example, run galleries or shops in the immediate vicinity of their offices. Changing to the service business should not be primarily interpreted as a second-best option or solely as a response to economic pressures. Product innovation is the result of architects' entrepreneurial and artistic creativity. Skills that have been acquired at university can also be productively applied outside the traditional field of building.

As a marketing instrument, the price is crucial for architects. On the one hand, planners in many countries are compulsorily organized in professional associations which specify service conditions and regulate prices, thus preventing price competition, through fee scales and codes of conduct. From the point of view of the suppliers, the architects, such regulation is attractive, since the necessity of competitive pricing tends to bring considerably lower fees, notably starting fees. However, better earning prospects entail that the market may be overrun by ever more would-be suppliers. You cannot turn one wheel at a time in the market system without having another wheel that is turning with it.

Another question is whether all this regulation business is worth the effort, since customers demanding planning services cannot really be called very price sensitive. As a commodity, planning services are comparable only with difficulty, and what is more, they are hardly substitutable. "Yes, fine design, but I can get the same for 120 Euros less on the Internet – I'm sorry. Goodbye!" is not a realistic scenario. Usually, it is other factors that influence the decision to buy, as long as we keep prices at the market level.

Web presence is important promotion. Studies show that buying decisions are often made on impulse, spontaneously and quickly. If access to an Internet page constitutes the first or second contact, then it may be here where a client relationship begins, or not.

Special attention should be given to the language we use in communicating with prospects. We should keep in mind that our (potential) clients have not studied architecture. Apart from the obvious need to make oneself understood, prospective clients should be addressed on an emotional level as well. Planning often is a kind of luxury article (e.g. an architect-built single family home), and luxury articles tend to be sold by soft skills rather than rational arguments.

Architects usually settle matters among themselves in their professional associations or institutions. As a rule, newspaper ads and other forms of classical advertising are prohibited as unfair competition. However, such forms of business communication are increasingly less effective anyway.

For this reason, other instruments are more interesting – and not only for architects: public relations and sponsoring are currently gaining in significance in marketing as a whole. Here the issue is finding ever-new interfaces for company communication.

These new marketing strategies are decisive for distribution policy: place – how and where do we find our clients, or how and where do they find us?

One reason for the success of networks (which, to some extent, people are still talking about) was the fact that various freelancers formed a kind of sales cooperative, and thus were able to address more potential customers. The more diversified the network, the more successful the distribution strategy. Since Wonderland encompasses almost exclusively architects, it is not really a good example of a diversified network. Yet when freelance graphic artists, computer specialists, artists, urban planners and geographers join in to cooperate with architects, then a good sales network develops.

However, cooperatives are often unstable, and since there is still no wholesale trade for planning services, we need to offer our skills in competitions and through direct distribution. In the case of young practices, social contacts are usually top of the list, i. e. close relatives and their friends are often the first clients.

For marketing people, this is quite unsurprising and by no means trivial. After all, it is a matter of trust. Architectural services presuppose a high degree of trust. Why is trust so important and how is it developed?

Architecture is a trust commodity – our clients rely on us to service them to the best of our ability and with all due care and diligence. Just as the customers of biodynamic farmers, surgeons or hair stylists rely that the service that they pay for is good, healthy, safe, or cool.

People and brands earn our trust through credibility (being authentic). It is not only in marketing that credibility is a core topic. In private matters, too, e. g. when entering into relationships with others, we check their credibility. Interestingly enough, in many cultures dancing is one of the most successful interpersonal rituals to get to know strangers and has been practiced for centuries. What can we do if we cannot go dancing or drinking with all of our potential customers? We become members of an association and draw up lists of reference projects. Is there anything else that we can do in order to be perceived as trustworthy?

From a marketing point of view, continuous social presence is of primary importance. Apart from factors of social influence, it is also important to activate others: building cultural, personal and psychological bridges. Civil engagement and a lively participation in social life are classical (marketing) activities used by successful entrepreneurs. Then, possibly, we will manage to take the step from an introverted to an extroverted practice. When we get into direct contact with potential clients, it will soon become clear whether we have done our marketing homework or not. ✎

FACTS

Pricing

62 % consider their pricing to be at market level, 21 % below, 11 % above. Nonetheless, only 17 % strictly observe the fee scales of chambers or other professional organizations. 96 % offers some work for free. At least 16 % take on jobs even if they know that this means incurring a loss.

Product

79 % of the surveyed practices say that they are ready to compromise between aspired quality and what is possible with a specific client. 30 % pose no conditions: all budgets and clients are accepted. 13 % exclusively go for high end design: if this is not possible, the project is canceled. 49 % are ready to work unpaid extra time to achieve the best possible design. Only 25 % limit effective working time to paid time.

Place

38 % work mainly in the local market, 42 % do not distinguish between local, national and international. 11 % mainly work on international projects.

Promotion

Only 4 % hire professional marketing or public-relations assistance. 7 % do not want to have anything to do with it, while 86 % try to get published and do the marketing on their own.

Source: Wonderland #1 Survey – by SHARE architects, 2005

PROJECT SURVIVAL

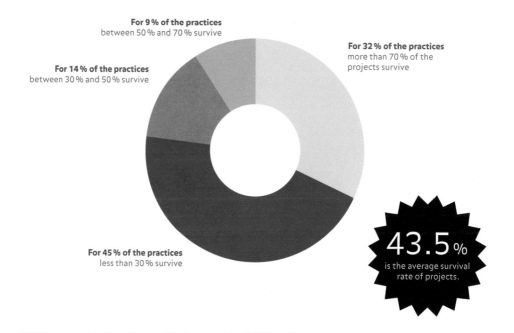

For 9 % of the practices
between 50 % and 70 % survive

For 14 % of the practices
between 30 % and 50 % survive

For 32 % of the practices
more than 70 % of the
projects survive

For 45 % of the practices
less than 30 % survive

43.5 %
is the average survival
rate of projects.

REVENUES

'Own' architecture

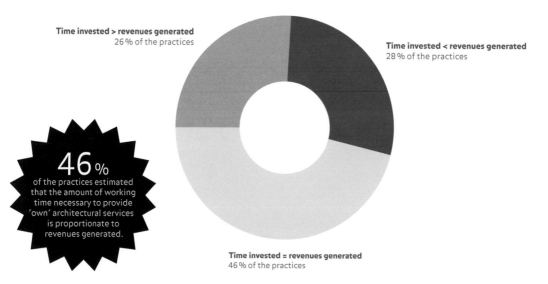

Time invested > revenues generated
26 % of the practices

Time invested < revenues generated
28 % of the practices

46 %
of the practices estimated
that the amount of working
time necessary to provide
'own' architectural services
is proportionate to
revenues generated.

Time invested = revenues generated
46 % of the practices

Source: Wonderland #1 Survey – by SHARE architects, 2005

WORKING HOURS

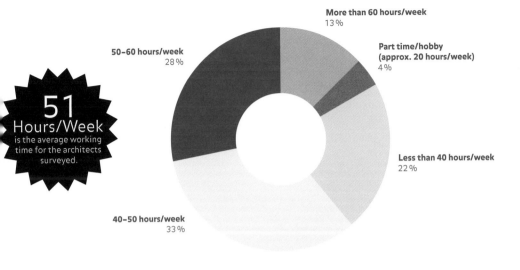

More than 60 hours/week
13 %

**Part time/hobby
(approx. 20 hours/week)**
4 %

50–60 hours/week
28 %

Less than 40 hours/week
22 %

40–50 hours/week
33 %

**51
Hours/Week**
is the average working
time for the architects
surveyed.

Working hours/week/country:

AT	CZ	DE	FR	HR	IT	NL	SI	SK	Average
46	63	40	63	45	46	57	56	56	51

PROJECTS PER YEAR

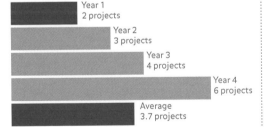

Average of realized projects/year

Year 1
2 projects

Year 2
3 projects

Year 3
4 projects

Year 4
6 projects

Average
3.7 projects

Including projects with no budget information.

**4 realized
projects**
is the average number of
projects per year per
practice in the first
4 years.

BUDGETS

Year 1
211,000 Euros/project
458,000 Euros/year

Year 2
341,000 Euros/project
824,000 Euros/year

Year 3
281,000 Euros/project
867,000 Euros/year

Year 4
596,000 Euros/project
2,457,000 Euros/year

**390,577
Euros** is the average
budget per project.

Source: Wonderland #1 Survey – by SHARE architects, 2005

Becoming Famous Won't Save You!

1923 Charles-Edouard Jeanneret published his book *Vers une Architecture* under the pseudonym of Le Corbusier.
He was 36 years old at the time.

1953 Ivan Chtcheglov, using the pseudonym of Gilles Ivain, wrote *Formulary for a New Urbanism*, a radical manifesto for the Situationist International.
He was only 19 at the time.

1953 the term Team X was created at the CIAM (Congrès Internationaux d'Architecture Moderne) congress in Aix-en-Provence.
Peter und Alison Smithson, the youngest of the group, were 30 and 25 years old at the time.

1961 David Green, Peter Cook and Michael Webb (joined in the following year by Warren Chalk, Dennis Crompton and Ron Herron) published the first edition of *Archigram*. At that time, they were between 21 and 34 years old.

1963 Hans Hollein and Walter Pichler wrote their manifesto *Absolute Architektur*, supported by collages and designs that they published at the same time.
They were 29 and 27 years old.

1966 Aldo Rossi published *L'architettura della città*.
He was 35 years old.

1966 Adolfo Natalini and Cristiano Toraldo di Francia founded Superstudio in Florence. (Gian Piero Frasinellli, Roberto and Alessandro Magris joined in later). The founders were both 25.

1967 Peter Eisenman founded the Institute for Architecture and Urban Studies.
He was 35 years old at the time.

1978 *Delirious New York*.
A Retro-Active Manifesto of Manhattan appeared.
Rem Koolhaas was aged 34.

1983 Zaha Hadid won the competition for the The Peak Leisure Club in Hong Kong.
She was 33 years old at the time.

These were all start-ups of one kind or another. At the time, the people involved surely had little intimation of their later success, but as no-names they had nothing to loose and everything to win. And they did have something to say (without judging what they said). But above all they first expressed themselves in a medium which, in contrast to a built structure, had a different form of autonomy (artistic or scientific) and that was subject to different laws of economic feasibility: they scored their early successes in the world of discourse. Like all branches of cultural production, the discipline of architecture also exists in parallel spheres – in the sphere of the production of the work or event on the one hand, and on the other in the sphere of the construction, dissemination, and reception of meaning. Specialized journalism (and only later the mass media) has become a power that can transform the discourse of a small group into a global one, or a small building in a remote Swiss alpine valley into a potential classic. But this happens as the result of the interaction of clearly defined rules and historical accidents, which, while being reconstructable with hindsight, are not easily predictable in advance. When Malcolm McLaren, inspired by the Situationists, founded the Sex Pistols together with Johnny Rotten to pull off *The Great Rock 60'n' Roll Swindle* (and only shortly after, together with Vivienne

Westwood in her first shop with its always closed doors, experienced the calculated bankruptcy that reverberated throughout the media), the media echo of the destruction and inversion of all symbols by Punk was one possible but not the inevitable outcome. The winners of the game always tend to reforge the chain of causality.

However, the relationship between these two spheres in economic terms – expressed in its simplest form in the taboo question: "How did they make a livelihood?" – is a phenomenon that is rarely discussed. How does media success change the profession and the circumstances of production? What implications does the "economy of attention" (Georg Franck) have for young teams? What were the changes caused in this respect by the pushing of the boundaries of the discipline?

1776, Adam Smith wrote in the *Wealth of Nations* that, whereas almost all craftsmen in the mechanic trades could make a living, in the so-called liberal professions only one in twenty would be in a position to live from his work. And yet, so it seemed to Smith more than 200 years ago, it was the professions that attracted the best and the brightest minds. The philosopher offered also a reason for this: the public success enjoyed by the few winners and their extraordinary self-confidence and belief in their own abilities and in luck[1]. Interestingly enough, uncertainties seem to have changed over the centuries, for when making a similar comparison in his book entitled *Freakonomics*, Steven D. Levitt uses the architect (with whom we are dealing here) as an example of a safe, albeit specialized profession with very slight (economic) chances of success in contrast to the prospects of a prostitute or crack dealer. Levitt was interested to find out why, in heaven's name, there should be so many people in the United States who make a living from dealing in crack at an hourly wage of 3.30 dollars and with a 25% likelihood of dying on the job. The answer to this question is the same that is given by Adam Smith (the fact that the public success of the crack dealer is clearly confined to a rather small segment of the public makes little difference here). In this area, the rules of the game follow those of the free market. When there are many potential providers of a service, the amount of money each of them can earn declines. But this amount is also dependent on the degree of specialization, the disadvantages involved in exercising this profession and the demand for this particular service.

For Levitt the main issue in all the professions he describes as "mythical" is always the same: a persistent obsession with achieving recognition, money and power (the architects among my readers will rather quickly point out the unlikelihood of achieving at least two of these goals within their own profession ...)

So much for the economist's viewpoint. In the field of cultural production, the process seems a little more complex. In *Die Ökonomie der Aufmerksamkeit* (The Economy of Attention) as well as in his subsequent book *Mentaler Kapitalismus* (Mental Capitalism), Georg Franck has described the far more subtle phenomena and the new rules of the game according to which our society has worked ever since the emergence of the media. In a mediatized world, the accumulation of 'attention' leads to the development of a social capital that creates its own markets. It is "not the financial turnover but the attention income that has helped certain directions achieve world-wide importance."[2] Architecture therefore uses two different kinds of markets: in one, "professional services are offered in exchange for payment", while in the other "published opinion is exchanged for the attention of those interested in culture."[2] But what Franck did not show was that, although following the victory of the "functionalism of attention", architecture can be seen as a paradigmatic discipline in which the relationship between achieving recognition and exploiting it in economic terms (the star architect and the global company, the branding of cities etc.) is clearly evident, the so-called win-win situation remains restricted to the sphere of discourse even for many prominent exponents of the

profession. The economic disaster suffered by the offices of Jean Nouvel and Rem Koolhaas in the 1990s may serve as a first small example here.

In his lectures, Rem Koolhaas made a point of presenting diagrams which show the curious discrepancy between media success and its economic impact in the world of architecture and other professions involved in the production of culture. Conscious of his role as a global superstar in the current architectural scene, he raised the question (also with regard to himself) of the economic implications that fame can have in the world of the arts and the media or in the architectural world. Whereas in the case of Koolhaas' artist colleagues (painters, sculptors, film-

makers, actors, football players, etc.), the exponential increase in recognition was matched by a corresponding increase in economic value, things are different in the world of architecture. Even in the case of top stars such as Gehry or Foster, there is certainly a clear accumulation of attention but, most interestingly, this is not directly reflected in the financial rewards (which is partially due to the fee scale that regulates architects' incomes, but even if fees were doubled, incomes would still remain ridiculously small in relation to the increase in value that results from fame in other branches). This striking discrepancy led Koolhaas to suggest that, following the completion of the Guggenheim Museum, Gehry should be given a percentage of the annual returns for Bilbao; after all,

his building apparently is the reason for the media attention and the subsequent strengthening of the city's economy. But, with regard to the Bilbao effect, Ernst Hubeli has pointed to the dangers of the media trap: "the inflation of (media) singularities has led to their self-destruction." In other words: in the beginning, there is a lot of money in the game thanks to the Koolhaas markup, but it quickly runs low for good old Gehry and his successors ... The laws of the "economy of attention" mean that, as a result of the architect's accumulation of acclaim, the work increases in value "... we value that which we pay attention to and we pay attention to what we value ..."[2], but for the architect this increase in value is largely expressible in terms of reputation only. "Reputation itself takes the form of capital. It is the capital that results from the accumulation of an income consisting in attention from experts."[2]

But Franck's theory, which is based on the assumption of a general narcissism, tends to obscure the fact that even the greatest moments of reputation only very rarely have direct economic consequences for architects. When Haus-Rucker-Co rocketed to fame in the late 1960s, they participated twice in the documenta (in the art world the equivalent of being raised to knighthood), but behind the scenes, their professional life still was a constant search for survival strategies, for jobs here and there, with the final possibility of teaching (which also strengthened the possibility for the discourse). What was particularly striking in the case of Haus-Rucker-Co was the difficulty that the public had to place their work in precisely defined context (that of architecture or, alternatively, art) and the associated evaluation of these works. With the extension of the boundaries of the discipline, this phenomenon has increasingly gained ground in the works of various architects and groups of our generation. As it was, primarily, the art scene that took interest in working at the interface of the disciplines and, particularly, in the subject of public space, generally is in the field of art that various works have found, and still find, a wide forum. Interestingly though, they have most often found little more than a forum, for it is not always the case that these works are understood as belonging to the field of art (whose mechanisms were precisely described by Pierre Bourdieu in his work *The Rules of Art*). The reverse situation also applies – merely because a work or event in the area of 'art' is perceived as pertaining to questions of (social) space does not automatically make it a work of 'architecture'. Consequently, it is its positioning within a 'field' that defines the value of a work or event.

Unsurprisingly, there is no easy way out of this dilemma. From the experience of our own practice, we know about the interaction of perceptions within one discipline or another. Ephemeral urban interventions – which, above all, addressed notions of public space and were made with much individual initiative and idealism, but without any profit interest – found an echo in Austrian architectural discourse as well as at the interface to the world of art. This in turn earned us lectureships and invitations to exhibitions, biennales, while, on the other hand, works that were developed in parallel and, from the start, tended to be perceived as 'architecture' were seen in the context of these strategies (and vice versa) and were expanded in that direction. Publications and (art) awards led to invitations to put these means to test in a broader context, so that these experimental works, originally created with a great deal of personal effort or public subsidy, suddenly also saw an increase in economic value. As the 'architecture' was publicized in parallel, the question of what generates which conditions and chances increasingly becomes a kind of chicken-and-egg situation.

Since the emergence of the pop phenomenon in the architecture of the 1960s, much, and yet little, has changed. What has in fact changed is the heterogeneity of the diverse scenes, the simultaneous existence of contradictory discourses, and the fact that a many of the young generation discussed today fights a battle on several fronts. Theory and practice are seamlessly interwoven, with all opportunities and all inconsistencies that this involves. From the perspective of the start-up generation of the 1960s, anyone starting today seems immeasurably overinformed and clear-headed; they are aware of which directions the heroes of their youth have taken and what has become of them in the

market. We all know the mechanisms of the media (although we remain their victims); we know that an examination of the spatial and social conditions in the favelas of South America – after making its way through all sorts of publications – can generate 'favela chic' for the apartments of London Dinkies promoted by, for example, Wallpaper. At the same time, we – the (perhaps unconscious) children of Umberto Eco's call for a "semiological guerilla" (1967) – were also born with an innate plan of action against these effects of the mass media.

We all know that media attention works like a gigantic telescope that can blow up a small phenomenon to a colossal, world-changing one, and somewhere in the back of our heads, we suspect that we could direct this telescope to the real spatial and social crises. Attention will most probably not fatten our wallets as architects, but the discourse it generates could possibly alter our view of the world. It's a question of relevance.

P.S.: The Yale Art Gallery was opened in 1952. It was Louis I. Kahn's first important recognized building. He was 51 years old at the time. Architecture is starting-up. Forever. ◼

Notes:
1) See also: 'The Willing Suspension of Disbelief' by Mark Gilbert and Kari Juhani Jormakka in *#5 – why make competitions*.
2) Georg Franck: Mentaler Kapitalismus. Eine politische Ökonomie des Geistes, Hanser: Munich 2005 (excerpts translated by the author).

making mistakes

why
make
mistakes

where
things can
go wrong

what to do
when things
go wrong

WHY SO MANY MISTAKES?

617,000 accidents per year in the construction industry cause nearly **800** deaths and entail costs of **75** billion Euros in the European Union.

Experts explain this high accident rate as a consequence of a relatively underdeveloped industry, consisting of small companies using inadequate building methods and technologies and generating low profit margins, which stands in the way of investments to improve productivity and efficiency. Nonetheless the sector remains important and employs 1–4 % of the population, with a total of 15 million people working in construction in the EU-28.

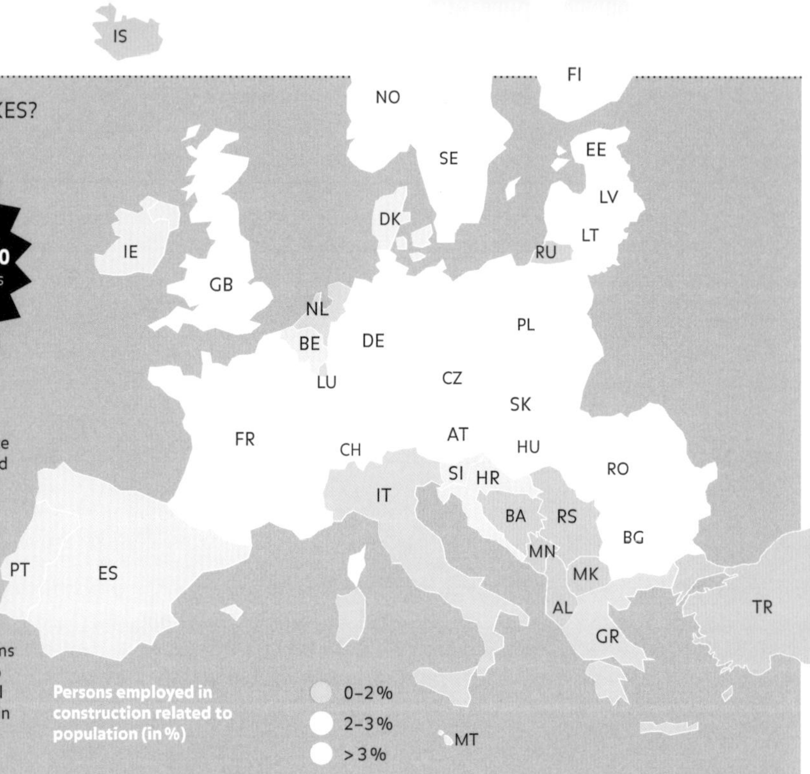

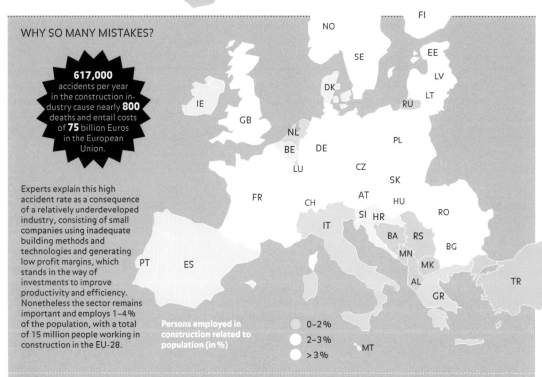

IS
FI
NO
SE
EE
LV
LT
RU
DK
IE
GB
NL
BE
LU
DE
PL
CZ
SK
FR
CH
AT
HU
RO
SI
HR
IT
BA
RS
BG
MN
MK
AL
PT
ES
TR
GR
MT
Persons employed in construction related to population (in %)
0–2 %
2–3 %
>3 %

WAGE ADJUSTED PRODUCTIVITY RATIO

The wage adjusted productivity ratio measures the relation between value added and wages (personnel cost). In other words, it is a profitability indicator. The average value added in the construction sector of the EU-28 covered personnel costs by 125 %, which means that the surplus value generated per employee exceeds the cost of wage for that employee by 25 % only. This is one of the lowest among non-financial-business segments of the economy. By comparison, the wage adjusted productivity ratio for the real estate sector is 290 %.

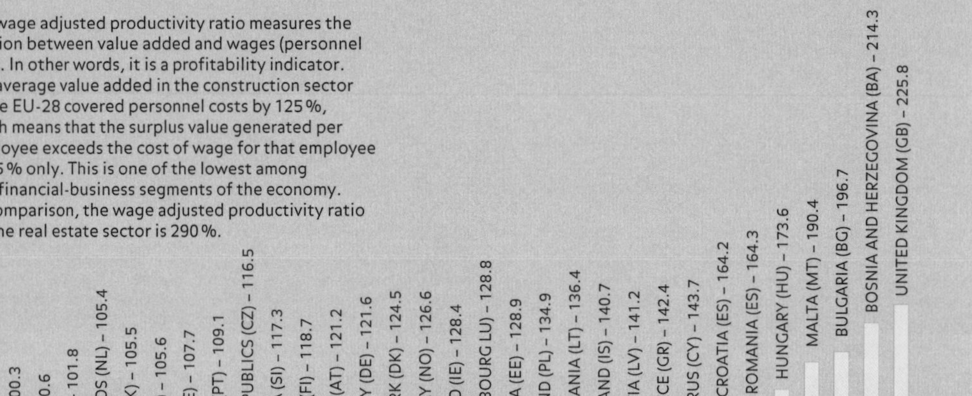

SPAIN (ES) – 100.3
ITALY (IT) – 100.6
FRANCE (FR) – 101.8
NETHERLANDS (NL) – 105.4
SLOVAKIA (SK) – 105.5
SWEDEN (SE) – 105.6
BELGIUM (BE) – 107.7
PORTUGAL (PT) – 109.1
CZECH REPUBLICS (CZ) – 116.5
SLOVENIA (SI) – 117.3
FINLAND (FI) – 118.7
AUSTRIA (AT) – 121.2
GERMANY (DE) – 121.6
DENMARK (DK) – 124.5
NORWAY (NO) – 126.6
IRELAND (IE) – 128.4
LUXEMBOURG LU) – 128.8
ESTONIA (EE) – 128.9
POLAND (PL) – 134.9
LITHUANIA (LT) – 136.4
ICELAND (IS) – 140.7
LATVIA (LV) – 141.2
GREECE (GR) – 142.4
CYPRUS (CY) – 143.7
CROATIA (ES) – 164.2
ROMANIA (ES) – 164.3
HUNGARY (HU) – 173.6
MALTA (MT) – 190.4
BULGARIA (BG) – 196.7
BOSNIA AND HERZEGOVINA (BA) – 214.3
UNITED KINGDOM (GB) – 225.8
%
100 %

Source: Eurostat 2015/ European Agency for Safety and Health at Work

making mistakes

Everybody wants to be known for his achievements, rather than his mistakes, and so everybody tends to play down or pass over in silence whatever mistakes he has made, or failures suffered.

So why, out of all things, did we choose 'making mistakes' as the focal theme of this second chapter of this manual for emerging architects? Because we are not interested in dwelling on the more glorious aspects of life as an architect; instead, we want to cast some light on the everyday challenges that one is in for, and ought to be up to, as an architect.

At the start of their career, self-employed architects are frequently confronted with unpleasant experiences such as error, failure, or prejudice. Particularly, young architects are likely to be suspected of insufficiency by clients. And, honestly, hardly anyone is really prepared for each and everything that they may be expected to know or do as self-employed architects. It is comforting therefore to see that even experienced professionals make mistakes – in fact, the building industry on the whole is rather mistake-prone, understandably so, considering the intense pace of work, the low level of investment in research and development, and slender profit margins.

Mistakes need not result in fatal consequences, but can also be a source of new ideas. In scientific research, 'trial and error' is an acknowledged method, but in architecture, a one-time error may cast a long shadow on future trial. Some of these aspects are discussed in our first section, 'Why make mistakes'.

The thing an architect has to be aware of is the special responsibility he or she is taking on. This may differ considerably from country to country, as is shown in our second section, 'Where things can go wrong'.

And finally: architects will be recurrently confronted with mistake prevention and crisis management – hence the theme of the third section, 'What to do when things go wrong'.

A questionnaire poll conducted in 2006 brings together a range of views on the subject, of different approaches and strategies, with architects from 60 practices in 18 European countries participating. ▬

TOP TEN THINGS THAT WENT WRONG

PR
36 % of the respondents

Office financing
43 % of the respondents

Timing
28 % of the respondents

1. Office financing
2. PR
3. Timing
4. Client
5. Budget
6. Execution
7. Expectations about the product
8. Design
9. Partnership
10. Details

Client
26 % of the respondents

Budget
25 % of the respondents

Execution
25 % of the respondents

Details
17 % of the respondents

Partnership
19 % of the respondents

Design
19 % of the respondents

Expectations about the product
23 % of the respondents

THE AVERAGE ARCHITECT

▶ considers the business acceptably risky (67 %).
▶ considers him or herself experimental (90 %) and concentrates on experimentation in design (60 %).
▶ takes risks with regard to the money flow in the office (41 %). Together with getting the wrong PR with clients, this is what he or she is most commonly afraid of. Practical experience shows that both fears are justified.
▶ is mainly afraid of not fulfilling expectations and budgets, but in the end is most likely to get the timing wrong. If quality control systems are used (only 53 % do), they most likely relate to design or human resources (both 30 %), but not to time management.
▶ sees a risk in keeping the balance between private and professional life (31 %).

See reality check #2 / page 89

Source: Wonderland #2 Survey – by SHARE architects, 2006

why
make mistakes

Exploiting the potential
Making mistakes can be devastating. At the same time, not all
failures are mistakes as criteria may change over time, making
a success of what looked like a failure, or vice versa. Still, if the
intention is experimentation, the only choice is to accept the
chance of failing.

Portals of Discovery

The idea that the source for creativity is to be found in error or failure is plausible enough.

James Joyce famously claimed that "a man of genius makes no mistakes. His errors are volitional and are the portals of discovery." The idea that the source of creativity is to be found in error or failure is plausible enough. In *Notes on the Synthesis of Form*, Christopher Alexander points out that if things work well, we have no particular desire to change them; design is called for at the face of failure.

An example is provided by Bernini's masterpiece, the Piazza S. Pietro in Rome. In 1586, the pope commissioned Domenico Fontana to erect an obelisk in front of St. Peter's basilica but unfortunately, Fontana missed the central axis of the church. To hide that mistake, Bernini shaped an oval piazza around the obelisk, flawlessly deriving the shapes from a narrow street leading to the church, the corner of the Vatican palace and the diagram of *vesica pisces*.

Here, the mistake was made by one architect and the masterpiece by another. Joyce's statement, however, implies something more radical: an error that turns out to be a blessing in disguise. The idea is not that the creative process is provoked by a failure but that it results in an apparent failure that in reality opens doors to unimagined opportunities. In this spirit, Nobel Prize laureate Richard Feynman once stated: "To develop working ideas efficiently, I try to fail as fast as I can."

A famous case of creative failure or accidental innovation is the invention of vulcanization. Since the early 1830s, Charles Goodyear experimented systematically with ways of treating india rubber so that it would not be sticky in hot weather and crack in the cold. After a number of failures, including a nitric acid treatment, he bought the process of Nathaniel M. Hayward who had discovered that rubber mixed with sulphur was not adhesive. In 1839, or so the tale goes, Goodyear accidentally dropped a piece of rubber treated with sulphur and white lead on a hot stove; the next day it was soft and flexible. In 1844 he patented this process of "vulcanization" but had to fight numerous infringements of his rights in the United States and in Europe. In France, a factory that vulcanized rubber according to his invention failed, and he was imprisoned for debts which by his death amounted to $200,000. In his two-volume book *Gum-Elastic and Its Varieties*, Goodyear denies that the invention of vulcanization was an accident, but it continues to be mistakenly quoted as such.

Another story concerns a rubber substitute. During World War II, James Wright, a chemical engineer at General Electric, mixed silicone oil and boric acid to develop a new bouncy polymer, but it was not firm enough for rubber. Although a patent was granted in

Text by Kari Juhani Jormakka, Prague, Czech Republic

> Most mistakes in art and architecture are simply failures.

1947 to McGregor & Warrick, no application for the substance was found. Two years later, Peter Hodgson borrowed $147 to purchase a batch of it, named it "silly putty" and sold it in plastic eqqs. Today, Binney & Smith produces 20,000 eggs worth of Silly Putty a day. In addition to its use as a bouncing toy, it has been used to strengthen hands in physical therapy and make casts of gorillas' feet. Similar stories of accidental innovation are regularly told about another toy, the Slinky, as well as popular food products, such as Coca-Cola, for example.

In architecture, by comparison, such cases are relatively rare. One example might be Alvar Aalto's decision to clad the facades of the Finlandia Hall in Helsinki with thin plates of Carrara marble – with the consequence that the plates curved this way and that in the harsh Finnish climate. Not realizing that this effect was just a technical error, many critics and aficionados called special attention to the curved marble plates, regarding it as another sign of Aalto's sensitive use of materials.

Most mistakes in art and architecture are simply failures. Leonardo's frescoes *Last Supper* and the Battle in Anghiari are a case in point. The artist wanted to invent a new painting technique but created a disaster: the paint on the *Battle in Anghiari* was boiling off even as he was painting it. If these famous mistakes led to anything positive, it was the opportunity for Dan Brown to make lucrative misreadings. While Leonardo, then, did not err in a productive fashion, Freud's celebrated reading of Leonardo is an example of an incredibly productive error. Freud starts with a note found in Leonardo's scientific notebooks:

"it comes to my mind as a very early memory, when I was still in the cradle, a vulture came down to me, opened my mouth with his tail and struck me many times with his tail against my lips."

From this apparently innocent remark Freud embarks on an amazing psychoanalytic journey. The reference to a tail is for him a clear indication that Leonardo was a homosexual, dreaminq at once of fellatio and of nursing at the mother's breast. The reason why the mother was replaced by a vulture is according to Freud to be found in ancient Egyptian religion. Uncovering a minor female deity with many heads (one of them that of a vulture), the psychoanalyst points out that the name of this goddess was pronounced *Mut* and asks "whether the sound similarity to our word mother (*Mutter*) is only accidental." Without presenting any evidence, Freud implies that the artist was aware of such similarities between ancient Egyptian and modern German as well as myths that associated vultures with the mysteries of birth. He concludes that the dream shows that Leonardo became a scientist because he missed his father and created his masterpieces due to sublimated homosexuality. As further proof of his interpretation, Freud later added an observation made by Oskar Pfister who claimed that Leonardo's painting *Anna Metterza* contains, in the drapery of Mary's robe, the outline of a vulture with its tail leading to the lips of Jesus. Prior to Pfister, C.G. Jung had already detected a vulture elsewhere in the picture, and later Raymond Stites saw a number of fetuses, in varying stages of development, beneath Anne's right foot. Sadly for all vulture-watchers, however, Freud's innovative interpretation was based on an error made by the German translator of Leonardo's notebooks: the bird in the dream was actually not a vulture (*avoltoio*) but a kite (*nibbio*, or as Leonardo spells it, *nibio*), a small hawk-like bird.

Although he was informed of this slip, Freud never expressed any doubts about the correctness of his reading. Similar self-confidence in the face of contradictory facts also characterized the theorizing of Le Corbusier. In 1943, the great architect gave his assistant Gérald Hanning the following instruction:

"take a man-with-arm-upraised, 2.20 m. in height; put him inside two squares, 1.10 by 1.0 metres each, superimposed on each other; put a third square astride these first two squares. This third square should give you a solution. The *place of the right angle* should help you decide where to put this third square."

Hanning worked hard on the problem of how to derive the golden section from the double square, and arrived at a complicated figure which combines the golden section, a rectangle derived from the square root of two, as well as two diagonals that are supposed to mark the place of the right angle; however, the solution is false as the angle is not a right one. The problem was in the original instruction since the only place of the right angle in the double square is in the middle – which does not lead to the golden section. Still, Le Corbusier refused to acknowledge that his original intuition was mistaken. When the Sorbonne mathematician René Taton finally convinced him that his original diagram involved an error of 6/1000, Le Corbusier concluded that these 6/1000 were of "infinitely precious importance" and they were the space of architecture. (Later an error

A mistake is a kind of failure, but not all failures are mistakes.

in Taton's estimate was found by Robin Evans who demonstrated that the mismeasurement was in fact 12/1000.)

Perhaps it is not incorrect to assume Ronchamp is one of the designs unfolding in this narrow space of architecture, as it seems to be very difficult – despite Le Corbusier's claims to the contrary – to derive its design from the Modulor. However, it should be pointed out that Le Corbusier himself may have felt that the Modulor itself was a failure, at least if used as a design tool. Only one week after he handed out measuring sticks based on the Modulor to each of his *Mitarbeiter* in the office, he forbade their use.

And yet, Joyce is right in claiming that errors can also be portals of discovery. To see why this must be so, we have to make a few distinctions, firstly between mistake and failure. A mistake is a kind of failure, but not all failures are mistakes. Assume I fail in my effort to break the world record in 100 m dash. The probable reason for the failure is not that I would have made a mistake – such as running in the wrong direction, for example – but that my physical shape does not allow such accomplishments. By contrast, a mistake – or an error – is a transgression or a deviation that presume the existence of some kinds of rules. If Hanning thought he had derived the Modulor from the double square figure, he had made a mistake by violating the rules of logic.

Moreover, Joyce further distinguishes between a mistake and an error: the former is inadvertent and involuntary while the latter, for him, is a deliberate transgression, a conscious departure from the correct path – which is the etymological meaning of *errare* in Latin.

The idea of erring in this sense has been a popular recipe for making art at least since the Romantics. Both the *Lyrical Ballads* of Wordsworth and Coleridge in 1798 and the notebooks of Novalis from the same year suggest looking at ordinary things in a way that makes them strange. More philosophically,

> Many of the stories of accidental innovation concern children's toys, soft drinks, desserts and other things.

> James Joyce further distinguishes between a mistake and an error: the former is inadvertent and involuntary while the latter, for him, is a deliberate transgression.

Schopenhauer argued that "to have original, extraordinary, and perhaps even immortal ideas one has but to isolate oneself from the world for a few minutes so completely that the most commonplace happenings appear to be new and unfamiliar, and in this way reveal their true essence." These ideas were adopted by Arthur Rimbaud and the *pittura metafisica* as well as the surrealist movement, leading to the glorification of the unconscious and also schizophrenia. With the Situationists, the spatial technique of the *dérive* extends

this method of systematically erring or straying as a way of recovering lost essences. Indeed, the deliberate transgression of whatever rules may be popularly held is the essence of the avant-garde.

Occasionally in academic research, one talks about serendipity as a method, as in Anselm L. Strauss and Barney G. Glaser's Grounded Theory in sociology. Referring to Robert K. Merton, they define a "serendipity pattern" as the experience of observing an unanticipated, anomalous and strategic datum which becomes the occasion for developing a new theory. Also some techniques of generating ideas in the natural sciences and technology stress that one should not shy from making mistakes. Still, Edison's statement that invention involves one percent of inspiration and 99 percent of perspiration seems to hold for most research in the sciences and engineering. It is not an accident that so many of the stories of accidental innovation concern children's toys, soft drinks, desserts and other things of limited functional value.

The case with art and architecture is similar to toys. Art is inimical to function: if something really functions well it becomes a technical solution and thereby no longer belongs to the domain of art. To give an example, John

> Thus, the problem of the new in the arts and architecture, as Boris Groys has suggested, boils down to a process of revaluation.

Ruskin contrasts construction as a form of scientifically based engineering with architecture as artistic creation, remarking: "I suppose no-one would call the laws architectural which determine the height of a breastwork or the position of a bastion. But if to the stone facing of that bastion be added an unnecessary feature, as a cable moulding, that is architecture." Howard S. Becker has pointed out that new art works, even new art forms, have often been developed out of craft traditions by making the objects non-functional – and thereby violating the essential rules of the craft. One example is Marilyn Levine who achieved a considerable reputation by making very realistic ceramic sculptures of shoes, boots, and other leather objects: visually indistinguishable from the originals, Levine's objects differ from the craft products precisely because they are unusable and hence 'about' representation, in the manner of art.

Related to this devaluation of banal functionality is the tendency of critics to take it for granted that works of art or architecture are perfect and complete according to their own rules. For example, W. K. Wimsatt and Monroe C. Beardsley state as axiomatic that in a poem, "all or most of what is said or implied is relevant; what is irrelevant has been excluded, like lumps from pudding and 'bugs' from machinery." In a similar manner, Arthur C. Danto takes it "as categorical with Warhol that there are no accidents." This can be taken as axiomatic, since the perfection of the work of art is not only demonstrated but actually constituted through the interpretation: unlike the workings of a machine, the functioning of a work of art is internally motivated rather than subject to some external criterion or a Kantian *Begriff*.

Because there are no independently definable or measurable criteria that a work of art or architecture has to fulfill in order to be successful, the question of discovery or creativity in art is less a matter of producing new forms or new solutions in an abstract sense than of convincing the art world that what has been produced is both new and relevant or valuable. Thus, the problem of the new in art, as Boris Groys has suggested, boils down to a process of revaluation. What is being valued anew are the rules or expectations that would determine a solution as an error, or instead a triumph. Hence, errors are the portals of discovery in a very particular sense: the discovery is that we have made a mistake about which things are errors.

Right mistakes and wrong correctness

Text by Eric Pöttschacher, Berlin, Germany

Mistakes: Everyone has his or her own experience of mistakes; apparently, they are found everywhere. If one were to believe the anonymous experts on mistakes, every article on the subject theme could be radically shortened: "It's easy to stop making mistakes, just stop having ideas." Sounds good, but makes little sense for creative people, including architects, who want to earn money professionally with their ideas. For them, we should approach the art of making mistakes from a different perspective. The usual one is that errors of any kind should be avoided.

If you search the Internet, you will find lots of sites containing a top ten of mistakes and how to avoid them, from the 'Top Ten Legal Mistakes Made by Entrepreneurs', collected by the Harvard Business School https://hbswk.hbs.edu/item/top-ten-legal-mistakes-made-by-entrepreneurs to 'The Top Ten Mistakes New Fiction Authors Make' www.writing-world.com/fiction/mistakes.shtml.

Naturally, there is a list of architectural errors, for instance the tips on tried and tested blunders made by church planners, 'Twelve Mistakes to Avoid when Building a Church' www.churchplansforless.com/ten_mistakes.htm. This Top Twelve contains as Mistake no. 3 'Relying on the architect's cost estimate', as no. 8 'Allowing the project to overwhelm your life' and no. 9 'Not praying for the construction workers'.

Sites like these lead us all to the assumption that we can avoid problems of any kind. All right, we can try to avoid errors our whole lives through, or alternatively, dedicate the time to a completely different question.

By looking at the faults in a more differentiated way. The management mentor Peter Drucker made the following distinction, which makes a difference when dealing with errors: "You can do the right things and do things right." The conclusion is: One can make mistakes doing things absolutely correctly, or do the right things in a completely wrong way.

Two examples: it's common knowledge that some architects do not find it at all difficult to invest hundreds of hours finding the perfect solution to a problem that the client actually does not want solved at all. That is one type of mistake. Drucker: "There is nothing so useless as doing efficiently something that should not be done at all." The other type is of a more operational nature. The assignment, the ideas and the plans are all in order – but the client presentation is so bad that it all looks like a huge mistake.

Knowledge about the different kinds of mistakes doesn't make them any fewer, nevertheless, one can learn from them in a more differentiated way. Which is something.

In his book *Ganz im Gegenteil* (Quite the Contrary) the scientist and systems analyst Matthias Varga von Kibed offers a lateral-thinking perspective that challenges the usual view of mistakes. He differentiates between correct errors and wrong correctness. Correct errors are still errors, but they lead to new insights that would not have been gained without these mistakes. Being eliminated from similar architecture competitions 10 times in a row should, sooner or later, become a mistake in this category.

Wrong correctness is rather different: here everything appears to be in order, at least on the surface, although any form of substantial development just does not happen. Many a correct procedure distorts the picture of the things that really go wrong.

Inventor Edwin Land allegedly had a little sign on his door that said the following: "A mistake is an event the full benefit of which you have not yet turned to your advantage."

What does all this mean in practice?

Mistakes happen. But how I creatively deal with them is as much my concern as sensibly distinguishing between mistakes of different kinds. ■

Experimentation
appears to be a natural
and integral part of the scope
of the profession. Only **10 %** admit
to keeping experiments within limits.
The amount of experimental work and
the time dedicated to it varies from
practice to practice. And so does the
admitted success rate: more than **1/3**
of the respondents estimate that their
success rate is about **50 %**,
but almost as many see
it below **20 %**.

Practices considering themselves experimental

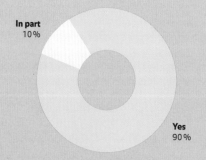

In part
10 %

Yes
90 %

Experiment success rate

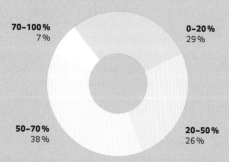

70–100 %
7 %

0–20 %
29 %

50–70 %
38 %

20–50 %
26 %

**Work considered
experimental**

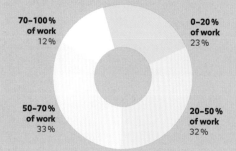

**70–100 %
of work**
12 %

**0–20 %
of work**
23 %

**50–70 %
of work**
33 %

**20–50 %
of work**
32 %

**Working time dedicated
to experiments**

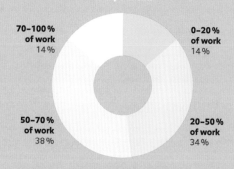

**70–100 %
of work**
14 %

**0–20 %
of work**
14 %

**50–70 %
of work**
38 %

**20–50 %
of work**
34 %

Source: Wonderland #2 Survey – by SHARE architects, 2006

WHERE DO YOU EXPERIMENT

Mainly program

Research teaching, cultural exchange

The main field of experiment is design itself, and the main declared motive is 'finding appropriate solutions'.

Fields of experimentation

Design
60 %

Materials
33 %

Collaborations
27 %

Project initiation
27 %

Entering other fields
25 %

Process
23 %

Other
18 %

Interaction of design and processes

Design, materials, collaborations, project initiation, entering other fields, process – all of it, or a combination, depending on the type of project.

Why experiments?

To solve given problems in the best possible way
59 %

To provide innovative products
29 %

Because architecture is experiment
20 %

In response to clients' wishes
4 %

To realize micro-utopia.

New way of life

I try many configurations of collaborators, the best so far are with family members and friends.

Materials, use of CAD/ CAM in production and building, collaboration

Theory

All kind of experiments

Source: Wonderland #2 Survey – by SHARE architects, 2006

DESIGNING AGAINST FAILURE

On the success of the late-modern architects of the 1960s and '70s in Bratislava

Errors made by young architects working in the 1960s and '70s in Bratislava in the conditions of the socialist economy are difficult to grasp in terms of success and failure by today's standards for the young generation of architects. At that time, the state forced architects, in an enormous number of projects, to take into account errors deriving from innate flaws of the system, from construction industry products which were not subject to free-market competition, and from a frequently absurd censorship of building materials available. While it is perfectly natural to design for success, the era condemned architects to design against failure, so to speak, which becomes obvious in many aspects of the completed constructions today, and nonetheless to try to produce architecture in such oppressive conditions.

Today's enthusiasm for the work of architects of the 1960s and '70s in Eastern Europe is an understandable reaction to the inadequate reception that their architecture had had to date. These architects were young in just that era when their peers in Britain and France, to name just two countries, had already rebelled against the inflexible anonymity of the late-modern planning championed by the established older generation. The many differences between socialism (the official term denoting the status quo in societies under communist regimes) and open society with regard to the phenomenon of 'mistake' in architecture in entirely different working conditions make for an illuminating insight.

Their careers in the early 1960s in Bratislava seemed truly faultless. They were only 30 years old and designed the best local late-Modern architecture.

Based on designs by this generation of architects, it was also the beginning of the mass production of precast-concrete-slab housing in and around cities, for groups of occupants among whom no distinctions were made. Immediately after graduation, these architects had entered established architectural offices (state-project firms) and thus were able to avoid many of the risks and mistakes that come along today with starting up one's own small practice, the risks of doing business and trying to get clients and commissions. Viewed from outside, it may seem that it was not too different from the situation today, when a young architect joins a renowned big firm, and the only source of failure, the only thing he may be held responsible for is a mistake in his work or a lack of knowledge and skills, while the business risks of the organization and dealings with clients do not rest on his shoulders.

However, this comparison does not hold: when the state financed architecture tailored to clients' wishes, that client wasn't the user – the occupant of a flat, an employee – but the state itself. The architect after all was an employee of the state, and yet at the same time had to supply his ideas and concepts to that state – or rather, to fellow state employees; his position was more than usually disadvantaged and dependent. It may seem that the

Text by Mária Topolčanská, Prague, Czech Republic

architect's position was simpler then; it was however, at the same time, quite absurd to expect that, from such a position, the architect could become successful without great difficulty.

Responsibility for failure and credit for success were portioned out anonymously among the dozens of uncreative staff who made up the colossal apparatuses of the state project offices and studios.

The more regulations by the collective authorities of the large state offices influenced projects, the less freedom there was for an individual architect, and the more likely it was that one or several of the many restrictions would be violated.

To work against these conditions and produce good architecture often meant coming up with strong experimental forms that impress visitors to Bratislava still today: be it the Hotel Kyjev and Department Store (designed by Ivan Matušík in 1964–68), the concrete UFO restaurant high above the suspension bridge across the Danube river (Jozef Lacko, Ladislav Kušnír, Ivan Slameň, 1972), the Slovak National Gallery with its wide-spanning bridge structure (Vladimír Dědeček, 1962–69), or the up-side-down pyramid form of the State Broadcast Company (Stefan Svetko, 1963–71).

The successful architect of that time experimented with risks arising from the conditions he had to work in. Only a very small number of studios under the leadership of a few of these key architects enjoyed a kind of artistic latitude. Atypical concepts (the much-favored circular ground plan, inverted pyramids, wide-span bridges, which so greatly defied the conventional and cheap rectangularity of the mass-produced construction of that time) were by far in the minority within the overall volume of construction, but their quality and expressive strength somewhat made up for the image of the state building industry. The question was not guaranteeing against architectural mistakes; rather, it was guaranteeing against a loss of face of the state itself.

In those times, the only permissible way for an architect to express his creativity in private commission projects was to build a single-family house, for oneself or for someone else. Thus architects like Ferdinand Milučký, Ilja Skoček or and Ivan Matušík who had been obliged to supply designs for large state commissions as their first creative achievements created for themselves austere and prototypal modern classics, which could, in the privacy of one's own fenced plot, finally be built with materials officially 'not recommended' for construction – traditional bricks. It is precisely these later houses, which prove that, if they had not been young right then and in Bratislava, these architects of '60s and '70s would probably have created good architecture anywhere and under any other system.

A Case for the Mistake

Mistakes in architecture projects have latent potential, depending on how they are seen: as real mistakes that are corrected by the book (these are the most boring), as mistakes that might be mistakes, as mistakes that might become such, as mistakes that are imputed to a project later, as mistakes that are not really mistakes but are created by fault-finding and norms (these are the most common), and as mistakes that are not any at all.

A very obvious, if dated, example of this range is the 'Hafnerriegel' Students' House, a tower construction and the first high-rise in Graz, built 1959 by the Werkgruppe Graz (Gross, Gross-Rannsbach, Pichler, Holomey). It had an exterior emergency staircase where 'the architect had forgotten the stairs' (what an idiot!), as I was repeatedly told with a smirk, quite some time before I studied architecture myself. Those exterior stairs did indeed look a bit like a later addition, and were not used. In fact, though, the high-rise Students House was based on what was a very innovative architectural concept at the time. Four stepped units on each floor spiral upward around an elevator and stairwell so that there is no circulation through corridors, but a continuous rise in levels. The landings in front of the rooms are wide enough to allow social interaction.

After the completion of the building, and partly as a result of it, the fire regulations were revised so that a building that had complied with the regulations at the time of construction had to be equipped with an additional emergency staircase. The reduced monolithic aesthetic of the building had to be changed. The then very young architects used the task, which seemed difficult to accommodate the given building concept, for a shift of aesthetic paradigms, articulating the emergency stairwell as an expressive application that can be seen today as a successful and very early precursor of the Grazer Schule.

Mistakes happen or simply emerge. I do not want to discuss the situation when actual mistakes can have a existence-threatening consequences for the architects involved, but speak about the apparent mistake that perhaps is not one at all, the mistake that triggers innovation. Planning mistakes arising from self-contradictory or constantly changing parameters are unavoidable in architecture, or they are a matter of opinion. A straightjacket of norms and standards today makes every deviation from them look like a mistake, even though it may add to the aesthetic or technical quality by going beyond the norm. In the case at hand, changing standards created a 'mistake' where there had not been one before. The 'repair' of the mistake construed afterwards then provided the stimulus for an innovation that could be defined as the productive force of a cultural dividend. To attain this bonus today, it takes more than a textbook approach to a commission. It calls for more creative reinterpretation of parameters and norms, which means that under certain circumstances mistakes may seem to arise that actually are novel solutions.

Whatever the case may be, mistakes are the harbingers of innovation regardless of whether they actually are mistakes, or risky solutions that are just interpreted as mistakes. They are the results beyond the norm, and hence a step into the unknown. They are the motor behind and the value intrinsic to all architectural developments. ▪

Text by Paul Rajakovics, transparadiso, Vienna, Austria

Taking responsibility

Architects want the power and freedom of decision, and this entails being able to face the responsibilities that go along with it. Even with a common EU framework increasingly gaining contour, the purview of architects strongly varies from country to country. And with it, the likelihood of making mistakes.

To be an architect is not enough anymore

To be a good architect, you also need to have managerial competencies.

In an interview with the Harvard Business Review[1], the founder and chairman of Foster + Partners, with 15 offices and 1,000 employees working on projects in 40 countries, answered the question what makes a good architect in a pretty non-architectural way: *"An open mind, energy, an appetite for hard work, a willingness to explore new solutions and push boundaries. A sense of humor is also helpful. […] Feedback, whether positive or negative, is given during regular reviews with the design board […]. Listening is vital, as is asking the right questions."* In fact, there is more management in this answer than architecture.

Even – or probably even more – in the "real" world outside the world of the archistars, architects are increasingly aware that their role is changing and becoming more complex. Architects are not only professionals who need technical competencies, they are also entrepreneurs and managers who need managerial competencies to define their business model, get new jobs, manage projects and project teams, deal with clients, reach artistic as well as financial results. In brief, to run their business.

The way architects run their professional practice contributes to its success, especially in the medium and long term.

Text by Beatrice Manzoni . Milan. Italy

Managerial Competencies

Managing is about making decisions to lead and guide the architectural practice through planning, organizing, leading and controlling. Managerial competencies are knowledge, skills, behaviors and attitudes that a person needs to be effective in a wide range of positions and organizations. Management scholars describe managerial competencies in several ways. In this article, we use the model developed by Hellriegel et al.[2] who grouped them into 6 categories and 19 dimensions.

Competency	Dimensions	What is it about?
Communication competency	• Informal communication • Formal communication • Negotiation	Communication competency is about managing informal and formal communication, building strong interpersonal relationships with people and negotiating effectively.
Planning and administration competency	• Information gathering, analysis and problem solving • Planning and organizing projects • Time management • Budgeting and financial management	Planning and administration competency is about gathering and analyzing information, planning and organizing projects, managing time, managing project and business economics.
Teamwork competency	• Team building • Creating a supportive environment • Managing team dynamics	Teamwork competency is about properly putting teams together, assigning goals, staffing people, managing dynamics, and creating a supportive environment that encourages collaboration.
Strategic action competency	• Understanding the industry • Understanding the organization • Taking strategic action	Strategic action competency is about understanding the industry in terms of threats and opportunities, knowing the competitors and the organization's distinctive competencies. It is also about defining strategic goals and working towards their implementation.
Multicultural competency	• Cultural knowledge and understanding • Cultural openness and sensitivity	Multicultural competency is about being sensitive to different cultures, understanding them and being open to integrate and make the most of cultural differences.
Self-management competency	• Integrity and ethical conduct • Personal drive and resilience • Balancing work and life demands • Self-awareness and development	Self-management competency is about integrity and ethical conduct, personal drive towards organizational goals and resilience. It is also about balancing work and family demands and self-awareness.

How about practice?

So much for the theory, but how about practice? To what extent do architects have these competencies in their daily life? How effectively do they use them?

In Italy, we surveyed a sample of 493 Italian architects (57 % male; 9 % under 30 years old, 27 % between 30 and 39, 44 % between 40 and 49 years old, 16 % between 50 and 59.4 % older than 60), asking them about how they believe they master these 6 competencies and 19 dimensions on a scale from 1 (lowest) to 5 (highest).

Across the board, the competencies considered to be the strongest are the multicultural competency and self-management. The ones considered to be the weakest are strategic action and planning and administration. There are almost no differences observable between male and female architects, although female respondents tend to rate themselves slightly higher on four of six competencies. But overall the difference is really small.

Similarly, there are no great differences between respondents of different ages. Ratings tend to level out for respondents from the age of 30. Experience only slightly weighs in as it makes respondents more confident with regard to their managerial competencies.

Six competences – Average (Italian sample)

Communication	3.88
Planning and administration	3.59
Teamwork	3.78
Strategic action	3.45
Mulitcultural	4.31
Self-management	4.14

Taking a closer look at the dimensions of managerial competencies, the weakest is budgeting and financial management (2.75), while the strongest one is integrity and ethical conduct (4.46) with almost a 2-point difference between them.

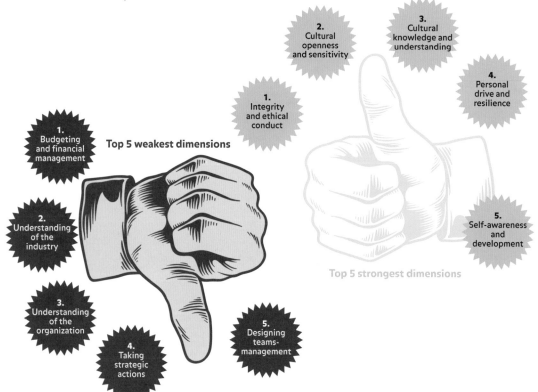

Top 5 weakest dimensions

1. Budgeting and financial management
2. Understanding of the industry
3. Understanding of the organization
4. Taking strategic actions
5. Designing teams-management

Top 5 strongest dimensions

1. Integrity and ethical conduct
2. Cultural openness and sensitivity
3. Cultural knowledge and understanding
4. Personal drive and resilience
5. Self-awareness and development

What if architects don't have and/or use these competencies on a daily basis?

The following table illustrates potential mistakes/pitfalls in each case.

What if you don't have/use...	Potential mistakes
Communication competency	• You are less able to convince clients and sell the intangible value of your work, which consists not only in the final building but also in the process and in the architect-client interaction. • You are less effective in managing the people you work with: what you say and how you say it can be an extremely powerful motivational driver for people. • You forego the chance to sell your design proposal at the 'right' price, because you fail to understand your counterpart and their needs.
Planning and administration competency	• You don't know whether your projects and firm are performing well. • You don't know which projects you should continue doing and which not: you lack information based on which you can make proposals to clients and informed business decisions. • You overrun budgets and timelines and/or fail to meet the agreed quality.
Teamwork competency	• You underperform on a project, because team members have no clear goals, roles and work standards and/or the wrong skills and an incompatible mindset. • You spend your time managing conflicts and negative group dynamics instead of aligning them towards doing the work. • You create a "toxic" workplace where people, including yourself, feel dissatisfied.
Strategic action competency	• You have an "all-you-can-eat" business model, meaning that you do everything (any type of projects) for everyone (any type of client) in a world where what really pays is specialization. • You don't know who you are competing with at the local, national and international level. Keep in mind that this also makes it impossible for you to occasionally establish "coopetition" (cooperation + competition) relationships with your competitors. • You are unaware of what your distinctive resources, that is, specific organizational capabilities, are: you don't know what you are better at than your competitors, which implies that you can hardly exploit, and monetize, these capabilities.
Multicultural competency	• You forego any opportunity of working abroad and opening yourself to international clients, projects and collaborations. • You face difficulties in managing nationally culturally, or ethnically diverse people and teams. • You find it hard to interact with clients and to understand why and how they act in a certain way if their background is different from yours.
Self-management competency	• You lose credibility and trust as a professional with clients and relevant stakeholders. • You are overwhelmed by your job and are in danger of burnout. • You miss out on opportunities for self-improvement as a professional.

Practical recommendations

We conclude with some practical recommendations for improving on the weakest dimensions: budgeting and financial management; understanding the industry and the organization and taking strategic action; team building.

All of those things should be ongoing processes. They are not something for architects to take care of when they are in the startup phase or at the end of the business year or when they acquire an important project and the firm suddenly grows. They are something that should be a constant over the life cycle of a firm.

85

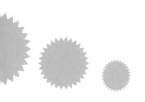

First, budgeting and financial management feeds on numbers from projects, clients, people on a daily basis. Knowing how to collect, analyze, and interpret numbers, also compared against the past and against competitors, is key. Moreover, it is not something the principal of the firm or accounting can do alone, it requires collaboration and input from all project stakeholders. Finally, it takes (a lot of) time, so it is rather better to be selective, choosing to collect less but being committed to do it well and consistently, so as to transform numbers into input for strategic action.

Secondly, strategic action should be about defining a unique value proposition that distinguishes the firm or professional from the competition. This implies reflecting on 'who' we serve, which means understanding who the clients and what their needs are, on 'what' we offer, meaning the services we provide, and on 'how' we do it in terms of required skills and organizational resources. Knowing the market and the competition and having clear benchmarks in mind is important to develop a value proposition and a business model that is economically sustainable, not only artistically.

Thirdly, teams building should be first and foremost about recruiting the right people. They are the ones with the right skills and, what is even more, with the right mindset. Every practice has its own "culture" (shared values and norms): the more of the people working there are in line with the specific culture, the better its teamwork is. Team building is also about setting the stage for team members, defining and communicating goals, assigning roles and responsibilities, and ensuring proper communication and coordination rules. In brief, it is a role that takes a good people manager and not just a project manager.

Now, let's switch the perspective: the data we have presented so far are the result of a self-evaluation, illustrating how architects see themselves. But how do their employees, colleagues and clients see them? Are outside perception and self-perception aligned? And if not, what needs be improved? These are interesting questions that architects should be asking themselves.

1 Alison Beard, "Life's work: Norman Foster", *Harvard Business Review,* March 2011.

2 Don Hellriegel, Susan E. Jackson, John W. Slocum, *Management: A Competency-Based Approach,* Cengage Learning, 2008.

CROSSING BORDERS
Temporary professional licenses within the European Union

Architects can apply for a temporary license to be able to provide professional services in another EU member country. The question is: which regulations apply, those of the architect's country of origin or those of the country where he or she wants to work? Dr. Stefano Nicolin, expert of EU law, has given us the following answer.

Text by Stefano Nicolin, Treviso, Italy

Architects who are nationals of a EU Member State can exercise their profession in another Member State under the right of establishment, or exercising the freedom of circulation of services as defined by the Treaty. In order to facilitate the exercise of these rights, the institutions of the Community have adopted the Directive 85/384/EEC. According to Article 2, each Member State shall recognize diplomas, certificates and formal qualifications obtained through education and training by the standards defined in Articles 3 and 4 of the same Directive and awarded to nationals of other member states. The Directive furthermore defines architectural activities as such usually pursued under the professional title of architect. The Directive 85/384/EEC was superseded the Directive 2005/36/EC concerning the recognition of professional titles, but the new provisions reaffirm in substance the principles expressed in that previous Directive.

However, the formulation is not 100 % clear, as it remains doubtful whether the term 'usually' refers to the licensing member state or to the state where the service is provided. The European Court of Justice ruled that a German architect working in Spain may provide all the services usually provided by Spanish architects, without the need to hire a local architect. This also applies if the services in question are not part of what is usually provided by German architects. **This means that an architect working in a EU member state outside the one where he is licensed may provide whatever services architects licensed in this state usually provide.**

It is reasonable to assume that this should also work the other way round: an architect exporting his services should be able to export whatever services he is usually providing in his country of origin, no matter if these are usual in the 'destination' Member State. In this regard, the European Court of Justice has recently ruled that access in Italy to the activities referred to in the second subparagraph of Article 52 of Royal Decree No 2537/25, i.e. activities relating to buildings of artistic importance, may not be refused to persons holding a civil engineering diploma or similar qualification issued in a Member State other than the Italian Republic, if such qualification is included in the list drawn up pursuant to Article 7 of Directive 85/384 or expressly listed in Article 11 of said directive.

Relevant regulations:

Council Directive 85/384/EEC of 10 June 1985 on the mutual recognition of diplomas, certificates and other evidence of formal qualifications in architecture, including measures to facilitate the effective exercise of the right of establishment and freedom to provide services, OJL 223, 21.8.1985, p. 15–25;

Directive 2005/36/EC of the European Parliament and of the Council of 7 September 2005 on the recognition of professional qualifications, OJL 255, 30.9.2005, p. 22–142;

Judgment of the Court of Justice of the European Communities, 23 November 2000, in Case C-421/98, Commission of the European Communities v. Kingdom of Spain, Rec. 2000, p. I-10375

Judgment of the Court of Justice of the European Union, 21 February 2013, in Case C-111/12, Ministero per i beni e le attività culturali and Others v. Ordine degli Ingegneri di Verona e Provincia and Others, CLI:EU:C:2013:100.

IN DETAIL

It is only through working in different countries that you really discover how the role of the architect can differ from one country to another. We talked about advantages and disadvantages of different systems with an architect who works in two European countries.

Greece – Austria
Buerger Katsota Architects, founded in 2005 by Stephan Buerger and Demetra Katsota, with offices in Athens, Greece and Vienna, Austria. www.buerger-katsota.com

Stephan Buerger is Austrian, Demetra Katsota is Greek. After studying in the GB and USA and a sound working experience in international firms in London, New York and Shanghai they set up an office together in Athens 2005. A year later, they established a second office in Vienna. This Interview was conducted in 2012 and updated for the second edition with an additional question about the current situation in Greece.

wonderland: How different is the work of an architect in these two countries?

Buerger: In Greece, the architect's role and responsibility is more loosely defined and thus often misinterpreted or misused. In fact, the architect has to "perform" many more roles than in Austria, which has its advantages and disadvantages.
In Greece, the architect operates, in the initial stage, as designer and planning negotiator of the project and may also become the main contractor as well as project manager, on-site architect, etc., during the execution. Usually the owner of a plot is compensated for the value of his land with a few apartments and/or shops by the "developer", who might be the architect him/herself, a civil engineer, a contractor or any investor. Thus the scale of such operations is small and solely based on private initiative. The architect who wishes to operate in such a context needs a relatively large amount of capital, a reliable team of contractors, and experience. In return, of course, he gets control of the entire building process.
In other cases, especially with small residential projects, the architect may be involved solely in the design stage and during realisation is forced to retreat to the so-called "artistic supervision". In such circumstances, the building is built according to the planning documents, therefore with the "design development and construction documentation" stages silently omitted, and the architect solely offering his consultation during occasional site visits. The architectural outcome can then be described as a loose approximation to the original design.

And in Austria?

In Austria, the design processes and professional engagement are more explicitly defined by law and common practice. It is rather a more "classical" role of the architect, who is involved as a key member of the consultant team at all planning stages.

Which approach to the profession do you prefer, the Greek one or the Austrian?

Difficult question to answer. It is the difference between the two contexts that makes work challenging and continually develop. In Greece the loose margins in the definition of the architect's role are disturbing, but at the same time open to many interpretations, even innovations. At times we appear inflexible, if we insist upon a clear-cut professional exchange with the client, collaborators and consultants. In Austria, the prescribed role at times appears limiting and unchallenging; but, after all, one may question the norm and propose other options.

And what about professional insurance in Greece?

Our Greek colleagues are always surprised when we tell them that we have liability insurance coverage. In Greece where any disputes are settled "in the street" and only larger practices are insured, it is uncommon for a young, small practice to have a professional insurance. In our case, the Austrian liability insurance covers our professional activity in both countries.

How did you respond as an architect to the financial crisis in Greece in recent years?

The Greek pie of construction contracts has shrunk dramatically in the last couple of years. In concrete terms, it is now only 10–15% of the pre-crisis construction volume. This means enormous financial and professional challenges for every architect and will inevitably lead to tensions and professional cuts. The construction work that we do in this difficult environment is mainly rebuilding, e. g. converting an office building into a student dormitory, or buildings for tourist purposes, such as holiday homes on the islands or a hotel. Of course, we try to get as many projects as possible outside Greece. ■

Interview by Anne Isopp

REALITY CHECK #2: MAKING MISTAKES

How do architects look upon the potential for failure and mistakes inherent in their professional activity? We made a questionnaire poll on the subject and received 60 responses from 18 European countries. The questions asked mainly focused on the issues of risk, experiment, and the experience of getting things wrong. The answers that we received revealed common concerns and a wide range of different approaches to the problem.

Common characteristics include seeing oneself as experimental, awareness about business risks, and happiness with the choice of profession made. The most common experience (shared by more than 40 %) is getting the finances wrong in the office, while design going wrong is relevant for only 20 % of the respondents.

Differentiation begins with the question of how and why do things go wrong: here the answers provided cover the full range. The most common reasons named concern approximately 30 % of the respondents. These include expectations, level of execution, timing and budgeting for the actual projects done by the practice. Other factors that were similarly rated are wrong client selection and private problems.

The resultant strategies are also quite differentiated; readiness for risk-taking can be roughly categorized in three groups: 1/3 moderate (taking calculated risks), 1/3 ambitious (whatever it takes to get innovative results), and 1/3 'whatever' (do not want to think about it).

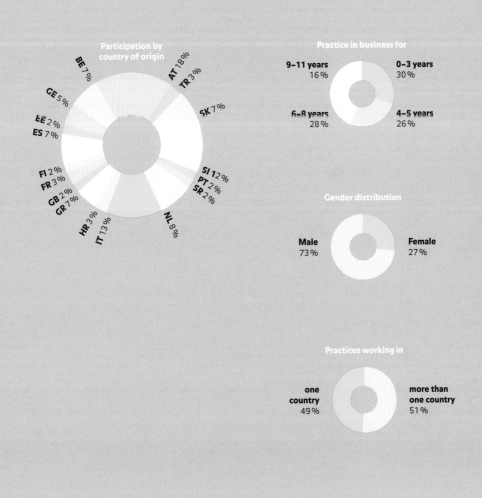

Participation by country of origin

BE 7 % AT 18 % TR 3 % GE 5 % SK 7 % LE 2 % ES 7 % FI 2 % FR 3 % GB 2 % GR 7 % HR 3 % IT 13 % NL 8 % SR 2 % PT 2 % SI 12 %

Practice in business for

9–11 years 16 % 0–3 years 30 %
6–8 years 28 % 4–5 years 26 %

Gender distribution

Male 73 % Female 27 %

Practices working in

one country 49 % more than one country 51 %

Source: Wonderland #2 Survey – by SHARE architects, 2006

ISSUES OF DISPUTE

Interview with lawyer Hannes Pflaum

Most often, the 'mistakes' that architects are taken to court for are related to delays and/or money; this includes disagreements over additional services and fees and suspension of payment.
When conflicts arise and litigation between client and architect ensues, legal advice often comes too late. Hannes Pflaum shares with us his knowledge about recurring problems and the insight he has gained through his practice; what is needed, he says, is better knowledge of contract law among architects, greater care in preparing commissions, and a more professional attitude on all sides.

wonderland: You represent many building clients as well as international architects: Where do they come from, and is their approach to building projects different from that of, say, Austrian architects?

Pflaum: I deal primarily with architects who work in Austria. They come from countries such as France, England, America and Germany and are regarded as foreign 'stars' in the first place, which puts them in a distinctly special position compared to Austrian architects. Of course, there are differences: Americans, for example, are very careful in preparing a commission, particularly with respect to contract formulations.

What are the problems that crop up regularly at the beginnings of a commission?

The fact that clients generally hold the stronger position leads to a situation in which truly undignified treatment of architects has become an established bad habit among clients. The architect is treated like an adversary from the very beginning.

Rights for the client – duties for the architect! How professional are clients? Do they also have duties, and what kind of mistakes do they make?

Of course, clients also have duties. Their noblest duty is payment in due course. Another one is making the necessary decisions and not revising them. The costliest term in architecture is 'users' wishes. This 'user' may be the client's spouse who wants an additional sauna, or it could be a group of clinic heads and professors who want to see all their special wishes met. This either leads to massive cost overruns, which are event-ually held against the architect, at the very latest when he presents his fee statement, or the planning has to be trimmed down to meet the cost limits, which in turn leads to arguments about who will pay for the time spent on unimplemented designs. To avoid such conflict, the project must be extremely well prepared. The program must be defined prior to the sketch design. Major corrections should be made in the preliminary design phase so

Interview by Astrid Piber

that the architect can complete the project professionally in the subsequent phases. Speaking about professionalism of building clients: I know a number of large institutional clients who have a great deal to learn. Real cost savings can be made in the preparatory phase, not by curtailing architects' fees!

In contract negotiations, the question of fees is always in the foreground. Why is this so?

Simply because there is immense distrust on the client's side. Basically, the fee is calculated as a percentage of the construction costs. This leads to the suspicion – which unfortunately is justified at times – that the architect has little interest in saving costs. This is one of the main points of conflict. In fact, this has come to be such an 'established truth' that even first-time clients already have a negative attitude about this. There are various attempts to resolve this conflict, for example the use of a bonus/penalty system. But this generally leads to debates about who is responsible for cost increases/reductions. There are also agreements based on a fixed fee. This only works if the project is very well prepared, if cost estimates are correct and no changes are made; otherwise, someone – generally the architect – will get the dirty end of the stick.

Is it possible to avoid mistakes by better preparation of a commission, the way American architects operate, for example?

This would be a great help. However, to achieve this, the services provided by the architect must be defined more clearly. Occasionally, I have the feeling that architects are quite happy with this 'grey area' in which the architect's services are not fully detailed. But this is where the next source of disagreement lies! There is always the discussion about whether a particular service is part of the contract or an additional service. How to draw the line between repeated contractual service and additional service? What is covered by the contract and what is not? I generally advise architects never to refuse a request to provide an additional service, but always with the reservation that it may (later) be charged for.

Do architects request your services during the contract phase, or only if problems arise?

In earlier times, clients considered it an unfriendly act if an architect requested the presence of a lawyer in the contract negotiations. This situation has improved, but there still are clients with a certain phobia of lawyers. But the lawyer just offers professional help in drawing up a contract which is intended to lead to problem-free collaboration. I don't represent architects only, but also clients. If one is called in to help in a dispute, it is often very late in the day, as the causes of the conflict generally lie far back in time and documentation often is very poor. This leads to problems in providing proof for either side and makes it very difficult for the lawyer to give a legal assessment; so this is risky business for both sides.

What are the most frequent 'mistakes' that architects are sued for?

Delay is the most frequent charge, followed by disputes over fees for additional services, increased services, repeated services etc. Design mistakes are rarely an issue; a great number of technical mistakes happen, but these are almost always covered by

insurance. There are also conflicts regarding threats made in the construction stage, as when the client withholds payment with the allegation that he has a right to compensation. These blackmail scenarios generally occur in the final phase of the project. For architects, this may be disastrous, as in general there are substantial sums at stake.

We know that 'failure to deliver plans on time' and 'not planning within the budget' are good reasons for firing an architect.

It is true that there are such cases, but they are rare exceptions. If the client terminates the contract, this may entail considerable risks. The question of project authorship, whether a new architect may continue the planning on the basis of the existing design, depends on the contract. If it is the architect who is to blame for the termination of contract, the client can of course continue the planning. But if the client throws out a 'disliked architect' without justification, for example, simply because he wishes to give the contract to somebody else, this can have very serious consequences. I general advise against one-sided termination of contract – if things have really come to a deadlock, there must be an amicable settlement in which all possible consequences are considered.

How good are standard contracts? What should be taken into account in contract negotiations in any case?

We drew up a model contract for the Austrian Chamber of Architects – but I have no idea if it was actually used. In any case, I don't believe that model contracts will come into wider use, since the major clients have their own standard contracts that they are willing to change only marginally. These contracts often are really terrible, which is due to the fact that every previous bad experience is integrated into the next contract as an additional cautionary clause, but these changes are never properly harmonized with the rest of the contract. The result is a contract that is full of gaps and contradictions. Generally, contract clauses can be divided into three groups: the first is clauses that are unproblematic and perhaps only need to be made more precise, at the most; the second group is clauses that ought to be amended, but may be accepted, if this is inevitable, while the third group comprises clauses that are not acceptable, so-called 'deal breakers'.

What kind of clauses would you describe as 'deal breakers'?

'Deal breakers' involve incalculable or uninfluenceable risks. I call them 'lucky chance contracts' – 'If I'm lucky it will turn out fine, if not, then not'. There are many such clauses: for example, penalties regardless of responsibility and with no limit, or cost guarantees that are dependent on factors that cannot be influenced or controlled. I strongly advise against signing such contracts – but they are always signed.

Architects often start providing service before a contract has even been thought of. Can this lead to problems?

There is no other profession, not even in the construction industry, where a professional works without having a contract. But with architecture things are different, as the client first wants an idea and says: "Show me a sketch design." The client is unwilling to commit himself, and the architect wants to play it cool. This game may go on for a long time. The client believes that, without a contract, he can get out of the project anytime if, for example, financing poses a problem, and the architect hopes that he has a better chance to land the commission after all he has already done for the client. Sometimes it is indeed better for the architect to delay the contract since, first, the legal assumption is that, in business relations, services are generally provided against payment (unless the

provision of services free of charge has been expressly agreed), and secondly, after a certain stage in the planning the client is no longer in a position to start again with a different architect, which weakens the client's bargaining position. However, it is necessary to closely examine each individual case. I remember one case when we signed the contract in an office building that was the subject of the contract.

If you were to advise young architects who are dealing with their first commission, what would you tell them?

Architects are taught technical and design competence and specialist knowledge, but they learn nothing about business management and contract law. Even in architectural practice, opportunities to take part in contract negotiations are rare. I would strongly recommend young architects to cram up on business management and contract law!

Hannes Pflaum, Vienna, Austria
Lawyer and emeritus founder of Pflaum Karlberger Wiener & Opetnik in Vienna. He was president of the Architekturzentrum Wien. He is specialized on building law, building contract law, real estate law, damages and warranty law, and commercial law. Books published by Hannes Pflaum include: *Der Architektenvertrag* (Orac: Vienna, 1991), *Bauvertrags- und Bauhaftungsrecht* (Manz: Vienna, 2001), *Handbuch des Ziviltechnikerrechts* (Orac: Vienna, 2007); www.pkp-law.at

LOSING A CLIENT

The biggest challenge at the beginning of every career as a self-employed architect is getting clients. Or at least one client to start with. And landing a commission certainly is a reason to be happy. But beware: the euphoria may not last until the completion of the project, and a rude awakening may follow. We present two cases in which the client prematurely ended his collaboration with the architect.

Project stopped for cost overrun

"We felt too young for a project of this size", the architects on the team say. Hence, to carry out their competition-winning project – a 2,000 square meter single family house on the coast –, they looked for an experienced architect as partner. Above all, it was the client's wish to use passive house technology that led them to make this move. However, the contract was made between the client and the partner architect, and the young team was left with no way of influencing decisions regarding materials, technology, scheduling or anything else. All they could do was to make suggestions.

It turned out that the partner architect had just as little experience with passive house technology as they had. In fact, the technical solution he suggested resulted in very high costs so that, after seeing the tenders, the client decided not to build the house.

Today, the young architects are convinced that they could have built the house at a far lower cost. They blame the partner architect for being unable to provide the expertise and experimental attitude that they had expected from him. After a number of years of experience as self-employed architects, they are now in a position to undertake far larger tasks and thus would think twice before entering such a partnership again. And they would certainly never take a famous architect in as a project partner.

For the young team this was a very bitter experience – not only because they lost a client and an interesting project but also because it left them in great financial difficulties. As they had not expected the project to be terminated so abruptly, they had not acquired any follow-up commission and for a year had to keep their heads above water by working for other architects and university lecturing.

Text by Anne Isopp

Source: IFIP 2003 after Schulte 1998, 175

PROJECT DEVELOPMENT: COST LIMITATION POTENTIAL

COSTS

COST SCHEDULE

Costs of
building use

Construction
costs

Planning costs

START OF CONSTRUCTION

COMPLETION

Side costs

Planning
costs

COST LIMITATION POTENTIAL

TIME

| INITIATION | CONCEPTION | MANAGEMENT | MARKETING | BUILDING |

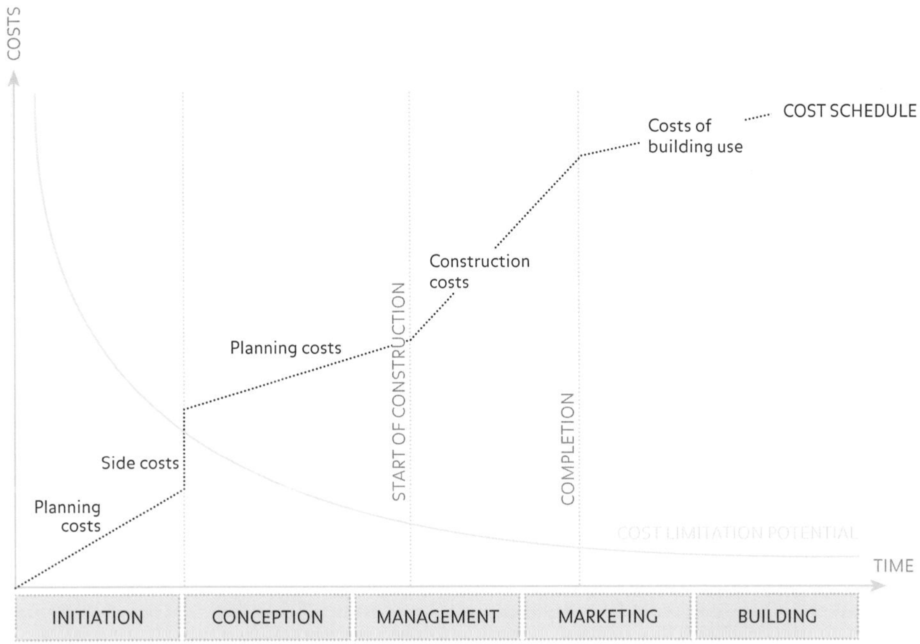

Cost limitation measures are best taken at early project stages. The further the process has
advanced, the less it will be possible to lower the costs.

Project stopped for cost underrun

This architect recalls that he was wondering about his client growing increasingly nervous
during the negotiations about awarding the construction contract. After all, he had battled
on his client's behalf, or so he thought, with the building contractor for the best price. He was
aware that the client and the contractor knew each other but it was only later that he realized
that at least one of the motives for the project was a dubious tax evasion scheme.

Construction was to start immediately after the contract negotiations. Instead, the client terminated his collaboration with the architect. The building had become too inexpensive. Behind the architect's back, he had made a deal with the building contractor that would allow him
to put part of the inflated tender price in his own pocket by channeling an agreed repayment
to himself, while paying lower corporate taxes, instead of higher income taxes. With the lower
costs that the architect had negotiated, there was nothing left for him to pocket and so from
his point of view the project no longer made sense. Of course, this was not the reason that he
gave the architect for his decision.

Contract negotiations are part of an architect's responsibility – and for this reason this architect says he is not going to change his approach in the future. But he has become more sensitive to possible hidden motives of the people he does business with: "Behind every commission, there may be a dimension that you never really see through." ▪

Buildings may fall short of their intended use because of a wrong planning concept or changing conditions. Read about five examples of buildings that went wrong and needed rethinking.

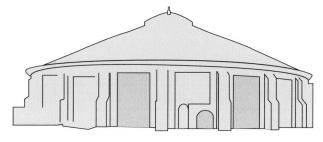

ROUNDHOUSE, LONDON

Celebrated as a feat of civil engineering, the Roundhouse was built in 1846 as a railway engine shed for the London and North Western Railway. With the introduction of new and longer locomotives, the building became obsolete only ten years later, and from 1869, was used as a liquor warehouse for Gilbey's Gin on a fifty years lease. In 1964, playwright Arnold Wesker took over the building for on behalf of the Centre 42 arts forum, named after the motion 42 adopted at the 1960 Trade Union Congress, which demanded 'direct promotion and encouragement' of the arts by the unions. Despite continuing financial difficulties, the Roundhouse remained a legendary performing arts venue throughout the 1960s and '70s. The Centre 42 closed in 1983 due to insufficient funding, and until the mid 1990s a number of proposals to revitalize the building failed. 1996, the Norman Trust bought the Roundhouse to bring the glorious building back to life and expand it with a new creative centre for young people, according to a design of architects John McAslan + Partner. The Roundhouse was reopened in June 2006.

MILLENIUM DOME, LONDON

The Millennium Dome was built by Richard Rogers in 1999 to house a major exhibition celebrating the advent of the third millennium. Following the closure of the original exhibition, several alternative uses of the building were proposed and, eventually, dismissed. It opened again in 2003 for the Winter Wonderland show, and in winter 2004 it was used as a shelter for the homeless by a British charity organization. 'The dome' was then redeveloped by an international investment group and converted into a sports arena. The venue, renamed 'The O2' after a British mobile phone company, was reopened to the public in 2007 with a concert by Bon Jovi. The remaining land around 'The O2' Entertainment District is planned to accommodate shops and offices.

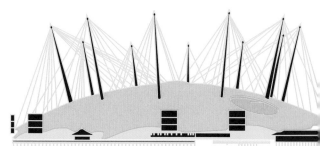

VITRA FIRE STATION, WEIL AM RHEIN

The Vitra Fire Station in Weil am Rhein, Germany, was Zaha Hadid's first built project. It was constructed as a company firehouse on the premises of the Vitra furniture design and manufacturing complex. The building soon became more or less redundant, because the Vitra-complex was eventually covered by a nearby public fire department. It was for this reason (or maybe because of the rumored planning error on Hadid's part of not allowing enough room in the building to house fire trucks) that the building was soon used by Vitra as an exhibition space for part of its permanent collection of chairs.

WORKERS VILLAGE, PISA

In 1954, the boron-producing Larderello SpA chemical company commissioned Giovanni Michelucci to build a workers' village on a hillside near Pisa. The architect developed a successful modern masterplan integrating a church and an elaborate circulation system with paths leading to the factories and all the facilities. Even though the houses were designed in a dynamic and heterogeneous way, most of them were never inhabited, as people at that time began to prefer a more individual lifestyle with more privacy. Some of the abandoned buildings came to be used by people from a nearby village to grow plants. They used basins, baths, and bidets as planters.

RYUGYONG HOTEL, PYONGYANG

The Ryugyong Hotel is a 330-meter-high, 105-storey concrete pyramid in the Potong-gang District of the North Korean capital. Planned as a hotel with 3,000 rooms and seven revolving restaurants on top and boasting 360,000 m² of floor space, it was a prestige project of the North Korean regime which was scheduled to be opened for the 1989 World Festival of Youth and Students. Construction began in 1987, but was delayed so that the appointed opening date could not be kept. In or around 1992, the project came to halt, presumably due to lack of funding, electricity shortages, and the famine in the country. Although the external facade was eventually completed in 2011, the unfinished building has stood as an empty shell ever since.

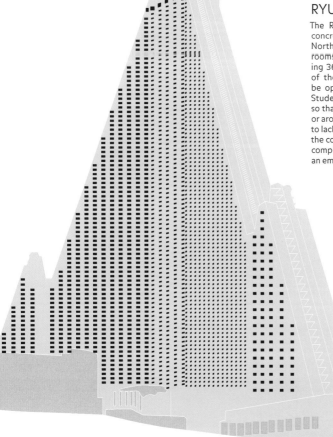

Text by Daria Ricchi, Florence, Italy

Source: RIBA Plan of Work (for the project stages) + personal experience. Compiled by Silvia Forlati

Unforseen work
Cost will rise

Poor finishing
Consequences range from litigation to bankruptcy, involving everybody. If the architect did the building supervision, he is at least in part responsible.

Wrong details bring unexpected surp
Responsibilities are difficult to pinpo
Consequences include litigation and possibly repayment to the client. Go
professional liability insurance is vita

Use
Involved: User

Forgotten or uncomplete positions in the specs
The nightmare of every architect.
The contractor will ask for more money.
The client will have to pay.

Wrong contractors
The contractor is not interested in doing a good job.

Involved: Client, Architect, Contractor

Construction

Financing crisis: client runs out money.

Abrupt end on the story

Discrepancies in the drawings
The contractor will go for one possible interpretation – usually the wrong one. Difficult to have it redone: the architect will have to live with it.

The architect is late
The contractor goes ahead and decides himself ... oops!

Critical Moments: What and where things can go wrong

Wrong idea
Rethinking is cheaper at the beginning; becomes expensive the more the project advances. Can stimulate creative solutions.

Wrong location
Idea and location are incompatible.

Insufficient funds
The client does not have enough money for what he wants: the project stops at some point. The architect will have problems getting paid and be accused of planning a much too expensive project.

Wrong client/architect matching
Experience teaches one to let go as s as possible. Beginners' mistake: try ● go on and make the relationship wor

Wrong brief
The real needs are not considered. The building comes out too small/big The user is unhappy and blames the architect for having designed a wron building.

Start

Conception
Involved: Client

Briefing
Involved: Client, Architect

Unexpected users/use
The design does not really fit the needs. How much unexpected can be accommodated before the design is considered a failure?

Wrong maintenance
From bad to dangerous. Lack of, or improper, maintenance will do damage to the building. Common opinion will somehow tend to hold the architect responsible for it.

Change of context
The building becomes obsolete and needs reinvestment to be given a new use.

End of the story

Tendering
Involved: Client, Architect

Client changes mind: project is cancelled

Budget raised: go ahead

Wrong details
From bad aesthetics to legal liability.

Wrong choice
The chosen bid is too low. The contractor goes bankrupt. Construction is delayed or stops.

much higher than estimates. Back to the drawing board!

Wrong design costs
Over-budget design forces rework. Time pressure rises, and so does tension between architect and client.

New requirements appear: more time is needed.

Planning and building permission denied: starts again!

Tight timeline (always too short)
Mistakes made entail loss in quality.

Lingering decisions (architect, client)
Lead to delays and continual redesigning. Risk of contract breaching.

Go back to the start!

Design to permission
Involved: Client, Architect

HOW MUCH RISK

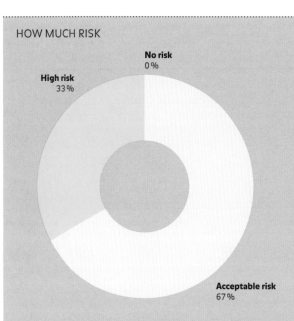

No risk
0%

High risk
33%

Acceptable risk
67%

The majority regards the profession as acceptably risky:

At least **1/3** declare to calibrate risks to desired results. The rest: **1/3** are ambitious (take whatever risk it takes to get innovative results), **1/3** are indifferent (do not want to think about it). The main concerns, however, are not about design, but about financing the office (**1**), stress (**2**), balancing private and professional life (**3**).

Risk handling strategies

take calculated risks to get acceptable results
38%

take all the risks necessary to get an innovative result
32%

do not think about it
25%

limit risks to the minimum
5%

WHERE DO YOU SEE MOST RISKS

Multiple answers were possible

Personal situation

Stress situations
32%

Imbalance of professional and private life
31%

Lack of money
25%

Dissatisfaction with the job/profession
3%

Office management

Money flow
41%

Time management
31%

Project acquisitions
19%

Workload
10%

Team conflicts
7%

Design and implementation

Projects budgets
29%

Construction stages/Technical issues
25%

Feasibility of the design
22%

Project timing
15%

Source: Wonderland #2 Survey – by SHARE architects, 2006

what to do when things go wrong

Dealing with mistakes

Mistakes require management – to facilitate mistake prevention in the first place, and, if it is too late for that, to cope with the ensuing crisis. Architecture education, however, hardly deals with this issue. Still, quality control, project evaluation, crisis management, and good professional indemnity insurance can make a difference. As can an honest look at one's own qualities and shortcomings.

Learning from your mistakes
How to do a project evaluation

You work, you learn. But do you exploit your learning experiences to the full? Learning is very important, but hardly ever urgent. How do you find the time to reflect when you are working your socks off to meet your deadlines and the client's demands? The answer to that question is very simple in theory, but may be very difficult to put into practice: you make the time, you organize project evaluations.

When?

For most people, evaluation comes after the event. But why not maximize the learning effect and evaluate a few times during the project, on completion of a specific phase, for example? Of course, the evaluation frequency and timing has to correspond to the size and complexity of the project and to the number of people involved.

ORGANIZE

Step 1: define scope and goals

To evaluate your project, the first thing to do is to determine the scope and goal of your project evaluation. You can think of the following scopes and corresponding goals. Obviously, it is possible to set multiple goals. The general goal of a project evaluation is to learn in order to improve current or future projects.

Design quality	Learn from users of buildings (functionality) Learn from other architects (aesthetics)
Design and construction process	Streamline the process to improve efficiency Gather best practices to prevent mistakes
Cooperation in the project	Improve your relationship with the client/cooperation partners
Profit or loss in a project	Improve financial control by learning from the cause of profit or loss
Personal development	Improve the skills of the individual team members regarding: • designing and drawing • communication and decision making • project management

Step 2: choose the participants

Who needs to be involved in the evaluation? Do you want to include external cooperation partners or the client? One thing is certain: having more people participating means pooling more opinions and experiences. From a learning point of view this has a surplus value.

Step 3: set the questions

In compliance with the goal set you can now choose your evaluation questions. Don't forget to reflect on cause and effect.

Questions

1. What was the goal of the project? Has this goal been realized? Why (not)?

2. Is the client satisfied? Why (not)?

3. Are you satisfied with the quality of the project design, process and results? Why (not)?

4. Are you satisfied with the results in terms of planning and project budget? (Compare calculations with the actual numbers)

5. Are you satisfied with the cooperation with internal and external parties (including the client)? Why (not)?

6. What were the mistakes made and successes achieved?

7. What lessons did you learn personally?

8. What experiences/knowledge/lessons learned from this project can be used in future projects? And how?

9. What concrete follow-up actions will assure the implementation of the lessons learned? Who will take action?

10. How are you going to share the things you learned with your colleagues?

Step 4: select the working method

Decide on the working method: you can organize a regular project meeting to evaluate, keep a file of best practices, use a questionnaire, organize a workshop, or you can ask an independent third party to do the evaluation.

Step 5: perform the evaluation

EVALUATE

Step 6: share results

LEARN

Step 7: implement lessons learned

Evaluation results or the identified lessons learned can be written down in a report. Define concrete follow-up actions to make the evaluation consequential. Unfortunately, most evaluation reports are filed and, after a while, forgotten. As a consequence, lessons learned are not shared, and different people keep making the same mistakes over and over again. This is a pity, but on the other hand, it is something that goes with the territory: learning by 'feeling' is something every person has to go through himself/herself. Apart from the more concrete outcome of the project evaluation, the process of performing an evaluation together is valuable in itself, as it contributes to team building and the strengthening of working relationships.

Start evaluating now!

Now you know how to perform a project evaluation. The first hurdle you have to get over is to make the time to reflect. So check your calendar now, reserve some time to organize the project evaluation and go for it!

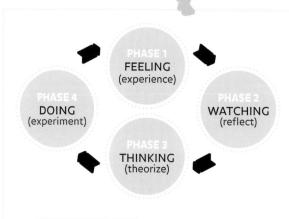

PHASE 1
FEELING
(experience)

PHASE 2
WATCHING
(reflect)

PHASE 3
THINKING
(theorize)

PHASE 4
DOING
(experiment)

KOLB'S LEARNING CYCLE
People learn in different ways. David Kolb did research on the way how people learn and defined four phases. For effective learning you must go through all of them. People have a natural preference for one specific phase. So the project evaluation is an ideal method to make sure you address those phases of Kolb's learning cycle that tend to be neglected.

Source: Kolb, D. A. and Fry, R. (1975) 'Toward an applied theory of experiential learning', in C. Cooper (ed.) Theories of Group Process, London: John Wiley

QUALITY MANAGEMENT IN ARCHITECTURAL PRACTICE(S)

Pro and contra ISO 9001

Text by Ulrich Beckefeld, osa, Vienna, Austria

Since 2000, quality management certification requirements have been specified in a number of standards under the common heading of ISO 9000ff. However, these standards do not prescribe working methods and processes, but rather call for individual and company-specific, and yet transparent and consistent process management. It is the individual adaptability of this system which makes the ISO 9001 useful for service industries; meanwhile this sector accounts for roughly one third of the certificates issued.

Formulation and documentation of relevant work processes provides a basis for evaluating and designing the interplay of a business's various internal processes. Under an ISO-9001 certificate, a firm undertakes to adhere to the self-defined work methods in daily business and, at the same time, to make regular inspections and promote further development.

Here is also where the problems with ISO-9001 lie: every company organizing its internal workflow and organization will do so in a way considered necessary and meaningful. But this is also possible without certification. With ISO-9001 certification – the only quality management system that is recognized across industries and countries – conscious process management is made transparent and communicable to third parties. But as ISO certification is not a criterion in awarding commissions in most countries, the question of its usefulness for architectural practices arises. In addition, certification by external auditors involves increased financial and administrative expenditure.

ISO 9001 also has certain advantages. These are mostly largely the result of the 'view from outside'. Existing blind spots in one's own practice often are revealed for the first time; here, it is essential that the auditor have a good knowledge of the usual ways of working in the particular industry. This level of expertise, though, cannot be taken for granted, particularly not in an area such as architectural planning. The choice of the 'right' auditor therefore is highly important. For architectural practices, which generally have only a limited amount of economic and business administration know-how, ISO certification only makes sense when the internal processes are developed in close collaboration with the auditor. This, however, requires willingness on both sides.

Only then can the external constraints associated with ISO 9001 come into play. Without doubt, most practices will understand the necessity to regularly review, and if necessary, revise their working structures – though in everyday business life this is generally paid not enough attention, in particular by small and younger practices. But during the office's first consolidation phase, at the latest, a chance arises to shape internal processes more consciously than was possible (or indeed even meaningful) in the founding phase.

WHAT IS ISO-9001?

ISO 9001 is a family of standards, designed by the International Organization for Standardization for quality management. To officially incorporate ISO 9001 in your (architecture) practice, you will have to undergo certification by a designated registration/certification body and submit to regular checkups. In exchange, you will receive an official and internationally recognized certificate that your office is run in compliance with ISO 9001 (to be precise: ISO 9001:2015).

The core concern of ISO 9001 is not product quality control, but to make sure that the underlying process is consistently carried out. Initially developed for the manufacturing sector, it is today mainly used by the service sector, including architects.

The applying organization, in this case your architecture practice, is required to produce a quality policy and a quality manual to ascertain that your "production" process meets a number of given quality criteria. The standard, however, does not prescribe a method, but leaves it up to the applying organization and the certification body to ensure that the goals of the standard are achieved. These requirements of ISO 9001 ranges from control of documents, control of records, internal audits, control of nonconforming product, corrective action, preventive action and include measures for continual process improvement.

A list of accreditation and certification bodies can be found on the Internet at **www.iso.org**. In some cases, these bodies will not only be authorized to certificate your practice, but also be able to provide business consulting services. Few of these bodies, however, will be specialized in architecture.

 SCHNEIDER + SCHUMACHER, FRANKFURT/MAIN, GERMANY AND VIENNA, AUSTRIA
ISO CERTIFICATED SINCE 2003

The German office schneider+schumacher received the first ISO 9001 certification in 2003. In 2018 they updated they certification to ISO 9001:2015. The decision to apply for the certification coincided with a period of strong growth, which made it possible and also necessary to carry out an in-depth restructuring of the practice. The office consists of circa 180 people and offers services ranging from urban, architectural, and product design to building and project management.

Originally, one of the reasons for the certification was to give the restructuring and the resultant organization an official status that could be taken into account by potential clients and in formal tender procedures. Today, the biggest advantage is seen in the inherent pressure to develop strategies to sharpen the office profile, to develop working tools and rules, and to enhance the planning process and design quality through regular self-monitoring processes.

The certification process was supported by an organization-development consultant who is also responsible for the yearly checkups for the required renewals. These checkups involve the presence of the certifier in the company for about 3 days each year; the necessary expenditure includes renewal fees, additional costs, and energies. For the whole thing to work, it has shown to be very important that cooperation with the accreditation body works well, as it is not always easy to find a certifier able to deal with the specificity of an architecture practice.

The ISO standards were introduced in a consolidation phase when the core competences of the office had become clear. According to managing director Ralf Seeburger, an earlier introduction only makes sense if the certification process focuses more on the development of the practice than on the standardization of the design process.

www.schneider-schumacher.com

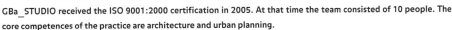

GBa_STUDIO received the ISO 9001:2000 certification in 2005. At that time the team consisted of 10 people. The core competences of the practice are architecture and urban planning.

Architect Gianluca Brini, who leads the practice, gives as main reasons for the certification the general desire to improve quality with regard to the final product and ensuing client satisfaction, and to improve organizational efficiency. One further reason is a more specific Italian situation: the legislation for public tenders requires construction companies to have certified quality management. This requirement may eventually be passed on to other actors in the construction process, such as architecture practices.

The consultant hired by the practice had never worked with architects before, but accepted the task with enthusiasm. The first steps involved auditing the practice (2 half days) in order to evaluate how it worked and how close existing processes came to compliance with ISO-9001 standards. The second phase was the design of the quality management system. It involved six weekly meetings involving the whole team and resulted in the quality manual. In the following phases, the manual was tested and the certification body was contacted, as in this case the consultant did not issue the certificate himself. The entire certification process took approximately 9 months, and the costs were acceptable, even for a relatively small practice as this one.

After approximately one year, the certification cannot be said to have led to an increased number of commissions. Nonetheless, architect Brini was definitely affirmative about it when asked if he would advise other offices to consider certification. The practice has experienced an efficiency increase in both organization and workflow. And what about the quality of the final products? "Either it is in the head, or nothing can be done about it", was his reply.

www.gbastudio.it

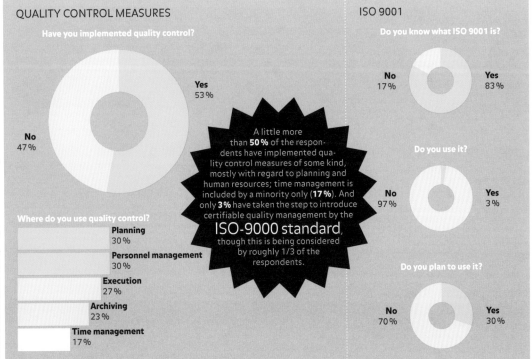

Source: Wonderland #2 Survey – by SHARE architects, 2006

QUALITY CONTROL MEASURES

Have you implemented quality control?

Yes
53%

No
47%

Where do you use quality control?

Planning
30%

Personnel management
30%

Execution
27%

Archiving
23%

Time management
17%

A little more than **50%** of the respondents have implemented quality control measures of some kind, mostly with regard to planning and human resources; time management is included by a minority only (**17%**). And only **3%** have taken the step to introduce certifiable quality management by the **ISO-9000 standard**, though this is being considered by roughly 1/3 of the respondents.

ISO 9001

Do you know what ISO 9001 is?

No
17%

Yes
83%

Do you use it?

No
97%

Yes
3%

Do you plan to use it?

No
70%

Yes
30%

WHAT DO YOU DO WHEN THINGS GO WRONG

Get fired / leave the job
0 %

Find a solution by ...
12 %

Other
20 %

Hire a crisis manager or get external help
7 %

Manage the problem within the office
69 %

> Prioritize!
> Never compromise!

> Find a solution by ...
> discussions on site with contractor,
> if not solved – to court!

> NLP-coaching by
> professional coach two
> to four times a year

> Flexible number of freelancers,
> very high level of co-specialists:
> graphics, PR, photographers,
> writers, scenographers.

> Broadening my field of
> activity from architecture to
> research, journalism, and the
> making of short films on archi-
> tecture, exhibitions, etc.

> I have learned to calm down and think things
> through in risky and stressful circumstances. And I
> do believe that, if you want something and work hard
> for it, you will succeed, and if things still do not work
> out the way you planned, this might have a reason and
> you should not insist. This works for everything –
> clients, process, expectations ...

> Somehow solutions are always
> found, you never know what will
> happen and how you will solve the
> problem but until now nothing
> has remained unresolved.

> I share my problems with
> architecture friends.

> We learn from
> our mistakes.

> Do a specific pro-
> ject about new
> conditions.

> Trying to find a solution
> that is acceptable for the client and every-
> body else involved to successfully continue
> the project, or abandon the project
> altogether and withdraw name.

> To sum up, I'm very pessimistic about
> the profession of architecture nowa-
> days. We have left Wonderland!

Source: Wonderland #2 Survey – by SHARE architects, 2006

FEARS AND REALITY

Not every problem that you are afraid of really occurs, and conversely, **not every problem that occurs is what you were afraid of**. The latter seems to be particularly true in three cases (see ●): problems with **office finance, clients,** and **timing**. These are included by less people in their 'afraid of' lists, but experienced by many more as actually occurring.

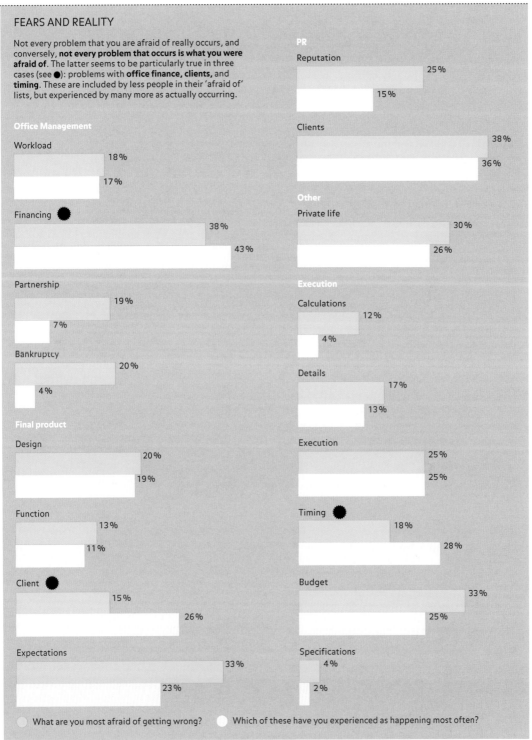

Office Management

Workload
18%
17%

Financing ●
38%
43%

Partnership
19%
7%

Bankruptcy
20%
4%

Final product

Design
20%
19%

Function
13%
11%

Client ●
15%
26%

Expectations
33%
23%

PR

Reputation
25%
15%

Clients
38%
36%

Other

Private life
30%
26%

Execution

Calculations
12%
4%

Details
17%
13%

Execution
25%
25%

Timing ●
18%
28%

Budget
33%
25%

Specifications
4%
2%

● What are you most afraid of getting wrong? ○ Which of these have you experienced as happening most often?

Source: Wonderland #2 Survey – by SHARE architects, 2006

CRISIS COMMUNICATION

What kind of crisis requires you to communicate actively? Well, if business is slow this may represent a severe crisis for your office, and to acquire new commissions you should definitely communicate the skills and services you can offer, but this is not the type of crisis we wish to focus on here.
Crisis communication is specific media work that handles mishaps, accidents or blunt faults that could be of public interest and therefore could have an impact on your professional reputation.

Public institutions and large companies use crisis communication, e.g. in the event of terror attacks, damaged goods, natural disasters, or other grave misfortunes. Why should a small architecture office consider applying crisis communication?

There are a few reasons: first, the field of business – architecture – is particularly prone to mistakes, second, we are superstitious **wonderland** folk who believe that it won't rain as long as you carry an umbrella, and finally, personal stress can increase dramatically in crisis situations – if communication can be kept under control, it will be to the benefit of the public image of the office and the internal working climate with staff and partners.

Be prepared

Take action

There are **3 simple rules** to be followed:

Communicate

How to prepare?

In the preparatory phase you need to make sure that you are still able to communicate in case of an emergency. Architects essentially think and act a) as business people and b) as creative people. Both viewpoints are inevitably linked with a risk, and this risk is what makes architecture an exciting creative process in the first place.

Emergency numbers on the fridge door and people responsible for safety on the building site are reasonable precautionary measures that can be taken without putting the brakes on innovation. Yet they alone are not sufficient; and as everyone knows, avoiding a mishap is better than having to clear up the mess afterwards. The approach you take to something unexpected happening is more important than having the right phone numbers to call. Looking at the dangers that may arise from your activity as an architect and taking them seriously is starting to avoid mistakes. Furthermore, such anticipation ensures that you can become aware of mistakes as soon as possible and that, in the best case, they will not take you by surprise. Thus preparation starts with your mental attitude. An old custom in Russia says that before undertaking a journey, even if in haste and with one's hat and coat on, one should sit down on a chair to keep still for a moment. Integrating such moments of composure in your work as a kind of control system may perhaps help to anticipate mistakes. Practically speaking, simple means such as check-lists may be useful here.

As a further step, you can plan your crisis communication. To do this, you reflect on all the important steps in crisis communication and, at the end, make sure that there is a clear priority list of all contact partners. This is a central aspect of the preparations, as you are determined to avoid information about mistakes being spread inaccurately, or accidentally.

What action to take?

On being alerted to a problem, you should make a determined effort to collect every imaginable piece of information about its extent, cause, and possible consequences. One great danger is the 'grapevine effect' (meaning that when facts are passed on they may – unintentionally or not – be twisted or distorted. In oral communication, this may start as early as with the third person in the chain. Exaggerations and confusion of facts, as well as incomplete information are continued by this chain of communication, leading at times to a completely distorted account of the situation.) To avoid such problems and to later be in a position to provide credible and reliable answers the best thing for you to do is gather the information personally. This means that *you should go to the site, look at the plans yourself or personally* calculate the whole thing a second time.

Before you make any hasty press statements, it is of absolute importance to ensure that the mishap is not continued or repeated and that any immediate danger is being dealt with. As soon as the extent of the calamity can be assessed you can decide on how far your crisis communication must extend. Whom should you talk to? Only my office staff? Or also others involved in the project? To further multipliers such as public authorities, manufacturers, or colleagues? To the press?

The greater the potential scandal, the more carefully you will have to choose the people you talk to. In the action phase, you collect information and then communicate it. Everybody involved and interested, now or in the future, should be aware that you take the problem seriously, that your crisis management is competent and that you will do everything necessary to make sure that something like this is not going to happen again in the future, neither to you nor to others.

All misfortune is the result of carelessness.

Proverb of the ancient masters of Japanese martial arts

How to communicate?

The aspect of learning is particularly important with regard to communication, and it begins with the action phase. This provides an opportunity to communicate a meaningful message that diverts attention from issues like human failure or apportioning of blame. In public-relations jargon, this is known as theme management (theme management or issue management – the term is used to describe the deliberate wording of headlines for news reports. It is widespread in politics and business communication; however, small offices may as well choose the central concerns of their communication in an equally focused way.)

For example, after a mistake with serious consequences you could communicate that

1) the site of the accident has, in the meantime, been made safe

2) that an internal workshop will examine how this kind of thing could happen, and

3) the results of this workshop will be published later.

This productive approach is likely to turn the interest of target addressees from the search for scapegoats to the search for (generally applicable) solutions. But this should not develop into diversionary manoeuvring. Only if there is a sincere interest in learning from what has happened, outside perception will correlate theme management with competence and responsibility. If this can be ensured through active communication and if everybody concerned can become aware of your competent and responsible response to the problem, then the crisis is, at least partly, mastered. ●●

Architect's Liability and Insurance

A European overview

In most European countries, the performance of architectural services entails a number of responsibilities; these vary from country to country, and so do architects' liabilities.

Compulsory or not, professional indemnity and office insurance can cover a wide range of risks arising from the work of an architectural professional and are frequently required by clients. In addition, architects also have responsibilities for construction workers, maintenance personnel, and people using a building designed to serve as a workplace.

Current legislation and other regulations regarding liability and insurance protection still widely vary in the different European countries. Information is scattered and scarce, and hence difficult to compare, and regulations are changing fast. The following list can therefore only provide a provisional overview.

Compiled by Anne Isopp

AT – AUSTRIA
Insurance: not compulsory
Liability period: 3 years for real estate/immovable property, 2 years for movable property (warranty, i.e. strict liability); after that, for compensation for damage (fault-based) 3 years (from the knowledge of damage and damaging party) for a 30-year period

BE – BELGIUM
Insurance: compulsory
Liability period: 10 years (from handover), 20 years (non-contractual liability)

BG – BULGARIA
Insurance: compulsory
Liability period: 5 years for interior fittings, insulations etc.; 8 for refurbishment works; 10 years for structural part including foundation

CH – SWITZERLAND
Insurance: not compulsory (professional liability insurance may cover injury, material damage, and damage to buildings
Liability period: 5 years

CY – CYPRUS
Liability period: 2 years (from date of occurrence or discovery of damage)

CZ – CZECH REPUBLIC
Insurance: compulsory (for members of Czech Chamber of Architects with permanent or temporary registration)
Liability period: 10 years

DE – GERMANY
Insurance: compulsory
Liability period: 5 years (from handover, other terms of liability subject to contractual agreement)

DK – DENMARK
Insurance: not legally compulsory but mandatory for members of Danske Arkitektvirks Omheder (Danish Association of Architects)
Liability period: 5 years for professional client, 10 years for consumer client (from handover)

EE – ESTONIA
Insurance: not compulsory
Liability period: 2 years standard warranty for construction work, 5 years limitation period for claims, 10 years for claims in cases of criminal intention

ES – SPAIN
Insurance: compulsory in some regions
Liability period: 1 year for rectification of defects, 3 years for functionality, 10 years for structural solidity

FI – FINLAND
Insurance: not compulsory but often required by client
Liability period: 2 years (from completion of professional service, standard warranty); 10 years for damage caused by "intentional or gross negligence or incomplete performance"

FR – FRANCE
Insurance: compulsory (lack of insurance may result in suspension or even removal from the roll of the Order)
Liability period: 1 year for rectification of defects, 2 years for functionality, 10 years for structural solidity

GR – GREECE
Liability period: 10 years (for substantial defects)

HR – CROATIA
Insurance: compulsory

HU – HUNGARY
Insurance: not compulsory (general insurance or project-based policy)
Liability period: 3 years (main elements of residential buildings); 3–5 years (finishing works and long-durability building products), 10 years (building shell)

IE – IRELAND
Insurance: not compulsory, but recommended for members of the RIAI (Royal Institute of Architects of Ireland)
Liability period: 6 years for a contract signed under hand; 12 years for a contract signed under seal (from onset of damage)

IT – ITALY
Insurance: compulsory for all work since August 2013
Liability period: 2 years (from handover) for defects and non-compliance with project; 10 years for stability defects

LT – LITHUANIA
Insurance: compulsory
Liability period: 5 years (all building parts); 10 years (structural parts); 20 years (intentionally concealed defects)

LU – LUXEMBURG
Insurance: compulsory
Liability period: 2 years (from handover) for small works, 10 years for large works; 30 years for cases of wilful misrepresentation

LV – LATVIA
Insurance: compulsory since October 2014
Liability period: 2 years (from handover) legal defects warranty period; 10 years for damage under Civil Code

MT – MALTA
Liability period: 15 years (from completion) for defects affecting building stability

NL – NETHERLANDS
Insurance: compulsory for members of the Bond van Nederlandse Architecten (BNA)
Liability period: 5 years for latent defects; 10 years for defects affecting stability and fitness for purpose; under Civil Code up to 20 years from handover

NO – NORWAY
Insurance: not compulsory
Liability period: 5 years

PL – POLAND
Insurance: compulsory
Liability period: 3 years from handover; maximum 10 years from originating act

PT – PORTUGAL
Insurance: compulsory for members of Ordem Dos Arquitectos
Liability period: 1 year, with equal rectification period

RO – ROMANIA
Insurance: not compulsory
Liability period: 1 to 10 years depending on contractual or legal basis

SE – SWEDEN
Insurance: compulsory
Liability period: variable depending on contract; 10 years for defects caused by negligence

SI – SLOVENIA
Liability period: 10 years from handover (structural defects affecting stability)

SK – SLOVAKIA
Insurance: compulsory for those on the list of Authorized Architects with permanent or temporary registration
Liability period: 3 years under Civil Code, 5 under Commercial Code (from handover)

UK – UNITED KINGDOM
Insurance: compulsory
Liability period: 6 years (5 in Scotland) , 12 years (20 in Scotland) for secured contracts

Sources: ACE www.ace-cae.eu; Länderdatenbank der Universität Siegen www.architektur.uni-siegen.de/ipb/laenderdatenbank.html?lang=d

SHADES OF ERROR

There is no foolproof way of avoiding mistakes. Everybody makes a number of them in the course of his or her career. Five architects anonymously tell about what went wrong for them and what they have learned from their mistakes.

Too much trust

One has to trust the people that one works with on a building project. After all, what we hear from famous architects about successful projects often is: "We had a good working relationship based on trust." In the case of a team of young architects, however, the building contractor betrayed their trust. The architects realized this only about six months after the completion of the building when, during stormy weather, rain entered the building through the brand-new roof. The builder had used one third less roof tiles than building regulations required for a roof of this pitch. "He took advantage of us to get the job done more quickly and cheaply." This issue had to be taken to court. Both parties, the architect and the contractor, were held responsible. The architect as the client's technical advisor should have inspected the work on site to ensure that it was being carried out correctly. The contractor accused the architects of not having provided proper instructions. The architects cannot say whether this would have happened to them if they had had more experience. But they are certain of one thing: next time, they will be more cautious about whom they work with.

Tricked out of full payment

The brief had been precise, but throughout the design stage, the project became ever more comprehensive. Eventually, the client decided for a proposed larger, better-quality and, of course, more expensive design. Accordingly, the architect would have been entitled to three times the fee initially agreed upon. After some negotiation, the client agreed to double the original fee, with one part payable during construction and the rest as a bonus on completion. After the handover, though, the client changed his mind and said that he had never agreed to a bonus – so 60,000 Euros of the agreed fee are still outstanding. In the future, this architect's office will never again supply designs or drawings without conditions being clearly defined in advance and in writing. And it will never make a contract again without a lawyer, no matter how congenial the relationship with the client may seem. The motto now is: "Don't trust anybody."

Text by Anne Isopp

A forgotten document

All that the Italian team of architects had forgotten to enclose in their competition entry documents was a copy of an ID card. They had spent a great deal of energy and time on their proposal, but were ultimately disqualified from the competition because of this omission. "Well, this kind of thing can happen," the architects say, although it was a particularly bitter experience: speaking to one of the jurors later, they learned that the jury had regarded their project as one of the best, but that it "unfortunately" had to be ruled because of the missing document. And there was nothing that the architects could do about it.

Since then, the teams have made a point of keeping a checklist at the office, which they try to stick to very closely. "Even so, it's very difficult not to make a single mistake. They often ask for so many little things."

Faulty scheduling

A project deadlock: construction about to start, and the plans not ready; to make things worse, the main managing partner in the office not even aware of the problem. "The partners were, in a sense, blind", says the project-supervising architect who had pointed out on several occasions that there were not enough people working on the project. The client suggested commissioning another architect to help them out, and the architect in charge of the project threatened to quit. It was only then that the main partner realized the necessity to take action. The team was expanded, and the project was brought back on track without outside help. The supervising architect now says that her resignation threat was only bluffing, but she simply saw no other way of responding to the problem. "The best part of it was that we got to know each other better, to trust each other more". Since then, similar problems have not arisen in the office, and timetables now are more realistic.

Naive approach

The idea was convincing, and the team of architects won the competition for an art-in-the-building project. "It always takes a certain degree of naivety to create a simple, strong, convincing idea", the architects say today. "But in the end reality always catches up with you. So, what initially seemed to be a great idea, turned out to be rather difficult to realize."

One of the problems they were confronted with was cost estimates. When the construction company realized that the architects were serious about the project they quadrupled their cost estimate. But not just that: technical feasibility posed another problem. By eventually finding the "right" partner – the search for a specialized firm turned out to be extremely difficult – they were able to master not only the technical issues, but also the financial aspects of the project. In the end, they overran the budget by a mere one to two percent. For the architects, this was a success that encouraged them to embark on similar projects in the future. Next time, however, they will take a closer look at cost estimates, especially if they are made at such an early stage in the project.

Finally, the 1600 residents of the village had to be convinced, too. For days, the architects sought to engage the skeptical locals in discussions to explain the project to them. It was only after the first part had been completed that public opinion changed. What the architects have learned from this is that, in such a small village, it is vital to keep contact not only with decision-makers, but with the whole community. ∞

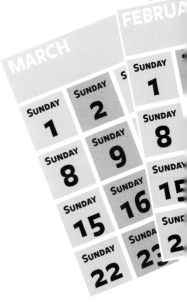

FACING YOUR FEARS

Interview with psychologist Eduard Brandstätter

Imagine a surfer riding a huge wave. One is not sure what is more dangerous: the wave itself, or the fear of making a wrong move and being buried under it. It would be hard to find an image that better illustrates the connection between the fear of taking a risk and the fear of making a mistake.
We talked about this complicated relationship with Austrian psychologist Eduard Brandstätter.

wonderland: Why are people afraid?

Brandstätter: Fear is a healthy natural emotion. It ensures our survival. Fear is the expectation that something bad will happen. This may be a mistake, a separation, a social embarrassment, or the loss of one's job. The goal is not to make people free of fear, but to reduce fear to a reasonable level. Part of this is the ability for realistic assessment of a situation. Do not attempt to avoid fear, but imagine what will happen if the particular situation arises. For instance, you have designed a building, and it is taken apart by the critics: What would then happen? In the context of a Socratic dialogue you should continue to ask this. Finally, you come to realize that your life would go on. Of course, it is not a particularly pleasant experience, but you no longer see it as a catastrophe.

How do people deal with fear?

Everybody feels fear differently. We know of innumerable ways of coping with fear: one of them is perfectionism. If you are very afraid of making mistakes, you can make an enormous effort to avoid them. Another form of behavior is ignoring the situation. In this case, the person concerned does not confront him or herself with the situation

at all. For instance, if he has a social fear, he simply does not leave the house any more. Then there is also defensive pessimism: here the person uses the assertion that something cannot possibly succeed as a kind of self-protection. And if things really go wrong he can always say: just as I predicted. He maneuvers himself into a situation in which he apparently cannot lose. But in the long term these are counterproductive strategies.

Can fear not lead us to make mistakes in the first place?

Let's take the perfectionist: for him fear is a strong motivating force. This kind of person invests a lot of energy and works very hard to avoid making a mistake. This can produce positive results. But as far as the individual is concerned, it is a different matter. Of course, there also is the kind of fear that has a paralyzing effect; fear that so incapacitates people that they can no longer think clearly. There is a good rule that was defined by Robert Yerkes and John D. Dodson: someone who has no fear at all does not make any effort at all. He or she is completely indifferent. If the fear is extreme, it also reduces performance. For instance, if you have to give a speech and are so afraid that you cannot

Interview by Anne Isopp

116

concentrate. On the other hand, a moderate level of fear seems to improve performance.

What is the relationship between fear and the readiness to take risks?

We can measure fear through personality tests – but this shows no strong correlation with the readiness to take risks.

Are there any professions that are particularly risk-loving?

Unless self-employment is an involuntary decision, a self-employed person is certainly more willing to take a risk than someone looking for a steady job. There is a study by Geert Hofstede according to which certain nations are more willing to take risks than others. He examined 50 countries. It showed that the willingness to take risks is very low for example in Greece and very high in the so-called Asian 'tiger states'. Austria is somewhere in the middle. Someone who is willing to dissent from the group opinion is also willing to take a risk. Although everyone seems to be doing things in a particular way, this kind of person is not afraid to say: "I'll do it differently." In his books, the American psychologist Robert Sternberg looks for creative personalities of whom people still speak 100 years later. Such persons often lived against the grain of the scientific establishment. They were isolated for a long time, took a great risk, but after a long dry spell came out triumphant in the end. Sigmund Freud, for example, went against the mainstream, including his own colleagues and profession. His research was initially dismissed by the entire field of academic psychology. To deal with this takes an enormous readiness for risk. Will he succeed, or will he be regarded as a madman?

How would you describe this kind of person? You surely cannot measure this in terms of willingness to take risks alone.

There is more involved, such as, naturally, a substantial amount of talent and creativity. These people do not conform to the spirit of the times. They listen to what is being said – but in fact follow their own inner voice.

Perhaps these are oppositional spirits who do not want to move along with the crowd.

But although, or even because, a self-employed person is willing to take a risk, he may fail and go bankrupt. How can one deal with this? There certainly are different behavior patterns. One kind of person might say: "I will try again", and another: "I will return to a safer way of life."

There are very great differences. I knew a man once whose company went bankrupt. He was a physical wreck; he had to take early retirement. An opposite example is Niki Lauda – from his racing car accident to an airplane crash, just think of what he has gone through. His airline, Lauda Air, went bankrupt; he was head of the Jaguar Formula One team and got fired; now he has his own airline again. The decisive question, of course, is what is right for the individual in the situation. This can only be answered individually. Resignation is not necessarily the wrong approach. If you realize that putting more time and money into something is just a waste of time, then you are right to give up. If you see that there is still a chance to succeed, you can certainly have another try.

But this needs a realistic assessment of the situation.

Exactly. What is the situation, what are my abilities to cope with it? In this context, we speak of the 'locus of control': if I feel that I am in control, I can influence what happens around me. Such people actively shape their environment. If control is outside of me, I feel like a puppet on a string. Behind this isa view of the world that says: "Everything comes from outside, if God does not want it that way, there is no point in making an effort." An internal 'locus of control' goes hand in hand with psychological health. The healthiest approach to life is that of the realistic optimist.

How do we deal with mistakes?

There are great differences here, too. There are people who are unable to admit mistakes and tend to put the blame on others. Sports

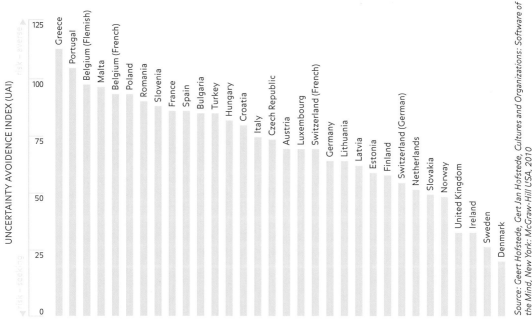

UNCERTAINTY AVOIDANCE INDEX (UAI)

risk – averse

risk – seeking

Greece, Portugal, Belgium (Flemish), Malta, Belgium (French), Poland, Romania, Slovenia, France, Spain, Bulgaria, Turkey, Hungary, Croatia, Italy, Czech Republic, Austria, Luxembourg, Switzerland (French), Germany, Lithuania, Latvia, Estonia, Finland, Switzerland (German), Netherlands, Slovakia, Norway, United Kingdom, Ireland, Sweden, Denmark

Source: Geert Hofstede, Gert Jan Hofstede, Cultures and Organizations: Software of the Mind, New York: McGraw-Hill USA, 2010

The avoidance of uncertainty is a measure of the extent to which the members of a culture feel themselves threatened by unclear or unfamiliar situations. This feeling can be expressed in the form of nervous stress, a need for predictability or for written and unwritten rules.

players, for example, are conditioned to react that way. They do not say: "We were the worse team, and that's why we lost", but instead say something like: "Today, we didn't play well". People should, of course, ask themselves where the mistake lies and then take a positive lesson from it. You learn from your mistakes. But, as we said in the beginning, there are also people who regard mistakes as a personal catastrophe. And then there is the phenomenon of over-generalization: that is the term we use if someone projects a single mistake onto his or her entire personality, the judgment being: "I am incompetent". If the mistake is clear and obvious, you have to admit to it; otherwise you don't have a chance. If, however, you react with a look to the future, you demonstrate a certain strength of personality.

What makes a person instinctive? What makes someone try to ignore mistakes, or admit them?

There are studies about this, too. People were asked to park a car. When they bumped into a neighboring car, their first reaction was to blame the other person, that is, the person who told them to park there. On second thought, however, they become aware that is was them who were driving and therefore are responsible. The spontaneous reaction is to suppress things.

There certainly are differences in understanding of what constitutes a mistake and what doesn't?

I would tend to make this dependent on the point of reference. The American scientists Victoria Husted Medve, Scott F. Madey, and

Thomas Gilovich made a study of medal winners at the Olympic Games. They used camera studies to compare the gestures of winners during the medal award ceremony. They noted that the gold medal winners – logically enough – were the happiest, but the second happiest group was not the silver medal winners, but those who got bronze. Why? Well, the runners-up were annoyed because they had missed out on the gold medal whereas those who made third place were happy that they had not ended up fourth. Although, objectively, those who came out second did better, they were less satisfied than those coming out third. They started from different reference points. We can draw an analogy to your question here: what is a mistake? The answer depends upon the point of reference. The perfectionist will always feel to have failed because of the high standards he sets for himself, even though he may, objectively, do better than someone else. Interpreting what is a mistake and what is not depends on one's point of reference.

Let's talk briefly about guilt feelings? When do these occur and why?

Do you mean guilt or shame? I would say that guilt is a moral violation, breaking a rule, doing what ought not to be done. Shame has more to do with a loss of status. Somebody going bankrupt is likely to be ridiculed by others. He feels that he has lost their esteem. This is not guilt, but shame.

And how to deal with such a loss of face? How does one behave in public with this kind of feeling?

I would suggest admitting to your mistakes, talking to someone that you can trust, asking other people for their opinion. Moreover, you should show your positive qualities and make sure that word gets out about them – in this way you can turn a weakness into a strength. To stay in the field of sports: the ski racer Hermann Maier once took a disastrous fall in an Olympic race in which he had been the gold medal favorite. Only two or three days later, he won a gold medal in another race. This enormously enhanced his advertising value in the USA. First the fall, then the gold medal; this was far better for his career than if he had won two gold medals in a row. Or take the case of Niki Lauda and his accident – this has become his trademark. People see that he overcame a difficult situation that would have caused others to give up. So you can move on from defeat to victory. I even go so far as to say that anybody with a successful career had to accept defeats. And it was precisely in those moments of defeat that they refused to give up. The decisive thing here is not success, but getting up again after a knockdown. ▬

Eduard Brandstätter, Linz, Austria
Studied psychology at the Universities of Innsbruck and Vienna and is now Professor at the Department of Social and Economic Psychology of the Johannes Kepler University in Linz. He has given coures in Applied Statistics, Consumer Behavior, Decision Making and General, Economic and Social Psychology.

Life after architecture?

The central triumvirate of Modernism, Mies van der Rohe, Le Corbusier, and Frank Lloyd Wright, all became architects without ever attending a school of architecture. The opposite may be true as well: people who started to study architecture and in some cases also completed their studies, but ultimately never worked in the profession. That is to say, for a short period of their life, they were considered 'failures' by conventional standards. The fact that they finally developed into the persons we know them as may be due to a number of factors, one of which probably was the 'mistake' of studying architecture (and the wide range of possibilities that an architectural education can offer).

John Cage (1912–1992)

After arriving in Paris in 1930, he began to study architecture with Ernö Goldfinger, but gave up soon as Goldfinger advised him that to be successful one must devote one's whole life to architecture. (A short time later, Yannis Xenakis, with his impressive achievements both as an architect in partnership with Le Corbusier and as a composer, was to prove the opposite). John Cage returned to America and became – John Cage.

Pink Floyd (* 1965)

Roger Waters, Nick Mason, and Rick Wright met in the mid-1960s while studying architecture at Regent Street Polytechnic. Nevertheless, this is not a reason to view *The Wall* as their musical comment on a principal element from the disdainful world of building ...

After the victory of pop culture, schools of architecture came to be regarded as a kind of breeding ground pop stars. However, it is impossible to detect any tendency toward a specific musical direction, as musicians of very different kinds such as Chris Lowe of the Pet Shop Boys, Edoardo Bennato, and John 'Country Roads' Denver all have the A-word in their CVs.

Luis Trenker (1892–1990)

The son of a mountain farmer from South Tyrol first studied architecture in Vienna and, after the First World War, in Graz and opened his practice in Bolzano – for a while together with

Clemens Holzmeister, one of the best-known Austrian architects of the 20th century. Originally only cast for the role of a mountain guide in Arnold Franck's film *Berg des Schicksals (Peak of Fate)*, he was eventually given the male leading role, as the actor originally intended for the part had no mountaineering skills. This was the start of his career in German-language films of the post-war period, both as an actor and director.

Max Frisch (1911–1991)

Max Frisch, the son of an architect, first started to study German philology at the University of Zurich, but after the death of his father in 1932 he was forced to drop out of university for financial reasons. After several years as a correspondent for the *Neue Zürcher Zeitung*, he went on to study architecture at the ETH Zurich from 1936 to 1941. In 1942 he won a competition for the Letzigraben public swimming pool (today known as the *Max Frisch Bad*) and opened his own architectural practice. In parallel, he built a career as one of the most important writers in the German language. It was only in 1955 that the author of books such as *Homo faber*, *Andorra* and *Stiller* finally closed down his practice to be able to devote himself completely to writing.

Siegfried Kracauer (1889–1966)

From 1907 to 1913, Kracauer studied architecture in Darmstadt, Berlin and Munich. At the same time, he also attended lectures in

Text by Michael Obrist, feld72, Vienna, Austria

philosophy and sociology and in 1914 completed his doctorate in engineering sciences. Until 1920, he worked as an architect in Osnabrück, Munich and Berlin before finally following his vocation to become a literary intellectual. From 1922 to 1933, he was a senior film and literature editor of the *Frankfurter Zeitung* (working alongside Walter Benjamin and Ernst Bloch, among others) and, in that time, also wrote one of his theoretical key works, *Ornament der Masse (Ornaments of the Masses)*. In exile (first in France, later in the USA), he developed into one of the last century's leading film and cultural critics.

Michael Cimino (1943–2016)

He initially studied art and architecture at Yale University with great enthusiasm (graduating with a master's degree), but his interest in the theater eventually brought him, in a roundabout way, to film-making. At the age of 39, he made *The Deer Hunter* which won three Oscars. Two years later, the economic disaster of his four-hour long monumental *Heaven's Gate* caused the bankruptcy of the legendary United Artists studio. It took five years before Cimino was able to make his next film. Among the number of architects who, despite completing their studies, turned their back on the profession to become film directors were Fernando Meirelles *(City of God)* and the great Italian master of film and theater, Franco Zeffirelli.

Anthony Quinn (1915–2001)

Following the death of his father, Anthony Quinn, who went down in film history as Alexis Zorbas in *Zorba the Greek*, was left to his own resources at the age of 12 and had to earn a livelihood by taking on odd jobs. He came to architecture from sculpture, and thanks to a grant was able to study art and architecture with Frank Lloyd Wright. Their close personal relationship led to Lloyd Wright paying for a tongue operation on the 17-year-old Quinn that remedied a speech impediment. Wright also arranged for the young man to attend a speech therapist. Here Quinn, who later won two Oscars, developed an interest in acting and changed his career direction.

Suzanna Arundhati Roy (*1961)

The Indian writer and political activist studied architecture at Delhi School of Architecture. She came into contact with the world of film through her second husband, the filmmaker Pradeeep Kishen, and started writing screenplays. 1992, she began to work on her first novel, *The God of Small Things*, which she finished in 1996. In 1998, it was awarded the British Booker Prize.

Arundhati Roy used her international fame to promote her political concerns and in recent years had developed into one of the best-known critics of globalization.

Adolfo Maria Pérez Esquivel (*1931)

Esquivel studied architecture at the Art University in Buenos Aires. Until 1974, he worked as a sculptor and held professorships of architecture at a number of universities. Political and social conditions during the military dictatorship of Juan Carlos Onganía led Esquivel to engage in opposition movements. 1973, he founded the newspaper *Pay y Justicia* that developed into a mouthpiece for the Latin American human rights movement. After abandoning his university career, he dedicated himself to the organization of these groups that also helped to educate the poor and started a campaign for the native Indian population that desperately needed land. 1977, he was imprisoned for 14 months and was put under house arrest for a further 9 months. In 1980 he was awarded the Nobel Peace Prize for his non-violent resistance based on the principles of Mahatma Ghandi and for his commitment to human rights.

Political circumstances also made two other former architects, Simon Wiesenthal, the founder of the Jewish Documentation Centre and world-famous 'Nazi hunter', and Ahmed Massoud, the Afghan national hero and opponent of the Mujaheddin (Wall Street Journal: *The Afghan Who Won The Cold War*) be remembered for achievements in fields far outside the domain of architecture. ■

going public

why
go
public

how
to go
public

where
to go
public

#3

ARCHITECTURE PRESS IN EUROPE

How do architects go public? Getting published in the architecture press is for many the way to go. We took a look at how many publications are potentially available by comparing the number of specialized periodicals in Europe to the number of architects. We have counted a total of 217 architecture magazines (not including the 'glossy ones'), which translates into an average of 1 magazine for every 2729 architects. The highest number of magazines per architect we found in Estonia with 1 magazine for every 133 architects. The ratio is lowest in Turkey with 1 magazine for every 10,000 architects, preceded by Germany with 1 magazine for every 7136 architects.

List of magazines based on Internet research, local know-how, and public library feedback. Estimated number of architects: Collegi d'Arquitectes de Catalunya, www.coac.net and other sources.
Our attempt should be considered a first try.
Cross-border magazine circulation has not been considered.

Average number of architects per magazine

Estonia (EE) **133**
Luxembourg (LU) **238**
Slovenia (SI) **338**
Lithuania (LT) **338**
Finland (FI) **389**
Slovakia (SK) **413**
Ireland (IE) **500**
Austria (AT) **578**
Malta (MT) **650**
Croatia (HR) **733**
Norway (NO) **748**
Switzerland (CH) **819**
Latvia (LV) **900**
Hungary (HU) **1050**
Sweden (SE) **1075**
Denmark (DK) **1111**
The Netherlands (NL) **1244**
Romania (RU) **1520**
Czech Republic (CZ) **1660**
Spain (ES) **1735**
Belgium (BE) **2517**
Greece (GR) **2600**
Serbia (RS) **2667**
Portugal (PT) **3171**
United Kingdom (UK) **3336**
France (FR) **3750**
Poland (PL) **4667**
Italy (IT) **7136**
Germany (DE) **7800**
Turkey (TR) **10000**

Number of magazines per country

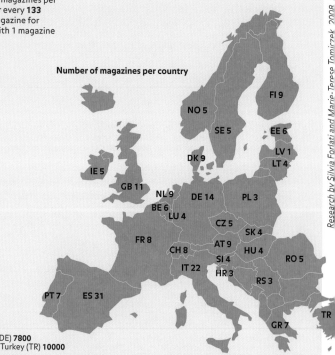

FI 9
NO 5
SE 5
EE 6
LV 1
DK 9
LT 4
IE 5
GB 11
NL 9
DE 14
PL 3
BE 6
LU 4
CZ 5
SK 4
FR 8
AT 9
HU 4
CH 8
SI 4
RO 5
IT 22
HR 3
RS 3
PT 7
ES 31
TR
GR 7
MT 1

---

a3 bau (AT) ▬ Architektur & Bauforum (AT) ▬ Architektur (AT) ▬ Architektur Aktuell (AT) ▬ dérive (AT) ▬ GAM. Graz Architecture Magazine (AT) ▬ Konstruktiv (AT) ▬ Wettbewerbe (AT) ▬ A+ (BE) ▬ Abstract (BE) ▬ Aktief Wonen (BE) ▬ DAMN° (BE) ▬ Dimension (BE) ▬ Renoscripto (BE) ▬ CIP – Covjek 1 Prostor (HR) ▬ Oris (HR) ▬ Prostor (HR) ▬ Architekt (CZ) ▬ Era 21 magazine (CZ) ▬ Stavba (CZ) ▬ Zlaty rez (CZ) ▬ INTRO (CZ) ▬ Ark Fokus (DK) ▬ Arkbyg (DK) ▬ Arkitekten (DK) ▬ Arkitektur DK (DK) ▬ Byplan (DK) ▬ Byplannyt (DK) ▬ KBH (DK) ▬ Living Architecture (DK) ▬ Tegl (DK) ▬ Akadeemia (EE) ▬ Ehitaja (EE) ▬ Ehituskunst (EE) ▬ Eramu ja Korter (EE) ▬ Maja (EE) ▬ Ruum (EE) ▬ Arkkitehti (FI) ▬ Arkkitehtiuutiset (FI) ▬ Arkkitehtuurikilpailuja (FI) ▬ Betoni (FI) ▬ Datutop (FI) ▬ Projektiuutiset (FI) ▬ Ptah (FI) ▬ Puu. Wood. Holz. Bois (FI) ▬ Teräsrakenne (FI) ▬ amc – le moniteur architecture (FR) ▬ Archiscopie (FR) ▬ archistorm (FR) ▬ D'Architecture (FR) ▬ L'architecture d'aujourd'hui (FR) ▬ L'Architecture de votre région (FR) ▬ Techniques & Architecture (FR) ▬ Urbaine (FR) ▬ AIT (DE) ▬ Arcguide (DE) ▬ Architektur & Wohnen (DE) ▬ Baumeister (DE) ▬ Bauwelt (DE) ▬ DAB – Deutsche Architektenblatt (DE) ▬ DB Deutsche Bauzeitung (DE) ▬ DBZ – Deutsche Bauzeitschrift (DE) ▬ Der Architekt (DE) ▬ Design Report (DE) ▬ Detail (DE) ▬ Häuser (DE) ▬ Topos (DE) ▬ Wettbewerbe aktuell (DE) ▬ Architecture in Greece (EL) ▬ Architektones (EL) ▬ Architektoniki os techni (EL) ▬ Domes (EL) ▬ Elliniikes kataskeyes (EL) ▬ Ktirio (EL) ▬ ek Architecture Plus Design Greece (EL) ▬ Alaprajz (HU) ▬ Átrium (HU) ▬ Octogon (HU) ▬ Régi-új Magyar Építőművészet (HU) ▬ Architecture Ireland (IE) ▬ Building Material (IE) ▬ House+Design (IE) ▬ Self Build (IE) ▬ Tracings (IE) ▬ 2a+p (IT) ▬ Abitare (IT) ▬ AND (IT) ▬ ARCHINT (IT) ▬ Area (IT) ▬ Casabella (IT) ▬ Case da Abitare (IT) ▬ Construire (IT) ▬ Controspazio (IT) ▬ D'Architettura (IT) ▬ Domus (IT) ▬ Domus d'Autore (IT) ▬ Giornale dell'architettura (IT) ▬ Interni (IT) ▬ L'Arca (IT) ▬ L'Architettura (IT) ▬ Lotus (IT) ▬ Materia (IT) ▬ OFArch (IT) ▬ Ottagono (IT) ▬ Parametro (IT) ▬ The Plan (IT) ▬ Latvijas architektura (LV) ▬ The Architect (MT) ▬ Åpent rom (NO) ▬ Arkitektnytt (NO) ▬ Byggekunst (NO) ▬ mur+betong (NO) ▬ Norske

arkitektkonkurranser (NO) ▬ Architektura – Murator (PL) ▬ Architektura & Biznes (PL) ▬ Archivolta (PL) ▬ + Arquitectura [mais arquitectura] (PT) ▬ arq./a (PT) ▬ Arquitectura e Vida (PT) ▬ Attitude (PT) ▬ ECDJ (PT) ▬ JA (PT) ▬ Nu (PT) ▬ A&B Arhitecţii si Bucurestiul (RO) ▬ Arhitectura (RO) ▬ Arhitext Design (RO) ▬ de arhitectura (RO) ▬ Igloo (RO) ▬ Arkhitektura, Stroitelstvo, Dizain (RU) ▬ Arkhitekturny Vestnik (RU) ▬ ArtChronika (RU) ▬ ARX (RU) ▬ Project Classica (RU) ▬ Project Russia (RU) ▬ Tatlin (RU) ▬ A & U Arkitektúra & Urbanizmus (SK) ▬ ARCH (SK) ▬ Building Research Journal (SK) ▬ Projekt (SK) ▬ AB – Architect's Bulletin (SI) ▬ Ambient (SI) ▬ Hiše (SI) ▬ Oris (SI) ▬ 2G (ES) ▬ A+T – Architecture & Technology (ES) ▬ Actar (ES) ▬ Archfarm (ES) ▬ Arketypo (ES) ▬ Arquitectos (ES) ▬ Arquitectura Viva (ES) ▬ AA Arquitecturas de Autor (ES) ▬ BASA (ES) ▬ Conarquitectura (ES) ▬ Constructiva (ES) ▬ DA – documentos de arquitectura (ES) ▬ dda – detalles de arquitectura (ES) ▬ El Croquis (ES) ▬ Formas de proyectar (ES) ▬ Matalocus (ES) ▬ Metapolis (ES) ▬ Neutra (ES) ▬ Oeste (ES) ▬ On Diseño (ES) ▬ Pasajes (ES) ▬ Postboks (ES) ▬ Quaderns d'arquitectura i urbanisme (ES) ▬ Revista de Edificacion (ES) ▬ Sin marca (ES) ▬ TC Cuadernos (ES) ▬ Tectónica (ES) ▬ Temas de Arquitectura (ES) ▬ Transfer (ES) ▬ Verb (ES) ▬ ViA Arquitectura (ES) ▬ Arkitekten (SE) ▬ Arkitektur (SE) ▬ Betong (SE) ▬ Forum AID (SE) ▬ Swedish Building Research Journal (SE) ▬ Architektur & Technik (CH) ▬ Archithese (CH) ▬ Bau & Architektur (CH) ▬ Faces (CH) ▬ Hochparterre (CH) ▬ Tec21 (CH) ▬ Tracés (CH) ▬ werk, bauen + wohnen (CH) ▬ Architectenweb Magazine (NL) ▬ Architectuur Lokaal (NL) ▬ De Architect (NL) ▬ De Architectuurkrant (NL) ▬ Frame (NL) ▬ Mark – Another Architecture (NL) ▬ OASE (NL) ▬ Scape (NL) ▬ Volume (NL) ▬ Arredamento Mimarlik (TR) ▬ Betonart (TR) ▬ Mimarlik (TR) ▬ XXI (TR) ▬ Yapı-Endüstri Merkezi (TR) ▬ AA files (GB) ▬ Across architecture (GB) ▬ AD Architectural Design (GB) ▬ Architecture Today (GB) ▬ Architecture Week (GB) ▬ Blueprint (GB) ▬ Building Design (GB) ▬ Icon (GB) ▬ RIBA Journal (GB) ▬ The Architect's Journal (GB) ▬ The Architectural Review (GB) ▬ Architecture Européenne (LU) ▬ Archiduc (LU) ▬ Revue technique luxembourgeoise (LU) ▬ adato architecture (LU) ▬ arhitekton (RS) ▬ Eko Kuća (RS) ▬ Enterijer (RS) ▬ Centras (LT) ▬ Namas Ir Aš (LT) ▬ Statyba ir architektura (LT) ▬ Archiforma (LT) ▬

going public

What is the role that going public plays for architects today? Is it an option or a must? And what is it all about? Getting published, getting new commissions, or defining the public role for architects within the communities and realities they work in? The issue is not clear but seems unavoidable nevertheless. Not only for those who are out there trying to make a living out of architecture, but also for Wonderland itself, the association behind this book, which started out with the aim of bringing the work of start-up offices to public attention.

It is precisely for such practices that the following applies: anyone who wants to get commissions must enter public awareness and cannot afford to hide away. Here the media are logical disseminators. Particularly the younger generation of architects well know how to use this instrument. Young architects are aware that, in the media, one has to come up with something to stand out from the mass. In addition to a good project and an interesting story, perfect photographs are playing an increasingly important role. We have gathered a number of expert opinions and have dedicated part of this book to trying to understand the mostly unwritten "laws of getting published" and the role of authenticity.

Dealing with the subject of going public we asked ourselves: are we not overrating the media? One can advertise oneself and one's concerns in different ways, too: "going public by shaking hands" is what Michael Obrist calls it in his text. And in fact the best-hired and best-earning architectural firms in the world still are those about which you hear next to nothing in the media. They acquire commissions the old way, through personal contacts.

'Going public', as we mean it, is not only self-marketing, but also public discourse, the discussion between the architect and non-architects. The more often it happens, the better the architectural understanding of the public – and the more likely new, good architecture is to gain acceptance. We also take a look at alternative strategies: taking an active position within the public realm, moving on beyond peer recognition through the specialized press.

The first section of this chapter focuses on the question that should precede the other two: why do it at all? What are the reasons for seeking publicity, for going public with an idea, a design, a building? The second section deals with what is perhaps the most pressing question: how to find a public and publicity, how to create a public image. This section is mainly about media and mediators, to those who help to give architects and architecture a public presence and significance beyond the mere fact that they are alive and in business. The third section takes a closer look at where public attention can be found, which media are relevant and at the different situations in various countries. ▨

GOING PUBLIC: THE AVERAGE PRACTICE

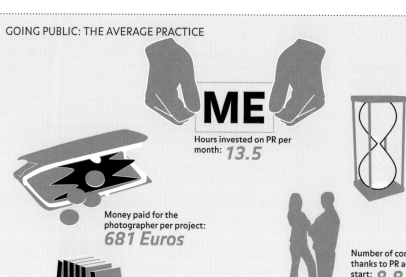

ME

Hours invested on PR per month: *13.5*

Hours invested on PR per project: *22.5*

Money paid for the photographer per project: *681 Euros*

Number of commissions received thanks to PR actions since the start: *8.8*

Number of publications per year: *6.1*

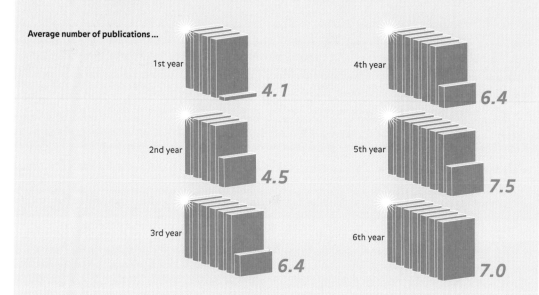

Average number of publications ...

1st year **4.1**	4th year **6.4**
2nd year **4.5**	5th year **7.5**
3rd year **6.4**	6th year **7.0**

- ▶ considers PR somehow important **(100%)**
- ▶ does some kind of PR work **(98%)**, but mostly does not have a consistent strategy **(75%)**
- ▶ does not consult a PR agency **(98%)**
- ▶ hires a photographer **(85%)**, but not somebody to help with texts

- ▶ sends press releases **(78%)**
- ▶ participates in collective PR formats, such as national architecture networks **(73%)**, group events **(73%)**, internet platforms **(74%)**.

Source: Wonderland #3 Survey – by SHARE architects, compiled 2006

See reality check #3 / page 133

why so public

Buildings need no publicity in order to function, architects apparently do. Confronted with increasing media power – a growing number and variety of media, growing reach and (not to forget) growing image quality – architects going public will have to ask themselves what they are really out for. Does publicity make better architecture?

A PARALLEL UNIVERSE

Carel Weeber, the award-winning Dutch architect (or "ex-architect", as he has referred to himself in recent years), once said that architecture only becomes architecture once people write about it. A building is just a building, and a design is just a design, but when people start talking and writing about it, it enters the domain of architecture. This definition seems to touch on the philosophical question of whether a tree falling in the forest makes a sound if there is no-one around to hear it. Is architecture still architecture if no one notices? As is often the case with Weeber, this sweeping statement may be debatable, but at the same time it encapsulates a deep truth, because these days, even though anything and everything can be classified as architecture, from a bike shelter to the Lincoln Cathedral, from an iconic structure to a tiny logo, from virtual space to theoretical construction, ultimately, only a small portion of architectural production makes the cut as architecture in the Weeberian sense.

Opinion-making is not a primary task of architecture. Its primary purpose, its self-legitimation, lies in the production of constructed substance. Without question, building for people prevails over building for publicity. A second source of architectural self-justification may be found in the contribution that architecture makes to its own discipline. Only then, a rationale of architecture as a public good begins to emerge, and this additional raison d'être applies to a very limited number of buildings and architects. The vast majority of the world of buildings is, to borrow a term coined by French writer Georges Perec, infra-ordinaire: although it exists, it is not consciously perceived, not even by architectural insiders (or if so, it is only at a most perfunctory level). The fact that, as a consequence, not only nothing is said about the vast majority of buildings, but in fact there seems to be nothing to say about them, would appear to create a great vacuum. As a result, the bulk of the world of buildings falls out of the realm of all public discussion, which architects, critics and historians alike have to blame themselves.

Ultimately, only a very small percentage of the world of buildings is actually perceived, and that fraction of the building production may be the subject of study, descriptive work, criticism and discussion – mind you, it "may", because not all, by any means, of what happens to rise above the infra-ordinaire becomes a topic in what could be called "public opinion" (a catch-all phrase for any and all attention generated via the media). From this perspective, one sees an ongoing struggle for attention, an urge to cross over into that parallel universe in which building production is not simply the world of buildings all around, but architecture: a universe in which buildings take on a public significance beyond whatever public function the building itself serves.

Text by Hans Ibelings, Montreal/Toronto, Canada

Why architects strive for a place in that parallel universe cannot be simply explained on grounds of some vague desire for recognition. To take a deterministic approach, using French sociologist Pierre Bourdieu's three-level structure, it is about acquiring economic, cultural and social capital. Recognition and fame can lead to new commissions, spotlights in the press lend a cultural sheen to an architect's activities, and architects who get a lot of public attention move higher in the social hierarchy than those who do not.

Normally, any publicity (except perhaps the very worst) boosts an architect's capital in all three areas, even if the precise impact and direction of this boost are impossible to determine. Media attention may not automatically lead to the next commission, but the higher social and cultural status that it entails does, of course, help.

Nonetheless, any architect who does public relations, or wants to, would benefit from distinguishing each of these three aspects. If the architect's main PR goal is gaining new commissions, then publicity means advertising and self-promotion. If this is what you want, you are better off with alluring images and stories in direct marketing to potential clients than with an intellectual, theoretical, high architecture exposé in an exclusive architectural journal. But the reality is often not that straightforward, and building cultural capital, a currency that seems to be earned primarily from professional journals, can also be worthwhile as a back door to new commissions. This indirect route means that defining PR and promotion purely in business-economic terms, with direct financial return, oversimplifies the equation. At the same time, just because any form of publicity has a cultural and social side, there is no reason not to approach PR activities from a cost-benefit perspective. It ultimately comes down to striking that balance between culture and economics that must always be sought in architecture itself.

Most if not all people with a message, including architects, focus primarily on getting the message out and much less on who the message is supposed to go out to. Going public is a two-way street with the sender at one end and the receiver at the other, and the medium, the vital connection between them, in the middle. But many architects who actively engage in PR seem to focus more on the act of transmitting the message than on the receiver and even those who manage to broaden their perspective beyond themselves and their brainchild of the moment still generally focus more on the media than on who might find the message interesting, relevant, or even vital. If, rarely, the target audience is considered, most attention is given to the segment of fellow professionals. Architecture sometimes goes over the heads of the people for whom it is intended, and by the same token, the world of architectural insiders seems to devote its publicity first and foremost to those same insiders. (Why else would architects make so much of an effort to get published in architectural journals read by other architects only?)

The struggle for public attention is not an issue for architects alone. For architects just about to start their careers, public relations processes may seem to be governed by arcane and inscrutable mechanisms and the media may look like an impenetrable fortress. The reality is almost certainly less daunting: the media is not a monolith. Individual media must also struggle for attention, and here architects and media can develop a sort of symbiotic relationship. Architects want to see their work published, and media are always looking out for new architecture to publish. This is definitely something that architects hunting for attention would be wise to take note of: that every journalist, editor and critic is hunting for news, scoops, spectacle, and surprises. ▪▪

HOW LOW CAN

ON THE MORALITY OF GOING PUBLIC

In the architecture scene, a legend has been circulating for some time that Erick van Egeraat once hired Grace Jones to perform at the presentation of one of his projects in Moscow. The aging diva belted out a few songs, before Van Egeraat himself presented his design on the same stage. Apparently his Russian clients clung like "slaves to the rhythm" to every word that fell from his lips.

Was this unlikely combination of performance and presentation an "indecent proposal"? Or does the end simply justify the means? Ultimately, this story causes such amusement at architects' parties because everyone knows that at the moment Erick van Egeraat has more work in Eastern Europe than many a young architect will see in his entire lifetime.

Admittedly, this is an extreme example of architecture marketing. But it cannot be denied that hardly any other group of professionals are as aversive to sales promotion as archi-

tects. According to architects, advertising of all kinds has an unpleasant smell to it. For, does it not mean admitting that the architecture is not good enough to speak for itself? And the reverse conclusion is often drawn, too: those who do not bother with any public relations work are telling potential clients that they have no need for this kind of thing. With the result that – for example, in Switzerland at present – it is regarded as chic not to have a website at all. The subtle difference is, however, that if the name of your practice happens to be Herzog & de Meuron this may be all be very well, but if your office is called Smith & Brown, you are running the danger of appearing arrogant or, in the worst of cases, unprofessional.

One background to this aversion probably is due to the fact that architects learn nothing about PR during their training. Their education is totally focused on the design of buildings. But nobody tells them that there are

Text by Anneke Bokern, Amsterdam, Netherlands

YOU GO?

a number of more profane things that also form part of an architect's everyday professional life. The result is a feeling of insecurity. Moving back and forth between service provider and artist, many architects prefer to see themselves in the latter category – and an artist does not praise his own products like a common salesman at a fair.

However, there is an essential difference between trying to pass off rotten grapes as choice quality and arranging one's fruit attractively on the stall and placing it in the best possible light. There is a difference between serious PR work and marketing stunts intended only to attract attention. It is always a question of substance and truth. Young architects' offices in particular are often confronted with the problem that they do not have any major successes to show for that could substantiate what they promise in advertising. Large offices in contrast generally have enough credibility for people to be taken in by their self-praise, at least initially.

PR is, however, a wide field. The most common form of publicity work, and one that is also affordable for young architects, is writing press releases about projects. If you want to do this professionally you need good texts and attractive photos. But how far must you go in remaining faithful to the truth? Some agree with H.G. Wells who found that "advertising is legalized lying". In such cases, the press is supplied with photographs that have about as much to do with reality as the serving suggestion on the instant custard sachet. But note: some journalist or another will always take the trouble to look at the project in real life. And then the "shoot and run

architect" must be able to run very fast indeed. A certain extent of realism cannot be harmful which, however, does not mean that you have to point out every sore spot.

In addition to the PR release, most young architects have their own website. And some even venture as far as the real-estate fairs in Cannes or Munich where they run around among potential clients with their tails between their legs, decked out in business suits and not daring to talk to anybody. But that's about it then. Creative advertising is very rare among architects – and in this sense one could actually learn something from the Grace Jones story. "Thinking outside the box" is never wrong. And this means thinking beyond one's own target group. Frank Peter Jäger, head of an agency for architecture marketing in Berlin, for example, finds that architects often focus too much on articles in specialist magazines read by other architects only. "The importance of the daily press is underestimated, and few architects include the magazines and innumerable trade and industry journals in their press relations work. There is an enormous unexploited potential here. If you have built a grape crushing and pressing plant for a wine grower, this may well be a suitable subject for a specialist journal about wine growing and agriculture."

It is important therefore to take a look over the fence from time to time and try to overcome one's reservations. After all, an architectural rendering is a kind of PR, too, as it is done in order to make a design appeal to the potential client and hence to sell something. In the best case, advertising simply means communicating one's own qualities.

Strategic silence can also be part of PR. It is true, there is that rumor that even bad publicity is better than no publicity. But just as star architects would rather not tell the whole world about their bread-and-butter jobs, there is no need for a young architect to present every less-than-successful design on his website, just for the sake of completeness. Every well-known architect has a few skeletons in his closet; which belong to the chapter "I was young and needed the money". And that is where they should stay.

Perhaps one reason why architects have a somewhat tense approach to PR is that their buildings often are supposed make PR for their client. Thus, if Zaha Hadid praises her BMW building in Leipzig, she actually makes PR for PR. That this seems kind of pointless cannot be denied. On the other hand, Hadid was only commissioned by BMW because she already has a certain status. In this sense, PR also stands for public recognition, and the dog bites its own tail. An ideal situation has been reached if architecture is its own PR, selling itself. Then you have what business analysts like to call a "win-win situation".

Public relations work, as we have seen, need not per se be unappetizing. How come, then, that one cannot get that fishy smell about the Grace Jones story out of one's nose? Because here the sense of proportion has been lost. PR measures may certainly be creative and have a certain entertainment value, but should never convey the impression that they are more expensive than the project itself. Otherwise this might arouse the suspicion that, beneath the sugar coating that makes the project go down so pleasantly, there is only a very tiny and useless pill. ●

REALITY CHECK #3: GOING PUBLIC

64 practices from 21 European countries responded to our e-mail survey. Questions focused on the role that PR plays within the practices' everyday work.

PR is considered important by all responding practices, though with some variation. Nevertheless, only few practices have defined a clear strategy for themselves, and only 20% feel that they are on the right track with their PR work (see also previous survey: PR was second on the top-ten list of things that go wrong).

The main difficulty is time – it is a job within the job, with teams investing up to 50 working hours a month on PR. Outsourcing is not an option for most (only 3 teams said that they work with a PR agency), except for photographers. Instead, what works for many of them is using collective formats, joining with other teams, joining networks, or being present on Internet platforms.

Is that enough? Most of the teams say that they are reasonably satisfied with their PR work. A small number of teams have given us hard facts, such as the number of commissions or publications they have obtained through PR. It seems that getting work through websites and other forms of PR is a possibility, but not for sure. On an average, 8.8 incoming commissions can be attributed to PR activities, over an average of 5 years of practice.

In the end, it is not quite clear whether all this is really worthwhile. What is clear, though, is that everybody feels a need to do something about it.

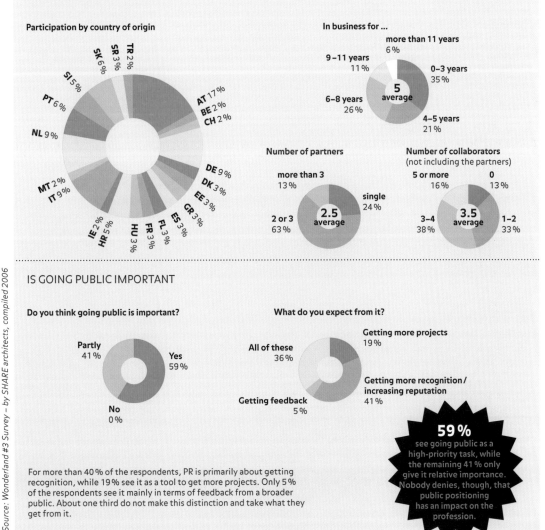

Participation by country of origin

In business for ...

Number of partners

Number of collaborators (not including the partners)

IS GOING PUBLIC IMPORTANT

Do you think going public is important?

What do you expect from it?

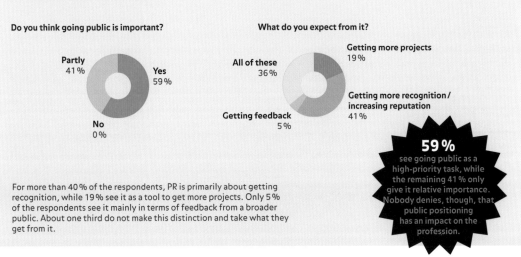

Partly 41%
Yes 59%
No 0%

All of these 36%
Getting more projects 19%
Getting more recognition / increasing reputation 41%
Getting feedback 5%

For more than 40% of the respondents, PR is primarily about getting recognition, while 19% see it as a tool to get more projects. Only 5% of the respondents see it mainly in terms of feedback from a broader public. About one third do not make this distinction and take what they get from it.

59% see going public as a high-priority task, while the remaining 41% only give it relative importance. Nobody denies, though, that public positioning has an impact on the profession.

Source: Wonderland #3 Survey – by SHARE architects, compiled 2006

How to ...

... disappear completely ... *(radiohead)*

About the (im)possibility of making publicity for an idea without making publicity for oneself ...

Text by Michael Obrist, feld72, Vienna, Austria

So I decided the way to do it was to become the invisible man, and that means a bank clerk – so I put on a black suit, bank clerk's clothing; then they would focus on what I was saying instead of my eccentricities. I said, 'I must get rid of continually making too much of myself'.

Richard Buckminster Fuller

When in December 2002 the teams invited presented their proposals for the rebuilding of Ground Zero, architecture and architects arrested the attention of the public like never before.

However, there was only one among the architects participating who managed to impress himself on the public's mind in a way that made him be perceived as more than "just" an architect: **Daniel Libeskind**. A lucky coincidence, as he said (others called it a clever PR strategy), had helped him who had previously been seen as a mere academician to a more conspicuous appearance – and this image of a man in a black leather jacket, wearing new Onassis-style horn-rimmed glassed, leather cowboy boots, and U.S. and New York State flag lapel badges kept appearing wherever he could be sure to raise attention. *Time* magazine and the *New York Times* gave extensive coverage to Libeskind and his new outfit.

He was even compared to Sprockets, the German nerd played by Mike Meyers on *Saturday Night Live*. Libeskind used every media occasion to bang the drum for his project, and not only by explicitly referring to it.

Rather, he spoke to people about visions and common dreams that were possible to make come true, as if he had not only memorised, but in fact written, that proposition by Saint-Exupéry: "If you want to build a ship, don't drum up the men to gather wood, divide the work and give orders. Instead, teach them to yearn for the vast and endless sea." At the same time, in panel discussions with realtors, he proved himself to be a great pragmatist, too. With the help of his wife Nina, who had previous organised election campaigns, led international organisations, and worked as a union mediator, he pulled off a smartly forged PR campaign. Consequently, what was circulated were not only suggestive renderings of his Ground Zero proposal: his office also sent out e-mails to potential opinion leaders asking them to promote his project by sending readers' letters to the *New York Times*. He went on every TV show that offered him a forum – and be it just because of his looks. Unlike all of his competitors, the architect once mildly ridiculed as a theoretician had succeeded in being perceived as both elitist and popular. When he finally

managed to win over New York's Governor Pataki, who launched a last-minute intervention for him, he eventually came out triumphant in the world's most noted architectural competition.

With his whirlwind tour of the popular media, Libeskind lost much of his reputation in the academic world – at the same time, the internal mechanism operative in this world also revealed its inherent weakness. It is a known fact that the public image of the architect in the United States is defined by two extremes: on the one hand, there is the great mass of those perceived as technicists, auxiliary agents, or simply corporate architects, and on the other, the small clique of elitist star architects who hold teaching assignments at ivory-tower schools to keep their heads above water while getting the heart-warming appreciation that they are denied in the USA by taking an annual bath in the crowds at European architecture biennales and symposiums. It is easier in the Old World for the stars of the architectural scene to transfer the capital accumulated in the "economy of attention" (Georg Franck) of the media world to the world of earning possibilities as a surplus value. The lead in public attention that Peter Eisenman held from the start in the discussion about the then-only-projected "Memorial to the Murdered Jews of Europe" was an advantage he did not have, nor was able to generate, in New York. While in Berlin an intellectually inspiring discussion took place (the public discussion held in the run-up to the several design competitions is seen by many as constituting the true Holocaust Memorial) in which Peter Eisenman of course succeeded in putting himself in an excellent position – with the whole discussion being an elitist matter (being elitist for once was admissible) – the mechanisms at work were of a different kind in New York.

"Architecture is big business today, and architects act like business people", says Peter Marcuse, an urban planning professor in New York, about the Ground Zero competition. "This means that they employ public relations firms, lawyers, and hire market researchers. In brief, they do everything that any company does to market their product. We must take care not to sell the right to build the World Trader Center to the firm contracting the best PR advisor."

In *Quand les cathédrales étaient blanches: voyage au pays des timides* (When the Cathedrals Were White: Voyage to the Land of the Timid), **Le Corbusier** had already written against the enormous PR machinery which was dominant in the United States, disguising public life. However, his own life, it seems, was formed by a not altogether unconscious talent to advertise himself and his cause in a highly effective way. As Gabriella Lo Ricco and Silvia Micheli have pointed out in *Lo spettacolo dell'architettura. Profilo dell'archistar©* (The Spectacle of Architecture: the Profile of the Archistar©), he knew to shrewdly combine discourse and business as early as in the era of *L'Esprit Nouveau*: presentations of his works went along with advertising for the manufacturers of the products used. And he used the magazine's pavilion at the *Exposition des arts décoratifs* not only for publicity purposes – in the archives a number of letters from exposition visitors were found to which Le Corbusier had replied with project proposals and cost estimates. At the same time, he showed great skill in getting out photos of himself which were supposed to convey a clear message: Le Corbusier, the urban intellectual, abreast of the period, in front of his new car, a Voisin 14 HP; Le Corbusier, the daring man of vision and foresight, with Ozenfant in a hot-air balloon high above Paris (in a photo montage of 1923);

Le Corbusier, surrounded by the greatest thinkers, artists, and political luminaries of his time; Le Corbusier in America with his dictum of "Much too small", addressed at the skyscrapers of New York; Le Corbusier with Le Corbusier with Le Corbusier. In *L'Esprit Nouveau*, as in all subsequent writings, he placed his own new ideas and works in the context of great achievements and the spirit of the past. He even resorted to downright manipulation to visualize the consistency between his theses propounded and his published projects – so, for example, there is evidence that the picture of the Schwob House published in the sixth issue of *L'Esprit Nouveau* was touched up. In his *Oeuvre Complète*, the early work – spanning, after all, a period of 16 years – is entirely missing; like all the others who have wanted to make their genius appear to have come out of nowhere, Le Corbusier obliterated all traces leading back into his past. He himself was one of his greatest inventions.

When in the early 1920s a journal was about to be founded (the aforementioned *Esprit Nouveau*) to expand discourse beyond pure art by incorporating thought from other fields, a consequential decision was made: as the board of editors seemed somewhat undermanned, the writers Amédée Ozenfant, Paul Dermée, and Charles-Edouard Jeanneret decided to duplicate themselves, without actually expanding the staff, by also writing under invented pseudonyms. Ozenfant chose his mother's family name for this purpose – Saugnier (for all conspiracy theorists inspired by Dan Brown – no, not *his* Saugnier). For Jeanneret, who was supposed to focus on architectural discourse, this possibility was out of the question, as his mother's maiden name – Perret – was already specifically associated with Auguste Perret. He chose the surname of a line of cousins, the Lecorbéziers, and split up the name, making it sound almost aristocratic with the prefixed "Le". Le Corbusier was born.

The greater his media success became through *L'Esprit Nouveau*, the more Charles-Edouard Jeanneret vanished, until eventually he was gone for good.

Frank Lloyd Wright, too, proved to have exceptional savvy in publicising his ideas by publicising himself. His autobiography, written at a time when commissions were in short supply (in 1932), is the cementation of his own myth, that of the hero who unfalteringly follows his own path against the ignorance of his time and comes out victorious in the end. A figure of this type also appears in Ayn Rand's bestselling novel, *The Fountainhead*, which was directly inspired by Wright: the main character, the architect Howard Roark, is a man who has liberated himself from public opinion to live for himself and his creative mission alone. Rand makes him the embodiment of her ideal of the human acting out his ethic of rational self-interest in her celebrated system of laissez-faire capitalism.

The book was explicitly dedicated to the "noble profession of architecture" and scored tremendous success, with six million copies sold to date and 100,000 still selling every year. The eponymous movie of 1949 starring Gary Cooper helped Rand and her theories to reach an even wider public.

This typification of the architect shown in the book and movie, and also instantiated (though of course in a less distorted way) by the real person of Frank Lloyd Wright, was, and still is, formative for the public image – notably as a cliché and wishful thinking within the architectural profession: the man who knows how and with what form of built self-expression a society should live, who is not understood at first and yet wins through in the end.

The bonus of being perceived by the public as redeemers of society, however, was gambled away by architects some time ago. Gone are the days when songwriters such as Simon and Garfunkel, in lyrics like "When I run dry / I stop awhile and think of you" ("So long, Frank Lloyd Wright"), could speak of architects as comforters of the soul.

The architect characters shown in the movies have changed as well, as has society, and with it the movies. While in the early 1960s, in films by Antonioni and other exponents of auteur cinema, the architect still was a wanderer between the worlds of art

and big money – a sensitive intellectual and bon vivant – Hollywood productions have in recent years been content to portray the architect as a middle-class protagonist with a susceptibility to strong emotions, which is likely to reflect the image that the audience has (also outside the cinema), since most of the characters in these rather commercial productions basically owe their existence to target-group research.

The images that we have of "the architect" are essentially media images. And the real-life experience that we have of our "neighbour-hood architect" can only complement, but not replace, these images. The media mean omnipresence and "truth through quantity". It is a sad fact that even if a good idea may eventually be sure to get through, the question of when this will happen strongly depends on the ability of the person communicating it. As long as the media space is full of attention to trash, all the more resolute clearing up is needed to make room for new views. There are architects who have made use of these mechanisms only to promote themselves and their works, while there are others who use the attention they have already earned to direct some media light towards some chronically underexposed zones. These discursive techniques introduced in the media space by Aldo Rossi, Venturi & Scott Brown, the actors around Team X, and, finally, Koolhaas, have significantly loosened the straitjacket into which the exponents of the discipline were put, or put themselves. But only those who have managed to get out of the professional and into the popular discourse have also succeeded in changing the image of the architect in society. The phenomenon of the "star architect" was perverted when what used to be the outcome of a development was turned into a promotion strategy. Today, it is not the most interesting figures who dominate in the public eye, but, tautologically, those who have aimed for this kind of attention in the first place. Storage space is limited in the short-term media memory – and in times when recognizability counts, any complex issue must be reducible to a simple or enigmatic image: what the "media

chancellor" is in politics, the "star" is to archi-tecture. Those who fail to attain that level of image will be the ones to fall by the wayside, irrespective of their claim to a dissemination of their ideas. Or who would happen to know the face of Christopher Alexander, the man behind the *Pattern Language*?

Beyond the economy of attention, how-ever, there still is the good old level of the "old boys' network", and obviously it still works: going public by shaking hands, so to speak. The projects in China which have been visually reported to us (Koolhaas's CCTV-Tower and Herzog & de Meuron's Stadium) are only part of that very small number of projects conducted in alliance with public attention giants for propaganda reasons. Most projects, however, are being pulled off by the usual suspects: huge firms of corpo-rate architects with good connections to the top mandarins. And although they plan the main part of the built environment surround-ing us, they have not (yet) changed the public image of the architect. It still greets us from magazines and TV screens, smiling and reas-suring us that everything will be fine. Just as Daniel Libeskind does after former World Trade Center leaseholder Larry Silverstein, with his in-house architect David Childs of SOM, eventually succeeded in pushing through his own plans for Ground Zero ... 🔚

P.S. The whole book you hold in your hands – and with it the self-organizing network of actors from all over Europe – bears evidence of an alternative way.

WHY NOT DO PR

For 72% of the respondents, the main problem is time. Only 36% see getting recognition as an easy consequence of doing a good job. Other factors considered to play a role are personal connections, related costs, or professional competition.

14%
"It is too expensive."

What are the difficulties?

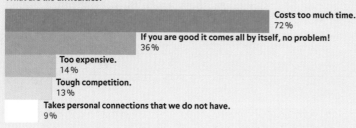

Costs too much time.
72%

If you are good it comes all by itself, no problem!
36%

Too expensive.
14%

Tough competition.
13%

Takes personal connections that we do not have.
9%

72%
"Costs too much time."

TIME INVESTED IN PR WORK (HOURS/MONTH)

13.5
hours / month
is the average time spent by the surveyed practices for PR-related work. In this case, though, the average might not say very much, as answers range from less than 5 hours estimated by 28% of the practices to more than 50 hours stated by 5%.

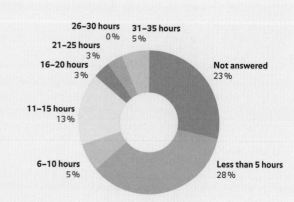

26–30 hours
0%

31–35 hours
5%

21–25 hours
3%

16–20 hours
3%

Not answered
23%

11–15 hours
13%

6–10 hours
5%

Less than 5 hours
28%

TIME INVESTED IN PR WORK (HOURS/PROJECT)

22.5
hours / project
is the average time spent for specific project promotion. Here again, the range is wide: from less than 10 hours for 30% of the practices to more than 50 hours for the top ranking 5%.

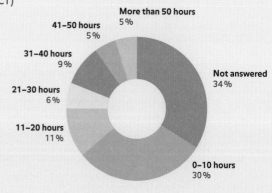

More than 50 hours
5%

41–50 hours
5%

31–40 hours
9%

21–30 hours
6%

Not answered
34%

11–20 hours
11%

0–10 hours
30%

Source: Wonderland #3 Survey – by SHARE architects, compiled 2006

EXTERNAL CONSULTANTS

Apart from the expenditure of one's own working time, help from external specialists may be considered. While only 3 of 64 practices have experiences with hiring a PR agency, 55 practices have already worked with a professional photographer.
The fee paid by two of the practices to a PR agency was between 1,250 and 1,500 Euros, while the third one paid less than 500 Euros per project.
680 Euros per project is the average photographer's fee on the basis of our survey. The range is again wide here, and it should be compared with the varying cost / quality requirements of the practices.

How much do you pay a photographer per projects?

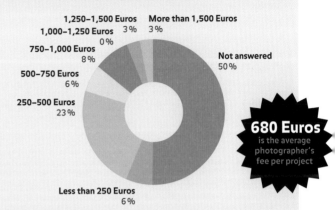

1,250–1,500 Euros 3%
More than 1,500 Euros 3%
1,000–1,250 Euros 0%
750–1,000 Euros 8%
Not answered 50%
500–750 Euros 6%
250–500 Euros 23%
Less than 250 Euros 6%

680 Euros is the average photographer's fee per project

OTHER COSTS

Famous architects sometimes get paid for permitting publication of their projects. By contrast, payment sometimes is asked from young and unknown architects to get their project published, although this is a not too common way to reach publication, at least according to our survey.

Did you ever have to buy a certain number of "voucher copies" in return for being published?

Yes 3%
No 97%

SUCCESS RATES

How successful?

70% declare themselves successful in their PR efforts, either reasonably (62%) or absolutely (8%). The remaining one third feels that results usually do not come up to their expectations (28%), or that they are not successful at all (2%).

How many press releases lead to publications?

The success rate of press releases varies: one fifth of the surveyed practices say that less than 20% of their press releases lead to a publication, three fifths claim to have success rates between 20 and more than 70%. And one fifth say that they do not send out press releases at all.

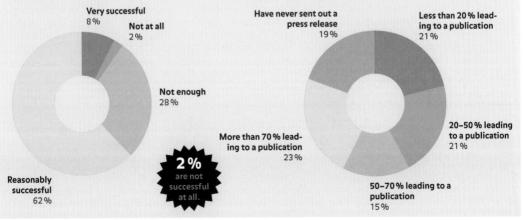

Very successful 8%
Not at all 2%
Not enough 28%
Reasonably successful 62%

2% are not successful at all.

Have never sent out a press release 19%
Less than 20% leading to a publication 21%
20–50% leading to a publication 21%
More than 70% leading to a publication 23%
50–70% leading to a publication 15%

Source: Wonderland #3 Survey – by SHARE architects, compiled 2006

WHITE NOISE

More and more architects are investing time and money in public relations. But what for? To win more commissions, help projects run smoothly, or simply polish up their own egos? Six architecture and PR experts discussed the pros and cons of this development with Wonderland.

wonderland: Do architects need public relations?

Czech: When a butcher opens a shop, he doesn't need to get that into the papers either. What's all this white noise supposed to be good for? And anyway, what's a client supposed to do with it? In my experience, being written about doesn't help you at all to get commissions.

wonderland: Nevertheless, architects keep trying. Often, it seems important to be published at least in professional journals read by architects only.

Zweifel: I think, this is indeed an interesting phenomenon. Today, each and every studio has already published a monograph as soon as the owners are 30 or 35. Isn't that redundant?

Steiner: There've been huge changes going on in the market. Formerly, architects used to hesitantly approach a critic asking him to express an opinion about what they had built and hoping that some favorable opinion was going to be published somewhere. In the 1980s, the question was no longer how a new building was judged, but how to get into the media most effectively. Matters of judgment or critical discussion have been replaced by propaganda. This has changed the entire profession. PR has become an integral part of the studios' work.

Roidinger: Of course architects need PR, no doubt, and of course they need publicity. I would not restrict PR to the press here. There are various possibilities of going public, various ways of communicating, from private lobbying to exhibitions, lectures, and media contacts.

Lengauer: We understand public relations, especially when it comes to architecture, as a service to architecture, and not primarily as a sub-domain of marketing or account development. These are architectural business promotion tasks. Getting media coverage for a new-built project accounts for probably twenty percent of our work only. The much more important part is about accompanying a project in terms of communications. Especially in the case of public building commissions, there are many who have a say in the decision. The redesigning of a town square, for instance, is a matter of politics and interest groups in the community; anybody who has ever built a house, or crossed that square feels competent to contribute an opinion. How should such processes be designed in order to aid in eventually bringing about meaningful and good architecture? How can the entire planning and construction stage be intelligently controlled, so that there won't be any stupid discussions afterwards and that as many people as possible will be happy with the outcome in the end.

Steiner: This takes place not only on a public, but also on a private scale. More and more companies planning critical construction projects now decide to have the project communication moderated in some way or another.

Lengauer: We don't only want to be there for architectural discourse. We try to explain projects so that they'll be understood by the general public—but without giving away their substance. This is our chief responsibility.

Steiner: There'll be an increasing demand to have projects communicated to the public. In this respect, the support of PR agencies is absolutely helpful. Architects often lack effective communication skills as this is something they haven't learnt in their professional training or from the social environment they normally move in.

Roidinger: The common belief is that architects are natural talents who can do this. Certainly there are personalities among architects who are super rhetorically, who appeal to people and have a high communicative competence. But not everybody is good at it. Some may need help from professionals.

Spiegl: Our studio has never done any active PR work, not so far. For whatever reasons, requests have arrived by themselves and relatively early–whether it was inquiries from the press or invitations to do lectures and exhibitions.

Steiner: Does that mean you don't do PR?

Spiegl: We have never actively positioned our-selves in the public arena.
Of course, a certain degree of narcissism plays a role here. I think that every architect loves showing to others what he or she has created. For many architects, the motive of presenting their own per-sonality may certainly be in the foreground, though this is often done under the pretext of serving the common good: we're doing this in order to give architecture more publicity or to promote a better understanding of it.

Steiner: That's really true. Compared to the 1970s, the situation has changed dramatically today–in all fields. Today, architectural studios are no longer studios in the classical sense. They are "start-ups"–business enterprises, firms that deal with the public in a different way from the very start. As far as I'm concerned, the classical architectural studio of the 1970s was an office waiting for clients to arrive. It was considered improper to offer one's services. This was the domain of architectural firms, business companies which always were rather aggressive in using public relations. But it was something that was not done by the so-called "content architects". How do the English put it so aptly? "Strong idea firms and strong service firms". The "strong idea firms" need patrons, and the others, clients. Of course, this old distinc-tion between "corporate architects" and "artistic architects" no longer exists today.

wonderland: Going public also has something to do with conveying content to the public.

Steiner: I've been missing "content" in our profession lately. It's not important any more. Formerly, architects built their reputation by think-ing about their work. This is no longer the case.

wonderland: Why?

Steiner: Because it's all about fashion, style, and being cool.

wonderland: It seems that the images of architecture that are being published today show a kind of architecture that doesn't really exist. The reality is totally different. We always present a sort of abstraction. Why isn't it possible to present things as they really are?

Czech: Never in my life have I sent material to anybody without having been asked to.

wonderland: Did you never try to win new clients actively when you were younger?

Roidinger: Reality can never be genuinely represented.

Czech: That's the next thing I was going to say: throughout my entire career, I've only received commissions from people who have approached me.

wonderland: What was your very first commission?

Steiner: Because abstraction provides a smoother, more spectacular image.

Czech: The first thing we did was a restaurant for my father. Everybody starts that way.

Spiegl: No, not any more.

Spiegl: But what we are talking about a choice here that is not always made by the architect himself. Those who decide are the ones print-ing or broadcasting these images. Ultimately, the magazines decide what's going to be printed, and these decisions are made on the basis of the market situation. One thing will sell well in my magazine, another, less.

Roidinger: That belongs to the past. In former times, there were not that many young architectural studios.

Czech: Yes, there are too many architects. There even are too many good ones.

Lengauer: This is where PR comes in. It is these reactions that we can anticipate. If I wish to publish something, the questions will always be: Where, for whom, and in what context? What's the effect that I would like to achieve? It takes some thinking about where the thing might fit in.

wonderland: So things are quite different today from what they used to be?

Steiner: Yes, of course!

Roidinger: We simply have more media today–good and bad ones–and thus much more information. We can't possibly read everything. The situation was different twenty years ago. Today people are much better informed. It's not true that everything was better in the old times.

wonderland: Just think of the old black-and-white magazines. Today we have many, many glossy pictures and very little text.

Spiegl: I personally am very much interested in glossy magazines. There I have an opportunity of presenting my things to an expert readership. In this way, I can start a discourse.

going public

Steiner: Let me give you a recent example: There's a design firm from Berlin, rather average in terms of content and quality. It's called "Graft". They've built a funny hotel. It's okay, although not much different from all the others. They've risen to international fame from Los Angeles to Beijing because they advised Brad Pitt, who is enthusiastic about architecture, on the reconstruction of his home. The truth is that he did everything himself. But there's no exhibition or project review about "Graft Architects" without Brad Pitt being mentioned.

wonderland: Can PR help you to take a big step ahead, to win major commissions?

Steiner: How do I advance from a single-family house to larger projects? Networking still plays a decisive role, I believe. Nothing much has changed here in the past fifty years. The busiest and best earning architects are those you don't know and who don't appear in the media. This is a local, personal network.

Czech: I don't see any chance that some intermediary could make up for this deficiency–my incapability of approaching clients. I can't imagine that anybody else could land a commission for me.

Steiner: I don't see either why getting clients for architects should be responsibility of PR agencies, not at all.

Lengauer: PR is not primarily about getting clients. Taking this approach means that you've already lost.

Czech: Why not?

Steiner: PR accompanies a project, which is quite important, especially with larger ones …

Spiegl: I think there are two types of architectural studios. The ones that wait till somebody comes along offering them a project, and others that think that they need new commissions and have to go out and get them. I believe that PR can naturally help both of them.

Steiner: I don't think it is necessary for a 35-year-old architect to publish a monograph about his life and work after his second built project.

Spiegl: All right, it's not necessary, but it's simply great self-gratification if you do it.

Steiner: If the point is to win commissions or get into contact with potential clients, you do need a portfolio. This can be produced for little money. However, all over the world, the majority of architects are certainly not entrusted with commissions because of images, portfolios, or PR, but through personal contacts and by talking to people.

Spiegl: I for my part would consider it positive if PR succeeded to promote an understanding of architecture on the part of the general public, or at least to stir people's interest. The whole profession would benefit from it. But this is a difficult thing. Effective and superficial nonsense just works more easily. You don't have to understand it; it's enough to say it's "cool" or not! But you're not obliged to deal with it in any depth.

Zweifel: Do you really need to publish everything everywhere? This will probably do more harm than good.

Czech: The more often something is published, the better, undoubtedly, for the project or its makers.

Zweifel: I was talking about that white noise …

Steiner: One should work out a strategy and find out what should be launched where, for this always entails costs and expenditure. However, I'd think that in the long run you succeed with a powerful identity, an attitude, and a concept, not with images …

Lengauer: I totally agree. If I'm convinced of what I'm doing, I will be able to communicate it convincingly.

Steiner: Actually I wanted to add that I'm afraid I might be wrong. This is something that goes far beyond the issue of PR and the role it plays in architecture. Our entire society is undergoing a fundamental change in that it tends to focus on "celebrities", which has generated a completely different type of public person – one that simply did not exist before. In trade and industry, too, there are figures that are perfect at selling themselves. Nobody cares to know what they can really do. They may lie, betray, and do all sorts of things, and yet they keep riding high.

Spiegl: If I could make a wish with regard to PR, it would be that the media should only publish what is worth publishing.

Lengauer: PR means convincing, not persuading.

Spiegl: If you send in three photographs to a newspaper and are unlucky, they might just select the one you like least, and completely rewrite the text.

Lengauer: This is where high-quality PR starts. Depending on the medium, I carefully select the photograph. I don't send in three for them to choose from, but decide myself which one they get. One has to be quite precise here.

Spiegl: So this is what they call the freedom of the press …

Lengauer: That's the way to do it.

Steiner: I'm listening to all this with amazement and a certain degree of teachability. Ten years ago, when an architect sent us material through a PR agency, it went right away into the wastebasket. This has changed profoundly in the past ten years. Architects' public relations work has improved, above all that of the young generation.

wonderland: It would really be exciting to know how you can plan your career as an architect.

142

Steiner: Today's generation of star architects have become what they are because of the authenticity of their stories. In the past thirty years, what made the difference was the personality, intellectual capacity, and creative power of an architect. I suspect that this is changing now.

wonderland: But how can I approach major investors with a publication about singe-family homes?

Steiner: That has to do with a certain system of social relations and differs from region to region. Look at the career of Herzog & de Meuron; you'll see that it was not only theoretical statements and architecture published in quality media, but certainly also their being rooted in the art scene. In the United States, it is all about art anyway. People like Steven Holl got to be commissioned with larger projects exclusively through that connection.

Spiegl: Let's hope that the best an architect can do in terms of PR is the quality of his or her projects. After a certain point, the potential of the press to hype up people and get them business is exhausted anyway. I hope this will not end up as it has in pop music, where many people who are excellent musicians don't have a chance to play, while others, who are not real musicians, are being passed off as such and backed up by some company or record label. If it were like that in architecture, those having the hippest PR agency would be getting all the good projects.

Steiner: That's an excellent comparison. If you think this through it means that it might also be possible for a PR agency to simply invent an architectural studio. Maybe "Graft" already is such an artificial product.

Spiegl: If I had the chance, I'd like to make the following experiment: take part in a competition every month with my studio and, at the same time, spend the same amount of money hiring people to simply go dancing at every party and talk about me with everybody they meet. Investing the money in people would probably produce better results. Shouting gets you a hearing – it's as simple as that.

Lengauer: I think in theory this is a great idea, but in fact the feasible solution is somewhere in between …

Steiner: We've already advanced much further, namely to the question of whether a young studio, a start-up, should invest in competitions or PR. When I was looking for a new press spokeswoman, one of the applicants pointed out what she was going to do for me. She had been the personal PR adviser to the director of a Viennese art institution for many years. She had set up his weekly schedules, telling him which events to attend and whom to invite for dinner, how to establish himself firmly in cultural, political, and social life so as to keep climbing up the ladder of success. This would not necessarily and automatically influence the quality of architectural production, but its perceived position. Young architects are confronted with the same question. Thinking of such phenomena as "Graft", one wonders if it wouldn't be better to live in Los Angeles for a year and do some celebrity hunting in Hollywood.

Hermann Czech, Vienna, Austria
Architect

Martin Lengauer, Vienna, Austria
Principal, "die Jungs" PR Agency
www.diejungs.at

Beatrix Roidinger, Vienna, Austria
PR expert

Herwig Spiegl, Vienna, Austria
Managing partner, AllesWirdGut
Architecture
www.alleswirdgut.cc

Dietmar Steiner, Vienna, Austria
Director (retired), Architekturzentrum Wien
www.azw.at

Kurt Zweifel, Vienna, Austria
Communications officer, proHolz Austria
www.proholz.at

For Wonderland:
Silvia Forlati , Anne Isopp, Elisabeth Leitner

This discussion took place on February 2nd 2007 in Vienna.

READING ARCHITECTURE
Layers of interpretation

According to Arthur C. Danto, a work of art – and hence also an architectural object – does not only exist in the eye of the public, determined by its material and formal aspects; but is also determined by the knowledge of art history and current events, as well as by interpretations (of the artist himself, or critics) which define it as art and incorporate it in world of art. As an artistic-technical endeavour, however, architecture is, in the aforementioned synchronic and diachronic coordinate system (geography and history), conditioned in a different way, ideologically and politically, than is "high art".

Today, when in the world of the arts the roles of the author (assuming he is still alive), curator, and theoretician are switched and inverted, the author-envisager still is, as before, a dominant and glorified person in architecture, and thus a role model for the young architect. The problematic question that arises is whether it is worth losing one's sense of calling by taking the position of star architect, and the idolization that goes along with it, as the goal to be sought after by every architect (particularly for one who is at the beginning of his career, mostly at around forty years of age). For in order to obtain a position of public recognition and the "completed house", the architect, more than other visual artists, is often forced, or tempted, to compromise between the commercial, political, artistic and academic spheres.

Two texts, one verbal and one architectural, can exist independently of one another, or can be incorporated in one another. Within this framework, it is possible that the verbal text dominates over architectural text (in contrast to the traditional hierarchy). Both texts are subject to interpretation.

The verbal text, regardless of what effect it seeks, is further reaching than the language of the object itself. The verbal text attempts to replace architecture, to take its place. The experience of project-making is not absolutely necessary.

Peter Eisenman: "Why I write such good books."
Jacques Derrida: "Why Peter Eisenman writes such good books."
Unknown architect: "Why Derrida says Peter Eisenman writes such good books."

Just as a verbal text can be written about architecture, or about a constructed architectural object or one that will never exist, likewise an architectonic text can exist as a constructed object, or as a collection of sketches and projects and thus function like an exposition. In this case "an exposition exposes itself" (Umberto Eco) since the underlying ideology of an exposition is that the packaging is much more important than the product itself.

The ideal (though not utopian) situation when the architectural text dominates the verbal one poses the question of how it can make itself heard. The architect draws public attention to himself by means of a constructed object without verbalizing, and hence must thank himself for his ability to understand the requirements and laws, and to find his place (without much servility) in the political life of the local community in which he builds and which, in turn, encourages him politically.

Jacques Herzog: "A building is a building. It cannot be read like a book; it doesn't have any credits, subtitles or labels like pictures in a gallery. In that sense, we are absolutely anti-representational. The strength of our buildings is the immediate, visceral impact they have on a visitor." 🙿

Text by Mariela Cvetić, Belgrade, Serbia

how
to go
public

Going public is a job within the job. Both in terms of know-how and time required. Strategic thinking is necessary to get out as much as possible of what you invest in effort, time, and money. Expert advice might help. Authenticity as well.

HOW TO GET NOTICED IN THE PRESS

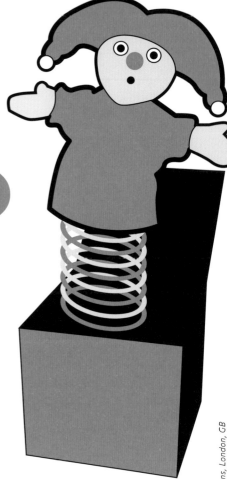

Text by Laura Iloniemi; Laura Iloniemi/ Architectural Press and Public Relations, London, GB

Young architects seeking media exposure usually say that it is for wholly utilitarian reasons – to get more and better work – and not for reasons of ego or vanity. Yet, some of the most prolific commercial practices around the world have relatively little exposure in the media. On the other hand, some of the smallest design studios with little built work are "big names" sought after by the magazines and lecture circuits.

Publicity in my experience is anything but a straightforward aspect of architectural practice. Other management tasks, such as human resources, accounting, IT, etc. can be quite clinically incorporated in the routines of a practice. Often, there is a desire that a practice's publicity department should act in the same crisply professional manner. It should

work like a well-oiled machine producing a smooth flow of promotional material that gets "out there" into the media and gets architects noticed at frequent intervals.

Usually, such publicity machines work best for practices whose partners are charismatic and influential leaders in their own right who have well-established useful press contacts and then delegate the job of informing the media to their press officer. In such scenarios, the partners still deal with the media personally, arranging for one-to-one visits to projects, etc.

Too often, practices without such charismatic figures think that if they only had a publicity machine like that of the latest sexy designer they would be sexy, too. Not at all. Publicity is about personality, just as celebrity today is wholly about the cult of personality. Of course, the architecture itself counts, too, but these days even architecture should have "personality" or a story to tell and it should not be same as that of any other building of its type. Why else write about it?

Press officers and publicity departments, however, need to tailor their work to the personality of both their senior architect and their buildings. If the architects they represent are charming/dynamic/interesting characters and their building is exciting or truly innovative, getting media coverage is not really a problem. If the architects and their projects are low-key, no matter how competent, and if there is, at one end, pressure from clients to see their buildings published, and at the other from partners wanting recognition from their peers and the wider public, then the publicity department is faced with a much harder task. Mass media – newspapers, radio, television etc – are rarely interested in stories of every-day professional competence. Both publicity departments and architects working in practices without obvious media appeal have to be realistic about the kind and extent of coverage they might receive outside the professional and specialist press.

Getting recognition

What, though, if the gifted architect is not interested in being a diva and is not well connected in the media and yet does interesting work with something to say and would like to see his projects get recognition through the press?

There are several key things to focus on. With no name about town or "brand", the most important thing is to have visual material to be made available to the press. Journalists are unlikely to visit the buildings of an unknown architect without seeing impressive renderings, drawings and a convincing overall presentation of a project. Moreover, sound

professional seriousness in looking at the material provided can be expected from the trade press only. This means that to get through to the mass media, such architects will first need to be championed by the trade or specialist press.

Trade and professional journals are looked at by journalists in the wider media, notably by specialist architectural and design writers, who may well pick out eye-catching projects and publish them. Articles by leading specialist writers are often taken up by other journalists, and so, bit by bit, an architect with something to say and with an interesting portfolio of buildings may well be "discovered" by the mass media and even become a "star"; although, this has its own dangers. A little publicity is a good and useful thing; too much of it, and the media may get bored and turn elsewhere for inspiration and stories.

In the beginning, visuals and ideas and how these are made available are key factors to get a foot in the media door. Finding a presentation style that substantiates what you want to say about your design approach is very helpful. It also helps if the images are eye-catching or, for example, of the highest standard of line or free-hand drawing. Drawings can become the personality of a practice, the way to help build your reputation amongst your peers. Photographs, too, should be produced in such as way as to suit magazines. Currently, there is a fashion for beautifully composed but extremely abstract photos that are like artworks in their own right; yet, they say little about a building to those looking at them, which makes it difficult to get them published.

One of the reasons why many practices fall short of their publicity goals is that in trying to reach out to a wider audience they tend to imitate the visual output, and even the designs, of the so-called star-architects. This may work for a lucky few in a fairly parochial way – the Foster of Finland, the Siza of Sweden, etc. In

particular, high-tech architecture has been watered down by second and third rate imitators of sorts. Now, everybody interested to get media coverage appears to be trying to be the next "green" architect. While, in practice, this is a good thing, in media terms it ceases to be something to write about unless it is done in an original, innovative, and truly creative way.

Telling a good story

Those who are successful at publicity REALLY understand what makes a story.

Those who are successful at publicity really understand what makes a story. The fact that a practice has its fifth or tenth anniversary or has launched new web-site is not really news. It may be worth throwing a party or bringing to the attention of clients and business contacts, but as more and more practitioners get media savvy, fewer and fewer editors are prepared to profile offices simply because of an anniversary, especially if they are not very established.

The same is true of books. It is usually a huge effort to publish a monograph on a practice, to get all the images and text right, to have all the pre-press work done, to pay the publisher, etc. – and yet, the whole effort and expenditure does not guarantee a review. There are just too many practice publications out there that do not differ significantly from one another for each to merit a review. Yet, from the perspective of an architect's client, it may still be worthwhile to be able to show that one has been published in a proper book.

The above really summarizes the two things that are central when setting out to get published. Having good visuals and recognizing the opportunity for a story. But what is a good story, and where to turn with it together with your visuals?

Good stories are easy when you are building a landmark building. A major monument, museum, concert hall, theatre, library, or church tend to be considered pretty sure hits. Even if you have done a lousy job, they tend to generate interest. The more important the city, the better your chances of getting wider media coverage. The more important your clients, the better as well, unless of course they refuse you the right to publicise your building.

There is a constant hunger for well-designed private houses, restaurants, and hotels. The more you have done, the better. Fully-fledged buildings tend to attract more interest than interior fit-outs, unless the client is very glamorous. The difficult stories are masterplans, office blocks, and all kinds of industrial buildings. Of course, there are exceptions to the rule, such as a current debate or exhibition that prompts coverage of, say, a new high-rise project. These are the windows of opportunity for press officers to get media attention.

The more likely it is to be the kind of design that might be included in a **sightseeing guidebook,** the more likely you are to get published.

You need to know **WHO** you are dealing with, journalists, editors and developers: they are not all the same.

Knowing who you are dealing with

You may even be able to claim that you have done a perfectly good office building which will improve the lives of hundreds of people and set an example for better office floor plan solutions from an economic and sustainability point of view, and yet the press may take no interest. Who defines the hierarchies of what deserves coverage and what not when half the stuff in the papers is rubbish anyway? Well, yes. Yet it seems that, as far as buildings are concerned, the more likely it is to be the kind of design that might be included in a sightseeing guidebook, the more likely you are to get published. Equally, a house or hip new hotel that has a "lifestyle" or ideological appeal is very likely to be published, and especially so in the popular media. Naturally, big-name clients – famous actors or plain old celebrities – help lift the stakes in the mass media.

As a rule, the specialized architecture and design press can be said to be a tamer version of the hierarchy of newsworthiness of the mass media. All the more reason for the trade press to be the ally of the young architect who may

not yet have prominent projects to show for. But beyond building typologies, good stories are stories that respond to current issues. Some architects have generated publicity by putting windmills on houses, others by creating inflatable structures. This is the type of story that can make it straight into the mass media and lift the profile of an unknown practice. The trick is to learn what the magazines and papers that you would like to be in consider worth publishing and to provide them with a story which looks like it may fit in. Of course, it helps if you take a news story to a news editor, etc. All this means that you will have to create the de facto tool of this business: a good database. You need to know who you are dealing with, journalists, editors and developers: they are not all the same. They may as well have intelligent ideas.

Good visuals with something to say to the right people at the right publications. It is quite clear, though, that there are many all-too common oversights or misunderstandings that frequently occur along the way. This is where some practices may be out of the game quickly. In addition to good visuals, they need to provide in the format and time-scale requested. Architects should resist the urge to have a hand in the layout or text editing unless invited to do so, or they run the risk of becoming unpopular. The right story for an architect may often be one that would work well at a cocktail party to entertain and engage others, such as about prospective clients or building projects. The right magazines, however, may also be trade magazines as these are often stepping stones to the mass media and also provide peers with information about a practice, peers who often act as advisors in competitions or even private sector short-lists.

One element in the game that I have not stressed enough yet is the relationship with the client. Sometimes clients benefit greatly from publicity on a project, and it is useful to collaborate with them regarding contacts and sharing costs of some of the presentation material or photographs. Sometimes clients have their own publicists who will either invite the architects to be part of the promotional campaign for a project or, as unfortunately happens more often, not quite see why the architect should at all be mentioned in a press release. If the latter feels more like your experience, it is best to discuss media expectations with your client early on. Discussing an architect's media interests is, more often than not, a delicate matter to broach towards the end of the project as the client is only interested in getting a building completed. Early on, trust on this front can be established, and public relations policies can be concerted in advance of any announcements. On a more major project, it is worth considering announcements at key stages of the project development: commissioning, planning, breaking ground, topping out, and of course, the opening of the building. Architects often miss out on simple ways to get more credit for their work by not offering tours of their new building for clients' guests, the media or even to their own business contacts. In a more public building, the architect may also arrange for a talk or information event on the project. And there are, of course, awards competitions that may help to attract media attention to a project.

When to go public?

Usually, it is worth waiting until you have a first project that somehow stands out; something that you feel you have a lot to say about and that would look good in a publication. Just to say that you have set up an office of your own is a bit weak as a starter; captivating work, however, is a strong starter. The professional and trade press trade may take interest while a project still is under way, as they usually scout for interesting new practices and offer slots for projects on paper, while the consumer media need a completed product.

Once a practice has enjoyed some exposure, it is good to take stock of all of the contacts made in the process of trying to achieve this. Keep a record of who was interested even if not willing to publish. These names, numbers and e-mail addresses will come in handy in the future when planning to send out material on the next interesting project or invite people to a party or lecture. It is good to keep the media contacts informed, make them remember a practice, even without a great new project under way. Alerts in the form of press notices just saying we have won X, Y or Z or have launched a new web-site without necessarily vying for coverage are fine to send from to time to time. However, the key to successful mailings is that they are targeted at those who might really be interested. The more failed attempts you make trying to get coverage, the more the office's media credit, or credibility, suffers so that even the good stuff may go unnoticed. ▰

PR STRATEGY

Not doing PR is an option shared by only **2 %** of the respondents; the remaining **98 %** are working on it, but do not necessarily give it high priority. PR strategies work for not more than **18 %** of the practices participating in our survey. For the remaining **80 %**, it is either a matter of reacting to what comes, or of having a strategy, but not following it through.

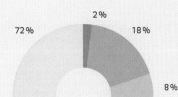

Do you have a PR strategy?

- We need no strategy, as we do not do PR!
- We have one and follow it through
- We have one, but never really manage to follow it through
- We have no strategy, we do PR as it comes

HUMAN RESOURCES

An external consultant or PR agency is an option for **13 %** of the respondents, but just to get started. **87 %** develop their PR on their own. Once the strategy has been decided on, implementation is seen by more than **50 %** as a responsibility of the partners that should not be left to employees. External help is an option for **3 %**, while for almost **39 %** it does not really matter: whoever is available will do the job.

We develop our PR ...

with the help of an external consulant
11 %

with the help of a PR agency
2 %

by ourselves
87 %

Who is in charge of PR matters?

Employee
5 %

External person
3 %

Specialized agency
0 %

Who ever
39 %

Partner
53 %

Source: Wonderland #3 Survey – by SHARE architects, compiled 2006

KEEP CONTACT WITH THE PRESS

Two opposing strategies are top of the list, each relevant for 58 % of the respondents: trying to get in contact with journalists vs. waiting to be contacted.

Outsourcing to a PR agency is an option for a minority only, while for at least 40 % of the surveyed practices sending out press releases is important.

How do you stay in contact?

■ high priority   ■ priority

7 % | 51 % — Send press releases to as many journalists as possible
58 %

19 % | 39 % — Wait to be contacted
58 %

11 % | 30 % — Send press releases to as many journalists as possible, and wait for a reaction
41 %

12 % | 26 % — Invite journalists to the office
38 %

12 % | 20 % — Invite journalists to building sites
32 %

5 % | 15 % — Show up at press conferences organized by clients
20 %

2 % | 14 % — Never dealt with journalists professionally
16 %

4 % | 10 % — Go to cafés where journalists hang out
14 %

2 % | 7 % — Hold regular press conferences
9 %

7 % — Have an agency, they do it for us
7 %

14 % go to cafés where journalists hang out

58 % wait to be contacted or send press releases to journalists they know

When do you do it?

For most of the respondents, press releases only make sense when they have something to show for it: a finished building, an exhibition, or a successful competition entry. Some keep the press posted during the process, while 22 % of the surveyed practices do not think press communications should have much priority.

Every time we finish a building
41 %

Every time we participate in an exhibition / event
36 %

Every time we get a prize in competitions
34 %

We often intend to send press releases, but then forget
28 %

Press releases are less important than our work, so we don't bother
22 %

At all milestone stages of a project
7 %

Whenever we have a new project coming in
2 %

22 % Press releases are less important than most of our work, so we don't bother

Source: Wonderland #3 Survey – by SHARE architects, compiled 2006

PRESS RELEASES

What do you include?

Digital photos
96 %

Text
95 %

Office description
41 %

Plans, line drawing
39 %

Sketches
30 %

Diagrams
29 %

Other, such as links to our webpage
11 %

WHAT TO INCLUDE AND WHAT HELPS?
No matter what is included in the press package, more than half of the practices seem to agree on what counts: ready-to-publish visuals and being already known by the journalists. The story or concept is important for 24 %. An equal percentage subscribe to the idea that it is the real building what counts, no matter how the press material looks like. Naïve?

There is more response from the press if ...

they have already heard about us
63 %

the material we send includes ready to publish photos/drawings
63 %

the material we send includes good text, so they can copypaste
44 %

the client is well known
25 %

the concept is good
24 %

the building is good, no matter how the press material is
24 %

the project has been designed to photograph well
24 %

We have no clue what journalists want!
5 %

63 % believe that ready-to-publish material works best with the press

It helps if ...

we do exhibitions
67 %

we are part of networks
65 %

we take controversial stands in panel discussions
22 %

we do not care, we just go on with what we are doing
15 %

65 % think that networking helps

Source: Wonderland #3 Survey – by SHARE architects, compiled 2006

A mirror to the outside

Interview with Thomas Manss

Design is not about engineering layouts, it is about **communicating ideas**.

Every business communicates, consciously or unconsciously, through its visual appearance. The goal should be to generate an appearance that harmonizes with the development of the business. A number of architects are content with a do-it-yourself visual identity, while others have recognized that visual identity can go far beyond traditional graphic design. What is important here is the choice of the right designer. Successful offices such as Foster + Partners, Grimshaw, and Zaha Hadid Architects have worked with designer Thomas Manss, a specialist in generating visual identities for cultural organizations, companies, and events. In an interview with **wonderland**, he let us in on some tricks of the trade.

wonderland: *Do you use a particular approach to generate a visual identity?*

Thomas Manss: Analyzing personality means looking and listening very closely. Maybe the practice has a very pronounced style, so you could start by looking at their buildings. It is not important what kind of style it is; the thing is that it is a style. This style must then be translated into other areas. If the practice is mainly guided by clients' wishes, this stylistically restrained approach should be reflected in the firm's identity. There are other things as well that one can look at when visiting the office: furniture, internal organization, location of the office, is it all creative chaos? Is this a practice where people wear their shirts outside their pants, so to speak, or where business suits are worn? The people who define the company culture generally are the partners. Are there certain explicit preferences, how do people talk about their firm? Are they team players, or are they figureheads who represent the firm? All this plays a role. Most visual designers do not take the trouble to search for personality, as this takes time and often leads to solutions that reflect the style of the client and not of the designer.

Is this approach any different with architects' practices, compared to other, not design-oriented companies?

Unlike many other business firms, architects are particularly aware that visual appearance is an expression of personality. They don't need to be filled in on it, and the awareness is located where a great deal of personality is created. The firm's personality should be located at the level of the partners or directors, and this is the case in most architects' practices that I have worked with so far. In architects' practices there is often a distinct visual culture, which of course exists in other businesses, too, but there it perhaps takes a different form. Architects do really have a good nose for this kind of thing, which sometimes leads them to think: "Yes, I can do that myself; all I need is a little help to get it right." This is certainly one kind of approach, but I doubt very much whether it can survive for ten years or so.

Interview by Astrid Piber

*How do you use these observations to
create a visual identity?*

We ask ourselves what can be distilled out
of them. In principle we work almost like
caricaturists. From one or two prominent
characteristics, a visual identity must be
constructed. For example, we worked on the
visual identity of Norman Foster: a firm which
wants to be a leader in terms of visual identity.
These are people who play in the top league
in terms of designing buildings that use the
latest technology. If my aim is to present a
firm like this as leading in its field, confidence
is the word to use, and self-confidence is the
most important characteristic.

Is this more difficult with a young practice?

In stylistic terms possibly, as the office probably doesn't have a distinct style of its own yet,
but for me the style is not so important. If
the goal is developing a personality, the kind
of DNA that it derives from can also be found
in young practices. As an example, I recall a
firm which keeps presenting itself as young
but that isn't really young any longer. In fact
it is middle-aged, a mature architect's practice. The people there are surprised that they
still only get smaller commissions. Through
its self-presentation, the practice can decide
where it wants to be in the future. One can
grow into a visual identity so that it does not
need to be changed every couple of years.

*Must buildings become a brand or are there
other successful strategies?*

In the case, say, of Zaha Hadid, the personal
approach and the architecture are one and the
same. There are many others where this is not
the case, for example, collectives or practices that are strongly influenced by clients and
their wishes. But this is something that I can
also get across through self-presentation. A
client of ours once started with a kind of
mannerism. He thought to himself that
architects are often blue or grey, and so he
chose pink as his "house color". There was
also another kind of wisdom involved here: I
can take things that I like personally, and if I
use them consistently then I can, in time,
generate a kind of "ownership".

Trends: designers always want to start,
or contribute to trends: this is crazy! When
I think about a firm, I prefer to stick with
Ludwig Mies van der Rohe who once said
that it is better to be good than original!

*Is it really necessary for every young
architect to have his own monograph?*

This has to do with the nature of the
publishing business. Printed material is
very important in the world of architecture,
whether it is brought out by a publisher
or by the architect himself. In the latter case,
though, I can make my own publications that
can be tailored to the personality of the
office.
For the new visual identity for Grimshaw
Architects we made a small square folder
intended to introduce the firm in only 100
words, while all the projects were put on a
CD for people to look at. Every small office
could do this kind of thing.
For Foster we are involved in the "Foster
Works", six volumes covering the complete
oeuvre. People wrote about these books that
they are a "publishing triumph", something
that nobody else could have done because
nobody else has the internal resources or such
a well organized archive.
For John McAslan + Partners we made an A3
volume: for example, they had a building that
was influenced by Morandi, therefore a
chapter about Morandi was included.
Another chapter was dedicated to the theme
of landscape. The issue was not so much
square meters, plans, elevations, and sections
but rather how the architecture interpreted
the region. The client has a small cheese-
making business where Parmesan is produced,
and so we included a story about Parmesan.
For another office with many different
projects that must be regularly re-compiled
in different ways we developed a system of
project documentation so that after each
new project a documentation can easily be
made, and after 20 projects we have a fine
little brochure. But, as I said, the printed
material used should be based upon the
personality of the office.

What might such printed material look like in the case of "start-ups"?

We have also worked a lot with "start-ups", for example, with the former director of Foster's office, an architect in Berlin who had just set his own office there. He had a fantastic CV, as he was able to say that he had worked on this big project or that, and these were all marvellous well-known buildings. His company brochure in the first two years was a CV designed as a time bar. Another example from London: a female architect had always presented her work in the manner of "Hockney-style photography". She made photographs and, when she needed a panorama, she put several photos together. This resulted in a kind of presentation that nobody else could have made. We took this and used it – but the idea belongs to her. Working in this way you can almost always find something that can become a kind of trademark if people continue to use it. A trademark can be anything; it can also be the logo.

It took me ten years until I had developed the self-confidence to go out and say:
we give companies a face!

How do you alter the visual identity of established firms?

We created a visual identity for a business that had, so to speak, shed quite a number of skins; a number of good designers had worked on it and had repeatedly tried to re-design their corporate identity in a contemporary way. When we got the contract we took a look at the original visual identity. The decision they had made on the signature of the business back then was so good that it had to be preserved. Over the years it had been papered over, and each designer had pasted on a new layer. We decided that all these papers had to be stripped from the wall, as it were, as they didn't make the wall any better. Where new elements are necessary we use them. There are also many architects who have a long history in which a great deal has happened. And in such a case one can

look at where the journey should lead. Depending on the situation one must adapt the visual identity cautiously or, at times, radically.

How important is the target group in this process?

It is decisive. When I moderate this process, meaning when I listen and observe, it is like a kind of role-play. You put yourself in the role of the architect and try to understand what he is trying to achieve. The second part is to put oneself in the role of the client. For me this is not difficult, I might well decide to build at some stage. Foster once told me a nice story that had a major influence on the design of his office's website. The office had taken part in a large competition, and three firms got on the shortlist. After the final presentation, Norman Foster wanted to know why his project had been selected rather any of the two others. According to the client this was very easy. The reason was two key statements. First, his project had a clear philosophy, and secondly, his was this only practice that had placed the team in the foreground. This was very important, as the client said: "We know that we will not work out the entire project with you but we wanted to know how you present your team." For many architects the issue also is other clients – this may come out in the process of discovering the personality.

Architects are often more interested in how they are seen by their fellow architects ...

It is far easier to build up a visual identity in one's own professional scene. Architects get quite a number of commissions through to the advice or recommendation of colleagues. The dual track approach of informing the public while also keeping fellow professionals informed about developments in the practice is also very important, but naturally, one can make priorities here. For me this has never turned out to be contradictory. You must try to address a very broad public. This is easier for the architect than for the graphic designers, as architecture is far more present in public space. There are no-ready made solutions saying you have to do it this way or another. It would be impossible to say anything like first of all you have to have a publication to show for. After all there are so many books that are never read. You will have to develop a vocabulary that is brings out the strengths of the practice.

How easily can architecture become corporate identity?

Architecture is a tried and tested but also a very difficult vehicle. There are successful implementations, the erco company for example. In their company building the issue was light, and it was developed precisely with this requirement in mind. Most business firms that I know have not recognized the potential of the building. A company must have enough self-confidence to "out" themselves. For customers, the seller's appearance has to suit the product; it is difficult to sell luxury cars in a warehouse. The car in which the architect arrives at his client's is also part of the visual identity, and generally speaking, discrepancies are not a good idea here. ✿

Thomas Manss, *Thomas Manss & Company*, **London and Berlin**
Founder and principal of Thomas Manss & Company, a multi-disciplinary design company. In 1993, he started his own studio in London, followed by the opening of a German office in Berlin in 1996. He has a longstanding affinity with architecture. This has resulted in him becoming the first choice for many leading British architects looking to renew their identity, profile their work, or provide wayfinding systems that are compatible with their architecture.
www.manss.com

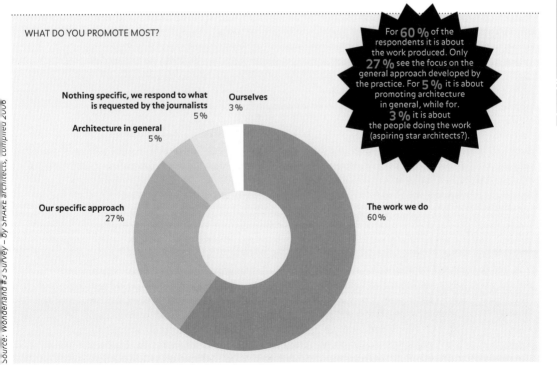

WHAT DO YOU PROMOTE MOST?

For **60 %** of the respondents it is about the work produced. Only **27 %** see the focus on the general approach developed by the practice. For **5 %** it is about promoting architecture in general, while for. **3 %** it is about the people doing the work (aspiring star architects?).

Nothing specific, we respond to what is requested by the journalists
5 %

Architecture in general
5 %

Ourselves
3 %

Our specific approach
27 %

The work we do
60 %

Source: Wonderland #3 survey – by SHARE architects, compiled 2008

How to ...

... CHOOSE AN ARCHITECTURE PHOTOGRAPHER

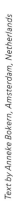

"Many architects owe their success to my photographs", Julius Shulman once said. Even though this may sound somewhat presumptuous and could, in fact, as well be applied the other way around – after all, Shulman only came to fame because of Neutra, Schindler and Wright – his statement is probably correct. As far as the success of a project is concerned, good photographs are worth their weight in gold. Architecture is a static, dry, and sometimes even unapproachable product that in its original state is noticed only by few but may be appreciated by many in the form of photographs.

But of course not every young architect is a Richard Neutra, whose office, even at an early stage, was generating sufficient profit to allow talented photographers to be engaged. But in the long run almost nobody can get around the need for an architectural photographer. Generally speaking, it is not a good idea to photograph one's own buildings – unless, that is, one is a multi-talent like Erich Mendelsohn.

For one thing, one is likely to lack the necessary professionalism, and for another, the necessary objective view. And, in addition, a well-known photographer can be a valuable help in getting one's projects publicized.

This can go so far that a famous photographer is considered to ennoble a project. If a building is photographed by Christian Richters, Hélène Binet, or Duccio Malagamba the editors of the specialist journals will automatically assume that it must be interesting. Photographers also help to spread the word about a project as they offer their photos of it to various editors. They are regarded as less directly involved than the architects themselves and often have far better personal contacts. "We often get information from photographers about good projects that we did not previously know of", says Felix Zwoch, editor-in-chief of the German *Bauwelt* magazine. "This is more useful to us than unsolicited press releases sent in by architects' offices." Malagamba keeps editors posted about his

Text by Anneke Bokern, Amsterdam, Netherlands

work by means of a newsletter that can be subscribed to on his website. And many editors looking for a subject to report on regularly check the websites of photographers who offer a database of newly photographed projects such as the Austrian Margherita Spiluttini or Jan Bitter from Berlin.

The style of photography is at least just as decisive as the reputation and the contacts of the photographer. "Most magazines prefer images with a straight view of the building, as this corresponds to their approach to describing buildings", Christian Richters believes. His photos are accordingly sober. "Architecture photography should not offer an interpretation or criticism, it should just describe. Therefore, as a photographer, I try to withdraw into the background as far as possible." An approach which is in marked contrast to the highly aestheticized black and white photographs by Hélène Binet, which are less purely documentary and more independent art works. This is why in architecture books

Binet's name generally appears in the title line, right next to the name of the architect.

And, finally, architecture photographers also move back and forth between the role of a provider of services and that of an artist – just as their clients – and as their client one will have to decide which role better suits one's own purposes. Unless, that is, one pursues a clever (but expensive) twin track strategy like UNStudio. Ben van Berkel likes to allow himself the luxury of having two photographers take shots of the same project. Conventional specialist magazines are supplied with photos by Christian Richters, and for hipper lifestyle journals the office provides experimental picture series, made by a photo-artist. This is done with the aim of ensuring maximum distribution.

If one wants to make sure that the project will be published in specialist magazines, classic objective photographs are still the best choice. This doesn't mean, though, that they have to comply with the cliché of frosty architecture photography devoid of any trace of human life. The Amsterdam-based photographer Allard van der Hoek, for example, tries to make mixed series of photographs: "Personally, I find the still and sober documentary photos that most architects and magazines want beautiful. But in the corner of my eye I also always try to see the special aspects of the place or situation. It can happen that you will find a building worker or a grazing horse in my photos." After all, each architect will have to know for himself whether people and trees disturb his architecture or not.

Van der Hoek is still relatively new to this business, and being not a big name yet such as, say, Christian Richters means that his prices also are more reasonable. He charges around 1000 Euros for 45 digital photographs of a project on a DVD. In terms of pricing, he is thus at the bottom of the range – in the case of his famous colleagues, prices may easily be several times that high. Generally speaking one has to reckon with 800 to 1200 Euros per working day, plus expenses such as material and travel costs. There are also photographers who charge per photograph delivered instead of having fixed, all-inclusive prices. In the case of analogous photography, material costs are really quite considerable, whereas digital photos require more working hours for the post-editing. For this reason, a number of photographers invite architects to select from the raw data what they want to be processed further. A real star photographer can spend an expensive working day just choosing the right angle for his handful of photos.

Licensing is handled differently by different photographers. In the case of Van der Hoek, the architect is free to use the photographs for all his or her own publications. But when a third commercial party, for example, a magazine, wishes to publish them, a license fee has to be paid. There are hardly any photographers who grant architects unrestricted rights of use for their photographs – and where they do so, this can be very expensive.

Some offices, however, do obtain a royalty-free license for one or two photos, which they then can pass on to the media, as appetizers, so to speak.

Generally speaking, publication fees amount to a maximum of 25 per cent of an architecture photographer's income. Basically, they live from fees that architects pay to them for the photo shoot. Nevertheless, architects can get themselves in a lot of hot water if they infringe a photographer's intellectual property rights by supplying a third party with photo material without expressly pointing out the photographer's right to a fee. On the Internet and in publications from countries where copyright law is rather slovenly handled caution is advisable. People often fail to understand that they must pay for architecture photographs submitted by the architect. But no matter how much pressure an editor may exert, the photographer's permission must be obtained for every publication of his or her work.

A small architect's practice really hits the big jackpot when a highly respected magazine finds one of the projects interesting enough to send their own photographer to shoot it. Then you get publicity free of charge and often also photos by a photographer that you could otherwise never have afforded. But waiting for this to happen is not such a good idea. Unless you have built a spectacle such as the Guggenheim Bilbao, you might as well wait for six right numbers in the weekly lottery. ▨

TEXT OR PHOTO

Even if text and photos are considered as equally necessary for a successful press release by almost all respondents, the related effort is different. Text writing is outsourced occasionally only, while hiring a photographer for at least some of the projects is common practice for 85 % of the respondents.

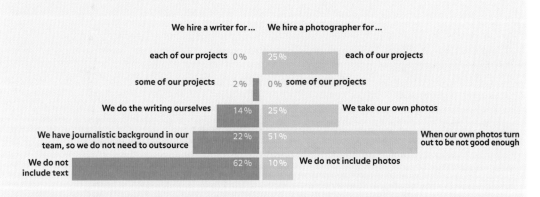

We hire a writer for ... We hire a photographer for ...

each of our projects	0 %	25 %	each of our projects
some of our projects	2 %	0 %	some of our projects
We do the writing ourselves	14 %	25 %	We take our own photos
We have journalistic background in our team, so we do not need to outsource	22 %	51 %	When our own photos turn out to be not good enough
We do not include text	62 %	10 %	We do not include photos

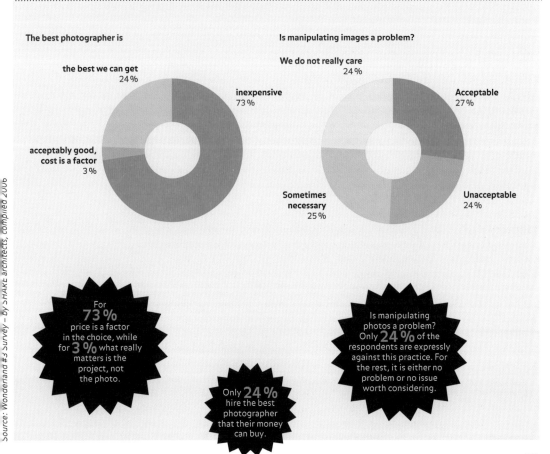

The best photographer is

the best we can get
24 %

acceptably good,
cost is a factor
3 %

inexpensive
73 %

Is manipulating images a problem?

We do not really care
24 %

Acceptable
27 %

Sometimes
necessary
25 %

Unacceptable
24 %

For **73 %** price is a factor in the choice, while for **3 %** what really matters is the project, not the photo.

Only **24 %** hire the best photographer that their money can buy.

Is manipulating photos a problem? Only **24 %** of the respondents are expressly against this practice. For the rest, it is either no problem or no issue worth considering.

Source: Wonderland #3 Survey – by SHARE architects, compiled 2006

ARCHITECTURAL COPYRIGHT

Interview with lawyer Thomas Höhne

Going public with a project or a design concept may not be a matter of getting publicity only. It can also be a matter of maintaining control and of making clear who the owner of the rights on the design or concept and on the visuals related to it is. We discussed the issue of architectural copyright with Thomas Höhne, a Vienna-based lawyer and expert in the field. And we found out that, in some cases, publicity may help you protect your rights.

Interview by Silvia Forlati

wonderland: *What exactly does copyright mean?*

Höhne: Anybody who originates a creative work automatically holds an exclusive right of use. This is similar to a property right. Although there are some European guidelines and conventions, the right of use remains a matter of national legislation in the end. The originator holds all rights on the work in the first place. In architecture, you may obtain the right to implement a construction design once or several times, to build it in Austria only or elsewhere, with or without any changes. Basically, all conceivable variants with regard to content, location, and time are possible.

You're talking about the rights of a client now. What about the rights of the architect?

As a matter of principle, the originator is the holder of all rights pertaining to the work. The notion of the work is central to copyright. It is the creative achievement. But not everything that is creative can be called a work. Certain qualifications have to be met. The originator is the person who made the creation. He has the so-called moral rights and the exploitation rights. Moral rights include the right of being named as author, the right of publication and access.

What are the criteria to define something as a work in the legal sense?

The law does not specify any criteria. It is possible that something is great, but may be nothing in terms of copyright. This is not a quality judgment.

Are publications relevant?

If several architectural critics review the work or architecture magazines report on it, I would say it is relevant. Under Austrian law, it is a solely law-based decision which means that the judge does not have to hear expert opinions.

Is it permitted to photograph the work?

Once the building is completed, unrestricted work use and the freedom of the public realm apply in Austria and Germany. When a film showing the work is broadcast on TV, it is permissible if I turn on my VCR and make a copy of it. It is not permissible, however, to make multiple copies for sale. And of course, replicating, or re-building, the built work is not permitted. However, it is allowed to represent the building in a painting, drawing, photograph, or film, and to distribute these pictures.

Should the author be indicated?

Although, of course, it should be done, it doesn't happen in the majority of cases.

It seems that the majority of architects are not fully aware of their rights.

As a matter of principle, indicating the author is obligatory. Some time ago, I read a detailed report on a recently opened restaurant. The owner and the chef were mentioned, the food was described, and it was also indicated who had taken the photos and written the article. However, the architect of the place went unmentioned. This is a lack of public awareness.

Yes, there is, but it doesn't play an important role. A patent protects technical developments and procedures. But architecture isn't primarily about technologies, but about design. A plan is not patentable. However, there are examples of patents in architecture: Buckminster Fuller took out a patent on complete detached houses using airplane technology. Jean Prouvé and Konrad Wachsmann did the same. The difference between copyright and patent lies in the fact that the copyright isn't registered anywhere. You obtain it by the act of creating something.

In architecture, there may also be a question of who was first ...?

Where is the boundary between inspiration and plagiarism? This is very difficult to determine. Of course, no architect works in a vacuum, or invents things from scratch.

What should architects be careful about? What can, or should, they try to settle by contract beforehand?

There is always a question of power which affects all creative professions. There are plenty of details, which can be agreed upon by contract. For example: where and in which form will I be allowed to put up a plate which identifies me as the architect of the building; when and how will I have access to the house? According to the law, I have the right to do so, but the details are always negotiable. The essential question is: How far does my authorship go? Is the client entitled to commission somebody else to revise or complete my preliminary draft? Will I be able to establish my legal position as the sole originator of the whole project?

What about changes in the building stage and after completion?

Austrian copyright laws entitle the client to make changes. The planner cannot insist on maintaining his design without any modification. Architect fees are ten to twenty per cent of the building cost. In this case, you have to be pragmatic enough to recognize that. If the architect succeeds to stipulate that the client shall have to consult him before making changes, then the architect has an opportunity to bring in his ideas. But there will be no contract, in which the client unreservedly commits himself to carry out changes only with the agreement or collaboration of the architect. In Germany, too, courts of law always weigh up clients interests and the architect's rights. It was a sensation when Meinhard von Gerkan won the case he filed about the Berlin Central Station.

Who is the owner of the plans?

This is something that should be stipulated in the contract. If the architect only provides the design and the client is responsible for the construction, the client will of course need the plans and will stipulate this in the contract. When the architect also does the detail planning or acts as construction supervisor, the client doesn't need to have the plans. And the client is not allowed to copy the plans.

When, and to which extent, will the architect have to share the copyright with other professionals involved in the building project?

Under copyright law, a simple idea is not considered a work. Ideas and wishes of the client therefore are not relevant. If the client's requirements are so strict that the planner's task is reduced to mere implementation of given specifications, then the client will be considered as the originator. This was a matter in dispute between Friedensreich Hundertwasser and the architect who actually did the detail planning of the "Hundertwasser House". It turned out, though, that not the complete work was attributable to Hundertwasser. ▄

Thomas Höhne, Vienna, Austria. Lawyer and executive partner of Höhne, In der Maur & Partner in Vienna. He is specialized in information law (including copyright, media and Internet), competition and trademark. He has published the book 'Architektur und Urheberrecht' (Manz, Vienna, 2nd edition, 2014) about copyright law for architects and engineers in Austria and Germany. www.h-i-p.at

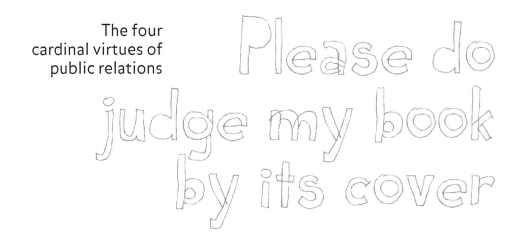

The four
cardinal virtues of
public relations

The saying "Don't judge a book by its cover!" means that one should not base judgment on outward appearance. Speaking in communication terms, it is frustrating both for the sender and receiver if there is a considerable difference between what is expected and what one gets in the end.
The four virtues needed to do effective publicity work in our highly competitive economy of attention are **timing, sensitivity, inventiveness, and authenticity.**

Timing

In some cultures punctuality is a crucial quality, whereas in others it plays a minor role. Regarding publicity work, it is necessary for survival. In a media-dominated environment, the clock is always ticking and the half-life of novelties and information is very short. But newsworthiness is the wave on which our public relations work rides.

One important step is timely preparation. Whether it is a project or an exhibition or anything else, one can prepare a news release in advance and send it to the press and post it on the Internet at the same time. The issue therefore is not necessarily to produce a lot of information but rather to spread the information widely.

For example, news reports on exhibitions or specialist lectures have almost died out. One must be happy to receive a mention somewhere in a list of events. Events calendars and appointments diaries are full, not only in magazines and newspapers. Personal invitations should be sent out in time as well. In fact the best solution would be to get events in the diaries of those invited a long time in advance. This is possible with iCal or vcf-files that can be downloaded or e-mailed. I always also send a last-minute reminder on the day of the event itself, just to make sure.

Then there are those events that people do not necessarily wish to attend but like to be kept posted about, such as cornerstone ceremonies or the completion of a building, etc. Readers of special-interest newsletters or RSS feeds like to read about this kind of thing as long as it is topical. A week later the interest has gone, and the news value has vanished into thin air.

Timing is essential for office communications in general. Many clients are under time pressure and need our services or tenders extremely quickly. Here again preparation is most important. This includes optimizing one's own homepage for search engines. Google, for example, gives valuable tips and offers free tools for webmasters. A listing in online yellow pages is often available free of charge. Even though the chances of finding customers this way are slight, each entry raises the search engine ranking. Internet surfing habits are becoming increasingly restless. We should therefore make sure that information about our practice is quickly found.

In addition to short-term punctuality, it is equally important to make one's presence known regularly over extended periods of time. Continuity in approaching former, current, and prospective clients is appreciated and establishes a feeling of trust. The communications industry often uses the term "customer relationship management" here, along with expensive software solutions. For an architect's office all that is needed is an up-to-date address book, a diary of appointments and events to schedule long-term communication, as well as a pen and paper to take notes and tick off the points on one's agenda.

Since the 1960s, punctuality along with accuracy have no longer been as highly valued as they were by previous generations. But these are things that can be learnt and they continue to be appreciated. Just think of how we, as customers, react with annoyance if we feel that a seller is hard to contact or keeps disregarding our wishes.

Sensitivity

Sensitivity is a key virtue in public relations and sounds more appealing than "customer orientation". What is the difference? Sensitivity takes into account the fact that, through my office, I get in contact with many other people who have completely different interests. So I do not only have to know the needs of my target group(s) but must also respect the interests of the editor, the chance reader, and other "third parties".

Relativizing one's own line of argument is far from easy. Often, it has developed over years and is based on building regulations, the table of fees, or personal aesthetics. Nevertheless, one should try to accommodate it to the perspective of the person one is dealing with. The issue is not to denying or hiding, let alone abandoning, one's standpoint. But admit-

ting that it is a personal viewpoint makes a positive difference. Instead of proclaiming iron laws – "That's the way it is!" –, one should explain personal views – "The way I see it is ... because ..." Similar applies to contacts from other industries: people coming from other fields of business appreciate it if one avoids technical or specialist jargon.

One should also respect people's natural need for entertainment. The right balance between factual information and entertaining elements can decide whether a reader or radio listener will remember the contribution later or not.

Sensitivity – like punctuality – is a virtue of politeness in public relations, a basically friendly approach to the rest of the world. So far, so good. But will polite friendliness get you anywhere, given the rat-race competition? The next section deals with strategies of dealing with competitors.

Inventiveness

Generally, practices do not have to think long about what distinguishes them from competitors. But coming up with ideas of how to convey this difference may take somewhat longer. First, I need to define my unique selling proposition. The next step is thinking of ways to communicate this to as many people as possible. This is where inventiveness comes into play. Should I use a textual presentation or a visual office portfolio? Or can I succeed to find new unusual ways to explain and convey what the real focus of my practice is?

In addition to the Internet and the classic portfolio, alternative media such as film or Podcasts naturally are also interesting here. A number of offices are also highly inventive when it comes to tapping, or building, effective publicity networks. They cooperate with groups or institutions that do not really have much to do with architecture but act as disseminators to reach people outside the logical target groups. Examples of this include collaboration with people from the world of theater, fashion, or music.

Networks of this kind are fun and may also enrich the architectural work proper. They are sustainable in the long term if the cooperation relates to a number of clearly distinct themes of maximum social relevance. Incidentally, it need not always be ecological building. In any case, what is needed here is inventiveness with regard to the choice of media, but there is a number of successful examples ranging from the virtual space of video games [Raumtaktik, Berlin] to outer space [Liquifier, Vienna]. Perhaps some of the Wonderland offices may provide inspiration for the reader, as they have found their own way of reaching the public through this magazine.

Even though savings coupons or scratch-and-win cards are out of the question for architects' offices, it is worthwhile observing how other industries combine media, themes and partners. Perhaps one can adapt the approach of one's favorite boutique or band for one's own communication strategy.

In a world where the distinction between lifestyle magazines and magazine-style advertising catalogues is blurring and TV documentaries are not only sponsored but sometimes actually scripted by business enterprises, credibility and realness are not only ethical values but also an important commodity. Precisely because the services we offer as smaller offices are pure luxury, the authenticity of our office "branding" is not quite unimportant. *(In this context see also "Dance of the Marketing Mix" in chapter #1).* As consumers, our potential clients are overloaded with information on the personal background of fashion designers or musicians, whose marketing experts keep frantically searching for content that can provide a meaning to be associated with the brands. Therefore it is not enough for us just to have a decent logo on our office stationery. But it should be said that the point is not to imitate a flashy image but to convey a holistic impression of ourselves and the values we stand for.

In times of Web 2.0, this is certainly becoming easier although architects are reluctant to make use of the new possibilities. There are many things imaginable, social networking on *facebook* and *MySpace*, or serious architecture criticism in video format on *YouTube*. A variety of contact points creates a more complex image of the practice and provides security. Ultimately, these are opportunities to provide proof of expertise and social competence, almost like personal encounters.

where to go public

Going public is a two-way street: at either end you have the sender and the receiver with the medium in between, providing the connecting link. If the sender is more or less given (after all, you are what you are), there still is a wide range of media and receivers to choose from. Whatever choice you make, it will reflect back.

Where is it leading to?

Four practices share their views

Does PR help to acquire new commissions?

An analysis of publications in architectural magazines shows that there is a tendency to publish a limited group of architects more often. It is even so that the same projects keep re-appearing in different magazines. The status of the published architect rises, and more of his or her work is likely to be published. Even less interesting projects or fragments of an architectural discourse are publicized – a phenomenon that, we think, OMA reacted to in a witty way by showing in its "content" exhibition a heap of rubble with a puppet's head floating above with architect's face projected onto it, mumbling in riddles and in an incomprehensible way.

Publications about architectural centers in the Netherlands show a similar phenomenon: press releases and articles about activities are taken over by different media and widely disseminated. Extensive media coverage generates positive feedback and a favorable impression of a center's "very interesting activities", even with people who, if asked, say that they never attended a single event. The mere fact that the activity was published suggested quality.

A second example is interesting. A fellow architect's office published, at its own expense, a monograph on its own work. This book won a prize for its design and getup. Subsequently, a number of articles appeared, primarily reporting the fact that the book had won the prize. Secondly, articles about the projects in the book were published. Even a magazine from central Russia contacted the office. They had never seen any work and had never had any contact with the office. They just knew earlier publications.

Contrary to what is commonly assumed, we do not think that PR leads directly to new commissions. We think that commissioning an architect is a personal matter. Either you know someone, or you are introduced to him or her. A real-life personal network, by the way, is not the same as a virtual Hyves or OpenBC network. It is not the same as knowing, or being known, from publications and exhibitions. PR may extend your network and facilitate better knowledge of what you do and stand for. In fact, we do believe that it is less the publication itself, but the reactions you get and the conversations you have about it which make the important part of going public.

There is no recipe for acquiring commissions by means of PR. There is no direct relation observable between PR and new work. The only thing sure is that there is a snowball effect: publicity creates more publicity.

Johanna Gunther and Mathias Lehner
lehner en gunther architecten LEGU, Amsterdam

Banging the drum is OK!

A rising number of architecture practices in the market, changes in client structure, fewer competitions, and the ongoing concentration tendencies in the building industry all make entirely new self-marketing demands on architects.

Austrian architects spend 63 million Euros annually on competitions; which means that each competition entry costs the participant practice some 18,000 Euros – while the average chance of seeing one's design realized is only 0.8 per cent. This makes it clear that focusing on competitions alone cannot be a productive strategy.

Given this situation, the question should no longer be "How can I/we find clients?", but "How can clients find me/us?" One answer is marketing and public relations. Here the idea is to take a diversified approach, addressing different segments of the public. Beyond networking in one own 'natural' professional environment – which is important for the more serious architectural publications and hence for one's reputation in the scene –, one must, more than in former times, also go where the clients are. This requires a great deal of initiative, courage and, not least, creativity. It is vital to provide precise information about the services offered by an architecture office and to point to the benefits that clients will have from commissioning a particular architect or team of architects. This is quite simple in the case of what are called "single architects", but with larger teams involving a number of different personalities and abilities, things become more complex. What all this boils down to is that architects will have to start seeing themselves more as entrepreneurs and to develop necessary managerial and business skills – something which, to date, has hardly been taught at universities at all.

An architecture practice cannot afford reluctance in marketing its own work and should be prepared to seek professional advice, as hiring experts in the field full-time is practically unaffordable. Anyone who takes marketing seriously must be fully aware that this is 'real work', that it ties up staff resources, time and money, and should be handled by experts. But, done in the right way, the effort is likely to pay off. See it as it is: it takes work to get you work.

Roland Gruber
nonconform, Vienna

Ar[t]ogance!

The issue of arrogance is directly linked to the image that the public has of our profession. It is not necessarily objective, but clearly indicates certain problems relevant for the profession.

First, the architect does not listen to the public!

He suffers from the same superiority complex as many liberal professionals. He tends to neglect the service nature of his profession and to abuse others for his purposes. By neglecting it, he forgets that the main objective of his discipline is the Human Being.

Second, he does not talk with the public!

The image that the public has of architecture is more or less monopolized by a handful of star architects. But they are not representative of the rest of the profession: they do a different job. They can choose their commissions. They are hired by special clients because of the image they offer and for their signature style. In fact, they provide a publicity image, an expression of status rather than a response to a need. They do an artists job and de facto belong to a completely different category than their colleagues who are confronted with quite different realities.

Dominated by this marginal architecture, which appears far exaggerated compared to the bulk of everyday production, the debate is reduced to the aesthetic component. What is discussed and defined is what allegedly is beautiful and what is not. Architects have succumbed to this aestheticizing discourse and have accepted architecture being reduced to art.

Confining themselves to the artist status, architects have forgotten that their discipline is much more rich and complex. They are neglecting the political debate, the issue of territorial management in all its social or environmental aspects. They have taken themselves out of the construction market: whom should a client refer to if all he wants to build is a space to live in? Certainly not to an artist, whose is far from practical economic, social, ecological, etc. considerations. Because art is purpose-free, the architects are useless! This explains why architecture is in demand for prestige buildings only, and why architects are little by little ousted from the construction market.

Why, then, is there no communication between architects and public?

Because art needs no justification. Thanks to their artist status, architects can conveniently get around explaining their choices. They refuse to talk about what they do and become arrogant. And considering a building that somebody else pays for as a personal creation instead of a useful response to needs is really arrogant!

Architecture is by nature a communication discipline. Isn't our main job to translate social language into a spatial one? Is justifying our projects not what we were taught in school? But what this usually comes down to is communication behind closed doors and in a closed circuit: architects talking with other architects about architecture! The problem is that the amount of work for architects is di-

rectly linked to the good relations between them and the public. Without clients, there are no more architects! And on the day when we will possibly be re-appreciated for the forgotten useful services provided by our discipline, it might turn out that there are no architects left to provide them.

The whole issue of professional arrogance is in fact a matter of communication, and the future of the profession depends on it. Architects need to say what they really do and how they do it.

Architecture schools and professional organizations should have a vital interest to maintain and defend an image of the profession that corresponds to reality and is not a phantasm (even if a cherished one). We surely will have to rethink our image, but we also need to communicate it effectively.

Laurent Guidetti
tribu'architecture, Lausanne

What do you stand for?

I don't really like architects! There are too many original creators, experts and consultants among us. We talk all the time about form and space. Every time I attend architects' meetings everybody agrees on how important we are for the city and how valuable our work is for its history, identity, image, for society in general, for the construction industry and so on and so forth. But we always end up speaking about shapes and volumes. I can see that in places where ecology is more trendy one can even invoke architecture as a way to fight global warming, pollution, or deforestation. In my country, architects consider themselves as "real professionals" if they succeed to use a modernistic style as an antidote against their clients' bad taste and, according to the national exhibitions of the last 15 years, if you manage to do that you will definitely get an award.

I always feel slightly uncomfortable when these arguments are used to demand more power over the city, more laws and regulations for "proper" architecture. It is

not only that mumbo-jumbo talk of the importance of image; it is that, in making our demands, we always turn to the people in power. Going public is on the agenda only when we speak about educating an incompetent public unable to understand the value of our work. Again, public talks are about form; apparently the main problem of my city is the lack of spatial coherence (yes, the towers that ruin the city skyline should be grouped together, so they will form an urban composition!) and about social progress in the form of support for the sacred private investments (we lack office spaces! without that, Romania won't develop!). Not a word about the public itself, nor about the rest of society, the ones that do not invest.

But maybe there is no public for architecture, unless we consider our clients as public. Or maybe there is a public only for public buildings. Though I think that in my case, what I do should be a public issue. The problem I address is extreme poverty.

The "fast, cheap, non-aesthetic" social housing project of Dorohoi is so simple, so "non-architecture" that it can be easily described without images: a long straight barrack on a wooden structure finished with PVC siding, housing three-room apartments of 52 square meters each, four in a row, using the simplest scheme possible. It was presented in exhibitions, published in a book, presented at various conferences, on TV and in a number of reviews. But why that? Nobody cares about barracks!

Well, the catch is that the cost of one apartment is 13,400 Euros, which means that for an investment of 500,000 Euros, 196 people can be housed in decent conditions in 36 apartments. This makes it around 2,500 Euros per person, and that was the kind of statement that I thought should be publicized. In the case of this type of "architectural object", the question was not how to present it to the public but why?

With less then 500 social housing units built by the government per year at "European standards" and almost at European prices, we won't solve the problems of the one million people, mostly Roma, living in shacks. We need cheap but decent houses; we need to legalize informal settlements. In absolute terms, the prices of Dorohoi are not much of an achievement in a regular poverty neighbourhood, where this is the top price for an informal house, but it was several times cheaper than the usual social housing investment.

Among architects now I am one of "the guys with the gypsies". There are very few of us involved in this and the award received for our study about extreme poverty did not help much to make the problem move up on the public agenda (alas, Mr. Sarkozy did more!), maybe because we don't stand for "good quality of design" i.e. "nicely composed volumes 15% more expensive then a compact form" or for "technical excellence" i.e. "a lot of concrete and useless metallic parts". We just stand for decent living conditions. What do you stand for?

Cătălin Berescu
architect, Bucharest

Internet platforms

Without having an Internet presence, you do not exist. Therefore, the first thing for architects starting their own practice is going online with their own website. Still, this alone is not enough. 52% of the practices participating in the Wonderland survey #3 are present in some way on an architecture-related Internet platform. The advantage: a much wider reach. Find here an overview of the most important architecture-related domains in the EU.

Countries	Platforms	Self-Definition	Language	For free?	How to enter?
AT–Austria	www.nextroom.at	Architecture from Europe, based on a rich database of buildings, pictures and texts, including daily press reviews	de	yes	Send project information by using the nextroom data sheet; various architecture institutions are responsible for the selection of the published projects
	www.austria-architects.com	Austrian section of world-architects.com; profiles of selected architects	de, en	no	
BE–Belgium	www.belgium-architects.com	Belgian section of world-architects.com	fr, en, nl	no	
BG – Bulgaria	www.citybuild.bg	Contemporary design and architecture	bg		
CH–Switzerland	www.vitruvio.ch	Information about architecture from primitive to contemporary	it	yes	Get selected by the editorial team
	www.arch-forum.ch	Platform for information and ideas exchange, with the possibility for any architect to set up an own webpage within the site and to be listed in the database	de		Registration required
CZ– Czech Republic	www.archiweb.cz	Daily updated information about Czech and world architecture. Offers architects an opportunity to present their work and products	cs, en	no	Contact via archiweb@archiweb.cz
	www.earch.cz		cs		
	www.asb-portal.cz	Internet platform for architecture, building industry and civil engineering in Czech Republic.	cs	no	Contact via asbporta@jagamedia.cz
DE–Germany	www.baunetz.de	Daily updates for the whole professional sector: news, specialized know-how, product news, legal information, etc.	de	yes, except for special services	Registration by e-mail at Kundenservice@BauNetz.de
	www.competitionline.de	Competition briefs and results from all over Europe, including architects search engine	de, en	no	Registration is free, subscription required to use the whole content
	www.arcguide.de	News, competitions, products reviews, blogs; offering architects and students a possibility for self-presentation	de	yes	Registration required
	www.archinform.net	Database of more than 14,000 international projects, mostly architecture of the 20th and 21st century	de, en, fr, es, it	yes	Proposals for publication by e-mail. Only projects published at least once in the specialized press will be considered
	www.german-architects.com	German section of world-architects.com	de, en		Registration required
	www.marlowes.de	marlowes – eMagazin about architecture and city	de	yes	
GR–Greece	www.greekarchitects.gr	Web magazine and architectural portal	el, en	yes	Similar selection criteria as for any other magazine
ES–Spain	www.plataformaarquitectura.cl		es, en		
FI–Finland	www.scandinavian-architects.com	Scandinavian section of world-architects.com	en, fi, dk, no, sv		
	www.safa.fi	Homepage of the Finnish Association of Architects	fi, sv, en		
	www.atl.fi	Homepage of the Association of Finnish Architects' Offices (ATL) with an office finder tool	fi, en		
FR–France	www.batiactu.com	Information about professionals in the construction industry	fr		
GB–United Kingdom	www.architecture.com	Portal of the Royal Institute of British Architects	en	yes	Only for members of the Royal Institute of British Architects
HR–Croatia	www.dezeen.com	Architecture and design magazine	en		
	www.d-a-z.hr	Webpage of Zagreb Architectural Association (DAZ); the site offers possibilities to showcase projects, built objects, research, or to write one's own column	sh	yes	Only for the members of the association

Country	Website	Description	Language	Registration required	Notes
HU–Hungary	www.epiteszforum.hu	Daily updated architectural portal	hu		Approx. 5 new items per day, open to nearly everything (more content, more visitors)
	www.epitesz.lap.hu		hu		
	www.epulettar.hu		hu		
IE–Ireland	www.ria.ie	Webpage of the Royal Irish Academy	en		Registration required
IT–Italy	www.italian-architects.com	Italian section of world-architects.com	it		
	www.architettura.it	Provides latest news about Italian and international architecture, competitions, events and a database	it		Choose between free or paid subscription
	www.europaconcorsi.com	Competitions, architecture and design	it		
	www.newitalianblood.com	An interactive architecture, landscape and design network that allows self-presentation (prizes, competitions, projects, ideas and texts)	en, it	yes	No editorial interference
LU–Luxemburg	www.oai.lu	Homepage of the Chamber of Architects	fr	no	
LV–Latvia	www.a4d.lv	Webpage about architecture	lv	yes	Everybody is welcome to publish their project
MT–Malta	kamratalperiti.org	Homepage of the Chamber of Architects	en		
NL–Netherlands	www.architectenweb.nl	Webpage about architecture including news, a discussion forum, media information and a data base	nl	no	
PL–Poland	www.ronet.pl	Webpage for architects to present their work	pl	yes	No other criteria than taking part in a competition
	www.architektura-murator.pl	Homepage and platform of the main architectural magazine Architektura-Murator	en, pl	yes	As in any other magazine
PT–Portugal	www.arquitectos.pt	Homepage of the Ordem dos Arquitectos	pt		
	www.arquitectura.pt	Discussion forum	pt	yes	Registration required
SE–Sweden	www.arkitekt.se	Homepage of the Swedish Association of Architects	en, se		
	www.trajekt.org	Discussion forum for information about architectural events, critical thought and regional planning	sl	yes	
SI–Slovenia	www.drustvo-dal.si	Homepage of the Slovene Architectural Association	sl	yes	Sometimes projects are published, but only from members of the association
	www.arhiforum.si	Homepage of the Chamber of Architects; publishes competitions and winning projects	en, sl	yes	
SK–Slovakia	www.komarch.sk	Homepage of the Slovak Association of Architects	sk	yes	Architects may submit entries to the "virtual gallery" of projects; selection is made by editor-in-chief Matus Janota; webadmin@archinet.sk
TR–Turkey	www.arkitera.com	Homepage of the Arkitera Architecture Centre; information on new projects both local and international, student projects, competition projects a.o. Online database of Turkish architecture AMV "arkitera architecture database"	en, tr	yes	Registration required for some sections
EU–Europe	www.mimoa.eu	MIMOA offers complete information on how to find and visit popular Modern Architecture in real life	en	yes	
Worldwide	www.archdaily.com	ArchDaily serves as architects' main source for tools, information and inspiration	en	yes	As a registered user you can publish your own projects

Countries in detail

Jānis Lejnieks, Riga, Latvia

LATVIANS HESITATE TO GO PUBLIC

How do Latvian architects feel about going public, compared to Westerners who are traditionally more familiar with putting together press packages and maybe are more confident that what was produced is worth being published, even unfinished projects, studies or concepts? The main difference is that our architects mainly regard it as "self-advertising" and hence are reluctant to send material to magazines. They are very busy; there is no unemployment among architects, and so there is little need for publicizing to get commissions.

On the other hand, corporate clients tend to see architectural designs commissioned by them as business materials and often prohibit publication. Similar cases apply to private clients who usually insist on the privacy of their houses and apartments. The situation has improved, at least as far as public buildings are concerned, with the establishment of the Riga Urban Planning Office in 2006 where designs and concepts discussed by the Board are open to the mass media.

From the late nineties, a few foreign offices have entered the Latvian market, mostly on a basis of collaboration with local architects. At the same time, there are a number of Latvia-based architectural practices that work in Russia.

The main event, which provides an opportunity for architects to get in the headlines of dailies and TV news, is the Annual Award of the Latvian Association of Architects, presented every year in spring for more than a decade now. For young offices, this may be a stepping stone to more public attention.

Another road to publicity is prestigious state-commissioned cultural buildings as were completed in recent years, such as the Latvian National Library, designed by Latvian-born American Gunnar Birkerts in Riga, or the "Great Amber" concert hall in Liepaja, designed by Austrian architect Volker Giencke. Such projects are strongly supported by the Minister of Culture and can be sure to receive good publicity.

By contrast, small and less conspicuous buildings remain largely unknown. In the last years, the bulk of built projects were supermarkets and housing, which are frequently presented in real-estate magazines and international web platforms, though architects mostly go unmentioned and stay anonymous in these publications. One exception is the bi-monthly "Latvijas Architektūra" magazine, first published in 1938 and relaunched after the 50-year Soviet hiatus, featuring interviews with foreign architects and reports from abroad.

Łukasz Wojciechowski, VROA!, Wrocław, Poland

Self-promotion, an inevitable task of the modern architect, is often humiliating and brings architects to pitiful acts. The desperate striving for attention implies the use of techniques that have their origins in advertising – which inevitably brings architects to use shortcuts, reducing complex and controversial issues to easy slogans and, even worse, glossy images. Architects in Poland are no exception to this global tendency.

Because popular media in Poland are not very interested in newly emerging architecture unless it is very catchy, big, corrupted or collapsing, rising stars mostly have to be satisfied with the attention of professional journals or very few art magazines. The architectural profession is still hermetic in Poland and the constructive public debate on urban space is not a common thing. Of course there are some exceptions – offices that force media attention by coming up with intentional projects – but such an approach is very rare. Polish architects not commissioning PR specialists mostly depend on their own abilities of self promotion – creating business connections or just taking parts in competitions. Thus – as a chance to build for the rookies not knowing the market – competitions can gain the respect of clients and fellow-architects and maybe even get some popular media attention if the building is somehow spectacular enough. But striving for spectacular effects often implies shortcut thinking.

Looking at Polish architectural scene which has been revived with more and more competitions – which of course is a perfect situation for young designers –, one can very clearly see a gap between what could be a possible opportunity and the proposed images. The gap seems to be the lack of any research concerning social or programmatic issues. Looking at published concepts, one finds that the vast majority of the designs is characterized by the use of common clichés and the adopting of repetitive patterns that are only carefully visualized – thus architecture becomes a hollow shell. The dummies

represent and even justify architectural projects and are a common 'shortcut self-promotion tool', whether it is the buildings themselves or people pasted in the images.

Examples of this come from the best – it is enough to look at the publications of the Mirador building in Madrid by MVRDV, where the social space is depicted full of happy people who on a second glance appear to be living models: creating an artificial social effect is used to help promoting the groundbreaking idea. But is it possible for Photoshop-pasted-people to become "The Purple Rose of Cairo" characters?

The real risk of such short term commercial strategies is to banalize architecture, as has already happened with private-house design in Poland. The idea of the house has been trivialized by the catalogues of typical projects sold at newsstands, and thus a canon was established – now the dream house is as much of a commonplace as the kitschy painting of a belling stag on the living-room wall inside.

Skipping social issues in the pursuit of commercial effect brings people to believe architecture is about images. Analyzing even the best Polish competition concepts, one can hardly find anything but a rational (or mechanical) approach to design and program. The organizational structure of space – the factor that begs to be constantly researched and revived – is an axiom. The competitions are often 'shortcut beauty contests' where spatial solutions are rather treated as a technical issue of how to put it together than as opportunities to redefine and rediscover potentials.

If it comes to the young blood – Polish architects are no exception in absorbing the ideas of the world's fanciest architectures. There is nothing wrong with learning from the best, but here come the dummies – clones of the images neatly placed on competition panels are mostly shortcuts that skip any attempt to come to a real understanding of the very core of the originals.

///////// PR IN RUSSIA: MARKET = PUBLIC /////////////////////////////////

Paul Abelsky, Moscow, Russia

When Don-Stroy, one of Moscow's biggest private developers at the time, set out in 2001 to promote Triumph-Palace, its then still projected wedding-cake complex, meanwhile Europe's tallest residential building, the company forged an impressive Western-style advertising campaign spun in a distinctly Russian way. Modeled on the Stalin-era Art-Deco high-rises that ring the center of Moscow, Triumph-Palace was publicized using tongue-in-cheek brochures made to resemble top-secret typewritten documents and radio commercials that poked fun at Western broadcasts of the Cold War. Now that advertising extends to all spheres of life in Russia, architectural projects have become subject to the same treatment. Only in the last several years has design been allowed to speak for itself, allowing lesser known but resourceful young architects to compete for sought-after commissions.

The fundamental rules of Russia's architecture and construction business started shifting in the late 1980s,

but the more outward appearances changed, the more the underlying basic constraints remained the same. Rigid government control, extensive bureaucracy, and the paramount importance of personal connections continued to drive the implementation of new projects. In the pursuit of quick profits, not much thought was given to design matters. Architects who were well-connected with government institutions and contractors enjoyed unwarranted advantages, cutting out the younger generation looking for a professional foothold. But the principal difference to Western practice is that open design competitions are still a rarity, and the few contests held in recent years were conducted under shadowy circumstances and often with predetermined results.

From 2003, the outlook on the part of developers and realtors started to change. A construction boom in many of the large cities has saturated the market, and quality design is now seen as a distinguishing mark which may also boost the project's commercial appeal and possibilities. While the importance of personal connections has not diminished, and local officials continue to exercise undue control over tenders and permits, a climate of greater architectural openness has created new opportunities for smaller design firms outside the closed circle of the establishment.

For all of the existing checks and regulations in Russia, the brisk pace of the construction business has brought a wealth of possibilities to enterprising firms. BuroMoscow, founded by a team of young Russian and Western architects, many of them OMA graduates, has been among those who were able to capitalize on the situation: just over a year into its existence, the firm completed its first project, creating a patterned, animated facade for a suburban residential block, whose novelty and cost-effectiveness prompted the developer to replicate it in other projects.

Another Moscow-based group, who call themselves Iced Architects, provides an even more revealing case study in self-promotion at such a volatile and promising time in Russian architecture. The firm has been at the forefront of Moscow's design scene for years. Endemic distrust of unproven firms, however, remained a constant challenge; so Iced Architects joined a government-run urban planning agency as consultants while preserving their creative autonomy. This framework allowed them both to gain experience and to win the confidence of influential developers. Ilya Voznesensky, the group's longtime leader, says some of their more utopian ideas were first published as concept designs in architecture magazines before interested investors approached them with construction proposals. The most famous project was a private mansion in central Moscow, built in the shape of a Fabergé Egg held up by spiraling Baroque volutes. Although innovative designs are drawing more attention from Russia's movers and shakers, allowing younger architects to compete with the established firms, some of the more outlandish projects still appear to be beyond market acceptance: the completed egg-shaped house was looking for a buyer for a long time.

"In general, clients are interested in our network of western consultants and suppliers and in our more analytical than artistic approach to projects," said Andreas Huhn, one of the firm's co-founders. "The building market is rather new, and it takes a big effort to explain the difference between 'good' and 'bad.' Once you managed to produce a result that stands out in quality, you get a lot of offers coming in."

Mária Topoľanská, Prague, Czech Republic

Doing architecture in Slovakia is still not a question of going public. The opinion is still very strong that what counts is the architect's built work and relations with clients (not so much public impact by publicizing one's work).

Take the situation as it is: there is a more or less limited set of twenty – my personal estimation – architects and teams in architectural offices who regularly produce architecture that meets the quality standards for being published in the two key architectural magazines – the PROJEKT Review of Architecture, edited by the domestic association of architects, and its private-owned counterpart, ARCH magazine on architecture and other culture. Then, there is an equally limited set of about fifteen architectural critics and reviewers who write about architecture produced in Slovakia by the first set of people in one of the two magazines on a monthly or bi-monthly basis. Most of the people know one another, and in many cases the two sets mingle.

It is highly improbable for an architect doing above-average architecture to starve for being published in Slovakia – this village community works on a principle that somehow is the opposite of public relations: the paradoxical thing is the minimum of pressure that architects put on the architectural media to get their work published. Architects – also the young! – stay passive in the process; it is the magazines that become active, and the teams of editors plus external writers hunt the limited ground for plans and photos of reasonably good architecture. Rarely, more thorough fieldwork is needed to discover new architecture, given that, in the rather small local architectural community, information quickly spreads by word-of-mouth and through personal connections. Magazines seldom have a chance to discover some unknown quality architecture or architect, and there only very few emerging architects that provoke the scene by having their new works published.

It is not only that architects remain inactive (the usual thing is not to provide editor's offices with material about their work); once their latest works receives some attention they often are even difficult to convince to go public with their work and cooperate on it. Architectural writers and publishers almost play the role of talent scouts in hunting for and portraying new faces and new stuff, in order to expand the range of publishable architecture and architects. Probably, architecture magazines provide the sufficient PR for architects who wait to be discovered without having any PR strategy of their own. The only way to open this closed circle of private personal connections to greater publicity is by widening the perspective. This means waiting until architects will want to go public on a larger than the Slovak scale (e.g. European A10, Czech or Austrian architecture media) and until foreign magazines will start to take more interest in the local architectural production.

Gonzalo Herrero Delicado, London, United Kingdom

When asked how they feel about PR, most Spanish architecture practices answered that they didn't really care about it, that it was something expensive if done properly and and not a priority on their agenda. They don't spend much time on the issue, but instead try to produce good architecture, hoping that media attention and public recognition will follow. As for emerging architects, only a handful of them have ever hired a professional photographer and prepared a press package, and almost none have commissioned a PR agency to run their communications. Leaving aside the question of affordability, the truth is that younger architects are much more aware of the value of PR than most established ones. They understand that going public is the only chance for them get commissions. Word of mouth and business card exchanges are the most powerful tools today.

However, younger architects are finding new tools for spreading their word in social media. Instagram, Facebook, and to a lesser degree also Twitter are most popular among the younger generations. Architecture blogs are now dead, and only a few international websites like Dezeen and Archdaily have a real impact in the Spanish context. Print media is also a thing of the past,

and after the 2008 financial crisis, only a few periodicals have survived. AV (Arquitectura Viva) and El Croquis are the only significant architecture magazines to be found at bookshops and newsstands. On the other hand, interior design titles are booming as refurbishments and small residential project commissions grow. Even lifestyle and trend magazines such as the Spanish editions of T magazine, Vanity Fair and Harper's Bazaar have started regularly covering architecture-related topics, which opens a new door for emerging architects.

Guido Incerti, nEmoGruppo Architetti, Florence, Italy

For some years now, a new creative task has occupied the minds and organization of Italian and European young architects' studios. What is becoming an increasing necessity, apart from research and the realization of projects, is to provide a media image for the studio, a communication strategy for its ideas and architectures, which exists independently of the architectural work proper.

Today, whilst continuing to take part in architecture competitions – in a country where, for under-40s, these are few and far between – and to get work in traditional ways, young architects in Italy have to perform a whole series of new tasks, such as developing a consistent corporate design for the studio, perfecting workflows, compiling mailing lists, and building the now indispensable websites.

The decisive factor for PR architecture is the importance of the media, whether it is the Internet or specialist magazines.

In Italy, it is mostly in the Internet where new names are launched. Specialist magazines, which usually confine themselves to featuring built projects and presentable front-cover names, are in fact the domain of already familiar faces, very foreign-oriented and quite slow in responding to the new. There are, of course, exceptions, such as the Spanish Actar, always on the lookout for novelties, and not just on the Iberian Peninsula, the Giornale dell'architettura as well as publications that are less specialist but more open to social dynamics, including supplements to daily papers such as CasAmica of the Corriere della Sera and D-Casa and D-Donna of the Repubblica, which often feature the "non-institutional" projects of young studios.

On the Internet, there is Arch'it, by Marco Brizzi, Luigi Prestinenza Pugliesi's Press Letter, the new "up-and-coming" section of Europaconcorsi and New Italian Blood.

Apart from publishing projects, these groups and institutions frequently organize exhibitions and conferences that provide a platform for the under-40 generation.

What young studios have to do, though – at least initially when they do not have many realized projects to their name –, is trying to get through to the public, using ways that are not at all foreign to the world of architecture, however remote they may seem from the system of competitions, standard professional practices, and the usual channels of information.

So, what we see from them is self-organized architecture-related cultural events, self-built and self-financed temporary installations, generally in abandoned and neglected urban zones which are thus transformed into places to meet, discuss, swap ideas, create networks and working collectives, sometimes international, thanks to knowledge and experience gained in the Erasmus program; a self-confident revolution, which finds first built expression in these emergent realities.

The aim of events originating in this way is to create a link – thought-provoking rather than "commercial" – with the public and political world, to demonstrate the often hidden potentials of the new studios and the new energies they are able to release; energies that are in fact needed for the renewal, cultural and otherwise, of our administrative institutions, faculties and cities.

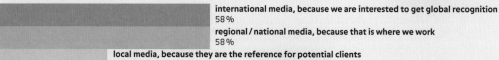
WHERE TO GO PUBLIC

Our main goal is to get coverage in ...

international media, because we are interested to get global recognition
58 %

regional / national media, because that is where we work
58 %

local media, because they are the reference for potential clients
30 %

Whatever, we do not have preferences
23 %

58 % are interested in more global recognition

The public we are trying to reach is ...

- specialized public / fellow architects – only they understand what we are talking about
- the general public – everyone could be our next client
- other industry professionals as developers and investors – we need big clients
- unspecified; we do not know our target group and they do not know us

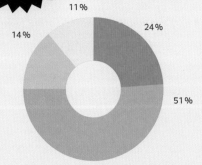

11 %
24 %
14 %
51 %

HARD FACTORS

324 commissions were gained thanks to PR activities by 37 practices answering this question, an average of 8.8 commissions per practice.

Where to invest if you are looking for commissions?

Webpage and publications are, according to our results, the most successful media to get work, each accounting for about one third of total incoming commissions.

Incoming commission resulted from ...

participation in exhibitions
16 %

office brochures
13 %

web pages
34 %

publications
33 %

other PR presence
4 %

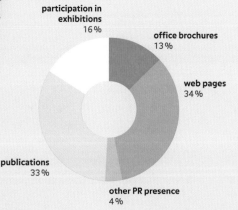

Source: Wonderland #3 Survey – by SHARE architects, compiled 2006

SOFT FACTORS

Which formats are the most effective to get your practice / your work known?

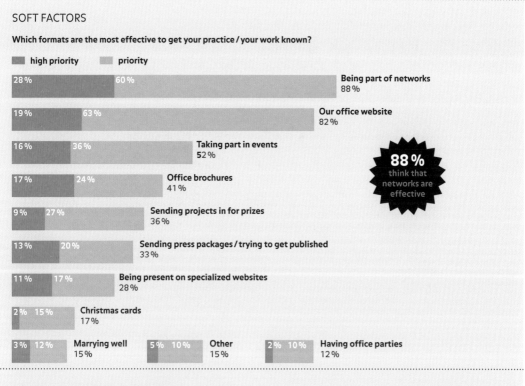

■ high priority   ■ priority

| 28 % | 60 % | Being part of networks 88 % |

| 19 % | 63 % | Our office website 82 % |

| 16 % | 36 % | Taking part in events 52 % |

| 17 % | 24 % | Office brochures 41 % |

| 9 % | 27 % | Sending projects in for prizes 36 % |

| 13 % | 20 % | Sending press packages / trying to get published 33 % |

| 11 % | 17 % | Being present on specialized websites 28 % |

| 2 % | 15 % | Christmas cards 17 % |

| 3 % | 12 % | Marrying well 15 % | | 5 % | 10 % | Other 15 % | | 2 % | 10 % | Having office parties 12 % |

88 % think that networks are effective

COLLECTIVES OR INDIVIDUALS

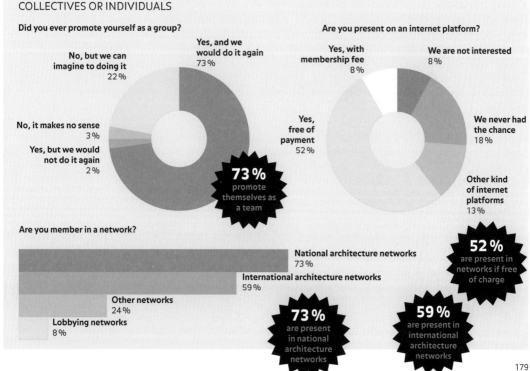

Did you ever promote yourself as a group?

No, but we can imagine to doing it 22 %

Yes, and we would do it again 73 %

No, it makes no sense 3 %

Yes, but we would not do it again 2 %

73 % promote themselves as a team

Are you present on an internet platform?

Yes, with membership fee 8 %

We are not interested 8 %

Yes, free of payment 52 %

We never had the chance 18 %

Other kind of internet platforms 13 %

52 % are present in networks if free of charge

Are you member in a network?

National architecture networks 73 %

International architecture networks 59 %

Other networks 24 %

Lobbying networks 8 %

73 % are present in national architecture networks

59 % are present in international architecture networks

Source: Wonderland #3 Survey # by SHARE architects, compiled 2008

SELFLESS SELF-PROMOTION

Most publicity in architecture can be seen as veiled or not-so-veiled self-promotion. This is not a criticism, but just an observation. However, not all opinion-making architects do so first and foremost to garner attention for their latest building or project. Not all PR need serve a direct, personal interest as its primary goal. There is also such a thing as "selfless publicity", in which an architect can (potentially, but not necessarily, using his/her own work as a starting point) draw attention to an issue of social, economic, ecological or political significance. A practically inescapable side effect of altruism is that the person calling for this kind of attention is not only perceived as having a higher moral fiber, but can also feel morally better. The world needs more of this selfless publicity.

There are many projects by architects engaged in promoting human quality of life where this is now in short supply, or making the world a better place for future generations, or helping to slow down the deterioration of the environment. This is something that often (all too often) happens outside of the public eye, and the media usually pays little attention to. This may be partly due to the modesty of those who devote themselves to such efforts, but in many cases it may also have to do with the lack of glamour. Projects of this type are not defined by the typical iconic building that fills the pages of every architectural journal. If buildings are involved at all they are much more likely to be low-tech and no-budget than the other extreme. And in some cases, the social factor – process and participation – is more important than the built result. As one example, in Romania, Cătălin Berescu is devoting himself to helping the Roma with publications to bring attention to the social and societal situation of this misunderstood people, and projects to actively improve their often deplorable living conditions by providing designs for do-it-yourself construction and extremely low-cost "catalogue construction" (modular housing). Because of the low glamour factor of his architecture, few journals give attention to his work, and even fewer outside Romania. And architects such as Berescu lack the star power to make people sit up and take notice of a design. (One notable exception is Shigeru Ban, who designed simple, lightweight emergency structures of cardboard and milk crates for earthquake-struck Kobe in Japan. His stature as an architect led to his architecturally refined emergency structures being published in journals and exhibited as models at leading architectural exhibitions).

The modest status of most altruistic designers makes it difficult to bring their essential designs forth from the background, where they are now frequently found, and shift them to the center of public attention. Doing good is something that anyone willing to make the effort can do, and the more people, the better. But in fact, it could, and perhaps should, be from the ranks of the traveling circus of superstar architects that an individual steps up and uses his or her personal fame and high profile to make a larger-than-life contribution. Beyond bringing attention to his or her own attention-grabbing projects, such an architect could raise serious issues, even through Prada T-shirts if necessary, in the same way that the glitterati have lent their efforts with much publicity, and much success, to issues such as a boycott on blood diamonds or the fight against AIDS, poverty and hunger. And by doing so, star architects, just like those stars, would also be helping themselves. ▰

Text by Hans Ibelings, Montreal/Toronto, Canada

getting specialized

why
specialize

what
to
specialize
in

how
to
specialize

#4

SPECIALIZED EDUCATION LANDSCAPE IN EUROPE

How specialized is the architecture profession? Our map, based on an extensive (but by no means complete) Internet research exercise, shows the distribution of specialized education courses – masters programs as well as postgraduate courses – throughout Europe.

We listed a total of **328 courses** in **30 countries**. **Sustainability** on different scales **(49 courses)** is the focus in the largest number of courses. **Urbanism (44 courses)** comes second. This is not surprising considering that urbanism is its own professional field rather than a specialization for architects.
Geographically, the highest number of courses in our list are to be found in **United Kingdom (138)**, where the bachelor-master system has been in place long before other EU countries.

Number of specialized courses per country

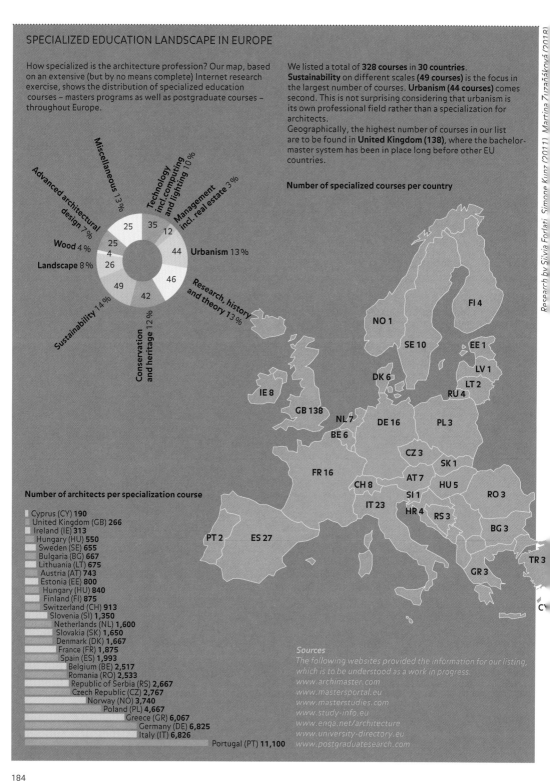

Donut chart (Number of specialized courses):
- Miscellaneous 13 % — 25
- Technology incl. computing and lighting 10 % — 35
- Management incl. real estate 3 % — 12
- Urbanism 13 % — 44
- Research, history and theory 13 % — 46
- Conservation and heritage 12 % — 42
- Sustainability 14 % — 49
- Landscape 8 % — 26
- Wood 4 % — 4
- Advanced architectural design 7 % — 25

Map labels:
FI 4, NO 1, SE 10, EE 1, LV 1, LT 2, RU 4, DK 6, IE 8, GB 138, NL 7, DE 16, PL 3, BE 6, CZ 3, SK 1, FR 16, AT 7, HU 5, RO 3, CH 8, SI 1, HR 4, RS 3, BG 3, IT 23, HR 4, TR 3, GR 3, PT 2, ES 27, CY

Number of architects per specialization course

- Cyprus (CY) **190**
- United Kingdom (GB) **266**
- Ireland (IE) **313**
- Hungary (HU) **550**
- Sweden (SE) **655**
- Bulgaria (BG) **667**
- Lithuania (LT) **675**
- Austria (AT) **743**
- Estonia (EE) **800**
- Hungary (HU) **840**
- Finland (FI) **875**
- Switzerland (CH) **913**
- Slovenia (SI) **1,350**
- Netherlands (NL) **1,600**
- Slovakia (SK) **1,650**
- Denmark (DK) **1,667**
- France (FR) **1,875**
- Spain (ES) **1,993**
- Belgium (BE) **2,517**
- Romania (RO) **2,533**
- Republic of Serbia (RS) **2,667**
- Czech Republic (CZ) **2,767**
- Norway (NO) **3,740**
- Poland (PL) **4,667**
- Greece (GR) **6,067**
- Germany (DE) **6,825**
- Italy (IT) **6,826**
- Portugal (PT) **11,100**

Research by Silvia Forlati, Simone Kunz (2011), Martina Zuzáňáková (2018)

Sources
The following websites provided the information for our listing, which is to be understood as a work in progress.
www.archimaster.com
www.mastersportal.eu
www.masterstudies.com
www.study-info.eu
www.enqa.net/architecture
www.university-directory.eu
www.postgraduatesearch.com

getting specialized

Sure he does exist, the generalist among architects, the one who does each and everything, from furniture designs to single-family houses to large construction sites. Not to forget the tendering and site supervision, which he likewise does himself, provided he runs a big enough office. However, to stand one's ground as a small office in competition with the other architects, it may be an advantage to specialize in a particular type of task, a special area within architecture, or only a specific approach to a task. This unique selling proposition helps sharpen an individual profile, stand out amongst others, and prepare better for the changing role of the architect in the future.

With 'Getting Specialized', we draw a realistic counter-image to the universalist know-all do-all architect. The question we ask at the beginning is: 'Why specialize? ' When architects think about specialization, it is always combined with a fear that this might turn out to be a dead end. Yet much depends on what we understand by specialization: this section shows that contemporary specialization has many different dimensions to it and should rather be understood as an opportunity and not a constraint.

In the second section, 'What to specialize in?', we have traced the paths and motives of the particular specialization of fourteen selected teams. We have come to notice, though, that traditional areas of architectural specialization, such as the ones based on building typologies, are not to be found in our research sample. What works is a multidimensional approach which combines specific fields of work with specific ways of developing the project or specific attributes of the final product offered to the client.

Which leaves the question of 'How to specialize?' A specialization may be actively pursued or deliberately chosen. But sometimes it also develops by accident or even inadvertently through an assigned task or won competition. Once one has consciously decided to concentrate on a particular area within architecture, there is a multitude of postgraduate studies to choose from. But note: taking an individual educational path may be just as successful as relying on traditional education institutions. ⬤

are **architects-only teams** (12 of 14 practices)

operate **between architecture and other fields** (11 of 14)

consider **learning by doing** an important source of its expertise (12 of 14)

work at least for 50 % of the projects **in their selected field of expertise** (11 of 14)

have **not** developed its specialization through **a top-down strategy** (13 of 14)

consider specialization an **advantage** (11 of 14)

see specialization as **only one possible way to go** , but not as the future of architectural practice in general (12 of 14)

Source: Wonderland #4 Survey – by SHARE architects, 2010

See reality check #4 / page 194

why specialize

In an increasingly competitive world, specialization may give you the edge you need to get enough work. Still, the ancient idea of the architect as a generalist has not altogether lost its lustre, even if the long-term perspective may still be an open question. Fast-changing conditions require flexibility, and this perhaps is more of a generalist quality.

QUALIFICATION REQUIREMENTS FOR ARCHITECTS

The discussion about generalism versus specialization in one's professional field always needs to be viewed in the context of the types of employment, fields of activity, and educational offerings available. In the following, Sigrid Mannsberger-Nindl takes an outside look at architectural education in relation to the traditional role of the architect.

The demand for a more generalist or specialized education of job-seekers, which is determined by the labor market, is always related to factors such as company size or corporate orientation.

The job description of the architect as a generalist has meanwhile given way to that of an interdisciplinary mediator in an interface position or of a specialized service provider. Moreover, architects today are also faced with the challenge of operating nationally and, in part, internationally: relevant in this respect are increasing internationalization and transnational networking of cooperation partners; projects are jointly developed and, once financing is provided, implemented. Regarding the requirements profile for architects, it is not only artistic-creative and technical skills, but also sociological, organizational, economic and socio-communicative capabilities that are expected from them. At the professional level, aspects such as technological innovation or the applicable legal framework need to be taken into account, which all makes a broad range of knowledge essential. It should be considered if a generalist qualification profile is still possible or desirable at all against this backdrop.

Text by Sigrid Mannsberger-Nindl, 3s Unternehmensberatung, Vienna, Austria

However, against the background of current and future labor market requirements the question remains whether a generalist or a specialized educational approach provides better job perspectives. Bachelor programs are usually associated with a more generalist-oriented education, which is then deepened in a master program; specialization is also possible by focusing study or research interests. But what conditions are in place now that would make a generalist or specialized architectural education more advantageous? Is generalist education still possible at all? While a generalist approach usually allows a wider field of professional activity, one can gain advantages on the job market by specializing in concrete areas of competence. By contrast, interface positions particularly call for interdisciplinary knowledge, i.e., the ability to act as a liaison between different departments or professionals.

Teaching basics vs. specialization in Bologna-style tertiary education

Since the fundamental change of the educational landscape to the bachelor-master system under the Bologna Process for the creation of a unified European Higher Education Area, the discussion about generalization versus specialization in education has been omnipresent.[1] With the introduction of a three-cycle modularized system of study, the first stage is a bachelor course, which teaches the basics of a given field of knowledge. By contrast, master studies are, depending on the country and the implementation of the Bologna Process, characterized by greater research or professional orientation.[2] Consecutive master studies should – as in the case of architecture – build upon knowledge acquired in the bachelor study and enable the focusing of study interests. As the third of the three stages, a doctorate, or Ph.D. program offers the option of a research-oriented deepening of knowledge and specialization. One goal of the Bologna reforms was to improve the international mobility of students and graduates. Mutual recognition of educational programs through the 'European Credit Transfer System' (ECTS) also contributes to this.

Architect's job description and field of activity

The job description of architects can be summarized in the most general terms as follows: "Architects design and plan buildings of all types (residential, office, industrial, or administration buildings, hospitals, senior citizen residences, museums, railway stations, etc.). If they receive the contract for a building project, they assume responsibility for the detail planning, the tendering of the construction work and the commissioning of construction companies (construction supervision), for cost controlling and project accounting. In addition to the erecting of buildings, architectural tasks also include maintenance and upgrading of the existent building structures (e.g., by adaptation and refurbishment, monument conservation), as well as the spatial planning, traffic planning and urban planning (creation of metropolitan area concepts)".[3]

In keeping with this description, the qualification of bachelor and master graduates in architecture, as summarized, for example, on the website of the Vienna University of Technology, includes "the analysis and specification of construction and planning tasks, drafting and designing, presenting and conveying planning-relevant information as well as the management of planning and implementation procedures".

This job description entails different employment possibilities, for instance, as an employee in architecture offices or as a self-employed civil engineer, also in group offices. Further employment possibilities offered are, e.g., jobs in planning companies, planning and building offices of public developers.

At the beginning of their careers, architecture graduates will have to reckon with temporary or atypical employment conditions; by contrast, permanent jobs are rare, not least because of the typical project-orientation of the profession. Smaller offices and one-person companies are becoming more and more common. Self-employed architects, however, are often confronted with a precarious income situation, unclear career chances, and high workloads.

The job description of architects has changed, compared to an earlier generalist-oriented perspective: architects are mostly seen as specific service providers who are no longer commissioned with full projects, from draft to implementation, but rather with parts of the process only. Consequently, architects also have to have skills in project development, project management, construction management and cost accounting and should have

teams of professionals on hand to be able to offer complete solutions (see more about this in the section 'Qualification Profile of Architects').

The role of the classical building contractor is on the wane – instead, real estate and floor-space management and the generation of project ideas based on market research and feasibility studies will become increasingly more important. Together with various other project collaborators, architects contribute to the development of projects and, on this basis, to the generation of contracts; at the same time they also carry entrepreneurial risks.[4]

"Today, the architect is no longer capable of taking over this multitude of tasks as the all-encompassing master builder. Owing to his/her education and his/her interdisciplinary knowledge, he/she is, however, the only one who can assume responsibility for coordinating the variety of participants and for the quality of the overall result. He/she is more of a guiding co-ordinator than a generalist. On the other hand, architects are also active as specialists, taking over subtasks in such planning teams. The generalization in regard to coordination and communication is contrasted with the specialization in partial aspects of planning in constructive and technical respects. Specializations are similarly evolving for certain planning tasks, as they are for subtasks such as drafting, design, construction management or project controlling and project leadership".[5]

Architects' qualification profile

In the expanding field of architectural tasks, a generalist qualification profile is hardly attainable any longer. Instead, interdisciplinary knowledge is called for: apart from artistic-creative and technical skills, sociological, economic and social-communicative abilities are expected of architects.[6] In the following, the subject-specific, methodical and interdisciplinary (social and personal) qualification requirements will be discussed in some detail.[7]

Subject-specific competence requirements

To secure cost control and project viability, architects need, in addition to project management know-how, knowledge and experience in construction work execution, cost calculation and accounting, construction testing and billing. Economic core competences required also include contract processing and the preparation of offers.

Sound product and implementation knowledge is indispensible for planners and architects. Qualification trends particularly concern the increasing importance of ecological building – materials and specialist knowledge – as well as transportation engineering knowledge. Population growth has an impact on the design of new housing estates, complete with workplaces, the challenge being to create affordable living space in strongly growing areas of high population density. Also relevant in this context is the issue of generation-appropriate construction.[8]

Environmental technology is becoming more and more important. Cost-effective new technologies and systems do not only involve research spending, but also optimized use of resources, which can, in turn, lead to lower costs and more competitiveness. Moreover, the ecologization of the construction sector is gaining in significance in light of the climate protection debate and consequent legal requirements.[9] Deployment of energy-efficient,

Architects today are also faced with the challenge of acting as supraregional and, in part, transnational service providers. In order to realize projects together, networking with international cooperation partners plays a role here, too.

As far as mobility is concerned, besides the accreditation of educational attainment through the ECTS credit point system, the Professional Qualifications Directive 2005/36/EG, which has been in effect since 20 October 2007, is particularly relevant as it guarantees mutual recognition of professional qualifications in the member states of the European Union. This directive is subject to constant further development and its applicability will also be extended to the new member states, e.g., to Bulgaria and Romania.

innovative and sustainable building technologies that could be marketed in the neighboring EU countries also opens up a perspective for the future. Residential and other buildings will have to be thermally redeveloped so as to meet ecological energy-saving standards. With concepts such as energy contracting, there is the possibility of refinancing energy-saving investments by way of utility cost savings.[10]

A study made for the Austrian Career Information System of the Austrian Public Employment Service (AMS) has shown that expert knowledge in architecture and spatial planning, CAD, job-related legislation and, increasingly, ecological building is particularly in demand.[12]

Legal qualifications particularly include zoning and cadastral law, private law, public law, EU law, building codes, trade regulations, drawing standards, protective regulations, etc. In order to be able to successfully realize larger construction projects abroad, profound knowledge of international building law is required.

Job-specific competence requirements

Architects are expected to be familiar with all project phases, from planning to preparation and actual construction. Project management skills are considered as essential to cost and construction time overruns. Mediation and conflict management skills to solve conflicts between the various parties involved (e.g., payment disputes) are equally helpful.

In view of increasing internationalization and the need for multi-directional project communication, strong communication skills, English and additional foreign language skills are becoming more important. With the opening of new markets in Eastern Europe, Eastern European language skills may be a decisive competitive advantage.

Social and Personal Competence Requirements

Besides technical skills, a good appearance and regular communication with clients as well as between planners and suppliers or contractors also play an important role in architecture.

Generalism, specialization, interdisciplinarity

At the qualification requirement level, it is essential for architects to be mindful of various different aspects. In addition to the core competence profile, which comprises technical, methodological and interdisciplinary elements, this also concerns recurrent knowledge updates with regard to, e.g., technological innovation or legal requirements. To some extent, specialization may result from focuses of study in higher university semesters and relevant practical experience. What is crucial is the post-graduate building of specific competence by working in a company with a specific focus or by individual priority setting as a freelancer. Above all, on entering professional life one should also be prepared to perform less qualified work in order to get a foot in the door.

Planning services are less a matter of generalism with respect to technical ability than with respect to the ability to coordinate the services of numerous professionals. The increasing number of task fields in architecture and their differentiation imply a diversification of the job description on the one hand, but also lead to demands made on the individual to specialize on certain services or tasks.

In a life-long learning perspective, continuing training and knowledge updates are essential. Generally, this goes for both trends and developments in architecture and framework conditions such as technological innovations, new products and processes, or legal provisons.[15] ■

Social and personal competences [14]

- Flexibility
- Leadership
- Innovativeness
- Ability to communicate
- Creativity
- Problem-solving orientation
- Spatial and mental mobility
- Stress resistance, resilience
- Ability to work in a team

1 See also: "The Bologna Process – Towards the European Higher Education Area",
http://ec.europa.eu/education/higher-education/doc1290_en.htm (18.07.2018; last retrieval date of all links listed).
2 Cf., e.g., the system of research-oriented "Master recherche" and job-oriented "Master professional" in France or consecutive master programs (in-depth study) vs. continuing-education master courses that require previous professional experience; see also, e.g., *Ländergemeinsamen Strukturvorgaben für die Akkreditierung von Bachelor- und Masterstudiengängen* in Germany at:
www.kmk.org/fileadmin/veroeffentlichungen_beschluesse/2003/2003_10_10-Laendergemeinsame-Strukturvorgaben.pdf.
3 Austrian Career Information System (Österreichisches Berufsinformationssystem), www.ams.at/bis/
4 Cf. The Association of German Architects (Bund Deutscher Architekten [BDA])
5 Ibid.
6 Cf., e.g., the description of the job outline of architects and city planners of the BDA (see endnote 4).
7 Cf. Austrian Public Employment Service (AMS) Qualification Barometer – Qualification Trends in the Professional Field of Planning and Architecture (AMS Qualifikationsbarometer – Qualifikationstrends im Berufsfeld Planungswesen und Architektur), online at:
http://bis.ams.or.at/qualibarometer/berufsfeld.php?id=255&show_detail=1&query=.
8 Cf., Gary, G. (2010): Die Zukunft des Bauens, in: Bauzeitung 12/2010
9 Cf. e.g., www.nachhaltigwirtschaften.at.
10 Cf., e.g.
11 Cf. AMS Qualifikationsbarometer (see endnote 8).
12 Cf. ibid.; on the basis of the AMS Large Firm Monitoring 2009. Report and evaluation of demanded and dynamic professions and qualifications, available online at:
www.forschungsnetzwerk.at/downloadpub/2010_Endbericht_Gro%C3%9FbetriebsMonitoring_2009.pdf.
13 Cf. AMS Qualifikationsbarometer (see endnote 8).
14 Ibid.
15 Ibid.

REALITY CHECK #4: GETTING SPECIALIZED

The Getting Specialized survey is based on 14 European practices from 9 different countries that have made specialization their main asset. The teams were directly selected.

With the exception of one, the practices were led by 2 to 3 partners and had an average of 5 employees/collaborators. They included mostly teams with more than 5 years business experience. Asked to define their specialization, all teams named multiple factors which related to their field of work, the kind of tools they developed and/ or the specific focus and thematic approach they applied to their projects.

The result is smaller offices providing a very specific kind of product, derived in most cases out of the traditional field of architecture. This product is not only defined by what it is – for example, in terms of traditional building typology or of specific qualities such as sustainability –, but also by how it

is developed – for example, through participative processes or flexible communication set-ups with the client or the users.

For the vast majority of our sample, their specialization was the result of a mix of chance and strategy and only in one case of a clear top-down business decision. Not all teams are able to keep their offices going with their specialized projects exclusively, and only two practices see the future of architecture in specialization. The others consider specialization as only one of several possibilities and even as a potential limitation for architecture in general.

To conclude: for the teams we surveyed, specialization remains a personal choice, based on personal interests, but is not a solution for the profession in general. One may conclude that, even for specialized architects, architecture is still more about a generalist approach.

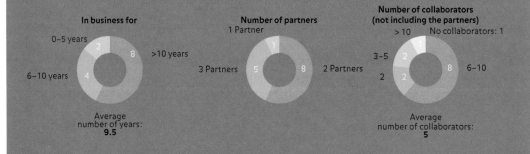

In business for

0–5 years — 2
8 — >10 years
6–10 years — 4

Average number of years:
9.5

Number of partners

1 Partner — 1
3 Partners — 5
8 — 2 Partners

Number of collaborators (not including the partners)

> 10 — No collaborators: 1
3–5 — 2
2 — 2
8 — 6–10

Average number of collaborators:
5

WHY SPECIALIZE

In the perspective of our sample, many teams would put a question mark over specialization. It is seen as advantageous by the most, but by only two teams as very advantageous. For most, it is just one way to go; merely two teams see the future of the architectural practice in specialization.

How do you see your specialization?

Very advantageous — 2
In-between — 3
8 — Advantageous

Is specialization relevant for the future of the architecture practice?

Yes, it is the future of the architecture practice — 2
12 — No, one of possible ways

Yes, because ...

... it can become a tool to communicate with a wider public about potential future projects and consultancies. (Zone Architects)

No, because ...

... in the future both specialization and a synthesizing approach to work will be important. (Servo)

... the way of doing business, arts and of course architecture constantly changes. There should be unlimited ways to proceed. (complizen)

... it would not be the best thing from a cultural point of view. Specialization reduces the intellectual complexity of architects, and the related problem-solving ability. (CZ Studio)

Source: Wonderland #4 Survey – by SHARE architects, 2010

GENERALIST VERSUS SPECIALIST

Who is more successful ?

The job description of the architect, as given by Vitruvius,
has changed a lot: being a generalist is not the only way to go.
Although many architects are afraid to call themselves specialists,
it is a good way for a young office to find its own profile.

> "A human being should be able to change a diaper, plan an invasion, butcher a hog,
> conn a ship, design a building, write a sonnet, balance accounts, build a wall, set a bone,
> comfort the dying, take orders, give orders, cooperate, act alone, solve equations,
> analyze a new problem, pitch manure, program a computer, cook a tasty meal,
> fight efficiently, die gallantly. Specialization is for insects."
>
> Robert A. Heinlein, Time Enough For Love, 1973

Text by Anneke Bokern, Amsterdam, Netherlands

If you google 'architect' and 'specialization', nearly all results turn out to be exhortative sermons delivered by specialized architects who preach to the rest of the profession to follow their example. Often they go so far as to predict the end of architecture as we know it, unless their stubborn brethren succumb to the power of specialization. "Our profession must let go of the romanticized ideal of the general practice architect", John Miologos, architect at retail design firm WD Partners, wrote in a finger-wagging article on the website of the American Institute of Architects.

"We need to mirror what is going on in our clients' businesses, reflecting the complexity of organizations, project economics and technologies." Sounds very business-savvy. The sheer number of articles dealing with this issue, however, suggests that the addressees aren't easily convinced. Most architects still refuse to specialize or only grudgingly accept specialization as a necessary evil if there's really no way out or if it happens by itself. Why are they so reluctant? And why are others so absolutely convinced of specialization as the one and only survival strategy?

195

Generalists by nature

First of all, architects like to see themselves as generalists by nature. Well-versed in the fields of art, design, technology, management, etc., they are true renaissance men and women, and architecture is the Swiss army knife amongst professions. At least that is the image that many an architect have of themselves. But, as typical party conversations show, the rest of the world does not necessarily share that image. "So you're an architect? What kind of buildings do you design?" is what unsuspecting non-architects would be likely to ask to strike up a conversation.

Equating architect with generalist has a long tradition, though. It goes as far back as the Ten Books on Architecture by Roman writer and engineer Vitruvius, who claims: "An architect (...) should be a good writer, a skillful draftsman, versed in geometry and optics, expert at figures, acquainted with history, informed on the principles of natural and moral philosophy, somewhat of a musician, not ignorant of the sciences both of law and of physics, nor of the motions, laws, and relations to each other, of the heavenly bodies." An impressive scope, which testifies to Vitruvius' intent of establishing architecture as the mother of all arts. But while this bold job description might be good for the prestige of the profession, it is not necessarily a good idea in modern business terms. Even the staunchest of anti-specialists will agree that, in an offer-driven market, young architecture firms somehow need to distinguish themselves from the competition, and generalism always carries the risk of becoming faceless and exchangeable. The solution is to create a clear profile and to set oneself apart from others. In business speak, this is called a unique selling point, which very often results in specialization. Of course, not every unique selling point is a specialism – but every specialism is a unique selling point.

Brown bears and pandas

Therefore, according to the finger-wagging articles, generalist architects are threatened by extinction – which seems a bit paradoxical if compared to the natural world, where specialists tend to be the endangered species, while generalists always find something to eat. Brown bears, for example, feeding on anything from berries to salmon to garbage, thrive all over the globe; panda bears, who eat nothing but bamboo shoots, are restricted to a small area and are on the verge of dying out. Of course, one might argue that zoos try their very best to breed pandas and resort to rather unsavory methods to dispose of all the brown bears being born every year – in short: specialists are pampered and coddled, while generalists run the risk of being considered a plague. If you have to fend for yourself, though, versatility doubtless has its advantages. As architect Oliver Thill of the Rotterdam-based office Atelier Kempe Thill explains: "We deliberately decided not to specialize, for economic reasons. As a specialist, you're finished very quickly if your main pillar breaks away."

This raises the question whether successful architects are specialists or generalists. When it comes to star architects, the answer is simple: they may have a signature style, but they are not specialized. Representing the very ideal of the all-rounder, they nimbly jump from designing a tiny pavilion to developing a huge station building and from commissions in provincial towns like Lelystad to projects in megacities like Singapore. Because star architects are promoted as role models for the entire profession, most young architects feel compelled to follow this path and think that everything else is a restriction of their freedom.

"No man can be a pure specialist without being in the strict sense an idiot", George Bernard Shaw once said, bringing grist to the mill of the anti-specialists. But on a closer look, this 'bon mot' may just as easily be turned into its opposite: no man can be a generalist without being superficial. After all, does specialization not offer a chance to dive deep into a subject instead of just scratching its surface? In economic history, specialization occurs when a business field matures. It is a sign of evolution and progress. This idea goes back to the industrial revolution, when production was fragmented into sub-branches, and specialization became an expression of, as well as an answer to, an increasingly complex world. Admittedly, the industrial revolution is not exactly a popular point of reference in a creative context. But that does not have to imply that all specialists are like assembly-line workers who do nothing but insert the ever-same screw into the ever-same car part all day long. The difference between a specialist and a one-trick pony is depth, expertise and, most importantly, versatility within the specialist scope of work. In addition, in architecture it is very well possible to be a specialist with regard to, for instance, materials or building technology, and at the same time a generalist when it comes to, e.g., design or typology. And to take this line of thought even further: maybe architects are not generalists at all, but rather specialists at acquiring and managing knowledge from all kinds of fields?

Parameters of specialization

Still, the mere word specialization makes many an architect shiver with fear of (self-) limitation – although it's a very malleable, sometimes even arbitrary notion. What exactly is architectural specialization anyway? Is Zaha Hadid specialized because all of her designs have a distinct formal language? Can we talk of specialization if an architect uses his knowledge about buildings to work as a location scout for TV productions?

If we leave aside architects who have taken up an entirely different profession, e.g. as photographer or journalist, architectural specialization can concern building typology (hospitals, prisons, family homes, interiors, etc.) as well as the architect's contribution to the production process (computer renderings, design, execution, etc.) and attributes of the architect's work, such as sustainability, low budget building, conversions etc. Here is an additional hypothesis: an architect or office can only be considered as specialized if at least two of these parameters apply. This minimum requirement draws a line between specialization and, for example, typecasting, which is only based on perception by others, or style, which is not a specialism in itself, but may eventually lead to one.

Specialization is a wide field, in which every architect can define his own limits and stake out his own field of expertise. Accordingly, architects – specialized or not – should rather see it as an opportunity, and not as a constraint.

SPECIALIZATION

Go for it!

Specialization does not confine, but extends the area of expertise. The following examples show that there are many different ways to go.

When I discuss the issue of architecture practice profiling with participants in the marketing seminars I hold for various architects' professional bodies, one question crops up regularly: should I specialize? And, if so, how can I develop my area of competence into a powerful unique selling proposition? Do architects who devote themselves to a special area give up clients from outside their niche? Specialization appears to contradict architects' self-perception as generalists, which in part is due to the fact that it is often inadequately understood as meaning concentration on certain types of building commissions, like apartment buildings, industrial buildings, or hospitals. The many smaller offices that, often out of necessity, have looked for a specialist niche for themselves, as experts in the construction process or as energy consultants, do not necessarily represent the true potential of systematic profiling. Many people associate with specialization a fear of ending up in a marginalized niche existence. Such worries, however, fail to do justice to the wide spectrum of conceivable expertise strategies. Actually, specialization can take place at very different levels: with regard to types of clients, areas of focus, and, not least importantly, the process quality of projects. One example of

an innovative process culture is the planning workshops that the Vienna-based nonconform office holds under the motto of "Architecture on site" with experts and the citizens of local communities (www.nonconform.at). The usual sequence – arriving at an idea, involving local citizens, and developing the final design – is given a more dynamic quality here with a short but intensive brainstorming workshop.

Specialization expands the area of competence

Therefore, is specialization a chance for small offices to assert themselves in the fiercely contested market for building commissions? The answer is yes – provided that specialization leads to increased professionalism and specialist networking, also beyond the immediate borders of the discipline. As a result, it promises to sustainably strengthen the profile and market chances of an office.

One example to demonstrate this is that of Berlin architects Tom Kaden and Tom Klingbeil: in 2008, their office attracted considerable media attention after they had succeeded in building the first timber-constructed seven-storey apartment house in Europe (since 2015 they work in a different setting). The commission came from a group of seven

Text by Frank Peter Jäger, ARCHIKONTEXT, Berlin, Germany

clients, including the architects themselves. When the time came to implement the planning, the architects and their fellow clients activated a wide range of external specialists, decision makers and institutions. They agreed upon a marketing cooperation with the wood industry lobbying organization 'Informationsdienst Holz' and the timber construction firms involved, commissioned the services of a PR professional and a graphic designer, conducted negotiations with banks, applied for subsidies from foundations, and actively sought political support. Their high level of professionalism was demonstrated by the fact that the two architects always treated their clients as partners at an equal level, without reservations. This was rewarded by considerable personal efforts made by the clients on behalf of the project. The 'first apartment building entirely of wood' achieved a maximum amount of public attention, which continued until 2009. One ingredient in the recipe for success was that Kaden and Klingbeil showed remarkable organizational skill in categorizing the tasks to be dealt with into three groups: first, things they could deal with themselves, secondly, things for which the office had to consult external experts, and thirdly, tasks which one of the fellow clients or another project partner could deal with.

On top of all this, Tom Kaden and Tom Klingbeil are also specialists in the conventional sense of the word – in timber construction and in wood as a building material. Combining specialized expertise with an approach that is generalist and network-oriented – their example makes it clear that, ideally, specialization is the opposite of self-limitation.

The case of architects Thomas Duncan and Noel McCauley, who also work in Berlin, is very similar (www.duncanmccauley.com). They have specialized in exhibition design which means that their work, for instance for the Berlin Centrum Judaicum or the Brandenburgische Stiftung Schlösser und Gärten, includes both building work in the usual sense as well as the concept, the spatial dramaturgy of exhibitions, and the visitor guidance systems. Apart from the exhibits on display, Duncan and McCauley also chose the media used to communicate the theme. They produce sound tracks, beamer projections and even short films, drawing on the services of a pool of professional partners, from sound engineers to actors. Their work aims at achieving a creative synthesis of different media, in particular film and architecture. Specialization in exhibitions and other staged spaces is combined with a generalist approach (everything from a single source), which, however, is informed by a marked interdisciplinary way of thinking.

Landmark buildings or building within an existing structural fabric is an almost classical area of architectural specialization – a tradition that goes back to Schinkel. The range spans from building research and the preparation of reports to producing and implementing own designs. One of the pioneers in this area is the Berlin office of Winfried Brenne (www.brenne-architekten.de). Together with Helge Pitz, Brenne began, back in the 1970s, with research into the buildings of classical modernism in order to secure their survival. In the field of monument conservation, it is precisely the small offices that have successfully established themselves as specialists throughout Europe. Despite their specialized focus, they remain generalists in terms of approach and working methods.

With areas of competence such as these, one can acquire a reputation among colleagues and clients, but many architects who specialize in certain areas admit that they would be quite happy if, from time to time, they had the opportunity to "carry out a somewhat larger building", as Tom Duncan puts it. The small-scale work on exhibition buildings monuments or conversions is so time-consuming that even fairly calculated fees do not get you very far.

Specializing in team cooperation

In recent years, it has become harder for small offices to compete against large offices with a staff of fifty or more – in restricted entry competitions as well in the direct awarding of commissions. In doubt, clients always tend to decide for large architecture firms, who claim extensive experience and efficiency for themselves.

In such a situation, there is much to be said for an 'alliance of convenience' between several offices who can then apply for commissions as consortium. The consortium ena (european network architecture, www.ena. ag), based in Baden-Baden, is made up mostly of larger offices but the example could easily be applied to smaller units as well. Six architecture practices and eight engineering offices from Baden-Württemberg, complementary in terms of profile and the range of services offered, make a joint market appearance under the ena brand, among them the offices Wilford Schupp and Knapp und Partner. Aside from the planners, a series of well-known office product suppliers are involved in this cooperation, too; without this network, both the individual offices and the supply businesses would stand little chance of gaining a footing in the Russian market.

Occupying themes

Being noticed and keeping a high profile: special competences and work focuses are closely related to an architect's office external self-presentation. As 'unique selling points', they facilitate focused client canvassing and help define distinctive differences from colleagues. And although the special competences that an office calls its own should not merely be assertions, they normally should not be dealbreakers either: presenting yourself as an expert in building for senior citizens, for example, should not prevent, or preclude, you from building completely different things as well. This also answers the question raised above. Clearly, nobody will lose clients just for having specialized expertise in one field or another. To put it positively: the issue is occupying thematic areas that an office is identified with in a constantly widening circle of the general and specialist public.

Specialization starts within the architect's office and here, for me, it becomes a synonym for 'professionalism'. If in an architecture office each task is dealt with by the person who is best at it, that is professionalism. This person can be an architect, but ultimately everybody running his own office would be well advised to call in external specialists or consultants to deal with all those tasks that lie outside the architect's core competence – such specialists may be urban planners, designers, graphic artists, PR specialists or economists. Trying to cover all these different fields oneself only betrays a fundamental misunderstanding of what generalism is, and can be, about. ✻

FINANCIAL MATTERS

For the majority of the teams, specialized projects make up more of the half of the commissions they work on, and for all teams, they provide at least 40 % of their annual turnover.

However, only 7 teams can actually make a living off them. For the others, specialized projects represent an investment, and other sources of income are needed to finance them.

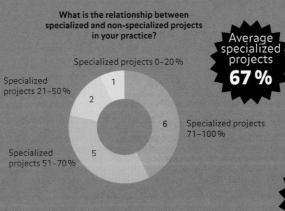

What is the relationship between specialized and non-specialized projects in your practice?

Specialized projects 0–20 %

1

Specialized projects 21–50 %

2

6 — Specialized projects 71–100 %

5

Specialized projects 51–70 %

Average specialized projects **67 %**

At least **40 %** of their annual turnover

What is the contribution of specialized projects to your turnover?

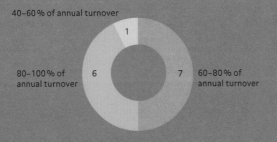

40–60 % of annual turnover

1

80–100 % of annual turnover

6

7 — 60–80 % of annual turnover

What role do specialized projects play financially?

We see our **future in specialization**, though at the moment we still have to invest additional resources. We think that they will be **sustaining the office** in the future: **3** teams

In order to be able to do specialized projects, we need to have money coming in from **other projects or activities**: **3** teams

Specialized projects are the main financial resource of our practice: **8** teams

what to specialize in

Clear-cut definitions have become blurred, as areas of expertise are increasingly open and multi-layered. Besides traditional, hardcore areas of specialization, such as building typologies, new ones have appeared, which are soft and more vague. What constitutes specialization in contemporary practices increasingly is a specific mix of ingredients. And the capacity to produce new and unique recipes for the production of space.

Other productions of space

How can one intervene in the production of space?
What are the values and skills that someone should
and could bring to such an effort?

Looking at how the architectural profession is evolving and what options are available today and in the foreseeable future, it might be useful to begin with Stewart Brand's famous provocation: "All buildings are predictions. All predictions are wrong"[1], as this reminds us that whatever is done or said now may be obsolete within a few weeks or months; if we are lucky, it may last a little longer.

The report produced by the Royal British Institute of Architects and Building Futures[2] in 2011, for example, presents the architect as a dying species that can only survive if adapting to the challenges of the future. The problem with the future as portrayed here is that it is outlined in market economy terms that recall colonial attitudes according to which architecture becomes, at best, another good for export into emerging areas around the globe and, at worst, a means of exploitation. Or else, in terms of branding: being different or setting oneself apart from the vast majority of practices, it is argued, will give clear advantages over one's competitors in the global marketplace. A discussion about responsibility and ethics, however, or a focus on how to engage with others and why is notably absent. Equally missing is an acknowledgement of the multiple crises – from local to global – that might call for or have already instigated other ways of engaging and working.

The form of the report and its focus may not be too surprising given that it was produced by an institution that has, ever since it was founded in 1834, done everything in its power to protect the title 'architect' and alleged architectural knowledge through a conflation of, as Jeremy Till argues, "architect (as expert) with architecture (as profession) with architecture (as practice) with architecture (as product)".[3] The self-serving operation of the RIBA has been attacked by many, but most notably the Architects' Revolutionary Council in the early 1970s, who campaigned, unsuccessfully, for "revolutionary changes within the architectural establishment and specifically for the replacement of the RIBA by a new architectural system"[4].

None of what the Architects' Revolutionary Council and other similar groups demanded ever materialized, but we seem still to be at a point in time, at which the very role of the architect is under question more than ever before; it has become almost fashionable to interrogate this role in public forums, lecture series, competitions, and exhibitions. However, the state *we* are or have found ourselves in mostly is an internalized discussion, which perpetuates the previously mentioned closed circle of architecture's self-referentiality. We are caught in debate after debate about the future field of practice and what

Text by Tatjana Schneider and Nishat Awan, Sheffield, United Kingdom does and does not constitute architecture. Discussions which, at best, reinforce existing divisions and, at worst, further deepen already existing chasms.

What if we were to step outside of this discussion for a moment? What if we were to leave the debates about the 'future' or 'future role' of the architect or architecture behind to focus instead on the world around us, on its various issues and crises? What if we were to look at this world afresh asking how one can intervene in the production of space and, if so, in what ways? What are the values and skills that someone should and could bring to such an effort?

> We are caught in debate after debate about the future field of practice and what does and does not constitute architecture.

What we might find is that these crises and issues cannot only be confronted with current knowledge, values, skills and tools inherent to the architectural profession and imparted throughout architectural education; that spatial production belongs to a broader range of actors; and, that it is dependent and contingent on external forces which can only be tackled by embracing more collaborative and ethical ways of working.

Entering the field of architecture, or rather spatial production, from questions such as these opens up, rather than bars, potentialities and opportunities for exchange. It leads away from the impasses of binary oppositions, opening the doors for a *third* way, which is neither about continuing, or abandoning, the 'old' one, but about a dialectical approach towards a new spatial praxis, which we have termed *spatial agency*.[5]

There are a large number of examples, historical and contemporary – the Wonderland network being one of them – that take this approach to spatial practice. One common thread amongst them is the desire to widen the scope of spatial engagement and to question its assumptions. Here, a number of key strategies have emerged, which are based upon a reconsideration of the sites and means of spatial production through the expansion of the scope and ethics of engagement, a focus on educational principles, the rethinking of resources, and finally, the reconsideration of disciplinary boundaries.

Ethical engagement

Whilst the responses from within the architectural profession have by and large refused to acknowledge the ethical dimension of spatial production, those practices who see the organizational structure and form of practice itself as their site of intervention and engagement necessarily take an ethical stance. These practices have the commonality of striving for more equity in the relations between architect and client, between members of a practice or other collaborators, embracing organizational structures such as social enterprises and taking on the status of non-profit organizations or workers' co-operatives.

The type of organizational structure also has an impact on the type of work produced. For example, the London-based practice 00:/[6] have expanded their work into strategic consultancy, designing systems and processes. Their work in the field of regeneration is characterized by an emphasis on creating micro-economies through supporting small-scale businesses and non-monetary forms of exchange such as swap shops. Indy Johar, one of the founding members of 00:/, speaks about creating "civic economies"[7] and emphasizes the need to "accrue micro-forms of capital" where "a new way of organising and democratising the finance of buildings ... starts to change the nature of form and the built environment."[8] This strategic work is combined with more traditional forms of design that create the spatial conditions necessary for social networks to thrive. Their project for the Hub Collective in Kings Cross, London, involved not only the interior redesigning of the building, but also the idea of a sharing economy where workspace was sold through time spent in the building rather than as desk space.

From a different perspective, the Paris-based group atelier d'architecture autogérée (aaa)[9], operate as a non-profit organization and an evolving and fluid network of individuals and groups. Being non-profit allows them to access social funds, such as those for skills training of the unemployed or young people, whilst connections to academic and cultural institutions provide aaa with access to research and other funding streams. Theirs is an explicitly activist stance that foregrounds the political nature of spatial production and emphasizes the importance of the micro-scale, as Doina Petrescu states, "politically also, this small-scale, local scale is important because this is the scale that is somehow accessible to everybody ... So, the micro is a scale of operation not opposed to the macro. It is a way of being active and through networks, through multiplication, through diversification, attaining also a macro scale."[10]

Transformative education

Arguably, a shift in spatial production will also require a change in direction for architectural education, whether this involves the introduction of forms of multidisciplinary practice that include a focus on management and practice beyond current norms, or the wider implementation of critical pedagogy and inquiry-based learning focused on experiments and questions rather than defined and determinable outcomes.

At one end of the spectrum is the Berlin-based group Baupiloten[11], who choose to challenge architectural education from within academia. Whilst their site of engagement remains the university, the means of that engagement are expanded outwards by facilitating students to work on real-life projects. Other than in traditional architectural education, students learn by doing and are involved in user participation from the very beginning. Although Baupiloten's approach leaves many of the assumptions of architectural practice intact, such as the relationship between architects and builders, or architects and clients, they question the way students are taught at university, pushing for a student-led approach to learning and open-

ing up a reciprocal relationship between student and teacher. Another Berlin-based group, Raumlabor[12], also view education as an important means of architectural intervention, but they shift the site of learning from the traditional university environment to a 'community' convened around a specific project. Primarily working with public space, Raumlabor see the task of the architect as highlighting problems rather than solving them, stating that: "It's never only about designing spaces, but it's about relating them to the public and generating reflections. We like to define ourselves as 'space planners' rather than designers: we encourage people to respond actively."[13] Raumlabor's projects are deliberately designed to open up a space of communication and learning where relations can be established and conflicts played out.

> So, the micro is a scale of operation not opposed to the macro.
> It is a way of being active...

At the other end of the spectrum is a collaborative project by the research program Sarai[14] and the NGO Ankur[15], based in Delhi, India, which brings together Ankur's long-term experience of alternative pedagogy with Sarai's open-source sensibility and interest in new technologies. Conceived as an empowering tool for children and young adults, the Cybermohalla project breaks down the power differentials between learners and teachers, while at the same time making space in the city for other types of inhabitation. The project operates through a network of neighborhood spaces set up in some of the most deprived areas of Delhi, which allow residents to carry out embedded research, take part in workshops and projects, and learn to use various technologies.

Rethinking resources

Environmental issues in particular require new types of knowledge and an emphasis on other skills and technologies, which places spatial production in a wider ecological perspective firmly based in the socio-economic and cultural context. This means that the attention shifts from the built object towards the uses of resources and the processes of spatial intervention.

An early example of such an approach is the Centre for Alternative Technology (CAT)[16] in Wales, which was set up in 1973 as an experimental community working towards self-sufficiency. CAT promoted a lifestyle away from urban centers and without dependence on industrial production by demonstrating alternative technologies and ecological lifestyles. Located in a disused quarry, the Centre operates as a cyclical, closed-loop system where waste from people, animals and crops is recycled and reused. Today, the Centre operates as an education and also visitor facility, a 'living laboratory' that continues to work on many levels demonstrating and implementing low-ecological-impact solutions as well as providing an educational facility that teaches principles of sustainable development. While CAT transformatively intervenes in the systems that enable spatial production and inhabitation, the Rotterdam-based group Superuse Studios (originally active as 2012 Architecten)[17] use an intimate knowledge of those resource systems already in place to design their projects and take their inspiration from the creative use of waste material that occurs every day in conditions of scarcity across the global South. By creating an inventory of the waste and productive cycles that a given site or situation is part of, including food, water, traffic, humans, and energy, Superuse Studios are able to produce products and spatial interventions that reuse and adapt freely available 'waste' material. Designing not just their interventions but the whole scenario of their production, the group aims to empower local exchange and production in order to help reduce the dependency on regionally or internationally imported goods.

A very different system of spatial production is the discourse that surrounds it: the traditionally closed realm of academia. The Berlin-based group An Architektur[18] open the discussion around the production of space beyond the subject's traditional boundaries, bringing in more contributors and a wider audience. An Architektur use several strategies, from operating as an independent publisher, hosting seminars and symposia, as well as organizing events, designing installations and exhibitions that are open and inviting. Critically analyzing spatial relations as a form of political agency, An Architektur, as a group and a publication, is increasingly becoming a hub for a network of progressive research groups and projects committed to a critical and political approach to spatial production.

Crossing disciplinary boundaries

One of the consequences of this enlarged field of spatial production is the need to work in explicitly transdisciplinary ways, bringing together 'traditional' specialists and professions, such as sociologists, engineers, anthropologists, computational experts and artists with residents, users and organizations connected to a particular place or event. An approach such as this, which focuses on the co-production of space, requires participants to be more self-reflective in their working methods and to acknowledge and work with the views and expertise of others.

Practices such as the Rotterdam based group Crimson Architectural Historians[19] utilize and appropriate methods from other disciplinary backgrounds such as story-telling and narrative modes of historical analysis as a means of engaging with space and location, weaving together a plethora of different voices and perspectives. Combined with on-the-ground ethnographic research, they design urban strategies that are embedded within the local context.

Other practices engage with the creative and artistic interpretation of building law and notions of legality. Some question and subvert by laws and covenants, whilst others are bringing international laws on territories and human rights to bear on the practices of architecture – both of which indicate a significant expansion of the understanding of spatial engagement. In the first group is Spanish architect Santiago Cirugeda[20], whose practice was born out of frustration with the disempowerment of ordinary citizens. He states, "I work from a citizen's point of view, because as an architect I can get the permission required for my installation. But really I want to be a citizen. I see architecture as a social art."[21] By showing citizens in step-to-step guides how to subvert laws, regulations and conventions, Cirugeda's practice reveals the possibilities for action available to everyone, while questioning the notion of the architect as sole author-designer. His is an open-source practice, distributed through his website Recetas Urbanas/'Urban Prescriptions', where his antidotes to capitalist, commodified space are freely available for anyone to replicate. On the other side of the legal spectrum is the work of Decolonizing Architecture (DA)[23], based in the Palestinian Occupied Territories, who have set out to challenge the occupation architecture of the Israeli state and at the same time to propose ways of reusing and adapting the colonizer's environment. Since pretentions to legality have so often been used as a tool of oppression in this context, DA choose to openly engage the legal and the political in their work through a series of propositional spatial interventions, discourses and legal challenges.

The expanded field of spatial production

Looking at these four key strategies – ethical engagement, transformative education, rethinking resources and crossing disciplinary boundaries – Rosalind Krauss's notion of the "expanded field"[24] comes to mind. In the context of sculpture, Krauss's seminal article investigates the notion of the "complex". She argues that "to think complex is to admit into the realm of art two terms that had formerly been prohibited from it: *landscape* and *architecture*"[25]. If we exchange her term *sculpture* or *art* with architecture, this expanded field gains crucial importance in the framework of this discussion here.

With the changes in styles over the past centuries simply camouflaging a lack of critical engagement with the world, architecture as a field arguably has remained a largely unreconstructed discipline. As mentioned in the beginning of this text: it seems that the recent global recession has served as a new reminder of about how fragile and contingent on other forces the field of architecture is. While a degree in architecture seems to be almost more popular than ever, we also see exhibitions produced by the Museum of Modern Art in New York entitled 'Small Scale, Big Change: New Architectures of Social Engagement' and competitions such as 'Resourceful Architect' initiated by the Royal Society of Arts and the Architecture Foundation. On the one hand, architecture still is popular. On the other, even large and powerful institutions seem to be advocating shifting the focus of attention. Although both examples, and there are many more, potentially are a step towards a different future that focuses on transformative effects rather than prioritizing functional requirements, it is important to be cautious. As long as architects, architecture and architectural knowledge remain the conflated synthesis of expert, profession, practice and product, other forms of spatial production, as discussed in this text, will remain entirely marginal.

One of the biggest challenges is the constructive deflation of this loop and the role that architectural education plays in it. Refocusing educational attention on how to tackle and work with the issues and crises referred to in this text may be one way out of this conundrum. The skills and tools needed to address ecological issues, uneven development, socio-spatial inequality, notions of collaboration, co-learning, reflexivity and the unknown versus the fixed are different from the skills widely taught in schools of architecture, which still focus on the production of form rather than the understanding of the field within which architecture operates.

> One of the consequences of this enlarged field of spatial production is the need to work in explicitly transdisciplinary ways.

Yes, architecture is a field that always required the collaboration with other people and other disciplines and from that perspective also always required external input and relationships. Yet, what the examples above have in common with many others that we have brought together under the term *spatial agency* is that each involves an ethical, moral and ultimately political choice about whom they work for, whom they work with and why. Rather than producing yet another prediction on what the future might hold for architecture or the architectural profession, we have to begin to act, which is what our spatial agents have in common: they act in the now, are less concerned with the future, with long term predictions or developments. They take small and concrete steps, on the small scale and with direct engagement.

Coming back to Krauss: her concept of expansion is an ideological as well as an operational one. It is concerned with ideas, with concepts. At the same time, it is also descriptive: she describes what has already happened and is happening in her field. And this is also true for spatial agency.

We understand architecture's expanded field as something that is expressed through its forms of operation and ethical dimension. One of the biggest challenges in this context – given the increasing privatization and commodification of education and knowledge in particular in England – is to contest, dispute and break down the traditional boundaries posed by architectural education. Giving the complex permission to enter might be the first step towards a more transformative understanding of the production of space.

1   Stewart Brand, *How Buildings Learn: What Happens After They're Built*, Viking: New York, 1994, p. 178.

2   Claire Jamieson, *The Future for Architects?*, Building Futures, RIBA: London, 2011.

3   Jeremy Till, *Architecture Depends*, MIT Press: Cambridge, Mass., 2009, p. 154.

4   Anne Karpf, 'The Pressure Groups', in: *Architects' Journal*, 166 (1977), p. 731.

5   Nishat Awan, Tatjana Schneider and Jeremy Till, *Spatial Agency. Other Ways of Doing Architecture*, Routledge: London, 2011. See also: www.spatialagency.net

6   See: http://architecture00.net/

7   See also 00:/'s work on this published as Timothy Ahrensbach, Joost Beunderman and Indy Johar, *Compendium for the Civic Economy. What the Big Society Should Learn from 25 Trailblazers*, 00:/: London, 2011. This document is also available for download on http://issuu.com/architecture00/docs/compendium_for_the_civic_economy_publ.

8   Indy Johar, 'Manifesting Change 21C', Talk at the Architecture Foundation, UK, 23 September 2010; www.architecturefoundation.org.uk/programme/2010/the-skyroom/manifesting-change-21c

9   See: www.urbantactics.org/

10 Interview with Doina Petrescu, in: *DESIGN ACT: Socially and politically engaged design today – critical roles and emerging tactics*, (International Artist Studio Programme Sweden (IASPIS): Stockholm, 2009

11 See: www.baupiloten.com/

12 See: www.raumlabor.net/

13 Raumlabor, interview by Silvia Franceschini, in: *Klat Magazine*, 19 May 2011

14 See: www.sarai.net/

15 See: https://ankureducation.wordpress.com

16 See: www.cat.org.uk/

17 See: http://superuse-studios.com

18 See: anarchitektur.org

19 See: www.crimsonweb.org/

20 See: www.recetasurbanas.net/

21 OneSmallProject, interview with Santiago Cirugeda, February 2004

22 See: www.decolonizing.ps/

23 Rosalind Krauss, 'Sculpture in the Expanded Field', *October*, 8 (1979), pp. 30–44.

24 Krauss, p. 38.

Field Focus Tool

How to categorize specialization?
14 teams analyzed in detail.

The way we understand specialization is linked to how we look at the profession as such. Traditional categories such as scale or building type will only work as long as we look at the profession within the traditional field of architecture. Once we broaden the perspective on the architect's field of action, other categories will come into play. The architect becomes an agent who walks the line between different professions and roles. The resulting specializations need to be described primarily in terms of the nature of the developed expertise, and not in terms of predefined exclusive areas of expertise. Our proposed categories Field, Focus, Tool follow this approach.

For most of the teams that we have analyzed specialization lies in the combination of two or more specific categories, for example by acting on a specialized field but with the maximum variety of tools – even unusual ones for architects, or specific tools for specific phases or specific fields.

Text by Silvia Forlati

Fields: the specialization lies in what the practice does. Small firms may find themselves pitched against too many big-scale competitors in the traditional field. For most, the way to go is unique expertise achieved by unexpected combinations: operating below the threshold of traditional architectural scales (Hütten und Paläste, Berlin), space architecture (Liquifer, Vienna), infrastructure (artgineering, Rotterdam) or 3-D branding (smertnik kraut, Vienna).

Focus: the specialization lies in the specific attributes of the products offered. Design strategies for social sustainability (ecosistema urbano, Madrid) or water self-sufficiency (Studio Marco Vermeulen, Rotterdam; CZstudio, Venice), or design based on specific materials (Kaden + Lager, Berlin) are possible options for this kind of specialized practices.

Tool: for a third category of practices, specialization lies in how the project is developed. These practices have developed specific tools to approach projects, such as the "on site ideas workshop", a participatory communication tool developed by nonconform, Vienna, or the "sportification" events devised by complizen, Halle. The London based leit-werk , who offer the aviation industry the slim communication structures of a small company while providing large-scale airport master planning, is also an example of how specific tools can help firms get a footing in the market.

13 teams are specialized in a mix of all 3 categories

1 team is specialized in 2 categories (field & focus)

0 team is specialized in only one category

Specialization also has to do with being able to communicate with specialist consultants and to act as a liaison between them, moving beyond technocratic solutions to 'real' ones. Being small and flexible can be made a competitive advantage, as it enables practices to adapt to non-standardized decision processes, as are practiced, for example, in airport planning in Sudan.

A 'romantic' view of the architectural profession (the architect as an artist) tends to see specialization more as a result of an inner artistic call on the part of the architect, thus a bottom-up approach. Few seem ready to go for a hardcore business, top-down approach hiring consultants to help them identify and define their specialization. Yet at least one of the experiences we collected shows that top-down engineered strategies, as are common in other industries, are also worthwhile to consider. ▄

Artgineering, Brussels, BE
www.artgineering.eu

Specialization:
Research and design
at the boundary of
urban planning and
infrastructure

Field Infrastructur / urban planning / public space	
Focus Sustainable public space – in the sense of long-lasting and flexible – (infra)structures / considering the role of structural elements in (urban) landscapes	
Tool Research by design / innovative participation processes	
Educational background Architecture	
Partners 2 (Stefan Bendiks / Aglaée Degros)	**Collaborators** 4
In business since 2000	**Percentage of specialized projects** 100 %

What type of specialization?

We do research and design in the area between urban planning and infrastructure. Our focus is on long-lasting and flexible, and therefore sustainable public spaces. We rather believe in specializing in a thematic field of work than in types of commissions. Our strategy can be described as 'filling the gap'. We devise and implement strategies for complex urban areas, with particular attention to the role of infrastructure and and active mobility (cycling and walking). Outside our office work, this specialization also extends into our academic work, for example, as head of the Department of Urbanism at TU Graz.

How did it come about?

This specialization was a result of our growing awareness of the importance of interdisciplinarity and the need to bridge gaps between sectors and disciplines. The process of specializing was accomplished by continually challenging ourselves, working towards certain commissions and expanding the body of knowledge step by step, often in collaboration with experts from other fields.

For us, it is very important to collaborate with consultants, partner offices or other advisers; we hardly do any projects on our own anymore. We are indeed highly specialized, yet versatile in this sense. Therefore we are, though loosely, connected to several specialization networks. We only take on projects within our domain of specialization, because we know what we are good in and what we want to develop further. Our specialization however, yields a huge variety of commissions.

Advantages/disadvantages?

We think specialization is important to build consistent expertise and a body of knowledge – and hence to develop as a firm. Also, it is important in order to be able to identify, and address, the relevant issues within tasks and to distinguish ourselves as an office. Our approach is very specific and certainly not a model for architectural practices in general: there are many approaches that are possible, and specialization is necessary in different fields and for different issues to cover the whole area of work. However, problems can arise with 'sectorial' specialization, when responsibility and commitment are limited to only some spatial or processual aspects of the whole.

Hütten & Paläste, Berlin, DE
www.huettenundpalaeste.de

Field Atypical building contracts on large and small scales / standardized product development

Focus Ecological materials / building and planning on limited space, maximum use of small spaces

Tool Architecture-related services like consultation / planning of new structures

Educational background Architecture / design / molecular biology

Partners 2 (Nanni Grau / Frank Schönert) **Collaborators** 2–3

In business since 2005 **Percentage of specialized projects** 70 %

Specialization: Alternative models for housing and living

What type of specialization?

In the beginning, we focused on planning small garden houses and other small-scale architecture with complicated requirements. Mostly, the scale of our work was below the threshold of what the building code would define as a 'house'. We work in areas that architects usually do not venture into. And these areas are mostly dominated by industrial products developed without architects. In our experience, there is a market here, as clients are looking out for higher-quality products. In recent years, the self-image and the position of Hütten & Paläste has further developed: we are and we will remain specialists for small-scale buildings, but we no longer define ourselves primarily in these terms; now, we interpret our specialization in terms of contents and issues. Our scope of work encompasses alternative models for housing and living. In our work, the city and the country are not opposites; we research and develop ways toward a conceptual reconciliation of urban and rural lifestyles. At the moment, we are planning a seven-storey apartment building which has over 50 % outdoor space on all floors. It is like living in a garden, so to speak.

How did it come about?

We started out in the last economic crisis. At that time, it was important for us to have our designs built directly instead of entering competitions. Prompted by an interest in urban issues, we began to do some research about the garden development in Berlin. The Allotment Gardeners Association took interest in our work and commissioned us to design a modern garden cabin type for a new kind of client, young families. We got the chance to realize this cabin type with one of the biggest German manufacturers of prefabricated housing. Considerable interest was shown by the media, so that other projects followed. As a result, we survived the economic crisis in good shape, thanks to our specialization. People began to rethink their own situation: as money in the bank seemed no longer secure, greater trust was placed in real estate, private property. A place with a special quality of life in the city or the country is timeless.

Advantages/disadvantages?

Specializing in small-scale building was a part of our path, but in the long term it is not of great relevance. At times, it was even a hindrance that prevented us from receiving bigger commissions.

We still consider specialization very important. However, things must always remain open to further development, as we wish to be able to provide topical answers to present-day questions – and these are constantly changing.

LIQUIFER Systems Group, Vienna, AT
www.liquifer.at

Field Space architecture, human factors, and habitability

Focus Economic and efficient use of resources and space, promoting human well-being and productivity / synergies between work (office / laboratory work) and life on earth and in space

Tool Systems and configuration architecture

Educational background Architecture / space studies / business administration / electrical engineering / product design

Partners 2 (Waltraut Hoheneder / Barbara Imhof)   **Collaborators** 6

In business since 2005   **Percentage of specialized projects** 50 %

What type of specialization?

We are specialized in interdisciplinary research with a team of experts from a broad range of fields, from space design and architecture, systems engineering, human factors, habitability and space technologies. We operate in Europe and India searching for synergies between work (office/laboratory work) and life on earth and in space. More than half of our team members have an education in design or architecture, some have had more years of education or experience to show for than others. Generally, the areas of expertise are complementary, they cover space engineering, space sciences, and design/architecture. Our associated consultants contribute further expertise needed, e.g. in technology, space mission planning and geological sciences. We are also part of the worldwide space architect network (www.spacearchitect.org).

How did it come about?

The specialization came from a personal interest in futures studies and social utopias. Issues related to sustainability in architecture are economic and efficient use of space and resources, dealing with minimal spaces, the fostering of well-being and productivity of the human being. Barbara Imhof obtained expert knowledge in the field in a master course of space studies at the International Space University, Strasbourg, France. She also acquired first-hand working experience during her stay at the NASA Johnson Space Center, Houston, Texas.

Advantages/disadvantages?

Our activities are focused on interdisciplinary aspects. We build teams with our associates and consultants and/or become part of larger industry teams to apply for research studies or projects. We have to compete with other teams and win the tender for proposals. We also initiate projects and look for funding. We definitely see our specialization as an advantage. However, specialization is only one option for the architectural practice. But it can create identification for potential clients. In the vast sea of architectural practices, it can help you stand out and be seen. On the other hand, it can also be a hindrance when it comes to applying for more conventional architectural projects or competitions.

smertnik kraut, Vienna, AT
www.smertnikkraut.at

Field Object and graphic design

Focus Shop concepts for brand-name stores / brand-building architecture / interior design

Tool Identifying project objectives and developing the basic idea in the project starting phase

Educational background Architecture

Partners 2 (Richard Smertnik / Johannes Kraut)	**Collaborators** 11	
In business since 2008	**Percentage of specialized projects** 60 %	

What type of specialization?

We are specialized in architecture for retail outlets: we develop innovative shop concepts for brand-name stores and create brand-building architecture and interior design for our clients which make brand identity a three-dimensional experience. The project start phase is an important stage of our work in which we have to identify or define the project objectives and develop the basic idea. Areas such as object and graphic design, which are outside the usual architectural field, are also done by our office. The new prototype store design for a cooperation of a supermarket with a gas station chain was just completed and furthermore, we implement the developed design of Bipa drugstores throughout Austria and Croatia.

How did it come about?

Richard Smertnik studied architecture at the TU Vienna, Johannes Kraut at the TU Graz. We set up our joint office in 2008. However, the path that our office was to take was already paved during our training: toward the end of our course of studies, we began to feel that a "classical" architect's career with public commissions was not of much interest to us. We are more interested in the reproducibility of a work, as well as in accelerating the working processes – an approach that is already widely accepted in the visual arts. We also developed our particular profile by collaborating with colleagues who already worked as specialists: we both worked in the same architect's office and went through all the important stages there, from project development to implementation.

Advantages/disadvantages?

We are not aware of any limitations that result from our specialization. Quite the contrary, in fact: the more projects we do, the greater our clients' trust in our work. With respect to competition, we know, of course, our competitors and have ties of mutual respect and recognition of each other's achievements with them. However, we do not accept commissions in our specialized field of expertise only; a broader range of commissions is important for the stability and continuous development of our business. We do not believe that specialization is a fundamental necessity for success. It is one of several options that our profession offers.

complizen Planungsbüro, Halle & Berlin, DE
www.complizen.de

Field Museums, schools, exhibition design, collaborative planning, quality of public places
Focus Special urban challenges due to structural change, low-cost/high-end architecture
Tool Communication and public relations in urban development planning,
strategies in shrinking urban environments/reutilization of vacant spaces/urban sports

Educational background Interior design/business administration
Partners 2 (Tore Dobberstein/Andreas Haase)   Collaborators 4
In business since 1999   Percentage of specialized projects 50 %

Specialization:
Architecture,
communication and
urban development

What type of specialization?

Aside from offering classical architectural services, we have specialized in developing strategies for shrinking cities with our complizen Planungsbüro. After all, we are located in Halle, a city in East Germany with a 20 percent housing vacancy rate. Our interest is focused on the reutilization of vacant spaces. We began with what we called 'sportifications', events where we hold bicycle races, Frisbee relays and other sports contests in empty stairwells or hallways. In this way, potentials that have previously been overlooked are detected and put to use. Moreover, we believe that new perspectives can improve the image of urban space. The list of our cooperation partners is long: associations, schools, local businesses and public institutions. For us, cities are like living creatures; they constantly change, and we have specialized in accompanying this transformation in which the human being always is in the center of attention.

How did it come about?

Andreas Haase studied interior design and Tore Dobberstein business. Working together as a small office, it is in our personal interest to address issues that are relevant for the local society. We have therefore always participated in local initiatives and cultural, artistic, or other projects. These activities have also broadened our professional horizon. And we have a passion for urban sports, such as skateboarding or BMXing. This passion has also informed our specialization.

Advantages/disadvantages?

We think the situation is ambivalent: most of our clients appreciate that ours is not a classical office profile. The disadvantage is that we do not have one specialization only. In the end, though, the offers contained in our 'grab bag' all fit well together one way or another. Nevertheless, the field of specialization also defines the values that the office stands for. If it is done right, many people and potential clients will remember specialized offices better than others.

However, we look into the future with optimism. Communication projects in particular are gaining in relevance, as the example of Stuttgart 21 has shown, which also has to do with a process of negotiating in an urban space. It strengthened our positioning. The very name of our office (in English: Accomplices Planning Office) indicates an essentially collaborative approach. We therefore are right on target with our persistent effort to improve communication. People's need to effectively participate in planning processes is increasing, regardless of whether or not a region, or the economy, is going up or down.

leit-werk, London, GB
www.leit-werk.com

Field Airports, passenger terminals, ATC towers, often XXL scale

Focus Introducing new materials, e.g., for ventilation / enabling new forms to be integrated in urban and suburban structures

Tool Collaborative communication / BIM – Building Information Modeling/space planning

Educational background Architecture / industrial design / interior design / textile design

Partners 1 (Henrik Rothe) **Collaborators** 10

In business since 1999 **Percentage of specialized projects** 80 %

What type of specialization?

We operate in the field of airport planning and design, predominantly in concept design and master planning in combination with regional and urban planning around airports. Often, we provide a master plan, which is then taken further by another team with another architect. Sometimes we receive designs from other consultants and architects, which we need to further develop to the next design stage. Since 2002 a big project of our office is being the lead architect in the design and implementation of the Khartoum New Internatvional Airport in Sudan. Our role is to cover all creative input with regards to the master plan and the design of the airport buildings and their arrangement on the airport, including landscaping and commercial landside facilities.

How did it come about?

Henrik Rothe studied Interior Design at Burg Giebichenstein University of Art and Design Halle. His diploma project in 1989 lead him from an initial interior material and colour concept to a new terminal concept. By chance, he got one type of project and others followed: "It was a result of the fall of the Berlin wall and the necessity to create airports in the former East Germany. This historic moment contributed to the specialization. I had to learn how an airport terminal would work. I drove to the five largest airports in Germany and spoke to their directors and managers who explained to me crucial concepts of airport planning, design and operation. From that moment the fascination of airports never vanished and the more one engages with the elements the more it becomes clear, how vast this field of airport design is." Maria Kramer and Anke Jakob are the other two of the three partners of leit-werk. Both have brought different values to the practice: Kramer is a proven airport design specialist, while Jakob is responsible for internal studio administration and management.

Advantages/disadvantages?

It is helpful being an independent organisation, because in large organisations communication is often a difficult issue. There are internal debates, which do not affect us so that we can focus on content rather formalities and politics. We like this kind of specialisation because with our work we cater to a relatively small group of potential clients, mainly the aviation industry, who appreciate our work as essential to design excellent airport environments. But we have to admit that we also feel a limit: sometimes we prepare airport master plans, which are then implemented by some star architect – a job, we would like to do ourselves as an inclusive part of our work.

As we are not star architects yet, we have to live in-between, building up our reputation and earning fees with our specialization and establish an image as architects and designers beyond this to be perhaps commissioned with the 'glorious job' one day. But it is also true, that this in-between is the only way to design first class airports, with ambition toward our specialization and toward architecture in general ... so hard work for many years to come and not too many completed projects to be expected.

nonconform, Vienna, AT
www.nonconform.at

Specialization: The "zero phase", the phase before the actual architecture project

- Field Working with the citizens of a community or town
- Focus A holistic view / sustainability
- Tool 'On-site ideas workshop' / formulating specific objectives for a construction project

Educational background Architecture / town planning / landscape architecture / cultural management / communication science / sociology

Partners 8 (Katharina Forster / Roland Gruber / Christof Isopp / Katharina Kothmiller / Christina Kragl / Peter Nageler / Caren Ohrhallinger / Sabine Weber) **Collaborators** 40

In business since 1999 **Percentage of specialized projects** 50 %

What type of specialization?

We have developed the concept of the 'on-site ideas workshop'. For a minimum of three days we 'set up camp', so to speak, on site and during this period work together with the citizens of a community or town or with staff members of an organization to find and formulate ideas for concrete future tasks. This joint ideas-pooling process generally focuses on formulating specific objectives for a construction project. Above all, villages and towns in the rural areas have turned out to be ideal clients for this approach: we notice that many of our clients need our method to learn to re-appreciate their town or village centers. In recent years, many of these centers have been neglected, but nobody actually wants to see them die. For us, the main issues are a holistic view and sustainability and not so much individual buildings. The project starts with working out in advance the 'right' scenarios and solutions for the future. The result is a course of action that can be implemented piecemeal with partial projects carried out over several years.

How did it come about?

We had problems to properly describe our work or philosophy and were tired of building single-family houses. As architects, we were often involved in projects in town centers, but generally in a re-active, never in a pro-active phase. Much about the tasks that we were commissioned with was poorly prepared and only cursorily agreed upon. In the course of Roland Gruber's studies for a master's degree in culture management, it became clear to us that these communities had to call in external specialists for a new project orientation. We talked to a specialist consultant from the creative industries area and worked with him for a year in order to arrive at a new position. In addition to intensive discussions with previous clients, we also took a look at the competition, considering general trends and developments, our own strengths and weaknesses as well as earlier milestones in our work. In the end, we developed a number of possible scenarios for the future. We wanted to move from re-active to pro-active planning and decided upon this new form of participatory development of ideas. The book 'The Idea Machine' by Swiss entrepreneur and writer Nadja Schnetzler, along with literature on open space technology and the development of scenarios, provided an important impetus to clarify and specify our new working method.

Advantages/disadvantages?

Before our specialization, the situation was more or less that each of us did everything; as a team, we did not concentrate on our respective individual strengths. Consequently, it was not only the strengths of the office as a whole that became more evident, but also the strengths of the individual members. Strengthening our strengths was a central guiding idea of our development process, for we believed that this was the only way we would stand a real chance of getting to the top in one area or another. In the last five years, our motto has been: 'Stay on the message – you have to repeat and repeat it until people understand this new kind of work'. This is attracting interest from more and more people, we have a growing number of inquiries, and new cooperative projects develop. Originally, however, we had not expected the path toward the new position to be so long: you need considerable perseverance and must be utterly convinced of the path that you pursue. There are enough obstacles that will come your way, and the market has, of course, been discovered by others as well – and not just by architects – and is fairly contested.

servo, Stockholm, SE & Los Angeles, US
www.servo-stockholm.com, www.servo-la.com

Field Interiors, installations and small scale buildings / architecture and product design

Focus Energy / environmental regulation

Tool 3D modeling / parametric design / pooling software / integrating interactive performance / speculative materiality / digital and analogue materiality

Educational background Architecture / landscape architecture

Partners 2 (Ulrika Karlsson / Marcelyn Gow)   **Collaborators** more than 10

In business since 2000   **Percentage of specialized projects**

Specialization:
Technical ecologies
and electronic
information
infrastructures

What type of specialization?

Servo explores the potential of networks, technical ecologies and electronic information infrastructures both as a way of organizing their practice and as a site of architectural research. As their name suggests, they operate on those sites where information and energy are transposed as they cross over from one system or circuit to another. The group's work focuses on the development of architectural environments, active design systems comprised of temporal conditions, shifting material states, and in general the ebb and flow of information in real time.

How did it come about?

We have gradually developed very specific knowledge and skills by testing various techniques and collaborating with other specialists: when we were students at Columbia University in the mid-1990s, animation software used in the film industry and digital fabrication processes were just being introduced. An interest in exploring the relationship between architecture, technology, and ecology became important for our practice and projects.

Advantages/disadvantages?

We see our specialization as an advantage in the sense that we can learn in depth from specialization. We think that specialization is important on the one side, and not important on the other. Today, complex architectural projects require expertise in very specific fields. At the same time, architecture is a generalist and synthesizing discipline, where expertise lies in the knowledge of how to make many different systems interact and produce an articulated larger whole. In this way, it is necessary that the architect is both highly specialized and, at the same time, able to correlate several systems to as to create a new whole. In the future, both specialization as well as synthesizing, generalist capabilities will be important.

CZstudio, Marghera, IT
www.czstudio.com

Specialization:
Water and energy
savings through
materials reuse

Field Themes related to infrastructure, mobility, energy and landscape · great buildings · public space			
Focus Water and energy savings · maximize opportunities for change while minimizing costs			
Tool Reuse of materials			
Educational background Architecture			
Partners 2 (Paolo Ceccon / Laura Zampieri)	**Collaborators** 5		
In business since 2006	**Percentage of specialized projects** 85 %		

What type of specialization?

In dealing with architectural and landscaping projects, we focus on saving water and energy by reusing specific materials like soil, water and, in certain cases, stones, gravel and sand. We try to build by using what we find on site, thinking of public spaces and buildings as unique man-made artifacts that begin with yard work so as to maximize the opportunities for change while minimizing costs. Projects of different kind and scale provided the training ground for us to understand the impossibility of organizing processes without problems, but also helped us to make problem solving our specialty.

How did it come about?

How this developed is difficult to summarize for us: we both had pursued different paths, but decided to work together because we both believe in a unified anthropic space, a space that is defined through how we act on different materials at our disposal, making waste processes a project resource. We both graduated in architecture in Venice, but were interested in the changing role of architecture. The energy generated from the transformation that this city has seen in the past 20 years has been a formative influence on us, our life, and our way of thinking architecture.

Advantages/disadvantages?

Specialized projects are the main financial resource of our practice. But in order to do such projects, we still need to make money with other projects or activities like teaching and consulting. From our point of view, specializing is important, because with specialist expertise available in your office you can provide the best client services. On the other hand, specialization reduces the intellectual complexity of architectural thinking and the related problem-solving ability.

ecosistema urbano, Madrid, ES & Miami, US
www.ecosistemaurbano.com

Field Multi-disciplinary approach	
Focus Social issues, energy and water, low-cost to create high-end sustainable architecture	
Tool Collaboration with urban planners, graphic designers, sociologists, anthropologists, and engineers	
Educational background Architecture	
Partners 2 (Belinda Tato / Jose Luis Vallejo)	**Collaborators** 20
In business since 2000	**Percentage of specialized projects** 60 %

What type of specialization?

We define our field of interest and specialization as Urban Social Design. For us, Urban Social Design means under-standing the make-up of the built environment, its space and dynamics in order to improve social relationships with-in the community. The objective of our team is to generate favorable conditions for interaction and self-organization between people and their environment. In order to promote this concept, we have started a non-profit organization to promote networking, free culture, the use of new technologies, and social innovation. Furthermore, we apply this specialization to projects according to the respective specific context, program, and needs. One example of a pro-ject we developed applying Urban Social Design is Dreamhamar, a participative design process that connects the city of Hamar, Norway, with the rest of the world by re-designing its city square with the help of 21st century tools.

How did it come about?

The positioning of ecosistema urbano is the result of a process of learning by doing: our orientation towards Urban Social Design evolved continuously while we kept defining the skills we acquired over the years by focusing on pro-cesses rather than outcome in projects. Along with our educational backgrounds, these various experiences helped us to define the statements that we use as guidelines in project development.

Advantages/disadvantages?

Cities today are becoming more and more complex, both physically and socially. We understand design as a mode of research and practice that shapes urban environments, responds to its problems and connects both social and physical forms in the city. The clear advantage of using Urban Social Design as a specialization is being able to bridge the gap between disciplines in order to address the complex issues of the city. Having a specialization also means applying an approach that is different from that of other architecture offices, which gives you an advantage of being unique.On the other hand, this approach is new, and not everyone is familiar with it. Also sometimes, when having a certain specialization, it creates a too specific image which gives potential clients a wrong impression of your work as architects, urban planners, etc. Thus, we have to learn from our mistakes and keep developing and adapting our specialization.

Kaden + Lager, Berlin, DE
www.kadenundlager.de

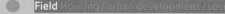

Specialization: From timber construction to urban renewal

Field Housing / urban development / social politics

Focus Timber construction / low energy architecture / cradle to cradle / urban renewal

Tool Nemetschek / Allplan / 3D / cellulose fiber for insulation

Educational background Architecture / design / art

Partners 2 (Tom Kaden / Markus Lager)   Collaborators 25

In business since 2000; as Kaden+Lager since 2015   Percentage of specialized projects 90 %

What type of specialization?

We are specialized in multi-storey timber housing and engage especially in projects that sit between the fields of architecture, urban development, and social politics. We often have to deal with issues of gentrification where one has to consider the social impact of the built environment and its consequences for different social groups.

Our architecture is distinguished by constructional and social responsibility. Anywhere in the urban fabric, but particularly in housing, the built environment has a major impact on the lives of residents and is not dependent on momentary interaction or short-term events.

Construction of housing – in many cases as a cooperative process with the future owners – became our central focus not by coincidence. Our office operates with low energy technologies and strives to stick to the cradle-to-cradle principle, which prioritizes systematic recycling and utilizes eco-effective products.

We mostly realize projects in Germany and have won several prizes abroad. One of our most significant projects is Germany's first high-rise building in timber construction, the 34m height– Skaio in Heilbronn.

How did it come about?

Mostly by self-teaching. We have an excellent network in the field of timber construction and are, for example, members of an association of timber-construction engineers, architects and consultants. With every new project, we develop timber construction practices further, trying to push the envelope. Practical implementation of new timber construction standards could, in the near future, improve usability and help increase cost savings in ecological urban residential projects.

Advantages/disadvantages?

One advantage of specialization is the increase of attention it helps you get in the industry. However, we do not only take on projects within our area of specialization, which means housing, but, on the contrary, try to extend our expertise to other building typologies. You should never allow yourself to be reduced to just one thing. Specialization in construction, however, can be important to create a stronger focus on the working process.

Studio Marco Vermeulen, Rotterdam, NL
www.marcovermeulen.eu

Field Large scale / business areas / urbanism and landscape

Focus Translating closed cycles (energy, water, and materials) into new spatial typologies / boundary conditions between city and countryside / parking / food production

Tool Focusing on concept phase

Educational background Architecture

Partners 1 (Marco Vermeulen)　　　　　**Collaborators** 2

In business since 2010　　　　　**Percentage of specialized projects** 70 %

Specialization: Self-sufficiency in water and energy

What type of specialization?

The interest of our office lies in boundary conditions between urban and rural areas. We mostly operate in large-scale projects in business or industrial areas somewhere between urban structures and the surrounding countryside; among them the 'Klavertje 4 – Greenport Venlo' or the 'Moerdijk Logistics Business Park' can be mentioned. They all are designed to be self-sufficient in energy and water supply. Another outstanding project that is currently being realized is 'Water Squares'. Living in the Delta Metropolis, the urbanized Western part of the Netherlands that includes cities like Amsterdam, The Hague, Utrecht or Rotterdam, comes with water-related threats, and these threats are increasing, due to the climate change. We can expect problems with water in more than one way: from the sea, from rivers, from the sky and from the ground. The rising sea level, combined with heavy rainfall, will have a direct effect on rivers. The current sewage system cannot deal with torrential amounts of rainwater. At the same time, these threats offer opportunities for the Dutch water cities: water threats can be a motivation to take on some of the urgent issues within the city. Perspectives for the future will not only have to come up with solutions to water problems, but will also have to create a more attractive urban environment.

How did it come about?

All the members of the office consider themselves, and were trained, as architects. Each project in our area of specialization led to, and informed, the following one. Currently, the office is involved in large-scale developments in the Netherlands, all of which are, at first sight, assignments that one would not want to get involved in as an architect in the quest for personal architectural expression. We like to call them neglected assignments: logistics businesses, greenhouse or pig-breeding units. These are the places where we use and waste enormous amounts of energy and produce half of all carbon dioxide emissions. And these are the situations in which we waste enormous amounts of space. Architecture has a long and rich tradition of optimizing density. There are hardly any architects involved in those neglected assignments, and much space is wasted. But in a country like Holland we cannot afford this any longer, and by now the issue has moved up high on the political agenda.

Advantages/disadvantages?

We do not only take on projects within our area of specialization, because our interests are broader, and work is scarce these days. Specializing may be important to sharpen the office profile, but it is only one of several possible ways: broadening the horizon also is vital for conceptual offices.

VIZE, Praha, CZ
www.vize.com

Field Large complexes / transportation and medical projects / urban and landscape designs

Focus Architectural visualization / still views / animated 3D movies

Tool Web-based communication / strict internal discipline concerning the file and project management

Educational background Architecture

Partners 2 (Miro Kurčík / Ondřej Tomášek) **Collaborators** 8

In business since 2000 **Percentage of specialized projects** 90 %

What type of specialization?

We have specialized in architectural visualization and produce views and animated 3D movies. Mostly, we come into play in the course of architectural competitions or in the preliminary design phase. The tools we use are standard 3D software like 3ds Max plus V-Ray, Adobe Photoshop, Fusion, or Sony Vegas. We cover a whole range of architectural projects, but have a preference for bigger projects, such as large building complexes, transportation and medical projects, as well as urban or landscape designs. Our clients and their projects are all over the world: therefore we have devised and developed a simple web-based tool for our international clientele so as to be able to clarify input information and revise planning processes through previews early on. We also work together with a number of remote collaborators, which means that we have to have very strict internal file and project management. Specializing in computer-generated imagery (CGI) means also having to develop a signature style, which helps to distinguish ourselves from the competition. We hope to have succeeded in creating a recognizable look of our images, which is what our clients hire us for.

How did it come about?

We both studied architecture, Miro Kurčík at the Prague Fine Arts Academy's School of Architecture and Ondřej Tomášek at the Czech Technical University in Prague. Basically, there was no course or training where rendering or visualization techniques were formally taught. It was all individual effort and learning by doing. However, the general rules of composition, lighting, and color interaction are more or less the same for architects, photographers, or painters. Most of the experience came from studying architectural photographs and computer-generated images published on Internet or in specialized books and magazines. Taking the step to specialize in architectural visualization was the result of identifying a market gap in the late 1990s and an existing demand for visuals for a couple of real projects. Miro Kurčík is the 3D Master, he is responsible for the creative work and the technological background, whereas Ondřej does project management and controlling.

Advantages/disadvantages?

If specialization is based on solid education and skills and, ideally, has been developed over time, the concentration of experience allows for a much faster and more competent reaction to any differences of opinion or unexpected requirements from the client. But specialization is not the only way for the future. With communication possibilities improving and new markets opening up, an increasing number of firms will be able to be active internationally in our area of specialization. We got most of our clients through references and recommendation. The nature of our work allows us to take on projects worldwide. Here is one general example of our workday: while working on scheduled projects, we suddenly have several parallel requests coming in from one to three long-term clients for various changes and amendments on their ongoing project. And, of course, "asap", as always … Without the internal rules and functionality of our virtual office system, which allows us to divide the work immediately among several collaborators, we would not stand a chance of keeping the required deadlines and quality at all.

FIELD – FOCUS – TOOL

All teams, with the exception of one, described their specialization as acting in a specific field of work, with a specific focus and tools. No team could, or wanted to, limit their specialization to any single field, tool, or focus.

Traditional architectural areas of expertise (such as building typologies) are combined with a broader interest for other non-traditional fields of practice in almost all teams.

FIELD: Are you specialized ...

11	in projects between architecture and another field
8	in certain typologies (housing, schools, airports ...)
8	in other areas that should be considered for specialization
7	in a certain scale of projects
6	in certain geographical locations

FOCUS: Are you specialized ...

10	in a specific issue, such as shrinking cities, aging society
9	in themes related to sustainable architecture
8	in other areas that should be considered for specialization
7	in low-cost or high-end architecture
4	in the recycling of materials

Aside from the more common focus on things like sustainability and low-cost, the teams of our sample have developed specific expertise and their own thematic approach. Specific issues include:

> Using an airport as a pump-primer for the economy in the region (leit-werk)

> Translating closed cycles (energy, water and matter) into new spatial typologies (Studio Marco Vermeulen)

> Synergies between work and life on earth and in space (LIQUIFER Systems Group)

TOOLS: Are you specialized ...

6	in working with a special software / method / technique
5	in services related to architecture
3	in working as consultant for other architects or designers

Similarly, the tools selected go well beyond traditional architectural know-how. Specific interest for communication has led some teams to act as consultants for other actors involved in the creation of urban – and other– architectural spaces.

> We are specialized in innovative processes of participation (Artgeneering)

> We offer strategic consulting for urban design by responding to environmental and social issues (ecosistema urbano)

> We are specialized in the "on-site ideas workshop" as a form of moderated user participation (nonconform)

getting specialized

225

SPECIALIZATION MAP

While traditional specialization is about what you do (field),
new specializations relate to the steering of the design
process (tool) and to specific priorities or attributes of the
design (focus).

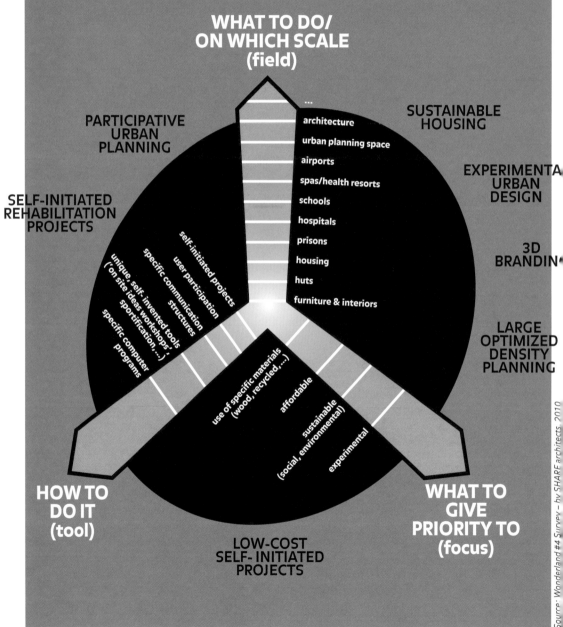

**WHAT TO DO/
ON WHICH SCALE
(field)**

PARTICIPATIVE
URBAN
PLANNING

SUSTAINABLE
HOUSING

SELF-INITIATED
REHABILITATION
PROJECTS

EXPERIMENTA
URBAN
DESIGN

3D
BRANDIN

...
architecture
urban planning space
airports
spas/health resorts
schools
hospitals
prisons
housing
huts
furniture & interiors

LARGE
OPTIMIZED
DENSITY
PLANNING

self-initiated projects
user participation
specific communication
structures
unique, self-invented tools
("on site ideas workshops",
sportification, ...)
specific computer
programs

use of specific materials
(wood, recycled, ...)
affordable
sustainable
(social, environmental)
experimental

**HOW TO
DO IT
(tool)**

**WHAT TO
GIVE
PRIORITY TO
(focus)**

LOW-COST
SELF-INITIATED
PROJECTS

Source: Wonderland #4 Survey – by SHARE architects, 2010

how
to
specialize

Specialization requires specialized know-how. But how to get it, and where? Through formal education, learning by doing, informal ways of learning? Is it strategic decisions or opportunity plus luck? While the continuing-education market increasingly offers prefabricated packages in various flavors, the way to go for many is a mix of readymade solutions and unique and personal biographical decisions. In other words, there is no ideal path that leads to specialization.

Chance or strategy

There is no reason to be afraid of being typecast.
You just have to find your own strategy.

Text by Hans Ibelings, Montreal/Toronto, Canada

How is it possible for an architect to map out a coherent path amid so much unpredictability? And how bad must things be if a star like Koolhaas feels he is at the mercy of chance? After all, he belongs to that top flight of designers who can afford to be selective about the work they take on and enjoy so much status that they do not simply have to serve clients. In addition, more often than not they deal with clients who realize that they have to accept that an architect *hors catégorie* decides for himself, to a certain extent, what he does.

Maybe now, more than a decade and a half since he wrote those words, Koolhaas feels less at the mercy of an "arbitrary sequence of demands". And it is beyond dispute that he also belongs to the elite group of architects who are able to bend client's wishes in such a way as to be able to explore the same or similar themes and motives in successive projects. There is no better example of this self-chosen route than the commission he landed in the late nineties for a residence near Rotterdam. The client, who had an obsession with clutter, wanted a house that was perfectly tidy. The design consisted of an object in the form of a rough diamond into which an orthogonal box was inserted like a sterile *panic room*, the perfect setting for the perfectly tidy life that the client so longed for. All the space around the box was defined as storage space, the contents of which could not be considered as clutter. After some time, though, Koolhaas turned down the commission because, he claimed, he had lost interest in this form of tidiness bordering on nosophobia, which in itself says something about his autonomy in accepting commissions or not. However, this independence was underlined all the more when the same configuration of an orthogonal box inside a rough diamond cropped up a short while later in the project for the Casa da Música in Porto, a totally different building, with a different program and a different context.

In the introduction to *S,M,L,XL*, the anthological monograph of the Office for Metropolitan Architecture (OMA), Rem Koolhaas writes that "incoherence, or more precisely, randomness, is the underlying structure of all architects' careers: they are confronted with an arbitrary sequence of demands, with parameters they did not establish, in countries they hardly know, about issues they are dimly aware of, expected to deal with problems that have proved intractable to brains vastly superior to their own". (OMA, Rem Koolhaas and Bruce Mau, *S,M,L,XL*, Rotterdam, 010 Publishers, 1995)

Relationships

While autonomous artists are free to choose their subject, theme and medium, architects are much more bound by the commission, the client, the site, and so on. Furthermore, there are so many individuals and parties involved in an architectural project who for good reason can claim part of the success for themselves so that it would be difficult to speak of any one single author.

For a start, it is the client (who often cannot be limited to a single person) who decides whether there will even be a commission at all; and the proverb "he who pays the piper calls the tune" very much applies to architecture.

Only a few individuals succeed in really turning this relationship around. Glenn Murcutt apparently keeps a celebrated list of clients who sometimes have to wait patiently for years before it is their turn and the master decides to accept their commission and money, in more or less the same way that Louis Vuitton demands patience from his clients as they wait for certain bags. However, most architects, let alone the entire community of professionals, do not succeed in giving potential clients the impression that their work ought to be valued as rare or rarefied. Most architects are like devoted pets, content with every morsel, any stroke they can get. That is the nature of the relationship, and in times of economic crisis it is clear that there are more architects waiting for clients than there are clients waiting for architects.

Stochastic variable

Even if the reality is that architects are in many respects more dependent on clients than vice versa, that is still no reason to view the architect as an obedient purveyor of services who can do nothing but wait and see what jobs are tossed his way.

The randomness Koolhaas wrote about – that commissions and clients can be considered as stochastic variables – may be what it looks like from the architect's point of view, but is usually not the case for the client. (Not always at least: I once asked a client how he went about choosing an architect, and it turned out that he was given an alphabetical list of names and simply phoned the first one whose surname began with a C and struck a deal.)

For many clients, though, there are more rational reasons for commissioning a particular architect. For example, if the architect in question has already distinguished himself with a similar project. That is a form of risk minimization, which is understandable in light of the investment involved in construction. It is also due in part to the limited imagination of many clients, who can only form an idea of what they have already seen or known before.

Typecasting

For that reason alone, the phenomenon of typecasting is very frequent, to the effect that the way a career starts often has a lasting influence on its further course. If an architect, whether deliberately or by chance, ends up in a certain area, a certain field of work, or deals with a certain type of client, he or she will often receive more commissions from the same or similar clients. Which is not to say that if a young architect wants to focus on large multipurpose complexes, he or she should never accept a commission to design a shop interior or convert a kitchen. Clients are also smart enough to realize that such small beginnings of a design practice may be no more than a prelude to bigger things. But as soon as the real work starts, the mechanism of typecasting will, in many cases, get started, too. It is just like some actors always get to play the bad guy, or the femme fatale – the very same thing happens to architects. Someone whose previous commissions mostly were for housing estates or private homes will not be a likely candidate to build a museum; and competitions are perhaps the only way to venture in a new direction. In some respects, therefore, typecasting even makes early fame gained through celebrated career-starting projects a risky development. For it will leave a lasting impression and before you know it you will only get similar commissions for years.

Eluding such typecasting is not easy, and current public tendering procedures in Europe do not make it any easier because they often require relevant experience with commissions of comparable program or size, which means that if you have never built a theater you are highly unlikely to ever get the opportunity to build one.

When it comes to typecasting, the person affected by it usually is convinced, rightly or otherwise, that he or she has been chosen for the wrong reasons or is unable to draw on some of his/her talents. (Incidentally, this is perhaps a general phenomenon: almost none of us are valued for the characteristics that we ourselves deem to be most important in us.) It is important to keep an eye on that mismatch because it may give rise to a second agenda in that an architect, while being commissioned to do one thing, all the while unfolds his own plan and carries it out, too, without the client becoming aware of it at all.

Local markets

Previous projects are important arguments for clients, but they are certainly not the only ones. Another reason to commission a specific person is proximity, both in a social and geographic sense. There is not one single market where all architects have to compete against one another for commissions. For a start, there are countless local markets. As is the case with dentists, plumbers and bakers, most architects find most of their clients in their immediate surroundings. Many architects find most of their employment, and their clients, in the city or region where they are based. That would be an argument in favor of building a local profile, in which an architect's social gifts are perhaps more important than architectural talent. A sports club membership, attendance at an exhibition opening, contact with other parents at the school of your children: such things can have more effect than an article in an international architecture magazine.

Local markets, however, are by no means reserved for local architects. And although local architects rarely operate in national, let alone international, markets, the reverse does not apply; at the local level, they have to compete against international stars. Herzog & de Meuron build all over the world, but especially in and around their home town of Basel. Siza is a world star, but has left his mark on his native city of Porto over the past half century. Apart from local markets, which can be considered as geographical niches, there are other sorts of niche markets, from the world of illegal money to a gay circuit from which certain architects succeed to secure the bulk of their commissions. The international vanguard also is something of a niche market, which just like any other niche market is an exclusive club with a strong 'like knows like' character and a stringent selection procedure, as described for example in *Architects: The Noted and the Ignored*, in which the author Niels Prak convincingly analyzes the fusion of social and cultural status. You do not have to be a sociologist to recognize the mutual relationship betweenclient and architect in particular markets like these, both of whom depend on the other for their status. Even though it might sound trivial, it is of great importance for architects to have a large network outside their own profession because it will contain more potential clients than their own discipline.

Equally trivial is the observation that, speaking of large networks, it is important to have a distinctive high profile in the form of a specialization or particular expertise or skill that lends itself well to self-promotion. Self-promotion can be effective, certainly so if there is a clear idea behind it. Thousands and thousands of architects show just about everything under the sun on their website, every single thing they can do, so as not to rule anything out. Such barraging is not necessarily the best way of attracting clients. 'A little bit of everything' is less convincing that 'everything of something'.

Individual initiative

If commissions fail to materialize, or if they are not those you would like to get, there is always the solution of generating your own work and developing your own initiatives. That is at odds with the habit many architects have of simply waiting for a client to appear, or of hawking their own work around in search of commissions, which, in neutral terms, is generally referred to as 'canvassing'. Only a small minority possess the inventiveness, courage and perseverance to generate their own commissions, which usually carries with it greater financial risk than is customary in standard architectural practice, for example by becoming a (joint) property developer, as Innocad and BKK in Austria, Paul de Ruiter in the Netherlands and others have done. Less financial risk is involved in conducting research and developing specific expertise on that basis. Those who succeed in securing subsidies or research grants can set their own course to a certain extent. A client often remains in sight, however, in the form of the individual(s) who represent the research-funding institution and expect a report at the very least.

Work generated by yourself can also lie beyond the realm of architectural design and research, for example in setting up an architecture center, a festival or a magazine, in the production of a book – Wonderland is a classic example in more than one way – or in exploring cross-disciplinary fields of work. In recent years, there certainly has been a boom in social engineering, in incentives and support for neighborhood initiatives, urban agriculture, workspaces for new creative businesses, workshops for youths and children, street festivals and other events that lie outside the domain of traditional architecture.

All such activities often concern issues of space, directly or indirectly, since they all concern the built environment, but on their own those issues rarely are of the sort that can be resolved in a reflex manner by building cubage. And this is something that is relevant, particularly now that the economic crisis, the ageing population, and the increasing awareness of ecological issues mean that building in such quantity is no longer a matter of course as it once was. It could even mark the end of the automatism of solving every problem by building something. And this, in turn, could mean that architects will have fewer clients no matter what, and thus their own initiatives could become more important. It takes a different professional attitude, which is not based on the traditional relationship between client and architect with all its vicissitudes, but on a very deliberate and considered strategy. Accordingly, we will have to redefine, certainly in Europe, how architecture can and should relate to that which it serves: society. ▪

HOW DID YOUR SPECIALIZATION COME ABOUT

Only one team expressly decided to specialize as a result of a top-down approach, hiring a consultant to define a specific profile for their firm. For the others, it was either something that developed over time without a clear initial strategy or a mix of strategy and chance that possibly happened during their education or in response to a time of crisis.

Research and theoretical work, or the simple fact of having two or more projects of the same type following one another are other possible key factors that resulted in specialization in our sample.

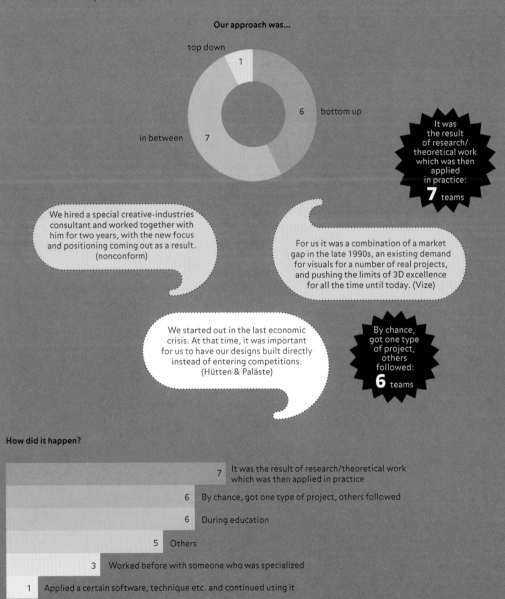

Our approach was...

top down 1

bottom up 6

in between 7

It was the result of research/ theoretical work which was then applied in practice: **7** teams

We hired a special creative-industries consultant and worked together with him for two years, with the new focus and positioning coming out as a result. (nonconform)

For us it was a combination of a market gap in the late 1990s, an existing demand for visuals for a number of real projects, and pushing the limits of 3D excellence for all the time until today. (Vize)

We started out in the last economic crisis. At that time, it was important for us to have our designs built directly instead of entering competitions. (Hütten & Paläste)

By chance, got one type of project, others followed: **6** teams

How did it happen?

7 — It was the result of research/theoretical work which was then applied in practice

6 — By chance, got one type of project, others followed

6 — During education

5 — Others

3 — Worked before with someone who was specialized

1 — Applied a certain software, technique etc. and continued using it

How to specialize in urban design

Text by Gabriela Barman-Krämer, Solothurn, Switzerland

For many decades in the twentieth century, architects gave much less attention to the design of cities and the urban environment than to the architectural object. It can therefore be considered a very important moment when in 1989–90, the first session of EUROPAN was launched, a biennial competition for young architects to design innovative schemes "between the city and the architectural object" for sites across Europe. This brought the discipline of urban design to center stage.

These tendencies had a strong impact on professional education: many architectural schools in Europe have introduced new master or postgraduate programs for urban design in the past 15 years; these included landscape architecture workshops, sociology seminars and lectures in urban design history, to name just a few. With the Bologna reform, graduates with bachelor degrees other than architecture were also permitted to enroll for these programs. Different academic backgrounds have not just extended theoretical discussion, but have also led to different approaches within the professional urban design practice. Probably some of the most coherent and successful urban design curriculums are run in schools with traditionally close ties to the actual political, social and topological context, as for example in the Netherlands. Since the dyked land, much of it below sea level, had to be protected and used sparingly and creatively, urban design primarily sought to find meaningful solutions to shelter cities from the threatening of water. At the TU Delft Department of Architecture large-scale projects are initiated, which also involve national and regional authorities, private institutions, engineers, and even bankers and lawyers.[1] Authorities in other European countries, among them France and Spain, launch urban design competitions with the intention to boost urban design as an element of cultural and economic development. In Switzerland and Germany, business companies commission famous architects to reconfigure the urban design sitting around their corporate headquarters. By contrast, urban design projects in Eastern European countries like Serbia are developed in government offices and attract local architects with an interest and talent in handling projects on the urban scale.

Although education, culture, politics and economy are important extrinsic influences, the intrinsic motivation is eventually most important for a career moving towards urban design. The fact is that many young architects have specialized in urban design without a specific educational background. They learn and incorporate principles and knowledge in the field by doing research and developing strategies in their practice. Other important skills to succeed with projects on the urban scale are consultation of clients and negotiation with all parties involved – qualifications that are hardly taught at school.

In practice, urban design is the material result of a number of conditions: the regulatory framework, social necessities, economic conditions or the development of traffic, just to name a few. These different interests are of a political nature and are represented by different public authorities. It is therefore evident that privately initiated urban design projects are supervised by officials or other representatives of public bodies who have a clear understanding of urban design processes and especially also of the qualities required for a successful transformation of the urban environment – an urban environment which offers people an improvement in the quality of life.

Architects specializing in urban design therefore potentially play a part in the urban design process not only as designers, but also as agents of those interests, which have a strong influence on the development of the design itself.

Should architects specializing in urban design call themselves urban designers? – 'Not only … but also!' As a job title, 'urban designer' simply is overused or misused by too many who do not care about the spatial qualities of cities, their peripheries and the areas beyond. The fact is that most architects who have specialized in urban design, among them EUROPAN winners[2] running a successful practice today, work on projects on all scales: installations and small buildings as well as large housing developments and new master plans for former industrial sites. From an architect's standpoint, urban design therefore is a specialization within architecture: however varied and diverse the responsibilities of the architects and urban designers are – at the core of the profession is, and will always be, the design of the city. ●●

This article is based on the author's conversations with several young professionals working as architects and urban designers:

Jan Schulz,
bb22 architekten und stadtplaner,
Frankfurt am Main, Germany
www.bb22.net

Ursina Fausch,
Zurich, Switzerland,
www.enf.ch

Suzanne Ewing

Sladjana Markovic,
Biljana Begenisic &
Sladjana Markovic Architects,
Belgrade, Serbia
AGBY architects
www.facebook.com/
agbyarchitects/

1   The projects are published in: Leen van Duin, François Claessens (eds.),
    Over Holland 7, 5x5 Projecten voor de Hollandse stad, Amsterdam, 2008

2   Editions Cité de l'Architecture + Europan (eds.), Europan Generation, the reinterpreted city, Paris, 2007

TEAMING UP

Is specialization about team work? Even if the educational background tends to be homogenous (see page 241) in the majority of the teams, partners develop different fields of expertise, or at least different roles.
Consultants may be important too, but only for some. Other teams never work with them.

> Generally, architects should be calling themselves something different, even though the word architecture is more and more becoming a term to describe complex structures. When you introduce yourself as an architect, clients often are nervous about whether you will be providing them with the right service. Calling yourself a consultant often clarifies the issue and everybody is expecting the result that you will actually get. (leit-werk)

> We hardly do any projects on our own anymore. (artgeneering)

> We hardly work with consultants. The expertise we have is self-taught or comes from practical experience. (Hütten & Paläste)

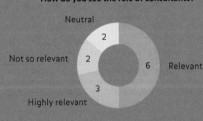

How do you see the role of consultants?

- Neutral 2
- Not so relevant 2
- Relevant 6
- Highly relevant 3

Is every partner of your team equally specialized?

- Not answered 1
- Every partner is equally specialized 2
- Partners have different roles 11

RADIUS OF ACTION

Getting clients in their local area and/or beyond, some teams are able to make their specialization their core business and a criterion for accepting or rejecting commissions. Sometimes it is not so difficult as many types of commission fit in with their specialization.

In other cases, it is a matter of quality and profiling. Yet, accepting other commissions also is a choice and not always a must: differentiation can help to put the firm on a sound economic footing.

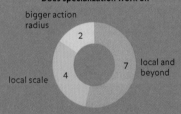

Does specialization work on

- bigger action radius 2
- local and beyond 7
- local scale 4

Are you only taking on projects within your specialization field?

- Yes 5
- No 9

Yes, because ...

> our field of specialization is quite broad. (CZ studio)

> you have to stay on the message – you have to repeat and repeat until people understand the new kind of work. (nonconform)

> we have joined resources and want to maintain our quality of work. (Zone Architects)

No, because ...

> there are not enough jobs available. (Liquifer)

> a diversification of areas of work makes sense for the sustainable stability and continuing development of our firm. (Smertnik Kraut)

BUILDING INFORMATION MODELING

NEW BUSINESS MODELS FOR THE ARCHITECTURE, ENGINEERING AND CONSTRUCTION INDUSTRIES?

The architecture, engineering and construction (AEC) industries are currently experiencing rapid digital transformation. Building Information Modeling (BIM) is increasingly becoming obligatory in public procurement procedures, and the establishing and standardization of BIM data is a major objective of the EU strategy for digitalization in construction.

How will digitalization and use of BIM affect small architectural offices?

Although the European AEC industry is characterized by high levels of design and engineering expertise, it is a highly fragmented small-enterprise industry. Based on the EU definition, the largest part of architecture offices are micro-enterprises (up to 5 employees). 72 % are one-person practices; less than 2 % employ more than 50 people (Architects Council of Europe, 2016). One of the central problems of the industry therefore is the traditional silo mentality, which prevents incremental innovation. New technologies such as BIM hold the promise of enhancing the integration and reducing the fragmentation of the industry.

Numerous advantages have been attributed to BIM technology, such as reduction of planning changes, costs, and planning time as well as improved design quality and building performance throughout the lifecycle with respect to resources and energy efficiency. But there also are many challenges and problems, such as a lack of data structures, insufficient using skills and competencies, and finally, a lack of interoperability between BIM tools; all these particularly affect small offices which do not have the resources for large investments in digital infrastructure or employee training.

Better integration of the different disciplines of the compartmentalized construction industry, however, is a necessity to make full use of the creative potential of collaborators on a

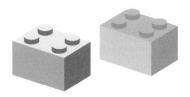

project. BIM could be an instrument that enhances integrated planning in that it facilitates closer cooperation of the individual disciplines and allows the collaborative establishment of, and work on, shared building models, which can be used for various purposes – architectural modeling, structural analysis, thermal simulation, life-cycle optimization, etc.

BIM research for practical planning

The potential of BIM as a catalyst for an integrated professional practice is yet far from being utilized to the full. Academic research has identified two major issues: individuals, or planning disciplines, seem to be bogged down by their respective role and thinking patterns, which accounts for a lack of cooperativeness even when working together with others on a team, and secondly, there is a lack of interoperable software and modeling conventions for shared use of models. This is indicative of some of the challenges that need to be tackled for a successful implementation of BIM. First of all, the skills of those involved in the planning process need to adapt to, or be brought up to the standard of, the changed BIM-supported interdisciplinary planning process; a task to be addressed by university curricula as well as by professional training. Moreover, confining BIM to the solemn realm of engineering technology has prevented it from yielding the expected benefits yet. Genuine innovation of the design and construction processes is closely related to the successful implementation of BIM on all levels: technology, people, and process.

Research at the so-called Integrated Design Studios (IDS) of the Vienna University of Technology shows that, while BIM tools are undeniably instrumental for analysis and quantification, actual process and design quality improvement also needs to take into account people-related issues such as working experience, interdisciplinary cooperation as a driver of creativity, and messy interpersonal communication. Thus a change in professional culture towards a more collaborative practice should be pursued in training and education to promote novel interdisciplinary approaches such as IDS. IDS research has shown that BIM tools can facilitate the transfer of tangible knowledge but are too inflexible to handle implicit knowledge. New tools and methods have to be found to support the creation and transfer of implicit, data-rich knowledge within interdisciplinary teams from the earliest planning stages. In this respect, one potential obstacle to overcome on the way to broader implementation of BIM was the negative response from architects who described intensified collaboration as "inhibiting creativity". Adopting BIM technology also carries a financial penalty in, especially for smaller offices. BIM-supported processes are more time-consuming and coordination-intensive than traditional ones. Significant effort has to be put in the pre-modeling and process-design phases to establish modeling conventions and standards; therefore the fee system for architects should also be reformed so as to make early design stages more rewarding.

A holistic approach to both process design and the integration of digital systems that would provide for smooth modeling and data-exchange workflows in accordance with the needs of local professional knowledge domains in project-based networks of professionals is still missing.

Establishing integrated digital design platforms would, however, allow for the integration of geometric and non-geometric data for, e.g., architectural, structural, energy and cost modeling and assessment, which, fed into mobile user interfaces or even robotic production, would enable significant process and quality improvement in construction projects. Moreover, the digital platforms do not only integrate various planning models, but also create networks of stakeholders, which is vitally important for small sized enterprises with limited personnel, financial, and technological resources. Specialization on the one hand and, on the other, the sharing of expertise and knowledge through digital platforms among designers, manufacturers, construction companies, facility managers, and software developers facilitate and enhance the creation of new business models for small enterprises like most architectural offices across the EU.

Practical advice and check list

The step towards BIM-supported design and planning involves a lot more than a software change. It will most likely require a comprehensive analysis of existing processes and systems in the office, as well as the careful designing of a future BIM-supported design process, including the structuring of data flows.

In general, there are two cases that occur most often in everyday practice: the office already employs BIM-capable software (such as ArchiCAD) but not as a 3D tool, or the office does not use BIM-capable programs at all (working instead with, e.g., AutoCAD) and needs to implement new software.

In the first case, the office should consider a thorough BIM training for all employees, as well as establishing BIM-structures in the office by appointing a BIM manager (who may, of course, come from the existing team).

In the second case, before deciding for a new software, a careful analysis should be made of a) design processes, and b) BIM software available on the market.

In the next step, it would be advisable to carry out a pilot project, using at least two different BIM softwares for the modeling and evaluating these in terms of usefulness, usability, interoperability, and ease of use. Software support should also be evaluated.

Any analysis of the design process as a basis to define
the requirements for a BIM software solution should include:

 a consideration of what planning stages the office is normally active in – competitions and preliminary design, or also further stages such as developed design, execution design, cost estimate, etc.

 a consideration of the types of project that the office specializes in, particularly with respect to project size and team size, global team distribution, complexity of geometry, building typology.

 a consideration of the network of consultants, of the software they use, and of the planning workflow. Knowing the workflow (the order in which a model will be used by different professionals involved in the planning process) is crucially important, as models for structural analysis have different requirements than those used for energy or cost modeling or assessment. This aspect is also important with regard to software interoperability.

Checklist:

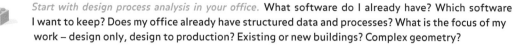

Start with design process analysis in your office. What software do I already have? Which software I want to keep? Does my office already have structured data and processes? What is the focus of my work – design only, design to production? Existing or new buildings? Complex geometry?

Which workflows do I serve? Only architectural modeling and/or data transfer to structural BIM, 5D BIM, 6D BIM? Consider what you are modeling for!

What are my financial capacities? How big is my team? Be aware that you will most likely need more than one software (e.g. Rhino for competition and handling of complex geometry; ArchiCAD for follow up developed design modeling).

BIM Management and Training You need to develop in-house BIM processes and structures (define the level of detail and level of development for each planning stage you participate in; define your BIM objects/families).

Do not overburden the model with an unnecessary level of detail regarding representation of geometry. BIM is not visualization (exact materials, light etc.). BIM needs avatars in terms of geometry, lots of information. Try not to use manufacturer's BIM objects—are too detailed in geometry, particularly HVAC objects. Keep as much information as possible outside the model (in a data base).

Try to start by testing a BIM software on a pilot project before definitely deciding for a solution.

The most common BIM-software tools

Architectural Modeling:	Revit, ArchiCAD, Allplan, Vectorworks, MicroStation (closed BIM, does not support IFC, data transfer not possible)
Parametric Tools:	Rhino, Grasshopper
Structural Modeling:	Dlubal RFEM, SOFiSTiK, SCIA, Axis, Revit Structure (modeling only, no calculation), TEKLA
Building Energy Modeling (BEM)/Energy Certificate:	ArchiPHYSIK, Saphyra, Energyplus, Transys (not BIM to BEM, only parametric)
Cost Assessment and Scheduling: iTWO, Vico, Nevaris	
HVAC:	Plancal, AX2000
Quality Control Tools:	Solobri, Tekla BIMsight

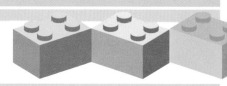

Useful links and web-sites:

BIMpedia:

Expert knowledge on BIM modeling and data transfers in various software tools

www.bimpedia.eu

BuildingSmart:

International Home of Open BIM

www.buildingsmart.org

BuildingSmart Data Dictionary:

Library of Object and their attributes

www.buildingsmart.org/standards/standards-tools-services/data-dictionary/

freeBIM Tirol Property Server (Merkmalserver) structured attributes based on Building Smart Data Dictionary

www.freebim.at/Info_2016

EU BIM Task Group

www.eubim.eu/about-the-eu-bim-task-group

ÖNORM A 6241-1 (in German)

Digital structure documentation – Part 1:

CAD data structures and building information modeling (BIM) – Level 2

ÖNORM A 6241-2 (in German)

Digital structure documentation – Part 2:

Building information modeling (BIM) – Level 3-iBIM

SIA 2051 (in German, French, Italian)

Building Information Modeling (BIM)

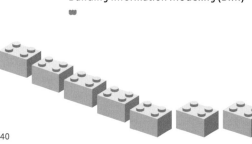

EDUCATIONAL BACKGROUND

Traditional architectural education was the starting point for almost all partners of our sample. Only 2 partners have a non-architectural background (management, textile design). 25 % have a formal education in other architectural fields, and another 25 % combine architectural education with postgraduate qualification in architecture.

For exactly half of the respondents their starting point was 'just' an architectural degree. Where did the necessary know-how come from? Aside from specialist education, possible sources of expertise were working experience in other firms and personal interest. And for all the teams, learning by doing is an essential tool in the specialization kit.

Educational background (partners)

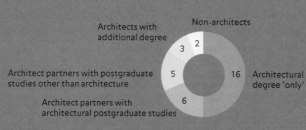

Architects with additional degree — 3
Non-architects — 2
Architect partners with postgraduate studies other than architecture — 5
Architectural degree 'only' — 16
Architect partners with architectural postgraduate studies — 6

Educational background (teams)

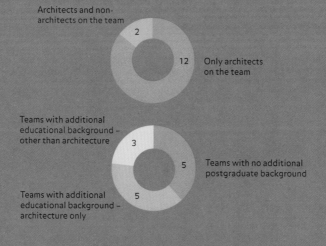

Architects and non-architects on the team — 2
Only architects on the team — 12

Teams with additional educational background – other than architecture — 3
Teams with no additional postgraduate background — 5
Teams with additional educational background – architecture only — 5

How did you, or your partners, get the know-how required?

12	Learning by doing projects in the own practice
8.5	Personal interest
8.5	Special education
4	Working experience in other offices or firms

How to specialize
An overview of available courses in Europe

Courses offering a specialization in ...
(Distribution by country)

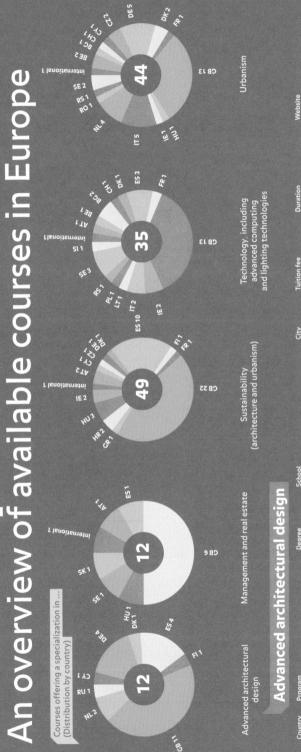

| Advanced architectural design | Management and real estate | Sustainability (architecture and urbanism) | Technology, including advanced computing and lighting technologies | Urbanism |

Advanced architectural design

Country	Program	Degree	School	City	Tuition fee	Duration	Website
CY	Architecture	MA	Eastern Mediterranean University	Famagusta	N/A	2 years	www.emu.edu.tr
DE	Advanced Architectural Design	M.A.	Staatliche Hochschule Fuer Bildende Kuenste – Staedelschule	Frankfurt	€ 17,000	2 years	www.staedelschule.de
DE	Architecture	Master of Arts	Beuth Hochschule für Technik Berlin	Berlin	N/A	4 semesters	architektur.beuth-hochschule.de
DE	Architecture	M.A.	Fachhochschule Frankfurt am Main	Frankfurt am Main	N/A	4 semesters	www.fh-frankfurt.de
DE	Architecture / Environmental Design	Master of Arts	Hochschule Bremen	Bremen	N/A	4 semesters	www.hs-bremen.de
DK	Design in Architectural Contexts	Diploma in Architecture (cand.arch)	Royal Danish Academy of Fine Arts / School of Architecture	Copenhagen	no fees	4 semesters	www.karch.dk
ES	Architectural Design	Master	University of Navarra	Navarra	€ 17,280	3 semesters	www.unav.edu
ES	Advanced Architectural Design Tri-Continental	Master	Universidad Europea de Madrid (UEM)	Madrid	N/A	1year (full-time)	www.uem.es
ES	Integrated Architectural Projects	Master	Universidad Europea de Madrid (UEM)	Madrid	N/A	16 months (full-time)	www.uem.es
ES	Innovation in Architecture, Technology and Design	MA	University of Sevilla	Sevilla	€ 821	1 year	www.us.es
FI	Architecture	MSc	University of Oulu	Oulu	€ 13,000 for non-EU/ EEA citizens	2 years	www.oulu.fi

Country	Program	Degree	School	City	Tuition fee	Duration	Website
GB	Architecture	MArch	Oxford Brookes University	Oxford	N/A	1 year	www.brookes.ac.uk
GB	Architectural Design Innovation	MSc	Robert Gordon University	Aberdeen	N/A	3 semesters	www.rgu.ac.uk
GB	Architectural Design	MAarch	The Bartlett Faculty of the Built Environment	London	N/A	2 semesters	www.barlett.ucl.ac.uk
GB	Architecture	MA	University For The Creative Arts	Canterbury	£ 13,540	1 year (full-time) 2 years (part-time)	www.uca.ac.uk
GB	Interdisciplinary Design for the Built Environment*	–	University of Cambridge Departments of Engineering and Architecture	Cambridge	£ 9,960 per year	2 years (part-time; students spend a total of seven residential weeks in Cambridge during the two years)	www.ice.cam.ac.uk
GB	Civic Design MPhil	–	University of Liverpool	Liverpool	–	–	–
GB	Design MArch	–	University of Nottingham	Nottingham	–	–	–
GB	Advanced Architectural Studies	MArch/PgDip degree	University of Strathclyde	Glasgow	N/A	MSc: 12 months full-time PgDip: 9 months full-time	www.strath.ac.uk/architecture/study/pg/
GB	Advanced Architectural Design	MArch/PgDip	University of Strathclyde	Glasgow	£ 1,820 (Scotland/EU) £ 9,250 (Rest of UK) £ 15,600 (International)	MArch: 24 months full-time PgDip: 21 months full-time	www.strath.ac.uk
GB	Creative Practice in Architecture	PHD	Cardiff University, Welsh School of Architecture	Cardiff	N/A	3 year (full time) 5 years (part-time)	www.cardiff.ac.uk
GB	Architecture	MA	University of Westminster	London	N/A	1 year (full time) 2 years (part-time)	www.westminster.ac.uk
NL	Advanced Studies in Architecture and Urban Design	MA	Berlage Center	Delft	€ 27,000	3 semesters	www.theberlage.nl
NL	Architecture, Building and Planning	MSc	Eindhoven University of Technology	Eindhoven	€ 7,500 (EU/EEA) € 15,000 (no EU/EEA)	2 years	www.tue.nl
RU	Architecture	MA	Irkutsk State Technical University	Irkutsk	RUB 150,000 (year)	3 years	www.istu.edu

Sustainability (architecture and urbanism)

Country	Program	Degree	School	City	Tuition fee	Duration	Website
AT	Future Building Solutions	MSc	Danube University Krems	Krems	€ 18.000	4 semesters (part-time)	www.donau-uni.ac.at
AT	Nachhaltiges Bauen	Certificate	Graz University of Technology	Graz	€ 10.000	2 semesters	nhb.tuwien.ac.at/home/
CY	Sustainable Environment and Energy Systems	MSc	Middle East Technical University, Northern Cyprus Campus	Güzelyurt	2.100 USD	4 semesters	www.sees.ncc.metu.edu.tr/
CZ	Buildings and Environment	M.Sc.	Czech Technical University	Prague		18 months	www.cvut.cz, no information about the master-programme
DE	ClimaDesign	M.Sc.	Technische Universität München Fakultät für Architektur	München	€ 5,000 each semester	4 semesters	www.bk.ar.tum.de
DK	Energy and Green Architecture (MEGA)	Master	Aarhus School of Architecture / Tsinghua Urban Planning and Design Institute (THUPDI)	Aarhus/Beijing, China	DKK 170,000 DKK / € 25,000 (includes tution, materials, food during courses, two travels)	4 semesters	www.aarch.dk
ES	Master in Advanced Architecture Self-sufficient Habitats Emergent territories, Self-sufficient buildings and Digital Tectonics	Master	Institute for Advanced Architecture of Catalonia	Barcelona	€ 28,500	18 months	www.iaac.net/educational-programs/master-in-advanced-architecture-2

Country	Program	Degree	School	City	Tuition fee	Duration	Website
ES	Sustainable Emergency Architecture – official	Master	Universitat Internacional de Catalunya	Barcelona	€ 9,480 + € 480 (enrolement fees)	1 year	www.uic.es/en/international-cooperation
ES	Architecture and Sustainability: Design Tools and Environmental Control Techniques	MA	Technical University of Catalonia	Barcelona	€ 6.600	1 year	www.arquitecturaysostenibilidad.com
ES	Master in Architecture, Energy and Environment	MA	Universitat Politècnica de Catalunya	Barcelona	€ 30,33 per ECTS credit	1 year	http://mastersuniversitaris.upc.edu/aem/info-general?set_language=en
ES	Architecture and the Environment: Integration of renewable Energy into Architecture	MA	Technical University of Catalonia	Barcelona	€ 6,400	1 year	www.talent.upc.edu
ES	Arquitectura Sostenible i Eficiència Energètica	MA	Universitat Ramon Llull	Barcelona	N/A	1,5 year (full-time), 1,5 year (online)	www.salleurl.edu
ES	Postgrau en Arquitectura Mediambiental i Urbanismo Sostenible	Post graduate	Universitat Ramon Llull	Barcelona	N/A	6 months (full-time), 6 months (online)	www.salleurl.edu
ES	Energy Efficiency and Sustainability	Master	Universitat Jaume I	Castelló de la Plana	€ 2,500	1 year	www.uji.es
ES	Sustainable Architecture and Urban Development	MA	University of Alicante	Alicante	N/A	1 year	www.ua.es
ES	Sustainable Architecture and Cities	MA	University of Sevilla	Sevilla	€ 820.00	1 year	www.us.es
ES	Creative Sustainability	MA, MSc, M.Ec.	Aalto University School of Arts, Design and Architecture	Aalto	€ 15,000.00	2 years	arts.aalto.fi
FI	Materials science for sustainable construction	MSc	Paris Institute of Technology	Paris	€ 600 (EU) € 1,200 (non-EU)	1 year	www.enpc.fr
FR	Architecture et Développement Durable	MAS	ENSA de Toulouse et l'Université catholique de Louvain	Toulouse and Louvain-la-Neuve	€ 4,500	2 x 2 mois	www.toulouse.archi.fr
FR/BE	Sustainable Environmental Design	MSc or March	Architectural Association School of Architecture	London	no information	12 months (MSc) 16 months (March)	www.aaschool.ac.uk
GB	Energy and Sustainable Building Design MSc	MSc	De Montfort University	Leicester	£ 5350 (EU) £ 13100 (non-EU)	1 year	www.dmu.ac.uk
GB	Sustainability and Adaptation Planning	MSc	Graduate School of Environment	Wales	N7A	18 month (full-time) 30 month (part-time)	https://gse.cat.org.uk/
GB	Architecture of Rapid Change and Scarce Resources	MA	London Metropolitan University	London	£ 5670 (EU) £ 10395 (non-EU)	1 year (2 days a week) 2 years (1 day a week)	www.londonmet.ac.uk www.arcsr.org
GB	Low-Energy Architecture MPhil		London Metropolitan University				
GB	Sustainable Building (Performance and Design)	MSc	Oxford Brookes University	Oxford	£ 9030 (EU) £ 13460 (non-EU)	12 months (Full-time) 24 months (part-time)	www.brookes.ac.uk
GB	Sustainable Heritage	MSc	University College London	London	£ 12380 (EU) £ 24420 (non-EU)	1 year (full-time) 2-5 years (part-time)	www.ucl.ac.uk
GB	Environment and Sustainable Development	MSc	University College London	London	£ 14520 (EU) £ 23540 (non-EU)	1 year (full-time)	www.ucl.ac.uk
GB	Sustainable Architecture and Healthy Buildings	MSc	University of Derby	Derby	£ 5202 (EU) £ 12227 (non-EU)	1 year (full-time) 2-3 years (part-time)	www.derby.ac.uk
GB	Environmental Sustainability	Mres	University of East London	London	£ 7080 (EU) £ 12480 (nor-EU)	1 year (full time) 2 years (part-time)	www.uel.ac.uk
GB	Advanced Sustainable Design	MSc	University of Edinburgh	Edinburgh	£ 10100 (EU) £ 20500 (nor-EU)	1 year (full-time)	www.ed.ac.uk
GB	Architecture of Rapid Change and Scarce Resources	MA	University of North London & London Metropolitan University	London	N/A	N/A	www.londonmet.ac.uk/pgprospectus/pgprospectushome.cfm
GB	Architecture, Energy and Sustainability	MA	University of North London & London Metropolitan University	London	N/A	N/A	www.londonmet.ac.uk/pgprospectus/courses/architecture-energy-and-sustainability.cfm
GB	Renewable Energy and Architecture	MSc	University of Nottingham	Nottingham	£ 4860 (EU) £ 11130 (non-EU)	1 year (full-time)	www.nottingham.ac.uk
					£ 7290 (EU)		www.nottingham.ac.uk

Country	Program	Degree	School	City	Tuition fee	Duration	Website
GB	Sustainable Building Technology (collaborative) MSc		University of Nottingham	Nottingham	N/A	N/A	www.nottingham.ac.uk
GB	Sustainable Tall Buildings	MArch	University of Nottingham	Nottingham	£ 7290 (EU) £ 16695 (non-EU)	N/A	www.nottingham.ac.uk
GB	Sustainable Cities	MA	University of Portsmouth	Portsmouth	£ 6500 (EU) £ 13200 (non-EU)	1 year	www.port.ac.uk
GB	Sustainable Architecture Studies	MSc	University of Sheffield	Sheffield		1 year (full time) 2 years (part-time)	www.sheffield.ac.uk
GB	Sustainable Engineering: Architecture & Ecology	MSc	University of Strathclyde Glasgow	Glasgow	£ 13850 (UK) £ 19600 (International)	1 year (full-time)	www.strath.ac.uk
GB	Architecture and Environmental Design	MSc	University of Westminster	London	£ 10500 (UK/EU) £ 12500 (non-EU)	1 year (full-time)	www.westminster.ac.uk
GB	International Planning and Sustainable Development MA		University of Westminster	London			www.westminster.ac.uk
IE	Sustainable Energy	MEngSc	University College Cork	Cork	6500 (EU) € 22000 (non-EU)	1 year	www.ucc.ie
IT	Sustainable Architecture and Landscape Design	MA	Politecnico di Milano	Piacenza	N/A	2 years	www.polimi.it
IT	Environmental Planning and Policy	MA	Università IUAV di Venezia	Venezia	N/A	2 years	www.iuav.it
NL	Architecture, Building and Planning	MA	Eindhoven University of Technology*	Eindhoven	N/A	2 years	www.tue.nl
NL	European Spatial and Environmental Planning	MSc	Radboud University	Nijmegen	N/A	1 year, full-time	www.ru.nl
NL	Environmental and Infrastructure Planning	MSc	University of Groningen	Groningen	€ 2060 (EU) € 14350 (non-EU)	2 years	www.rug.nl
SE	Architecture and Planning Beyond Sustainability	MSc	Chalmers University of Technology*	Gothenburg	N/A	2 years	www.chalmers.se
SE	Master's Programme in Architecture and Urban Design	MSc	Umeå School of Architecture	Umeå	N/A	2 years	www.arch.umu.se

Technology including computing and lighting

Country	Program	Degree	School	City	Tuition fee	Duration	Website
GB	Architectural Science	PHD	University of Wales Cardiff	Cardiff	N/A	3 years	www.cardiff.ac.uk
IE	Information Technology in Architecture, Engineering & Construction	MEngSC	Cuniversity College Cork	Cork	€ 7,000 (EU) € 18,000 (non-EU)	1 year (full-time) 2 years (part time)	www.ucc.ie
IE	Fire Safety Practice	PGDip/Cdip	University of Dublin Trinity College	Dublin	€ 6,115 (EU) € 13,396 (non-EU)	1 year	www.tcd.ie
IT	Building and Architectural Engineering	MSc	Politecnico Di Milano	Milan	€ 1,500 (EU) € 3,500 (non-EU)	2 years	www.english.polimi.it
IT	Industrial Design for Architecture	Master	Politecnico Di Milano	Milan	€ 13,500	1 year	www.polidesign.net
LT	Civil Engineering	MSc	Vilnius Gediminas Technical University	Vilnius	€ 2,910 (EU) € 3,900 (non-EU)*	2 years	www.vgtu.lt
PL	Road Engineering	MSc	Cracow University of Technology	Crakow	Free (EU residents) € 4,000 (non-EU)	18 months	www.bwm.pk.edu.pl
RS	Architectural Engineering	MSc	University of Belgrade	Belgrad	N/A	2 years	www.arh.bg.ac.rs
SE	Structural Engineering and Building Technology	MSc	Chalmers University of Technology	Gothenburg	Free (EU residents) € 20,400 (non-EU)	2 years	www.chalmers.se

getting specialized

Country	Program	Degree	School	City	Tuition fee	Duration	Website
SE	Infrastructure and Environmental Engineering	MSc	Chalmers University of Technology	Gothenburg	Free (EU residents) € 20,400 (non-EU)	2 years	www.chalmers.se
SE	Architectural Lighting Design	MSc	KTH Royal Institute of Technology	Stockholm	N/A	1 year	www.kth.se
SI	Traffic Engineering	MA	University of Maribor	Maribor	N/A	2 years	www.uni.mb.si
TR / NL	Computational Design and Fabrication Technologies in Architecture	MSc	Middle East Technical University (METU) / Delft University of Technology (TU Delft)	Ankara / Delft	€ 5,544 (EU)	4 semesters	www.fbe.metu.edu.tr

Urbanism

Country	Program	Degree	School	City	Tuition fee	Duration	Website
BE	Urbanism and Strategic Planning	MSc	University of Leuven	Leuven	€ 6,000	4 semesters	www.kuleuven.be
BE	Human Settlements	MSc	University of Leuven	Leuven	€ 6,000	2 semesters (full-time) 4 semesters (part-time)	www.kuleuven.be
BG	Urbanisme - Master's Programme	state diploma	University of Architecture, Civil Engineering and Geodesy	Sofia	N/A	no information	www.uacg.bg/UACEG_site/index-en.html
CH	EDAR Architecture & Sciences of the city	doctoral programme	Swiss Federal Institute of Technology	Laussane	N/A	k.A.	http://phd.epfl.ch/edar
CY	Urban Design	Master	Eastern Mediterranean University	Famagusta	N/A	1 year (full-time) 2 years (part-time)	www.emu.edu.tr
CZ	Architecture and urban design	Ing. arch.	BRNO UNIVERSITY OF TECHNOLOGY	Brno	N/A	1.5–2 years	www.fa.vutbr.cz/pages/studijni_programyDB.aspx?lang=en&menu=3
CZ	Architecture and Urbanism	Master	Czech Technical University	Prague	€ 4,130	2 years (full-time)	www.fa.cvut.cz
DE	Advanced Urbanism	MSc	Bauhaus Universität Weimar / Joint program with Tongji University, Shanghai	Weimar/ Shanghai	€2,000	4 semesters	www.uni-weimar.de
DE	Urban Management	MSc	Berlin University of Technology	Berlin	€ 11,000	3 semesters	www.urbanmanagement.tu-berlin.de
DE	Urban Agglomerations	MSc	Frankfurt University of Applied Science	Frankfurt	€ 3,000 (1st–3rd semester) € 2,000 (4th semester).	2 years (full-time)	https://typo3-alt.cit.frankfurt-university.de
DE	Architecture Course	March	HOCHSCHULE ANHALT (FH)	Köthen	€ 3,600	2 years	www.dia-architecture.de
DE	SPRING (Spatial Planning for Regions in Growing Economies)	Master	University of Dortmund	Dortmund	€ 3,600	2 years	www.tu-dortmund.de
DE / FR	Deutsch-französischer Doppelmaster in Architektur	Master	Fakultät für Architektur des Karlsruher Instituts für Technologie / Ecole nationale supérieure de l'architecture de Strasbourg (ENSAS)	Karlsruhe and Strasbourg	N/A	4 semesters	www.arch.kit.edu
DK	Urban Planning and Management	MSc	Aalborg University	Aalborg	N/A	2 years	www.urban.aau.dk/
DK	Architecture in Urban Context	Master	Royal Danish Academy of Fine Arts / School of Architecture	Copenhagen	N/A	4 semesters	www.karch.dk
FR	Ville, Architecture et Patrimoine	Post-Master	Ecole Nationale Supérieure d'Architecture Paris-Val de Seine	Paris	N/A	1 year	www.paris-valdeseine.archi.fr
GB	Projective Cities	Mphil	AA School of Architecture	London	N/A	2 years	http://projectivecities.aaschool.ac.uk/

Country	Program	Degree	School	City	Tuition fee	Duration	Website
GB	Housing and Urbanism Programme	MA/ MArch	AA School of Architecture	London	N/A	MA (12 months) March (16 months)	www.aaschool.ac.uk
GB	Urban Design	MA	Liverpool John Moores University	Liverpool	£ 6,250 (EU) £ 13,250 (semesters)	N/A	www.ljmu.ac.uk
GB	Architecture and Urbanism	MA	Manchester School of Architecture	Manchester	N/A	1 year (full-time) 2 years (part-time)	www.mmu.ac.uk
GB	Urban Design	MA	Oxford Brookes University	Oxford	£ 7,340 (EU) £ 13,460 (semesters)	1 year (full-time) 2 years (part-time)	www.brookes.ac.uk
GB	Urban Design	MArch	The Bartlett School of Architecture, University College London	London	N/A	1 year (full-time)	www.bartlett.ucl.ac.uk
GB	Building and Urban Design in Development	MSc	University College London	London	£ 14,520 (EU) £ 23,540 (semesters)	1 year (full-time)	www.ucl.ac.uk
GB	Urban Design	MA	University For The Creative Arts	Canterbury	N/A	1 year (full-time) 2 years (part-time)	www.ucreative.ac.uk
GB	Architectural and Urban Design	MA	University of Brighton	Brighton	£ 6,270 (EU) £ 14,580 (semesters)	1 year (full-time) 2 years (part-time)	www.brighton.ac.uk
GB	Architecture and Urbanism	MA	University of East London	London	£ 7,080 (EU) £ 12,850 (semesters)	1 year (full-time) 2 years (part-time)	www.uel.ac.uk
GB	Architecture and Urban Design	MA	University of Kent	Canterbury	£ 7,300 (EU) £ 15,200 (semesters)	1 year (full-time) 2 years (part-time)	www.kent.ac.uk
GB	Sustainable Urban Design	MArch	University of Nottingham	Nottingham	£ 7,290 (EU) £ 16,695 (semesters)	1 year (full-time)	www.ncl.ac.uk
GB	Urban Design	MA	University of Westminster	London	£ 7,000 (EU) £ 12,000 (semesters)	1 year	www.westminster.ac.uk
HU	Master In Architecture	Dipl. Ing. Arch.	Budapest University of Technology and Economics	Budapest	€3,500	2 years	http://portal.bme.hu/C13/Bulletin/Document%20Library/Architecture.aspx
IE	Urban Design	MSc	University College Dublin	Dublin	N/A	12 months	www.ucd.ie
IT	Master in Progetto dello Spazio Pubblico	MA	Masp	Lucca	€ 2,600 +IVA	N/A	www.masp.it
IT	Urban Vision and Architectural Design	Master	Domus Academy	Milan	N/A	12 months	www.domusacademy.com
IT	Pianificazione e progettazione urbanistica nel governo delle trasformazioni del territorio	Master	Università degli Studi di Napoli Federico II	Napoli	N/A	3 years	
IT	Pianificazione urbanistica	Master		Rome	N/A	N/A	
IT	Pianificazione Urbana e Territoriale Applicata ai Paesi in Via di Sviluppo	Master		Venice	N/A	N/A	
NL	Architecture, Urbanism and Building Sciences	MSc	Delft University of Technology	Delft	€2060 € 15575 (non-EEA)	2 years (full-time)	www.tudelft.nl
NL	Urban Management and Development	MSc	Erasmus University Rotterdam	Rotterdam	€ 13,900.00	1 year	www.ihs.nl
NL	Urban Regional Planning and Development	MSc	Saxion Hogeschool IJselland	Deventer	N/A	1 year	www.saxion.edu
NL	Urbanism (EMU)	MSc	TU Delft, Faculty of Architecture	Delft	N/A	2 years	www.emurbanism.eu/
RO	Urban Design	Master	"Ion Mincu" University of Architecture and Urbanism (UAUIM)	Bucharest	N/A	2 years	www.uauim.ro
RS	Integral Urbanism	MSc	University of Belgrade	Belgrad	N/A	2 years	www.arh.bg.ac.rs
SE	Architecture and Urban design	MSc	Chalmers University of Technology	Gothenburg	€ 20,400 (semesters)	2 years	www.chalmers.se
SE	Urban Planning and Design	MSc	Kungliga Tekniska Högskolan	Stockholm	N/A	20 months	www.kth.se

getting specialized

Getting ex-specialized
Taking the step beyond specialization

**Architecture is no longer only about buildings, as building is not just about architecture.
We need to invert the process of specialization. Rather than getting more specific inside the discipline,
we should step out of its center far enough to be able to understand and face the complexity of the reality
we need to work with, and the complexity of our own desires, background, education and influences.
We need to acquire a new status within the profession, breaking free of the limitations implied by the
discipline. Borrowing the term created by 'ex-designer' Martí Guixé and 'ex-architect' Carel Weeber,
architects now should not be specialized, but ex-specialized, with 'ex-' standing for the step beyond
and the embracing of decontextualization.**

The ex-specialization manual

1. Search: Asking questions is a goal
Question yourself, your tools and processes, and trigger new questions.

"Generally, evolution emerges not in the center of an eco-system, but rather on its edges. The same
is true for architecture", say STEALTH.unlimited, a practice whose area of work spans from urban
research to spatial intervention and cultural activism. "Stepping beyond is important as it exposes
you to what is going on at the fringe of the discipline, where it overlaps with other fields that may
provide you with significant insights or intriguing new tools or approaches to what you are doing."
The fringe offers a position to reflect, affording us the distance to question the Why, What and How
of our work. As Peter Lang, active member in several urban research groups in Europe, including
Stalker/ON, points out, "the education of the architect must extend well beyond the usual issues. I
don't see much choice in this new world disorder."

Taking a step beyond implies reflecting on the effects (and affects) of the tools we have used to
date. Alexander Vollebregt, program director at Spacelab/Urban Body research lab of the TU Delft,
a cross cultural platform aiming to generate urban sensibility through inter-professional engage-
ments, affirms: "We cannot solve problems with the same kind of thinking we used when we created
them. If the tools and language of the past had sufficed, our urban areas would all be prosperous
and blooming".

2. Move in unstable fields:
Work from and with the unpredictable

Architecture can operate as a dynamic tool, through which interaction, collision and uncertainty
may spark opportunities to act and react to a dynamic reality. It is only by taking a leap into the
unknown that you are able to transcend your learned discipline and knowledge. For STEALTH.un-
limited, "stepping beyond offers the possibility to experiment, to take positions that are hard to
take if you act solely within the perceived bounds of what architecture is supposed to be. It allows
you to take more risk and brings new concepts or tools to your practice. You push the development
of your practice from the fringes inwards, and this opens up new perspectives and indicates new
approaches."

Text by Alicia Velázquez, IN TRANSITION, Netherlands and Spain

3. Connect and get exposed

The influence of other disciplines may indicate new ways of approaching professional challenges. It will help to rethink our role within society and the city, to redefine our tools and language as well as relationships in teams or with clients.

"In our practice", says Aether Architecture, who create projects in peer collaboration with others, "our main focus is to develop systems, technologies, spaces that carry cultural qualities and explore possibilities in today's networked societies. I like the ability to switch between subjective and objective methods, to have a strong cultural standpoint and yet create complex systems."

4. Get surprised, also by, and about, yourself

Architects, however, may as well incorporate this dynamic and embrace multidisciplinarism, change, conflict and fluidity.

"I don't fit into standard definitions, I'm a little bit of all and none of it really", says Megla, a multi-skilled cross-disciplinary worker who does "mainly design", "I simply pursue projects and personal interests."

For In Transition, collaborative practice that utilizes the emotional power of architectural tools, "traditional (values of) architecture were not satisfactory: too static, too far from the human experience, too time-consuming to grasp. We had to find new relationships".

5. Be prepared to fail

Although some, like Aether, claim that things for them are "all fantastic", stepping beyond may make reality difficult at times.

It requires high time-investment, and the result is uncertain. Working from experimentation and questioning, although challenging and rich, is not always efficient. As Megla confirms, "you will take more time, and the result will probably not be superb".

Changing background and teams, as in the experience of Stealth.unlimited "may demand a lot of effort and time to understand the specifics of a different context or to develop a common language between different disciplines."

Project financing is not always linear and available. As Peter Lang knows, "a project needs a leap of faith, well before funding. And it requires an incredible amount of preparation."

Working relationships and processes need to be redefined. You may develop the project first, and then find the client and money. And often the two will come separately.

Ex-specialization is based on diversity. Even if the intentions are clear, the tools and language used go beyond the ones traditionally employed by architects. "People from the outside may not understand what you are doing or where you are heading", say Stealth.unlimited. "Working *beyond* borders creates confusion."

Although you will find that you are not alone, there are not always points of references available to help you direct your own practice. You work on a trial-and-error basis, leaving preconceived ideas and experience behind. "You need to go against your own realizations", say Modulorbeat, a practice of "ambitious urbanists and planners". And Megla quickly found out in her working processes that you are "likely very soon to touch the limits your own skills and know-how".

How to define (and therefore communicate) the undefined? The market asks for answers, and you work with conflict and doubt. Ultimately, as Megla knows, "you can never explain in one minute what is that you do." 🐛

Contributors to this article:

Aether Architecture
(www.aether.hu)

Modulorbeat
(www.modulorbeat.de)

Stealth.unlimited
(http://stealth.ultd.net)

Megla
(www.megla.org)

Alexander Vollebregt

Peter Lang
(www.petertlang.net)

In Transition
(www.in-transition.net)

making competitions

why
make
competitions

how
to make
competitions

what
happens
next

DENSITY OF COMPETITIONS IN EUROPE

Throughout Europe, (including Switzerland and Norway) architecture competitions held by public authorities provide extremely valuable opportunities of Europe-wide access to public commissions for emerging – and other architectural practices.

In order to evaluate the distribution of competitions we analyzed and mapped all such competitions running in Europe at a given date (June 18th, 2009). In absolute terms, the most competitions running when this map was produced were to be found in France (**23** competitions), followed by Germany (**14**), Italy (**10**), and Spain (**8**), for a total of **87** contests running in **20** European countries. In relative terms, it is in smaller countries such as Luxemburg, Slovenia, Austria, and Estonia that we found the highest number of contests per licensed architect. On an EU average, the ratio was **one competition for every 4003 architects**.

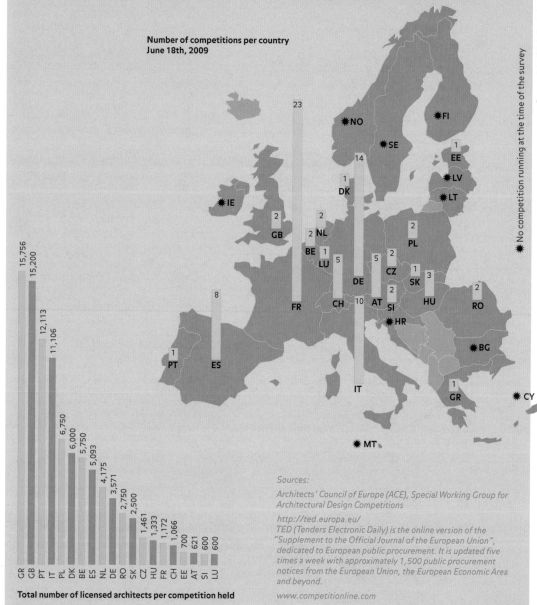

Number of competitions per country June 18th, 2009

* No competition running at the time of the survey

Total number of licensed architects per competition held

Sources:

Architects' Council of Europe (ACE), Special Working Group for Architectural Design Competitions

http://ted.europa.eu/
TED (Tenders Electronic Daily) is the online version of the "Supplement to the Official Journal of the European Union", dedicated to European public procurement. It is updated five times a week with approximately 1,500 public procurement notices from the European Union, the European Economic Area and beyond.

www.competitionline.com

See page 258

making competitions

Taking part in a competition is about testing one's abilities outside a predefined setting of personal connections, nationality, office size, or gender. It is about experimenting and developing a personal vision much more directly than in the usual architect-client relationship.

And winning a competition is much more than just getting a job! It is about the possibility of growing big in a day, of shortcutting years of slow growth, or of jumping scale in the size of projects the practice deals with, of getting a footing in a different national context, of specializing. And finally it is about publicity and recognition in and beyond the professional context – from colleagues to the general public.

However, competitions also mean making an investment of valuable resources – time, energy and money – with an uncertain outcome. Is the prize worth the effort?

To answer these questions, we put together a series of expert opinions on the issue, but also compiled more than 100 competition stories from all over Europe, which provided the data source for the survey 'Making Competitions' (2009), and a series of experience reports.

Thematically, we have structured the chapter into three sections. In the first, 'Why make competitions', we look at the mechanism behind architectural competitions and the motives that bring architects to take part in them. In the section 'How to make competitions', we focus particularly on how to deal with the brief and the limits defined by it, and examine what may be the basis of a winning approach. In the final section, 'What happens next', we take a look at the next stage: this includes individual experiences of the frequently long and winding path from winning proposal to the built project, but also the more general issue of what future approaches to architectural competitions and the specific know-how could, or should, be about.

THE AVERAGE PRACTICE

Number of competitions done per year since the office start-up **3.4**

Hours invested in competitions per year **1,891**

For every **10** competitions: **4** won a prize of some kind – of these **2** were winners

2 won other prizes,

and of the first prizes **1** was realized

Realized projects thanks to competitions: **2.5** over **8.4** years of practice and

29 competitions submitted.

Sees competitions as a way to develop the architectural thinking in practice **83 %**

Sees competitions as a necessity for clients who want new ideas **84 %**

Uses models to test ideas **50 %**

Has collaborators specialized in competitions in the office **74 %**

Is not so interested in the first-prize money when choosing a competition **71 %**

Sees the relationship between work required and compensation as problematic **76 %**

THE AVERAGE SUBMISSION

Hours worked on the submission project

568 by the team

94 by consultants (if part of the team)

253 by collaborating architects (if part of the team)

The team

3.5 People in the office team who worked on the project

3.5 People from collaborating offices (if part of the team)

4.6

Consultants (if part of the team)

8.4 months Time needed to get a contract

31 months Time needed to realize the project

Fee received for the commission

309,659 Euros

See reality check #5 / page 269

why make competitions

One thing is certain: participating in an architectural competition means making a substantial investment of time, energy and money – valuable and sometimes scarce resources – with an uncertain outcome. Is the prize worth the effort?

Wonderful Chances to Success and Abuse

The profession makes an enormous investment of time and human resources – at times a risky strategy and not necessarily conducive to safe and profitable business.

What is an architectural design competition and what types are there?

Architectural design competitions have a long history, going back to ancient times. In our "modern" history, design competitions as an architectural selection procedure came into use in the 19th century. Various iconographic buildings as well as thousands of profane/secular projects were planned and built as a result of a design competition. While, formerly, architectural competitions mostly were arranged for landmark buildings or urban designs, nowadays it has become a widely used procedure for procuring architectural services.

In the light of these figures, the profession can sarcastically be said to be competitive beyond reasonable limits. But since architects apparently are more afraid to fail with a design than to die, as a study conducted in Finland has shown, the phenomenon of going to great lengths for design quality in competitions is typical for architects, but hardly cherished by any other profession.

Architectural competition is a remarkable invention to contribute to the quality of the built environment. But at the same time, it serves another reasonable purpose, namely, to rise up the professional hierarchy. Many architects have started their career by winning a specific competition, and this in turn generates confidence and zeal among younger generations to participate in competitions and gain their own commissions in this most respected way.

Regarding the vast investment of Austrian architects, each participation has to be carefully considered. The

According to a study commissioned by the Austrian Chamber of Architects and Civil Engineers in 2009, no less than **1,637 architects** participated in architectural design competitions in that year. Altogether **1,422,259 working hours** were spent on **59,058 competitions**, and the cash value of the time spent was estimated to amount to over **80 million Euros**. For this investment, the winning competitors **won 18 million Euros** worth of prize money and landed **1,099 commissions** worth **324 million Euros**. The aggregate building cost of these projects came to just over **4,413 billion Euros**.

quality of the brief, the client, the adequacy of the task for your office, the necessary work-time investment, and the commission you might get are the main factors. And one more piece of advice: never participate in a competition if you do not have a clear, convincing idea, which allows you to do your best, with fun and enthusiasm.

What is a competition about?

Let us try to give a definition: Architectural design competitions are *quality-based, project-oriented* selection procedures to procure architectural services. Quality-based means that the decisions are made on basis of the quality of the submitted proposal. It is the opposite of a quantity-based, or even solely price-based, decision. Project-oriented means that the decisions are based on expectations for the future, as the basis is the upcoming project, and not on past achievements (as in the case of a team-based selection procedure).

Text by Georg Pendl, pendl/architects, Innsbruck, Austria

TYPES OF COMPETITIONS

Architecture competitions are selection procedures conducted with the aim of selecting a design proposal for a given situation and, usually, of contracting the architectural services to the winning architect. Competitions can be categorized on the basis of the kind of services requested, the number of stages or phases, or the type of procedure.

SERVICES

Ideas competitions: the service required from participants is a broad concept and the generation of new ideas, while no ensuing planning services are to be directly awarded to the winner.

Project competitions: the service required is based on a detailed program and precise performance brief, usually with the aim of awarding to the winner the further planning services necessary for the realization of the project.

STAGES OR PHASES

Two-or-more-stage competitions: the proposal is developed in two or more steps with intermediate feedback from the jury. Usually after the first stage, the number of competitors is reduced, and the selected practices are compensated at least for some of the work invested.

PROCEDURES

Open competitions are accessible to an indefinite number of participants – usually as long as they comply with professional licensing regulations. Economic and technical capacity criteria may apply, yet no economic offer should be required. Competitions may be held in several stages. The sole assessment criterion has to be the quality of the proposed design.

Restricted competitions limit the number of architects or multi-professional teams allowed to enter proposals. The selection can be made on the basis of given criteria, such as previous experience and/or economic and technical capacity. Very often, the requirement of having already realized building projects of similar size or budget is used as an effective negative selection criterion that excludes not yet established practices.

Both open and restricted design competitions can be integrated in a negotiated procedure, when the intention is to commission the winner for the implementation of the project. In a **negotiated procedure**, the contracting authority negotiates the terms of contract with the successful candidate/s.

In **competitive dialogues**, the contracting authority conducts a dialogue with selected candidates to develop a planning solution and select the architect for the project. This kind of procedure, however, is strongly opposed by the Architecture Council of Europe, as it involves a high risk of ideas copyright infringement.

Architects might also play a significant role in **design-developer competitions**, such as competitions held by public or private project promoters, in which the winner (usually developers in cooperation with planning professionals) is awarded the contract for the design and building of the project in question.

This definition already indicates several advantages that this procedure has not only for architects, but also for clients:

● *Design quality and project maturity* are higher in architectural design competitions. No single planner can ever cover the range of possible solutions that unfolds in competition entries from numerous participants. And holding a competition is less expensive in any case than commissioning several offices to provide alternative designs. Selecting the best from a range of proposed solutions, clients can make sure to get the best-suited result.

● *Transparency of procedure.* Public contracts – and this applies to most architectural design competitions – are financed from taxpayers' money. We all are taxpayers, and decision makers have an obligation to use this money carefully and responsibly and to make sure that contract awarding procedures are reasonable and transparent and that access to them is not unfairly restricted. Architectural design competitions usually meet these criteria at a high level. Depending on the type of competition, access is open to all planners or architects, in some countries even to students. The decision of the jury is based on defined criteria, there are jury protocols and exhibitions of project proposals so as to make decisions transparent and traceable. These public presentations also address the general public and thus meet public information duties about the planning process and the project development.

Which competition type is the best for a specific task?

There are hazards, too, both for competition participants and for clients: for the architects, competitions require an investment of time and resources, with only a small chance of winning; for the clients, competitions involve the risk of hiring an architect with insufficient resources and/or getting an expensive project.

How these potential pitfalls might be dealt with gives us a set of fundamental rules for holding competitions:

- ● prepare as carefully as possible;
- ● define financial limits;
- ● define precisely the needs and options, make preliminary studies to check that those needs can be met in the given circumstances;
- ● take care to get the best participants and the best jury possible.

For all this, a proven architecture expert is needed to prepare and to direct the procedure. All these factors imply an investment of time and money and on the one hand are a precondition for a competition to be successful, and on the other a safeguard against failure.

One basic decision to be made is the choice of the adequate type of competition.

It is important to say that the best solution both for architects and clients is an adequate mix of all these variants. To create this mix, it is helpful to have an active architects' organization, which can be a responsible partner for clients to make these basic decisions concerning an architectural design competition.

It is of crucial importance that certain rules are observed. Regulations for architectural design competitions have a long tradition and are in place in all European countries. A European standard was defined by the Architects Council of Europe (www.ace-cae.eu) with 10 basic rules and a model brief for architectural design competitions.

Observance of these fundamental rules is a necessity to justify the time and work investment made by architects in competitions, as described by the Austrian example at the beginning of this article.

If they follow the above rules and recommendations, clients/competition promoters can be sure to launch competitions that will get them the right project for the given task, the right planning for the project, and the right team for the planning.

OPEN VERSUS RESTRICTED PROCEDURES IN THE EU

The chances for emerging practices much depend on which competition procedure is eventually adopted, and, in case of a pre-selection, on the selection criteria. Out of the 87 analyzed competitions, slightly more than half were open competitions, the rest were restricted competitions.

A generalizing EU perspective is misleading, as the ratio of open to restricted competitions varied strongly from country to country. While France had the highest number of competitions in absolute terms, almost all of them were restricted in one way or another. In Germany, the ratio was fifty-fifty, whereas in Austria and Spain the share of open procedures was slightly higher; Italy stood out because there were virtually no restricted competitions at all. Even if the premises are shared, competition realities in different member states are far from homogenous.

Distribution in selected countries

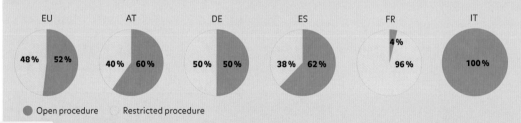

EU: 48% / 52% AT: 40% / 60% DE: 50% / 50% ES: 38% / 62% FR: 4% / 96% IT: 100%

● Open procedure   Restricted procedure

See page 252

THE LANGUAGE

The language in which the brief is written presents a first and effective barrier to limit the number of international participants. Of the competitions analyzed, only 9% offered an English translation of the brief.

Competition language

National language plus English 9%

National language only (incl. English for GB) 91%

Research by Silvia Forlati and Marie-Terese Tamirzek, 2009

WHAT ABOUT THE PRIZE MONEY?

The total prize money is often calculated on the basis of the preliminary design fee and then split among the winning entries. In some cases, the first prize is considered part of the actual fee, once the contract is awarded.

The average prize money in our selection was **19,259 Euros**. On the basis of an estimated average of **568 worked hours** per competition, this roughly corresponds to **34 Euros per hour** in case of success. Yet the range is broad: prize money varies from 2,326 to 230,618 Euros, and the majority is **below 10,000 Euros**.

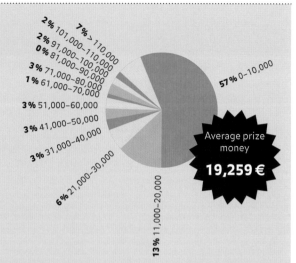

2% 101,000–110,000
7% > 110,000
2% 91,000–100,000
0% 81,000–90,000
3% 71,000–80,000
1% 61,000–70,000
3% 51,000–60,000
3% 41,000–50,000
3% 31,000–40,000
6% 21,000–30,000
13% 11,000–20,000
57% 0–10,000

Average prize money
19,259 €

TOP TEN REMUNERATIONS

Ranking	Prize money (EUR)	Competition name	Country	Deadline
1	230,618	Zürich Europaallee – Baufeld H, Pionierprojekt für das energieeffektive Bauen	CH	19 June 2009 16:00
2	164,727	Centre de détention pour mineurs à Palézieux	CH	31 July 2009 23:59
3	120,000	Scheme design for the ESOC Site Evolution Project "Callisto"	DE	19 June 2009 12:00
4	115,309	Neubau Bildungs- und Kindereinrichtungen Brünnen	CH	26 June 2009 16:00
5	114,000	Gartenschau "Natur in Tirschenreuth 2013"	DE	22 June 2009 16:00
6	112,000	Neubau Gymnasium Wendelstein	DE	30 June 2009 18:00
7	109,800	Neubau der Messehalle Süd	DE	18 June 2009 16:00
8	108,000	Erweiterung Stadthalle Heidelberg	DE	3 July 2009 18:00
9	100,000	"Erinnerungsstätte an der Großmarkthalle"	DE	19 June 2009 17:00
10	100,000	Concours d'architecture Parc des expositions / Luxexpo + Gare Kirchberg	LU	26 June 2009 16:00

Top
Highest prize money
230,618 EUR
(350.000 CHF)
Restricted two-phase competition
"Zürich Europaallee – Pionierprojekt
für das energieeffektive Bauen"
(CH)

Flop
Lowest prize money
2,326 EUR
(2.000 £)
Open ideas competition
the "London Bridge 800"
(UK)

WHAT YOU HAVE TO DO FOR IT

A) Be admitted to the competition

B) Design the most innovative and energy efficient building complex in Zurich combining high quality of life with sustainability and lowest energy demand; creating a functional, economic, energy-efficient and design-orientated building for mixed hotel and residential use, as well as areas with flexible use for services.

C) Submit (stage one)
- Max. 6 plans (A0), including urban situation (1:1000, 1:500), floor plans/sections (1:500), selected elevations (1:200, 1:50), text ● Strategies and detailed data about sustainability and energy efficiency ● Digital copy on CD-ROM ● Declaration of authorship ● Physical model (1:500)

D) Submit (stage two)
- Max. 7 plans (A0), including urban situation (1:500), floor plans/sections (1:500), selected floor plans, elevations (1:200, 1:20), materials, visualizations ● Strategies and detailed data about sustainability and energy efficiency ● Digital copy on CD-ROM ● Declaration of authorship ● Physical model (1:500)

WHAT YOU HAVE TO DO FOR IT

A) Imagine a new version of the inhabited bridge

B) Submit
- One A1 board, content left to competitors' discretion (it may include architectural drawings, plans, elevations, three-dimensional representations and supporting text, physical models will not be accepted!) ● Digital copy on CD-ROM ● Declaration of authorship.

THE WILLING SUSPENSION OF DISBELIEF

About the irrationality of doing competitions

"Meeting (excessive) of efforts.
Existence (accumulative) of diverse (and different) ideas, wills or occurrences.
Wasting (generous) of energies.
Help (ignored) in achieving an end.
Excuse (surprisingly habitual) for not facing or following up on decisions." [1]

Definition of the architecture competition,
Manuel Gausa, The Metapolis Dictionary of Advanced Architecture, 2003

Each of these points is commonplace among architects: a competition produces a remarkable variety of ideas, but at a tremendous cost for the participants who usually work for free and have to invest in expensive presentations; moreover, the jury is often blind to the richness of the ideas submitted and the client may choose not to realize the best project. Given this negative balance, it is surprising how architects nonetheless play along, willingly suspending their disbelief in the institution of competition. Indeed, in the same *Dictionary* as Gausa, Federico Soriano hails the competition as "an empirical method of distinguishing an advanced architect." [2]

The reasons for architects' interest in competitions – or what Pierre Bourdieu called *collusion*, namely the unconscious, invisible, collective readiness to be "taken in by the game" – must be sought in the *illusio*, the belief in the game. To understand the *illusio* it helps to contrast the architectural competition with other contests.

Citius, altius, forties

If we may believe Pierre de Frédy, Baron de Coubertin, the modern Olympic Games best exemplify the spirit of fair competition in athletics – and even in architecture and the arts. In 1912, de Coubertin started to award Olympic medals to sports-inspired works of art in the areas of literature, music, painting, sculpture, architecture and urban planning. [3] However, art competitions were abandoned in 1954

Text by Mark Gilbert and Kari Juhani Jormakka, Vienna, Austria

because the artists were considered professionals, while Olympic athletes had to be amateurs. As the rules of amateurship have since relaxed, the International Olympic Committee restarted the tradition of Olympic art contests in 2000. How doping issues will be controlled in the arts competitions is still open.

Some well-known architects received prizes in Olympic competitions. In 1928, for example, Jan Wils, a founding member of the De Stijl, was awarded the gold medal for designing the venue of the Amsterdam Games. In 1936, Werner March took home the silver medal in architecture and the gold medal in urban planning for his design for the Berlin Olympic complex. The other medals in architecture in that year went to Austria, to Hermann Kutschera and to Hermann Stieglholzer & Herbert Kastinger. The training of the Austrian architects was equally successful before the London Games of 1948, with Adolf Hoch winning gold and Alfred Rinesch silver. In the urban planning competition of 1948, Finns made the strongest effort, with Yrjö Lindegren receiving gold and Ilmari Niemeläinen bronze.

Olympic history recognizes at least two champions who won medals in both athletic and art competitions. Alfred Hajos-Guttmann of Hungary was the swimming sensation at the first modern games in Athens in 1896, and in 1924 he won silver in the architecture contest (the highest prize, as no gold was awarded). Walter Winans of the United States won gold in shooting in the London Games of 1908, and although four years later in Stockholm he only got silver in shooting, he received gold for his sculpture *An American Trotter*.

The idea of Olympic art competitions suggests that artistic achievement could be measured similarly to athletic performance. But there are fundamental differences as well. In sports, competitions have explicit, relatively unambiguous rules. In the 100-meter dash, for example, all participants start from the same start line at the same time, and whoever crosses the finishing line first is the winner. There are many additional stipulations to make sure the race is fair: early starts or the changing of lanes will be penalized; the use of doping leads to disqualification. As a result, both participants and viewers see the race as a fair and accurate means of identifying the fastest runner. Moreover, since the same rules are observed in many different sports events, it is possible to establish world records among athletes who have not participated in the same race.

Paul Valéry explained that "there is no room for skepticism where the rules of a game are concerned."[4] This is because rules are not only restrictive but also constitutive. Scoring a goal in soccer makes sense only if one first accepts the rules of soccer; if one rejects the rules, there is no point in delivering the ball in one of the goals on either side of the field. Hence, the rules are unquestionable because they are inseparable from the game itself. Analogously, Bourdieu argues that every established order tends to produce the naturalization of its own arbitrariness through the *habitus* that reproduces the *doxa*, a set of cognitive and evaluative presuppositions whose acceptance is implied in membership itself so that they cannot be called into doubt by any prospective member of the field. The capital, the *habitus*, and the *illusio* have no purchase except in relation to the field, and the field is essentially structured by the *doxa*.

If the architecture competition were similar to an athletic one, its rules should be equally sacrosanct. However, in the Olympic architecture competitions, the brief was so vague as to imply virtually no rules: one was only asked to submit a design that had something to do with sports. Normal architecture competitions are very different, and yet the rules never are as clear as in the 100 meters. This is evidenced by the very fact that architecture competitions need a jury to decide upon the winner: the selection does not follow automatically from applying defined criteria. Also, it is not unusual that participants in architecture competitions intentionally break the rules without being disqualified. In Vienna, for example, Hans Hollein won the 1994 competition for the Media Tower with an entry that violated the height limit specified in the brief. Because the rules are so malleable, there can be no world records in architecture.

Architects may want to break the rules of the competition for a number of reasons: the original program does not allow for what their particular strength might be; the brief is so ill-formulated that it cannot produce an ideal solution; a breach of rules will make their design stand out from the crowd and catch the attention of the jury. But what would be the motivation of the jury to allow this? It is accepted because it increases variety, and variety is what the *illusio* promises for a competition to produce. Bound by the *illusio* to prove the worth of competitions over and over again, the jury is often inclined to even premiate entries they would in fact not like to see built.

Varietas delectat

No matter whether competition projects will be built or not, the prizes increase the winners' symbolic capital within the architectural field, and the public attention given to competitions raises the prestige of the architectural profession in general. The public's confidence in the value of the projects chosen is also supported by the architecture competition's similarity to athletic ones, including the occasional emphasis on national success in the international field. Here, the variety of the competition results also corroborates another element of competition lore: the idea that by organizing a competition a client will find a better solution than by commissioning a single architect – perhaps even the objectively correct solution to the task at hand. Especially "ideas competitions" are expected to show the full range of possible solutions to an openly defined problem.

Again, this idea has a certain logic to it. The more different proposals, the more likely it is that the client gets what he wants or needs, especially if it is something new. One of the reasons why competitions were particularly popular in Victorian England was that there many new functions for architects to tackle and new typologies were needed for buildings for transportation, education and health services.

While it is undeniable that competitions produce a variety of solutions, it is also true that a certain kind of architecture is noticeably absent: the competition process privileges one-liners and passes over quiet and complex projects. It is like a monologue duel between Jay Leno and David Letterman; James Joyce and Marcel Proust don't need to bother.

Indeed, the main problem here is the kind of variety that a competition produces. For a client, it may not make any difference whether the building is clad in a minimalist or parametricist garb, all other things being equal. There is no necessity nor guarantee that the variety competitions tend to produce indeed addresses the issues that are relevant for the client (or for society at large). For one, Le Corbusier explained that "architecture begins where calculation ends" and it excludes the "practical man".[5] In this context, it is worth noting that the competition eliminates direct communication between client and designer just at the moment when it would matter most.[6]

Autopoiesis

The notion of variety is also related to the interpretation of the architecture competition as akin to economic competition in general. With globalization and the rise of neoliberalism in most Western countries, the abstract idea of competition has become more and more acceptable as a nostrum for all social ills. Adam Smith's postulate of the autopoietic and inerrant "invisible hand" of the market seems to have found new currency.

However, the architectural competition is very different from the liberal notion of unbridled competition. The law of supply and demand hardly applies in a situation where the contestants and the professional members of the jury operate with symbolic capital which is specific to their field and unintelligible to the client. Moreover, participation in competitions often is very limited. Typically, competitions are only open to registered architects, and recently more and more qualifying conditions regarding the size and experience of offices have been included in competition briefs. A good example of this is Finland, where architectural competitions used to be very prominent. The Finnish Association of Architects (SAFA) – to which 80 % of Finnish architects belong – insists that it has exclusive regulatory authority over the field of architecture in Finland. Consequently, the organization has aggressively sought, with considerable success, to gain complete control of competitions. Defining the concept, the organization unapologetically states that "an architectural competition must be organized in collaboration with SAFA."[7] It has also prohibited any SAFA member from participating in competitions not controlled by it. In 2004, however, the association was sued by two architecture offices, a design office, and a student housing foundation in the town of Lappeenranta, for breaching the Competition Act with such restrictions. In court, the representatives of SAFA argued that the free right of its members to participate in any competition they desire would undermine the promotion of national architectural objectives and lead to decreased standards in competitions, hence eliminating their benefits for developers.

The Finnish Competition Authority (FCA) was not convinced. It decided that design proposals submitted in architectural competitions qualify as bids given while conducting business, so that the competition act applies. Cooperation agreements, which aim for a restriction of competition by means of price fixing, output limitation or sharing of markets or customers, violate EU treaties. The immediate result of price fixing or output limitation is that the customers either pay higher prices or cannot obtain what or as much as they want. The FCA argued that SAFA's conditions tend to reduce the number of architectural competitions (and thus the chances of new offices getting contracts) because clients rather hire offices they have worked with before and can negotiate with during the design phase. The association's rules further entail a limitation of output, which distorts competition in the design service market. In the end, the FCA ordered the SAFA to revoke its regulations, as they were violating the Competition Act, under penalty of a €60,000 fine.

De gustibus

Architecture competitions may not be free in the sense that Adam Smith imagined markets to be, but this is not necessarily an argument against them: instead of the blind invisible hand, architecture competitions boast a jury of experts, and what can be said in favor of competitions is that clients benefit from an expert judgment on which project is the best.

At a concrete level, it is often claimed that competitions save the client money, because they offer a way of avoiding costly mistakes by multiplying architectural intelligence. However, it seems as possible that competitions do not lead to any savings because it is by no means clear that the winner follows the same economic rationale as the client. In effect, the contestants and the jury operate with cultural capital which means little for the client and whose laws in fact invert the logic of the economic world.

The most notorious, but certainly not the only, example of this may be the Sydney Opera House competition of 1956/57. Jørn Utzon won because his design contributed to the discourse on organic forms and complex geometries, which was also explored by one of the jurors, Eero Saarinen. The trouble began when the design had to be realized. Construction took sixteen years and cost seven times the original estimate. Nonetheless, the completed building did not provide the seating specified in the brief and, instead of operas, could only host concerts that do not require a large stage. Here, the client got a very expensive building that did not meet the original demand. However, as John Ruskin argued, irrational economic sacrifice may increase the cultural value of architecture: "it is not the church we want, but the sacrifice ... not the gift but the giving."[8] It may well be that it was the exorbitant cost, in addition to its flamboyant appearance, which made Utzon's building a proud emblem for Sydney and Australia.

More generally, one can expect an expert jury to identify the best of several solutions only on the assumption of that jury's verifiable expertise in the particular field. In science, medicine, or engineering, this assumption seems reasonable. However, architectural expertise does not relate to measurable qualities that allow for scientific reviewing. Once the theory of construction, for example, was formalized, it no longer belonged to the special province of architects. Instead of hard science, architects are experts in matters of taste. And that is the problem.

In his magnum opus *Distinction*, Bourdieu attacks the notion of a universal transcendent conception of the aesthetic and the notion of 'pure' taste in the sense posited by Immanuel Kant. Whereas the ideology of charisma sees in good taste a gift of nature, Bourdieu's empirical studies show that cultural needs and preferences are closely linked to educational level and social descent. This background is internalized as the unconscious *habitus*, which makes taste appear natural. Thus, taste can be defined as the unconscious "practical mastery of distributions which makes it possible to sense or intuit what is likely (or unlikely) to befall – and therefore to befit – an individual occupying a given position in social space."[9]

Moreover, Bourdieu identifies the mechanism which determines high taste as one based on distinction. In his opinion, "'pure' taste and the aesthetics which provides its theory are founded on a refusal of 'impure' taste and of aesthesis (sensation), the simple, primitive form of pleasure reduced to a pleasure of the senses."[10] Indeed, taste works diacritically: "It is no accident that, when they have to be justified, they are asserted purely negatively, by the refusal of other tastes. In matters of taste, more than anywhere else, all determination is negation, and tastes are perhaps first and foremost distastes, disgust provoked by horror or visceral intolerance ('sick-making') of the tastes of others."[11] As a result, tastes are the practical affirmation of an inevitable difference between positions in social space. The 'highest' forms of art are the most difficult and only satisfy the disinterested viewer whose understanding of the most obscure forms and cultural references make up the 'game of art', whereas the most popular forms of art offer satisfaction to viewers who expect the object to deliver 'representation' or 'meaning'. Hence, the taste of the elite inclines towards Kant's idea of disinterested formalism, while the lower classes tend to what is called *kitsch*, and theirs is the taste of necessity. Bourdieu concludes that "taste classifies, and it classifies the classifier. Social subjects, classified by their classifications, distinguish themselves by the distinctions they make, between the beautiful and the ugly, the distinguished and the vulgar, in which their position in the objective classifications is expressed or betrayed."[12]

To gain capital in the field of architecture, one has to internalize a taste that differs fundamentally from the taste of the masses. Should a sophisticated architectural concept become generally accepted and loved by broader sections of society, it will be immediately rejected by the architectural avant-garde as banal. To take an example: as the Jugendstil (which originally emerged in the mid-1890s) became hugely popular in the early years of the twentieth century, the avant-garde quickly distanced itself from it, and as early as 1901 Henry van de Velde vowed to stay away from Jugendstil ornaments.[13] Similarly, postmodernism started as a highbrow critique of the international style but soon became popularized, and its leading lights, such as Michael Graves, were thoroughly discredited.

However, we do not have to assume that taste is in any way objective to find a reason for clients to trust the judgment of experts even in matters of taste. To agree with or even internalize the taste of the elite increases one's cultural capital, even if that capital were only based on distinction.

A star is born

From the competitors' point of view, an architectural competition is analogous to the liberal market model in that it promises that every entry will be treated equally and through competition it is possible to succeed without the social support system that an office normally needs.

Indeed, competitions can propel newcomers to fame. Zaha Hadid is a good example of an unknown architect whose successful career started with a competition, the Peak in Hong

Kong in 1983. For years thereafter, she still had no buildings to show for it, but remained a star and ultimately received the Pritzker Prize in 2004.

On the other hand, there are not that many beginners who win a competition. Instead, there are offices that specialize in competitions and sometimes have consistent success.

Lockwoo & Mawson are an example of competition specialists in Victorian England, winning 20 of the 30 competitions in which they took part. However, they were not always commissioned to realize their winning designs and play only a very marginal role in architectural history. Twentieth century specialists include Eero Saarinen with 12 wins out of 20 competitions, and Alvar Aalto with 25 first prizes out of a total of 58 competitions. Today, Rem Koolhaas, Norman Foster, and Jean Nouvel are among the leading architects who often get commissions through competitions.

Given that the odds are against newcomers, why do so many architects expect a competition to help them make their breakthrough? In the Wealth of Nations, Adam Smith argues that in the mechanical trades, every craftsman is usually able to make a living, but in the liberal professions such as law, literature, or philosophy, no more than one in twenty will be able to live by the business. And still, these uncertain prospects seem to attract the best and the brightest. Smith suggests two reasons for this: first, the public admiration for the few who do succeed, and secondly, the overconfidence that everyone has not only in one's own abilities, but in one's own good fortune.

If even the ideologist of liberalism thinks that people tend to put themselves at a disadvantage by misjudging their odds in a competitive situation, it is not surprising that a critic of liberalism, Pierre-Joseph Proudhon, would condemn competition in much stronger terms. In his Philosophy of Poverty, Proudhon argues that the principle of competition in capitalist economy is the negation of itself. "Is there a theorem in geometry more certain, more peremptory, than that … competition destroys competition?"[14] Competition, he contends, overturns all notions of equity and justice; it increases the real cost of production by needlessly multiplying investment capital requirements, causing both the expensiveness of products and their depreciation; it corrupts the public conscience by putting chance in the place of right and disseminates terror and distrust everywhere. Proudhon sums things up by claiming that the competition's "most certain result is to ruin those whom it drags in its train."[15]

1 Manuel Gausa, Vicente Guallart, Willy Müller, Federico Soriano, Fernando Porras and José Morales, The Metapolis Dictionary of Advanced Architecture, Actar: Barcelona, 2003, p. 123.
2 Ibid.
3 Interestingly, de Coubertin himself won the gold prize for poetry with l'Ode au sport, submitted under the pseudonym of "Georges Hohrod and Martin Eschbach." It contains a wealth of observations, such as "O Sport, tu es la Beauté! C'est toi, l'architecte de cet édifice qui est le corps humain."
4 Valéry, Paul, Occasions, transl. by Roger Shattuck and Frederick Brown, Princeton University Press: Princeton, 1990, p. 35.
5 Le Corbusier, L'art décoratif d'aujourd'hui, Arthaud: Paris, 1980, p.86 n 2. Le Corbusier, Vers une architecture, Crès et Cie: Paris, 1924, p. 179.
6 Stevens, Garry, The Favored Circle. The Social Foundations of Architectural Distinction, MIT Press: Cambridge, Mass, 1998, p. 97.
7 For example, see Järvinen, Anne (ed.), Suomen arkkitehtiliitto. Finlands arkitektförbund r. y. Jäsenluettelo. Matrikel, 2001. Forssan kirjapaino: Forssa, 2001, p. 24.
8 Ruskin, John, The Seven Lamps of Architecture, Dover: New York, n. d., pp. 9, 13–14.
9 Bourdieu, Pierre, Distinction: A Social Critique of the Judgement of Taste, transl. by R Nice, Routledge: London, 1984, p. 466.
10 Bourdieu, p. 486.
11 Bourdieu, p. 56.
12 Bourdieu, p. 6.
13 See Jormakka, Kari (ed.), Form & Detail, Universitätsverlag: Weimar, 1997, pp. 18–21.
14 Proudhon, Pierre Joseph. System of Economical Contradictions: or, the Philosophy of Misery, transl. by Benjamin R. Tucker (originally published in 1888), The Works of P. J. Proudhon, Volume IV, Arno Press: New York, 1972, p. 223. http://etext.lib.virginia.edu/toc/modeng/public/ProMise.html
15 Proudhon, p. 240, 223. We are paraphrasing the translation from Marx's critique of Proudhon in The Poverty of Philosophy.

This text was published first in: "Wettbewerb! – Umbau 22", Österreichische Gesellschaft für Architektur, Edition Selene, Wien, 2005.

Competition systems: looking for the right one

What role can competitions play for emerging practices? What works and what should be rethought in the current system to make it work better?

On the occasion of the opening of the exhibition 'Deadline Today, 99+ stories about architecture competitions', Wonderland organized a symposium to discuss these questions.
The event took place on June 18, 2009, at the Architekturzentrum Wien.

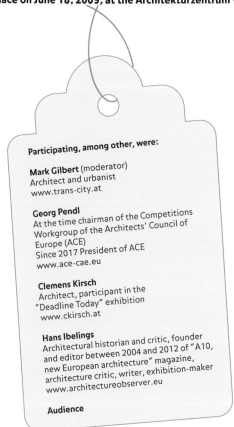

Participating, among other, were:

Mark Gilbert (moderator)
Architect and urbanist
www.trans-city.at

Georg Pendl
At the time chairman of the Competitions Workgroup of the Architects' Council of Europe (ACE)
Since 2017 President of ACE
www.ace-cae.eu

Clemens Kirsch
Architect, participant in the "Deadline Today" exhibition
www.ckirsch.at

Hans Ibelings
Architectural historian and critic, founder and editor between 2004 and 2012 of "A10, new European architecture" magazine, architecture critic, writer, exhibition-maker
www.architectureobserver.eu

Audience

Gilbert: Open competitions have a great value in that they arrive at quality solutions. But there is an economic cost to that: one competition with 200 entries – which, taken together, are tantamount to 400 months of work – this is a whole career's work for one competition. And if there is no decision, it's a whole career for nothing. So the issue is: are there ways to define competition rules, or restrict competitions, in order to increase economic efficiency? And how can we do so and still get good results but with more economic rationality?

Pendl: The whole system works well, if there is a good mix of open and invited or other kinds of competitions. If you have competitions for small jobs with many participants, sometimes you do not really get the best participants. It may sound a bit cynical, but it's the truth – the more advanced offices weigh their chances very carefully and decide after a clear evaluation of the procedure only. Even for very high-level tasks you often do not get enough high-level offices. The only way out of this is an agreement between architects, the potential participants, and clients. And this can only go well with the help of an effective, representative architects' organization. And here we get to yet another problem: sometimes these organizations are not professional enough. Then the client has difficulties, because he doesn't have a proper partner for discussion.

Kirsch: Competitions for small projects were my only chance to get commissions in the first place. I remember when I won a project for a school in October 2008, there were 26 participants in the competition, and two months later for a school in Bregenz, there were a hundred participants. That was the impact of the crisis. Private clients had just dropped their projects or put them on hold, so the architects all turned to public commissions. In half a year, it may be down to 20 participants again. It's not really predictable.

Gilbert: There clearly are two issues here: how does the contracting authority find a system to choose the right architect for the task? And secondly, how do architects decide when to take part in a competition, and in which type of competition ...

Audience: We should rather get into the methodical problems of competitions before talking about administrative ways of improving the system. With every winning example, there are half a dozen or more other entries that have a similar approach, sometimes are even better, but do not win. The jury only has a few minutes for each project. And this is the basic problem that should be discussed.

Kirsch: I think that is a natural quality of anonymous competitions: that a sheet of paper, or the competition entry, is the only way of communicating with the jury. You never show a finished project, you show a concept, a way of thinking that lies underneath or behind the project. I expect the jury to be able to see in which direction the project will go. In the jury report, the jury always adds things or makes recommendations about how to further develop the project. It's more like writing letters, there is no direct communication or discussion, but it's our task to make ourselves understood – by drawing lines, by giving descriptions or by creating images. Sometimes there are misunderstandings. There are projects where the jury doesn't get the point or others where I am not clear enough to make my point. That's part of the system.

Gilbert: The jury also performs a service, an intellectual service of considerable value. Anonymous or not anonymous, what sort of possible ways of communication between a jury, a client and an architect participating in a competition are realistic and possible?

Pendl: The preliminary design, as we normally call it, is the basis for the decision in the competition; it's not a final design. There's a long process coming after that. Perhaps it's just a kind of "snapshot", a picture of the process which then leads to the final building. But what you describe here, this kind of dialogue even has a name in this EU Directive, it's called competitive dialogue. And it is supposed to be used for highly complex tasks like computer programs. It means that the client is in continuous dialogue with all participants, and it includes a very critical issue, namely, author's rights. Because there always are additional questions that participants are asked by the jury, you can't avoid getting questions like "Wouldn't it be better if you put a door over there, as this proposal does it?" And so you get a total mess. The author's rights of the participants are not properly protected in these procedures, and therefore it is a common position in the Architects' Council of Europe that we do not want to have this competitive dialogue procedure in architecture.

Audience: So the variety of competitions is there, it's just which one to choose? I strongly support a mix of open competitions, restricted, invited, whatever. In invited or restricted competitions, you always have a certain minimum of young architects or young offices. But the compensation for a competition should be much higher, because when you look at the lifetime cost of a building, construction costs are about 25 to 30 percent, and then, if you break it down to the cost of a competition, it's ridiculous.

Kirsch: Sometimes there should be competitions for competitions. If you ask the wrong questions you will get the wrong answers. So there should be a preface. There are so many questions that need to be asked before starting the competition to clarify the needs of the client.

Gilbert: One of the issues I see being raised here is the issue of anonymity in any communication process. You can send a letter anonymously.

Gilbert: There's a whole set of decision to be made before the architectural competition really gets to the participar architects; there is a whole range of issues which need to be properly defined.

Audience: This question of anonymity should be also seen at different levels. In the EU Directive, there is not only the competitive dialogue, but also the electronic auction. And this is not appropriate for architectural competitions. What should be remembered is that in the Directive there is a difference if the jury decision is binding for the contracting authority or not. If not, the jury is just a kind of expert body. It can make its evaluation completely without discussion with competitors, and once the competition is over and the results are out, it's just the jury's opinion. And the contracting authority is free to decide whether they want to make a contract with the winner or start negotiations with several participants.

Pendl: As architects, we have one threat that's lawyers in architectural design cor tions. More and more, lawyers are gettin involved in architectural competitions, ar is awful because all they want is restrictic fact, this would be the beginning of the e architectural design competitions. Which me to the second point I want to make, na that we ourselves should continue to have hand in the system of design competitions This has to be done by architects, because architects understand the options, chances possible variations of a job.

Gilbert: One of the issues is how to make restrictions in order to rationalize the process. How do we define what good restrictions are?

Ibelings: The question is what the real benefit of a competition is for anyone other than the winner. If you're the winner you're lucky. But is this the only reason to build this whole system of competitions?

Pendl: I always fight for two-stage competitions, because if you want to reduce the number of participants, who have to invest a lot of work, and, on the other side, want detailed proposals, which require even more work investment, then this is a very good way. It's much better to have a preselection on basis of project proposals than of references and résumés, because actually you don't really get much out of a résumé.

Audience: It's for society, not only for us. Take an example from Finland: every two years, we have an exhibition that shows the best projects of these past two years in Finland, and the majority of these projects always come out of competitions. So it's a system which raises the level of architecture in the country, and for youngsters it's a way to get better and get ahead.

Audience: To reduce the workload, clarity of the brief is a key point. The clearer the brief, the better defined the task, the easier it is to work efficiently for the teams. And this is something that could be another means to reduce the workload of the teams. Personally, I have experienced two-stage competitions where in the end the workload was quite similar to an open competition and it was actually very difficult to understand the direction of the jury in the intermediate communication when you were selected for the second stage.

REALITY CHECK #5: MAKING COMPETITIONS

116 stories about 'the competition that changed your life' were submitted by practices from 25 countries at the beginning of 2009 in response to an open call. The survey framed both the general results achieved by the teams since the beginning of their independent practice thanks to competitions, and the specifics of the 116 entries. The respondents included both teams from outside Europe doing projects in Europe and European teams doing projects outside Europe.

Competitions represent a relevant investment for all responding practices, with an average of almost **2,000 working hours per year**, which is tantamount to the total annual working time of one full-time collaborator.

Many teams agree that the amount of work required is disproportionate compared to the possible prize moneys, yet the gain is also seen at other levels: the chance to stimulates architectural thinking within the practice, to experiment and to get acknowledged within the profession.

Consequently, the return on this investment is not easy to estimate. For all practical reasons, we can count the number of realizations achieved by the participants: **1** project for every **10** competitions done, which equals **19 %** of the projects realized by the practices since they started their business.

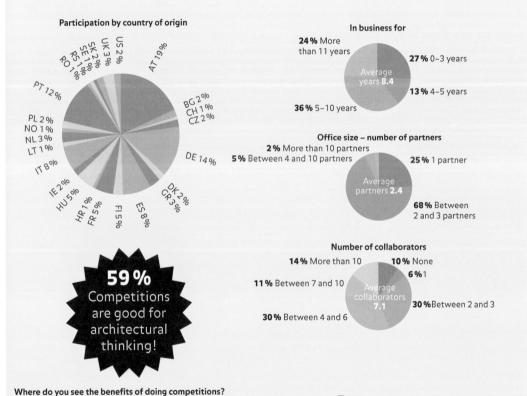

Participation by country of origin

In business for
- 24 % More than 11 years
- 27 % 0–3 years
- 13 % 4–5 years
- 36 % 5–10 years
- Average years **8.4**

Office size – number of partners
- 2 % More than 10 partners
- 5 % Between 4 and 10 partners
- 25 % 1 partner
- 68 % Between 2 and 3 partners
- Average partners **2.4**

Number of collaborators
- 14 % More than 10
- 10 % None
- 6 % 1
- 11 % Between 7 and 10
- 30 % Between 2 and 3
- 30 % Between 4 and 6
- Average collaborators **7.1**

59 % Competitions are good for architectural thinking!

Where do you see the benefits of doing competitions?

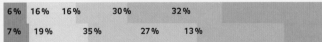

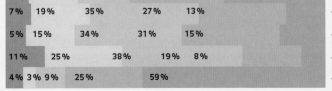

Not true at all	Not really true	Could be	True	Absolutely true		They …
6 %	16 %	16 %	30 %	32 %		… provide higher quality of design
7 %	19 %	35 %	27 %	13 %		… provide media attention
5 %	15 %	34 %	31 %	15 %		… are a good opportunity for getting new commissions
11 %	25 %	38 %	19 %	8 %		… are a shortcut to getting well known
4 %	3 %	9 %	25 %	59 %		… stimulate architecture thinking in the practice

● Not true at all ○ Not really true Could be True Absolutely true

WHY MAKE COMPETITIONS

All in all, competitions represent the most important source of commissions for 39% of practices taking part in our survey. More than 62% see the competition system working at least at some level. For the practice itself, they are for the most a good way to develop the architecture thinking within the practice.

39% of the practices lives off competitions

Does your office live out off competitions?
3% Not answered

39% Yes
58% No

Does the competition system work?
4% Not answered

37% Yes, there is a large number of competitions
34% No, in most cases clients try to avoid that
25% Yes, but only at national level

Where do you see the benefits that the project gave your practice?

79% Acknowledgement in the profession
73% Media attention
56% Material for exhibitions
52% New clients and commissions
51% Getting the job
16% Another project on the shelf

37% Projects usually don't get built!

WHY NOT

For the great majority of the offices, the problem is the amount of work required. Yet, for only 20%, direct contacts with clients are a viable alternative to get commissions. At least one third sees a problem in the uncertainty of the realization. They are, by the way, quite right!

Competitions are problematic because

75% … the prizes do not correlate with work required
37% … projects usually do not get built
33% … there is no guarantee for the copyright protection of your idea
20% … they are a loss of energy, our office relies on direct contact with the client
19% … most of the results are prearranged
6% … they are slowing down the process

TURNING POINTS

Competitions can be a reason to start an office, to take the next step, and venture into a new market – either in terms of geography, specialization, or project size.

Of the 116 projects surveyed, 37 (32 %) were the decisive factors to start up an own office. Still, one should be careful: the time between winning the project and signing the contract may be very long!

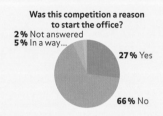

Was this competition a reason to start the office?
- **2 %** Not answered
- **5 %** In a way...
- **27 %** Yes
- **66 %** No

Getting started

Next step: location

One third of competitions surveyed were held in countries outside the home countries of the participant offices. And previous working experience in that country was not considered necessary by a majority (62 %) to decide to try one's luck in a new location.

Was the competition held in a different country than your own?
- **32 %** Yes
- **68 %** No

Taking the next step

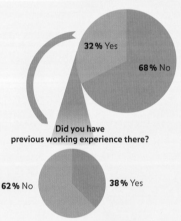

Did you have previous working experience there?
- **62 %** No
- **38 %** Yes

The EU public procurement system

The public procurement procedure put in place in the EU countries has brought positive improvements for the majority of the teams. Most of all, it has created opportunities for young practices and has contributed to the internationality of the scene.

24 %
Has brought no improvement

49 %
Has brought more opportunities for young practices

What did the EU system bring to your country?
- **49 %** More opportunities for young offices to emerge
- **42 %** More internationality
- **37 %** A stimulus for the discussion on architecture
- **33 %** Better quality of architectural design
- **29 %** More cooperation between architecture offices
- **28 %** A raise of public interest for architecture
- **25 %** More transparency in development
- **24 %** No improvements at all

EXPERIENCE REPORTS

Why make competitions

/ / / / / / **Because they fit a specific interest** / / / / / / / / / / / /

RMNO GEKRULDE RUIMTE ("WARPED SPACE")

DUS architects (NL)
http://houseofdus.com
Design methodology/national authority

 Ideas competition
10 participants
40 hours worked
14,000 Euros prize money

Status: completed

150,000 Euros worth of commissioned se

1st Prize

While founding our office DUS architects we decided NOT to take part in competitions. Instead we started to initiate our own urban projects. Gradually, our approach evolved into a design methodology in which we bring together everybody involved at a round table: the municipality, future residents, current neighbors, and the developer/building corporation. In 2006, the Netherlands Advisory Council for Research on Spatial Planning, Nature and the Environment (RMNO) issued a call for proposals for new ways of communication and design methods. We simply made a poster that illustrated our method and won first prize. **This competition was special because it provided a platform to present our approach – not a design.** After winning, our approach got dubbed "the DUS method" and brought us several commissions, like the project shown here.

/ / / / / / **Because they are a chance to develop** / / / / / / / / / / / /

INTERVENTIONS IN THE CITY – SAFE INJECTIONS CENTRE

Paulo Moreira (PT)
www.paulomoreira.net
Urban design/public private partnership

Ideas competition
170 participants
104 hours worked
2,000 Euros prize money

Status: unrealized
3.5 months to finalize the contract

1st Prize

In 2007 the Lisbon Architecture Triennale launched an ideas competition, inviting architects to make proposals for the rehabilitation of structurally and socially run-down urban areas. I decided to propose a building that everyone was talking about but nobody had ever seen – and invited my friend Diogo Matos to co-design this challenging task.

The commitment to architecture with a social purpose triggered by this ideas competition brought many opportunities for the start-up of my architectural practice. In fact, two of the consultant institutions commissioned an architectural workshop on equipment for drug addicts and other deprived communities, which I coordinated. As a result I was invited by a NGO to take part in a social development project in a slum area on the outskirts of Angola's capital Luanda, for which I designed a primary school. This competition was a remarkable moment for my professional education and an undeniable opportunity for personal development. **This project turned into a PhD by Design started in 2010 at the London Metropolitan University.**

CB3 – CHÙA BOC MIXED-USE DEVELOPMENT, HANOI, VIETNAM

ICE – ideas for contemporary environments (DE/HK)
www.icehk.com
Mixed-use/private investor

Invited competition
3 participants

2600 hours worked
0 Euros prize money

Status: unrealized
3 months to finalize the contract

The client provided us with the brief and site information, offered a site visit and told us that they would really want to work with us, but needed to see some ideas first. In the end, we found out that we had been in a competition with at least 3 other teams. On the day of the presentation of our conceptual ideas, we were appointed the winning team and started negotiating the contract. **We have completely embraced the fact that every commission might become a competition at any point (and vice versa) and we appreciate it as it keeps us innovative and self-critical.**

/ / / / Because they can be effective turning points of an architects career /

FINNISH SCIENCE CENTER

Heikkinen-Komonen Architects (FI)
www.heikkinen-komonen.fi
Educational & cultural/public institution

Open competition
70 participants
1,000 hours worked
5,000 Euros prize money

Status: realized
6 months to finalize the contract
36 months to complete the project
360,000 Euros worth of commissioned services

My partner Markku Komonen and I started our collaboration '68/69 in school. We had a small basement room with a tiny window where we spent the evenings after our daytime jobs and most weekends. After a nice start, no calls came in anymore from the competition juries. Our third partner quit in '78, fed up with useless competitions. In the mid-80s, we also started to have doubts whether this would ever work. It was in '85 when we decided that the national competition for the Finnish Science Center would be our last one if once again nothing came out of it. I can still remember heaven coming down on us when we heard that we got the first prize.

UNIVERSITY OF HELSINKI CITY CAMPUS LIBRARY

Anttinen Oiva Arkkitehdit Oy (FI)
www.aoa.fi
Education & cultural/public institution

Restricted competition
30 participants

630 hours worked
30,000 Euros prize money

Status: realized
15 months to finalize the contract

It was a really big one and immediately **changed our office profile**: we hired 3 new employees soon after that and 3 more in 2008. The commission brought us stability and credibility.

BANYA RESIDENCE

Fordewind architecture (BG)
www.fordewind.com
Residential & urban design/private investor

Invited competition
8 participants

700 hours worked
5,000 Euros prize money

Status: unrealized
9 months to finalize the contract

Although we have Bulgarian roots, we had spent most of our lives (nearly 30 years) outside Bulgaria in Austria and Germany. As a result of winning the competition within one year we decided to relocate our office and ourselves to Bulgaria. Living in Bulgaria now for the last few years, we found **this decision was very heavy metal**. We enjoy ourselves every day (almost).

AAA ARCHITETTI CERCASI 2008
DEMO architects (IT/NL)

Residential /private investor

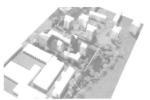

Ideas competition	Status: canceled
69 participants	
900 hours worked	
5,000 Euros prize money	

'Send it and forget about it' had always been our policy.

Then we won the first prize! Un-be-lieve-able, it was hard to imagine that this was real.

All of a sudden we realized that we were architects. All energies and potentials that had always been put into competitions **finally turned from a game into something serious**: to set up a space for work, launch the office website, and start thinking objectively about how we can survive.

ADBC – ADI DASSLER BRAND CENTER
querkraft architekten (AT)
www.querkraft.at
Commercial/private investor

Restricted competition	Status: realized
29 participants	3 months to finalize the contract
600 hours worked	24 months to complete the project
15,000 Euros prize money	1,000,000 Euros worth of commissioned se

It was the first big project and the first project in a foreign country. With the new commission we changed our payment system for our staff. It was the point when our practice began to be more professional. **Once the project was completed we knew that we would be able to handle any project of any size now.**

/ / / / / / **Unexpected results from lost projects** / / / / / / / / / / / / / /

URBAN IMPLANT
PARASITE studio (RO)
www.parasitestudio.com
Mixed-use/public private partnership

Competition	Status: unrealized
5 participants	
200 hours worked	
1,200 Euros prize money	

In a way that is characteristic for Romania, the design and the success of the project (2nd place) remained unnoticed in the context of Romanian architecture. The design was noticed abroad, and this is how we managed to draw attention to our architecture office.

BLOK 64 7 IJBURG AMSTERDAM
LOOS ARCHITECTS (NL)
www.loosarchitects.nl
Residential/private investor

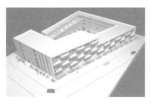

Invited competition	Status: realized
3 participants	5 months to finalize the contract
140 hours worked	42 months to complete the project
0 Euros prize money	330,000 Euros worth of commissioned ser

A year and a half before the actual decision, we were asked to present our vision on contemporary housing. After that, we did not hear anything for a while. Half a year later, we were invited to present our vision for a development in Amsterdam. We lost. Another year later, we were asked by the same client to make a quick sketch for two housing blocks. Two days after the presentation, we were told that we had been selected to design one of the two blocks. We have already started the real design process.

how to make competitions

Designing for a competition poses an extreme challenge: the project is not just about what one specific client wants, but more about what can be asked of an architectural design in absolute terms – it's a quest for the absolute design. Strategic decisions are therefore difficult: should the rules be respected or should one move beyond these limits? Conformity or radicalism?

An Order of Maria Theresa for Architectural Insubordination?

On rules and irregularities in today's design competitions in the EU

There is a notorious myth among architects, namely, that the ultimate feat is to win an architectural competition contrary to the specifications of the brief. One might well do the promoter, and oneself, good by surprising the prize jury with a planning solution that clearly ignores the limits defined in the competition documents. Admittedly, the freehand reinterpretation of the competition task – by including properties outside the planning area, by demolishing parts of a listed building, by ignoring cost limits and urban planning constraints as specified in the brief, etc. – does have some intellectual appeal.

The idea of an extreme response means to impute to the promoter a question that remained previously unasked but might be beneficial for the project. Architectural disobedience, the myth says, can win a competition and even a commission. Successful insubordination has much charm. It fuels the ambition of the competition participant to eclipse collective knowledge, as articulated by the public promoter in the competition brief, with allegedly better individual knowledge.

Such "heroic" competition behavior has a historical model in Austria, which is deeply rooted in public consciousness: that of successful military insubordination which not only entails no punitive sanction, but results in social ennoblement. Among the legends carried over from the Habsburg monarchy to the present day is the one about the officer who, disobeying his orders, takes the initiative and achieves brilliant success in battle, for which he then is elevated by the emperor into an elite circle of national heroes. Some competition participants are still trying their luck using this role model today.

Creating with courage and bravado a surprising configuration that could not have been created or would not even have been thought of without the intervention of an individual is a fascinating pattern of thought and action, which many competition entries seem likely to fall for. The servant would only be too eager to demonstrate to the master where the development is headed. Disregarding the declared goals of one's own chain of command and judging the situation independently often creates opportunity for surprising tactical action and has frequently led to success on the battlefield.

Text by Walter Chramosta, Vienna, Austria

276

At this point, it should be discussed whether it is opportune to follow this maxim in front of a competition jury. In the area of the planning competitions, heroic insubordination is directed against those who are fighting for the same thing: the best design, the commission, architecture. The enemies to overcome are not the competitors, but rather practical constraints of project feasibility, the public opinion, the cultural state of the user, etc.

In 1757, Empress Maria Theresa founded the most coveted Austrian military award, the Military Order of Maria Theresa. It was the highest decoration for bravery that officers could get in the imperial army and was awarded in two, later three categories, without regard to class and religion, for personal initiative of a military impact in battle. The sole criterion was bravery before the enemy, and only "the best of the best" were supposed to become members of the order. Those awarded were held in high esteem, received a life-long pension and were raised to nobility. The message of this decoration was: you can act on own initiative, violating rules, or even against an explicit command. And if successful, it may earn you the highest reward. The nimbus of the Order of Maria Theresa was that it gave sanction to disobedience and even insubordination as long they produced success.

The very fact that the violation of rules might be rewarded by the ruler himself, the maker of rules, in fact encourages the rarely satisfied desire for disobedience. The Order of Maria Theresa no longer exists. But in architecture competitions, the strategic question of whether intelligent rule violations are worthwhile is still being raised. Can the career and social status of an architect be based on an act of non-compliance in the system of architectural competitions?

Participants in architectural competitions in the European Union hope that juries will not award projects that go against the competition brief. The crux is: can a violation of rules be the basis for a good competition result? So much is certain: in the European Union, adherence to competition rules guarantees the best chance of success. No participant of an architectural competition should try to bypass, or overthrow, the rules with a heroic project.

To distort a contest with a bold non-conforming design is a form of old-style struggle. The competition rules seek to establish a fair contest of ideas and not to eliminate architects. Therefore, a competition brief has to define clear limits, formal rules and design boundaries.

The formal rules of well-designed architecture competitions reflect the best practice. They represent a centuries-old tradition of architecture competitions in Europe and are largely consistent with the contracting regulations in the European Union.

The best practice is summarized in the 10 Recommendations for Design Contests of the Architects' Council of Europe (ACE)[1] of 2016, which should provide an acceptable basis for architectural competition procedures for both contracting authorities and participants. These 10 rules ought to be respected in every architectural competition procedure.

10 RECOMMENDATIONS FOR DESIGN CONTESTS - ARCHITECTS' COUNCIL OF EUROPE (ACE)

1 DEFINITION OF AN ARCHITECTURAL COMPETITION
- Architectural competition means the procedure of a design contest evaluating the ideas of architects in a formalized procedure on a defined program and defined criteria, anonymously weighted by an independent jury.
- There are different types: project and ideas competitions, one or two-stage competitions.
- The procedure is anonymous until the final decision of the jury.

2 EQUAL CHANCES FOR ALL PARTICIPANTS
- Same information level provided to all participants at the same time.
- No individual exchange of information between participants and jury members.
- Representatives, partners or employees of the promoter or of any jury member are excluded from participation.

3 INDEPENDENT JURY
- The jury shall be autonomous in its decisions or opinions.
- Where a particular professional qualification is required from participants, at least a third of the members of the jury shall hold that qualification at a high standard and must be independent from the competition promoter.
- The jury shall examine the proposals submitted by the candidates anonymously and solely on the basis of the criteria indicated in the contest notice.
- It shall record its project ranking in a report, signed by its members. This report shall contain the merits of the projects and a clear recommendation on how to proceed with the result of the competition.

4 THE BRIEF
- The competition brief must be clear and unambiguous. Competition requirements must be clearly specified. There must be a clear distinction between requirements and non-binding guidelines.
- The evaluation criteria applicable must be stated in the brief.
- The brief has to be accepted by the jury prior to the launch of the competition.

5 TRANSPARENCY OF THE PROCEDURE
- The summary of the jury's discussion and the decision-making process have to be recorded in a report.
- The jury report shall be published or distributed to the participants and the public.
- There shall be a public exhibition of all entries.

6 ANONYMITY
- Anonymity must be kept until the jury has reached its final opinion or decision.

7 PRIZE MONEY AND REMUNERATION
- The prize money or remuneration has to be fixed and announced in the competition brief. For the calculation of the prize money or the remuneration, there must be an adequate relationship between the required performance of the participants and the fee that would be usually payable for that task.
- In the second stage of a competition, a remuneration, which is a part of the total prize money, is paid to each participant admitted to that stage.

8 CONSEQUENCES OF THE JURY'S DECISION
- There must be a fair and adequate compensation for the participants. There must be a declaration of the client to award a contract including a sufficient scope of work to the prize winner or to one of the prize winners in a project competition.
- If an ideas competition is not followed by a project competition, an adequate remuneration in the form of higher prize money has to be awarded.
- If the results of an ideas competition are used as a basis for the execution of a project, this has to be done in agreement with the author.

9 COPYRIGHT
- Author's rights for a competition entry remain with the author.
- The promoter is entitled to make use of the winning entries under the conditions that are laid down in the brief or agreed between the parties.

10 DISPUTE RESOLUTION
- Any disputes arising from or concerning competition procedures shall be examined by the competent national professional organization before legal procedures are taken.

Comparable rules for design contests exist in most of the EU member states as principles and guidelines for regional and urban planning and architectural competitions. By ignoring these rules, a participant puts his/her competition entry at an extreme risk: the project has no chance to be judged. If the promoter or contracting authority ignores these rules, they will only be able to muster a handful of participants for the competition. Violating these rules is not intelligent, because they guarantee the comparability of competition works.

Without a proper comparison, including discussion by the jury, quality assessment is impossible. A winning project that is based on disregard of the rules would lead any competition to absurdity.

Material limits in a competition are more difficult to define and evaluate than formal limits, because they are project-specific. This is the challenge for architects, who prepare and organize architectural competitions, and for the promoter, who has the final decision. It is very important to distinguish between hard criteria, to be observed in any case, and soft criteria, which allow leeway for the freedom of design.

Most important for the success of an architectural design procedure is the strict distinction between hard and soft criteria prior to the start of the competition. The definition of what the hard and soft criteria in the completion task are can never be left to participants as this would make competition entries largely incomparable.

Architectural competitions are quality-oriented and therefore, necessarily, procedures are governed by rules. They can only work on a solid foundation of formal limits. This formal regulatory framework is known throughout Europe and can hardly be improved. Nevertheless, these proven formalities need to be propagated further, as contracting authorities are all too fond of slimming procedures without being aware of the consequences. Formal issues in competition matters should in fact no longer be the priority in preparing competitions.

Architectural competitions cannot work without clear decisions made by the promoter between hard and soft criteria. Participants who think they have to overstep the line risk seeing their designs disqualified. Pushing the soft limits is the actual playing field of the competition. If the promoter wants to hold a project search and not a planner search, he will clearly stake out this field in his very own interest. But no public promoter today must arouse hope for a lucky shot – winning a competition by ignoring the brief – so, sadly to relate, there will be no Order of Maria Theresa for successful architectonic insubordination.

1 Quoted after: https://www.ace-cae.eu/uploads/tx_jidocumentsview/6.1.1_GA2_17_Compet-Rules.pdf

HOW TO SELECT A COMPETITION

Competitions with a challenging theme are particularly interesting. The location and a convergence with the existing specialization of the practice are relevant for more than the half of the respondents. Fewer teams find the reward for the first prize or the estimated chances to win relevant in this phase. And the jury? For at least 50 % of the teams, it is a factor to count in.

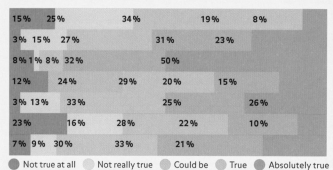

15 %	25 %	34 %	19 %	8 %	The competition is not so important but chances to win are better
3 % 15 %	27 %	31 %	23 %		It is an important competition
8 % 1 % 8 %	32 %	50 %			Theme is challenging
12 %	24 %	29 %	20 %	15 %	Our knowledge of the location
3 % 13 %	33 %	25 %	26 %		The jury!
23 %	16 %	28 %	22 %	10 %	It is the relation project size/prize
7 % 9 %	30 %	33 %	21 %		The theme fits our specialization

● Not true at all ● Not really true ● Could be ● True ● Absolutely true

82 %
It is
the theme
that counts!

COMPETITION SETUP

Doing competitions is a specialization in itself – more than 70 % have specialized people in the office to work on competitions. The majority rely on internal skills. Outsourcing of model-building and renderings is an option for roughly one third of the respondents.

Do you have a competition setup?

15 % No

85 % Yes

75 % We have collaborators specialized in competitions in the office
39 % We have someone external for renderings
31 % We have someone external for model making
28 % We have a filing system
21 % Other ways

39 %
outsource
renderings

WHAT ABOUT PHYSICAL MODELS

Only 50 % see them as a working tool to be used in the process!

50 % They are a working tool to check ideas
20 % We like to experiment with new model techniques
15 % We like to experiment with new materials
8 % Models are not important
7 % Models are an end product for presentation purposes

Source: Wonderland #5 Survey, by SCAPE architects, 2009

WITH WHOM TO DO A COMPETITION

The projects surveyed listed collaboration as key strategy to approach, develop and possibly win the competition project.

Was the project done in collaboration with specialized consultants?

5% Not answered

34% No

61% Yes

Of 116 competition entries surveyed 61% were done in collaboration with professionals from other fields and 29% in collaboration with other architects.

From the field of...

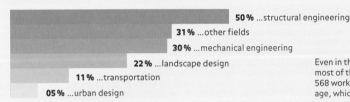

50% ...structural engineering

31% ...other fields

30% ...mechanical engineering

22% ...landscape design

11% ...transportation

05% ...urban design

Even in the case of multi-disciplinary teams, most of the work is done by the architects: 568 working hours per project on an average, which is 80% of the total workload.

Was the project done in collaboration with other architects?

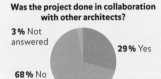

3% Not answered

29% Yes

68% No

Hours worked

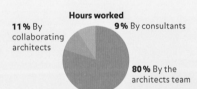

11% By collaborating architects

9% By consultants

80% By the architects team

84% Competitions are necessary for daring ideas

HOW FAR SHOULD YOU GO

Key decisions include the possibility of moving beyond the limits as a way to success. **Out of the 116 surveyed submissions, 6 came out winning because of such a strategy.**

Would you say that competitions are...

84% ... necessary for clients who want new daring ideas

72% ... good for iconic building designs

65% ... the best tool to experiment

47% ... less limiting than direct commissions

Source: Wonderland #3 Survey – by SHARE architects, 2009

A matter of approach

MISFITS – DIE CURRYWURSTBUDE WIRD GESELLSCHAFTSFÄHIG

Büro Popp (DE)
http://buropopp.com
Commercial/private investor

Ideas competition
26 participants
60 hours worked
50 Euros prize money

Status: unrealized

I tested a radical idea of proposing a do-it-yourself-building with a calculated very low price. I will continue to make radical proposals in competitions. **Architects should try not only to provide creative answers but ask creative questions.**

KINDERGARTEN SCHUKOWITZGASSE, VIENNA

Architekt Clemens Kirsch (AT)
www.clemenskirsch.at
Child-care/local municipality

Open competition
90 participants
150 hours worked
10,000 Euros prize money

Status: realized
1.5 months to finalize the contract
10 months to complete the project
140,000 Euros worth of commissioned ser

History: I opened my own office in 2006 with no contracts on hand. Working at home on my laptop, I tried to participate in as many competitions as possible. In retrospect, I would call this year 'the heroic phase'. In 2007, my design approach shifted into a more 'realistic phase'.

Approach: To me, doing competitions is a question of exercise and thinking. It is like playing the piano: you cannot play a piano concerto by only thinking of playing it. This special discipline in the field of architecture takes a lot of exercising. The composition of the jury is also an important indicator of how to set up your strategy. So with all the information given or decoded, you can make a conscious decision how far you want to go. Apart from exercising there is the thinking: my approach follows no strict concept, I would rather consider it an attitude. Ideally, a concept will be continually condensed and reduced until its individual essence becomes perceptible.

Featured project – 'Never compromise on a concept'

The competition entry it is the smallest project (2 mio. Euro building cost, around 1,500 m² building footprint) we have won so far. Situated on the outskirts of Vienna, the new kindergarten has the perfect mix of openess and enclosure to 'survive' in the surroundings and at the same time to be an enrichment to the tough environment.

I was astonished how efficiently in terms of working hours (less than 100 hours inside the office) we managed to get the competition entry done. This time, after the brief and unsatisfying consideration of a 'normal' kindergarten layout, I fell in a **long phase of meditation-like thinking. So, after some time without drawing anything, the 'inside-out trick' came to my mind, and luckily the whole scheme fit into the concept.**

//// A matter of collaborations ///////////////

JOHN PAUL II CENTER "DO NOT FEAR", KRAKÓW

¬parallelprojekt with
Agnieszka Anczykowska (DE)
https://parallelprojekt.jimdo.com
Religious/public institution

Open competition

100 hours worked
6,000 Euros prize money

Status: unrealized

Honourable Mention

I teamed up with a psychologist. We set up a style of approaching projects by inviting non-professionals to contribute ideas and thoughts. We developed the design in 3-D and frequently produced visualizations to discuss the images, moods, scenes, which created results more like a storyboard; then the usual plan, section, elevation.

The client finally commissioned a local architect to design the center in a style the Vatican liked better. The local media were mainly interested in the unusual team of a German architect and a Polish psychologist working together successfully.

JAMES USSHER LIBRARY, TRINITY COLLEGE DUBLIN

McCullough Mulvin Architects (IE)
www.mcculloughmulvin.com
Educational/public institution

Restricted competition
6 participants
1,800 hours worked
0 Euros prize money

Status: realized
6 months to finalize the contract
12 months to complete the project
1,200,000 Euros worth of commissioned services

1st Prize

The competition started in 1997 as a restricted competition of six practices from the UK and Ireland, including Norman Foster and Richard Rogers. We linked up with another practice – KMD Architecture – to enter it, wanting an Irish winner for the competition. The competition was the single largest project executed by the office to date and has directed much of our subsequent work towards the exploration of library design.

YORKSHIRE DIAMOND

Various Architects (NO)
http://variousarchitects.no
Cultural/public private partnership

Open competition
67 participants
400 hours worked
3,500 Euros prize money

Status: unrealized

Finalist

We had been chosen as one of 5 finalists. **For the presentation to the jurors, we were accompanied by engineers and by the inflatable-buildings manufacturer who would be able to produce the parts needed for the project**. We felt that this gave the project the necessary depth to convince the jury that it was feasible and could be built in time and on budget.

We received a follow-up email with further questions. We spent another two weeks answering the technical questions, which included a full computational structural simulation to assess the deflections of the building under gale-force winds.

GRAND EGYPTIAN MUSEUM
heneghan peng architects (IE)
www.hparc.com
Cultural/national authority

Open competition: two stages
1,557 participants
500 hours worked
176,850 Euros prize money

Status: realized
5 months to finalize the contract

> "There's no such thing as a blank slate. When you are faced with the UNESCO World Heritage site, that slate is heavily loaded, and how you respond to that becomes important."
>
> "The things that influence us are quite broad and mostly outside of what architecture can provide."
>
> "Consultants have contributed a lot to our projects. At times there are parts of the projects that almost don't belong to us but they all get brought together in the project itself. At the end of the day, there is no logic to the process. The project is everywhere, the process is everywhere, but you do end up with the project only because you have to deliver it on deadline day."
>
> *(Opening lecture for the exhibition "Deadline Today", Architekturzentrum Wien, Vienna, June 2009)*

We got shortlisted down to 20 from 1,557. We were quite happy when we received the mail; it was all fading because it was done on an ink-jet printer. We also kept the envelope that told us that we won. The project is adjacent to a World Heritage site, only two kilometers from the pyramids. It's basically Egypt's national museum and will house, amongst many other collections, Tutankhamun himself.

We had not only to address the past of the pyramids, but also needed to understand the museum as a living museum within the urban context of everyday life. The other thing is to understand Egypt's geography. The client chose a very good and interesting site: the cliff face itself, this condition or juxtaposition between desert and Nile, is what should become the icon. They have already given you, in some way, all the raw material in order for the project to start, hence not a blank slate. What's iconic here is not an object that is new and signature and different, but actually something embedded already in the Egyptian culture. By transforming that surface, we in fact produce an icon of what is already there. We wanted to try to actually bring the pyramids themselves into the space of the museum. So, instead of using cars, we hoped to actually take the gardens of the museum along an esplanade and connect it to the pyramids and out to Sakkara, with a kind of bus or train system.

When President Mubarak came to look at the competition schemes, his comment about this scheme was that from anywhere in the museum you can see the most important artifact of all, which are the pyramids.

There is a kind of simpleness to the scheme that actually allows people to understand the project very quickly, too. At the end of the day, the site is the architecture and what is on the site is what needs to be preserved. The question is how to construct an object that actually is sympathetic and works within that, but simultaneously has an identity of its own; it is not about the new, but about the transformation of what's there.

When we started the competition, we were three people in the office. We worked on it for four months, day and night, about 500 hours. When we met the consultants, we just locked the door and nobody could answer the phone. At the height of the project, there were 117 people and twelve consultants working on the project, which entailed the accelerated development of office infrastructure, both with regard to physical/technical and organizational/operational systems. The GEM project has shaped the way in which we approach and run projects now and in the future. Big change.

Note: assuming an average of 500 man-hours per submission, more than 700,000 man-hours were invested by architects and consultants for the first phase only of the GEM competition.

The 'Five Second Rule' of heneghan peng architects

The largest architectural competition in history was the two-stage open competition for the Grand Egyptian Museum in Cairo, Egypt, with 1,557 entries from 82 countries. The competition was won by the Irish practice heneghan peng architects from Dublin in June 2003, and their winning project is currently under construction.

When asked about the secret of their intriguing success, they refer to what they call the "Five Second Rule". Whether "an idea reads from a distance of five meters within five seconds" is their key on developing and winning such competition. As part of their approach, the architects keep their mind-set open at the start and engage consultants from the beginning. With their help, they put the proposal to the "Five Second Rule" test. Asked about other successful tools, they point out that, in parallel to their design work, they also focus on preparing and planning the process carefully, using spreadsheets, brief analysis, deliverables, design time, design freeze, sheet layout, production, red-marking, report production, signoff dates and finally, shipping dates.

1st Prize

REFURBISHMENT AND EXTENSION OF THE RESTAURANT PAVILION BY THE CENTENNIAL HALL IN WROCLAW

VROA ARCHITECTS with ch+ architekci (PL)
www.vroa.pl ; www.chplus.pl
Cultural & commercial/ local authority

Open competition
10 participants
480 hours worked
10,000 Euros prize money

Status: realized
5 months to finalize the contract
36 months to complete the project
770,000 Euros worth of commissioned services

At the end of summer, Marta and I were biking around our neighborhood as usual. The park, the river promenade, the pond, and the cappuccino on the terrace with the most idyllic view. We happened to meet Aga sipping espresso there. She had her office in the building that housed this decaying café. We were sitting there, chilling, as she told us about the announcement of a competition for this area – news from some radio station you never heard about before. Aga suggested that we should maybe try to work together. It would be nice to take a closer look at the area where you often meet or go biking with your friends ... we could all easily walk to the construction site from our homes.

Following Aga's suggestion, we met a few weeks later. Doubts about working together were overwhelmed by doubts about the competition brief as the chapter about historical reconstruction requirements appeared to be the most detailed ... Dammit, let's make a statement, no overreacting to the bullshit from heritage conservators ... no pumping up the volume to the limit ... We don't enter a winning project – we enter the project we want to experience here when hanging out and sipping beers in the park ... Our final proposition was the most restrained – just the background for the existing situation. We won.

The main concern about our winning project and the bone of contention of our competitors was the non-reconstruction of the 'phallic' tower in the center of the building. Instead of a literal reconstruction of the lantern, we designed a reflection of it in the existing water pond. Anyway, in the meantime the political decision was made to build the multimedia fountain in the pond. It would disturb the reflected image. Moreover, it drove away rare frogs that appeared to live in the shallow water. Some say their singing was quite nice.

THE EUROPAN CHALLENGE FOR YOUNG ARCHITECTS

Interview by Silvia Forlati

Interview with Thomas Sieverts, former President of Europan (2011–2015)

The Hows and Whys of competitions are not only an issue for participating architects, but also for the ones in charge of setting up such design contests. What does Europan, the Europe-wide competition for young architects, have to offer to emerging practices, and what are the challenges that it, as well as the competitions system in general, should be prepared to face in the coming future?

wonderland: *From your point of view, what is the role of competitions for emerging architecture practices?*

Thomas Sieverts: That is not a trivial question, as participation in a Europan competition costs time and money, so young colleagues intending to establish their office will have to strike a balance between costs and chances. I would argue: a Europan competition offers the young architect a chance to develop new and fresh ideas for difficult but nevertheless typical problems. His or her ideas and proposals will at least be discussed by a jury of professionals and – if successful – published at a European level. With some luck, his or her proposal will even be realized and may be the starter for the office! With this competition, they get the opportunity to contribute to the European architectural debate. I think this is an important experience for any emerging architect.

Is it possible to distinguish between competitions that are helpful and others that are not really helpful?

This question can hardly be answered in general terms, as circumstances differ too much. Europan competitions are especially helpful for young architects under 40, as the majority of competitions at present are 'invited' competitions with a pre-selection of participants, who have to prove that they have long and specialized experience in the tasks in question. Young architects do not stand a chance in this procedure as they cannot have such experience. Europan offers a format for young architects to work on complex programs with a good chance of success.

Does it make sense to hold competitions just for young architects?

I think it was, and still is, a good idea to create and defend a realm at the European level that is reserved especially for young architects, to help them start their professional career. It is a kind of 'positive discrimination', which meets with opposition from the European Commission, but has a positive influence on the profession as a whole, as it helps to realize unconventional ideas. Europan is a large institution for continuing architectural education! But the original Europan goal of giving young architects a direct chance to realize and build their winning proposal meets with growing difficulties, as the character of architectural practice has changed over the past decades: in many cases, there are several years between competition success and building process, as most Europan competitions at present deal with the complex transformation of the urban fabric. The political, administrative and economic procedures that are necessary before building can start take a long time, and generally, the winning team is not involved in these procedures: This has to be changed! The term 'implementation' has to be extended so as to include to this preparatory planning phase.

Does the idea of an open competition really make sense? Shouldn't one be looking for other ways?

The open anonymous competition is only one form of an organized and civilized struggle for the best ideas. Meanwhile, other formats have been developed and realized as well, for example, for problems which have no clear structure and no clear program yet: a 'call for ideas'; the professional, interdisciplinary workshop, special forms to integrate future users in the creative design process etc. But I am convinced that in most cases the anonymous open competition still is the best format; it is democratic and has a long, valuable tradition, with rules proven to work in all sorts of different situations. However, it must be seriously discussed if this traditional format of the open, anonymous competition should – in later stages – be combined with other competitive formats which should be part of the competition brief from the very beginning.

Our office has been awarded in 5 editions of Europan and in 3 different countries. But it was not before the latest one that we got a first prize. After only 2 months we were commissioned by the municipality for different urban planning tasks. The masterplan has gone through the democratic process and the detail plan commission should follow.

ZERO ARCHITECTS (ES)
www.areazero.info

Has the idea of Europan changed over time? Or is it going to change in the future?

In its basic structure, Europan has not changed as far as I know: it has developed a valuable, solid tradition with some evolution of its rules, but basically it has kept its original identity.

It may be, though, that the architectural profession itself has changed so much that Europan has to change, too: I have the impression that much work which originally was part of the architect's core responsibility has become a matter of various specialists. The whole procedure of construction planning has changed in the last decades. It has become much more complex. And it has a lot more political and administrative implications than just having a clear building program and then starting to build. In more and more cases, there is no clear building program any more. It just emerges in this long process. And it will be part of the architect's daily working practice to participate in this process. Also, Europan has to open its clients, municipalities and cities which are offering sites for Europan projects, so as to create acceptance for young architects to have a role in this procedure.

What you are talking about basically is a different set of tools, of skills that need to be developed both on the part of the client and the architect.

As just mentioned, we observe, on the one hand, a shifting of tasks from the architect to various specialists, and on the other, an

> The competition made us aware of how difficult is to get on with the realization of the project. We are still in touch with the municipality, hoping that some day realization will be in sight. We tried to organize a big workshop on the Poljane area, inviting other local architects and the municipality to start a discussion about our project and how we could eventually make it possible. In 2008 we found investors from the States, but then, due to the economic crisis, they withdrew from sponsoring.

NABITO ARQUITECTURA (ES)

EUROPAN 9

extension of responsibilities to the area of strategy development, including programming, political and administrative communication, moderation of people's participation, and last but not least, a mediatory role in conflicts. Architects have to develop a kind of creative procedural thinking.

Do you think that the role of the architect is changing?

In many cases, the architect has lost his role to specialists in building. I think that the role left for the architect still is that of a guarantor of the overall strategy, and this means that he has to be a very good communicator.

Maybe you are still a specialist as an architect, maybe even increasingly so, but not a specialist in creating buildings.

This development of the architectural profession may indeed lead to a fundamental change in the reality of architectural professional practice. But this does not at all mean that the core of the architectural profession – producing a design – is less valuable!

I think it rather is about strategic thinking and perhaps not technical solutions, or technical solutions within strategic thinking.

Learning conception and design, which takes as much time as learning music, leads to special skills and abilities of thinking in terms of space, form and time, which, in its extended form, also is the basis of strategic urban planning. These special abilities make the architect a specialist! Technical solutions play an important role in this strategic thinking.

Is there any approach that Europan is trying to develop for this new type of competition?

All the younger colleagues in the Europan Scientific Committee see the problem, but there is no real solution yet. What kind of work or task could we define? How can the results be evaluated? Is it really a good idea or just hot air? Is it a facade, a design? The real problem is how to define the stage of implementing a competition design. Implementation needs to be redefined in a way that includes these strategic phases, which are now part of the whole planning process. We have to do more about communication. How do we bring the ideas of young architects to the media debate, to the international debate? There are so many ideas, and many of them are worth discussing on a larger scale. Of course, a lot has been done, and Wonderland is also doing something with this book. But I think there might be more possibilities of how to build a media platform for younger architects.

And Europan can be one of these platforms.

Yes, we need to develop the very useful Europan tradition into the future.

One last question: Why did you decide to become president of Europan?

When I was asked by Europan if I would accept the Europan Europe presidency if I were elected, I agreed, because both as a planning practitioner and a university teacher for more than 30 years, I still feel an obligation to support the efforts of Europan to offer chances to young architects for creative thinking and working at a European level. ∞

I did the Europan 6 in 2001 with a friend. Like me, he was working in Siza's office when we met. It was an exciting moment: in the end the jury voted for our project, but it took two years to sign the contract. After we had won, there was some media attention and new clients appeared. We did not build this project, but other projects came up because of it.

Nuno Abrantes Arquitecto with Benjamin Barcel (PT)
www.nunoabrantes.eu
EUROPAN 6

"Thanks Gianluca!!! Thanks! We'll start next week."
This is what Mr. S., chief engineer of the municipality of Kotka, said before leaving from the Europan 9 Forum of Results in Santiago di Compostela, Spain, in May 2008. Since then, we have had the strange role of trying to understand and cope with the contrasting signals, mixing dreams of success, traveling exhibitions, media attention, and debates: the goal is there, only the paths to get there are different.

b4 architects with
Matteo Ossetti + Luigi Valente (IT)
www.b4architects.com
EUROPAN 9

WHAT IS EUROPAN?

Europan is a European federation of national organizations, which manages biennial architectural competitions for building or study projects launched simultaneously in several European countries on one common theme, with common objectives and rules. The objective of Europan is to bring to the fore Europe's young architecture and urban design professionals, and to publicize and develop their ideas. Another objective is to help cities and developers, which provide project sites, to find innovative architectural and urban-design solutions for the transformation of urban locations. The anonymous open competitions are public calls for ideas on a European scale. Teams may also include young professionals from other disciplines. All candidates must be under 40 years of age at the closing date for submissions.

A national jury, whose composition – 9 jurors plus substitutes – is published on the Europan website, reviews all projects entered in the respective country. The jury meets in two separate sessions. In the first one, the competition entries are evaluated for compliance with the competition rules and for the quality of ideas, and a maximum of 20 % of the projects are shortlisted and qualify for the second round. In the second session, the jury evaluates the short-listed projects for their innovative qualities and suitability for the urban context which they are intended for, awarding prizes to winning projects and runners-up and possibly considering other projects for honorable mentions.

Between the two jury sessions, a European forum with the members of the juries and the representatives of project sites is organized to discuss the projects on the shortlist in the context of thematically related project sites. The winners and runners-up receive a prize money of 12,000 and 6,000 Euros (including tax), respectively. The organizers undertake to publicize all prize-winning entries both nationally and at the European level through exhibitions, meetings and publications, including a European catalogue of results. Europan guarantees to use its influence to encourage cities and/or site developers to entrust the prize-winning teams with the project implementation.

Europan competitions are organized every 2 years.

The 2017 session of Europan received 1,000 submissions by teams from 35 different countries for 44 proposed sites.

www.europan-europe.eu

Thomas Sieverts studied architecture in Stuttgart, Liverpool and Berlin, and co-founded the *Freie Planungsgruppe Berlin* in 1965. Professor for Urban Design in Berlin, Havard, Darmstadt, Nottingham, Berkeley and Vienna. His work includes more than 300 publications in professional magazines and books. He has been president of Europan, the eponymous organization behind the biennial Europe-wide competitions for young architects.

ARCHITECTURAL COMPETITIONS IN EUROPE

European regulatory frameworks

In all EU member states, public commissions for architecture services above a certain threshold value (see table) are to be awarded through a transparent competition procedure ensuring fair conditions of competition for licensed architects throughout the EU (including Switzerland and Norway). These procedures – officially named *Architectural Design Contests* – theoretically provide extremely valuable opportunities of Europe-wide access to public commissions for emerging – and other – architectural practices. In some EU countries and in Switzerland, architecture competitions are also open to participants from member countries of the World Trade Organization that are parties of the multilateral Agreement on Government Procurement, yet with different thresholds. All contests can be found at http://ted.europa.eu/, with TED standing for Tenders Electronic Daily. This is the online version of the "Supplement to the Official Journal of the European Union", which is dedicated to European public procurement. It is updated five times a week with approximately 1,500 public procurement notices from the European Union, the European Economic Area and beyond.

The **Directive 2014/24/EU on public procurement** also regulates how to run the various admissible procedures (open, restricted and negotiated procedures as well as competitive dialogues) with particular emphasis on the public announcement of contests and on the anonymity of the submissions. Negotiated procedures are usual for contests under the European regulation, where the goal is to determine the best quality of design and, on the basis of this, the best offer (Best Value for Public Investments).

As both the design quality and the economic offer are evaluated to select the winners, better-ranked design proposals may still fall behind competing proposals with very low fee bids (a proposal selected for a second prize for design may actually be awarded a third prize because the proposed fee is higher than that for the third-ranked design).

Various national professional organizations, such as the RIBA in United Kingdom, the Federal Chamber of Engineers and Architects in Austria, the Finnish Association of Architects, have set up own additional guidelines on how to manage architectural competitions, with particular focus on the preparation of the brief, the management of the work of the jury, and the need of fair payment for participants or winners. At the European level, the Architects Council of Europe has also published a set of 10 rules deemed essential for every architectural competition (see page 278). At the international level, the UNESCO has, first in 1956 and then in 1978, issued a series of recommendations concerning international competitions in architecture and urban planning, and mandated the International Union of Architects to oversee the observance of these rules.

Text by Silvia Forlati

2017 thresholds for architectural services for public contracts (EU/EAA member states)

Contracting authority	Threshold
Central government authorities	144,000 EUR
Sub-central contracting authorities	221,000 EUR

http://ec.europa.eu/growth/single-market/public-procurement/rules-implementation/thresholds/

COUNTRIES IN DETAIL

BULGARIA

Text by Peter Torniov
Sofia, BG

Architectural competitions unfortunately are rare in Bulgaria, and if held at all, they are in most cases badly organized and non-transparent. Most public building projects are commissioned after competitions held under the Bulgarian law for public procurement, and the most important factor here is pricing and not project quality.

Formally, the applicable law went into effect in April 2009, but has in fact not really been operative since, because the Ministry of Economy raised an objection against the competition rules for architects. Obviously, in Bulgaria some lobbies close to the authorities disapprove of the law, and the Associations of Architects alone is powerless to change this state of affairs.

There can be no doubt that architecture competitions are currently seeing a renaissance in the Czech Republic. In period between 1993 and 2012, the average number of competitions per year was 15. But from 2013 to 2016, the average was 36 competitions per year, and in 2016 alone, there were no less than 56, four of them fully bilingual with English as a working language and an international jury. It is yet hard to say how rapid the growth will be, but there are indicators that this is a trend that is here to stay.

One of the preconditions for this boom is the growing active role of architects in the organization of design competitions. The mere fact that—according to a 2013 survey—more than 80 Czech cities, towns and municipalities are currently employing municipal architects generates a good portion of public discussion about the quality of urban planning, public space, and architecture, which in turn leads to urban planning, public space design, or architecture competitions. Even if creating such a position at the municipal level is not required by law, there appears to be a broadening general understanding that it is beneficial to have one.

In analyzing the list of competition organizers, what is notable is the broad range of municipality sizes, their wide geographic distribution, and the diversity of public institutions involved. Other promising new aspects are the decentralization of competition organization, regional capacity building, new stakeholders, and an unfolding international dimension.

Also, a significant growth in the share of design as compared to ideas competitions is proof of a maturing commissioning system in the public sector. To illustrate this: between 1999 and 2012, there were 40% design and 60% ideas competitions, while in the period from 2013 to 2016, the average proportion already was 80% design and 20% ideas competitions, and in 2016 alone, it was 88% design and 12% ideas competitions. Still, only about 50% of winning projects get built (data from 1993–2012), others fail for political, financial, or other reasons, or due to investment strategy changes.

However, the massively prevailing model for public commissions in construction in the Czech Republic still are public tenders, in which the main criterion is price. Design competitions represent only a small fraction.

The vast majority of design competitions are open and anonymous, invited competitions are few and reserved to private investors (in the public sector, they are practically illegal). Combined competitions—partly open and partly invited with a participation fee—are legal but basically nonexistent, as a result of severe criticism from architects because of unequal competition conditions. The dominating trend in more complex project briefs is for two-stage competitions in order to eliminate the excessive waste of time and energy of large numbers of architects involved. In first stage, judgement is usually made based on design concepts and portfolios, in second stage—with a secured participation fee—on elaborated design studies. The first stage may also take the form of a qualification round based just on references.

Wider public participation in the formulation of design briefs is very rare; similarly, there is usually no participative element present in the final selection procedure. The entire process is controlled by professionals, and the competitions discussed here follow the Competition Rules of the Working Group for Competitions of the Czech Chamber of Architects. Architects registered in the chamber are strictly discouraged to take part in any design competitions not approved by the Czech Chamber of Architects, the goal being to create and maintain a secure, fair, just and transparent design competition environment. Most independent jurors recommended or delegated by the Chamber of Architects are trained and certified for this work. Any architect can take this training. Other jurors represent the investor or are invited experts. Independent expert jurors always have a majority over dependent jurors—by three to two, four to three or five to four, depending on the size and complexity of the project.

The project commission is not guaranteed to the winning team. The prize-winning participants are invited to negotiation procedures without public notice, pursuant to Article 23, Paragraph 6 of the Public Procurement Act, no. 137/2006 Coll. Negotiations are usually held in the order of the prizes awarded in the competition, but there are no obligatory rules. The criteria for these negotiations are defined by the competition organizer/investor.

Text by Osamu Okamura, Brno, CZ

Anonymous open architecture competitions always are like blind dates, with the announcement of the winner being accompanied by a certain nervousness of "Who did we get? Did we get a star?" Maybe the unknown youngster is the star architect of tomorrow, whose first building will be built in Estonia. Open competitions have been one of the cornerstones of Estonian architecture policy, and without its success, Estonian architecture would certainly not be what it is today. The construction boom and the award system have shaped the playground for young Estonian architecture offices, a result that their Western European colleagues of the same age can only marvel at.

And yet—where are the limits of this policy of openness in EU? Aren't competitions also a game of power and money? On the European scale, architecture—its formal vocabulary, technical requirements, aesthetics, and ex-

pected urban-design effects—is becoming increasingly uniform, and so open architecture competitions in a small country like Estonia, which is not very wealthy but nevertheless open-minded, provides a fantastic opportunity for architecture offices from all over Europe to go "fishing in foreign waters." For some reason, Estonian architects did not win most the important local architecture competitions held for large public projects. In this practical-minded Northern country, the practice, widely used in the world, of inviting star architects to participate in a competition has never established itself—for obvious financial reasons. So far, the winners have mostly come from lesser to well-known Scandinavia offices but also from other countries like Austria, except for Zaha Hadid Architects who won first prize in the 2017 planning competition of the Tallin harbor area. There is a number of

Text by Triin Ojari, Tallinn, ES

sad-but-true reasons for the lack of success of local offices. Joining the European Union meant that, with the policy of openness, competition markedly intensified. In a small area like architecture competitions, it increased manifold, and local bureaus neither had the experience for these competitions nor resources that were in any way comparable to those of larger architectural practices abroad. Competitions are like a team sport—success is predicated on having a large well-functioning team, where everyone has their own specific function, and it takes visual perfection to make a strong finish.

ITALY

Text by Beatrice Manzoni, Milan, IT

Unlike in some other European countries where architecture competitions are an established praxis, they are far from it in Italy. In the first three months of 2017, only 50 competitions were held in Italy, which represented a mere 4,84% of the total number of tenders for architectural design commissions, with or without implementation and detail planning, compared to 161, for example, in France. In 2017, "Il Giornale dell'Architettura" provocatively wrote that "the stage of architectural design competitions in Italy is already coming to an end without having ever gone into full swing." Few projects actually get built, and many of them undergo significant modification during the design phase.

Starting in the postwar years, there has been a number of exemplary competitions showing the good and the bad of the Italian system. One of the first significant competitions in Italy, held in1967 for the new offices of the Camera dei Deputati in Rome, ended up with nothing done: the proposal by Italo Insolera, which, contrary to the brief, located the offices in existing buildings, was eventually realized, undermining the credibility of the entire procedure and wasting the efforts of the other participants. In the 1960s, the ZEN Quarter in Palermo marked a turning point in the design of social housing, while competitions in the following decade were mostly were for university projects: Florence, Calabria, Cagliari all provided grounds for confrontation. From the 1980s onwards, confrontation reached an international level, and large competitions were often for projects with a cultural focus. See, for example, the competitions for the Parco Navile in Bologna, for the new Bicocca district in Milan, for Bocconi University, for the MAXXI Museum in Rome and the new ENI Headquarters. One last example: in the international ideas competition, the 2017 "Blueprint Competition", aimed to pool proposals for the port, industrial, planning and social development of Genoa, none of the 69 projects admitted actually reached the minimum points to be awarded the first prize. This is another case showing that the present competition system may well be in need of revision.

NETHERLANDS

Text by Anneke Bokern, Amsterdam, NL

To say that there are not too many open competitions in the Netherlands is quite an understatement. In a spot check in April 2018, the Dutch architecture website ArchiNed listed a total of four competitions in the Netherlands, of which just one was an actual project competition.

One of the reasons why competitions are so rare is that Dutch housing corporations and project developers prefer invitational project planning procedures with only a handful of candidates. That is nothing new, and in the past the system worked fine, as part of an informal architectural culture with a lot of advantages for young offices. However, since the introduction of the European tendering directive in 2004, public planning and construction projects are no longer commissioned on the basis of competitions either. In the Netherlands, reference-project and firm-turnover requirements are far more strictly implemented than in neighboring countries, which makes it almost impossible for young firms to get a foot in the door and enter tender processes. As a result, the few remaining open competitions are fiercely contested. In recent years, it has become a trend among young Dutch offices to team up with more established firms in order to improve their chances in competitions. This, of course, generates turnover and adds valuable building experience to the portfolio. But the drawback is that the bigger office usually gets all the credit, while the smaller firm is often overlooked in publications and media coverage. Accordingly, if young Dutch architects get a chance at all to participate in a competition, it is mostly for small scale conversions or interior designs, or it is an ideas competition, or it takes place abroad.

SPAIN

Text by Gonzalo Herrero Delicado, London, UK

Today, architectural competitions in Spain are mostly held by public institutions and can be categorized into two types: small and large scale. The first ones are what recent graduates and emerging practices battle for in order to land their first building commission, putting in long hours and what limited resources they have. Often a few dozen participants compete for just a single contract, with the best-case scenario being winning a commission that only pays a meager minimum fee, which potentially won't compensate the long hours spent on meetings, traveling and endless negotiations with clients and contractors. The situation is even more problematic for the non-winners who will have spent hours and hours of work without any compensation at all. In order to make such procedures economically viable, many practices "employ" unpaid interns to do the competition submissions, but that's a separate matter. On the other hand, participation in large-scale competitions is generally restricted to practices with a proven track record of similar projects, which means that, while being the most profitable and having a wider media impact, these competitions are mostly inaccessible to emerging practices. If open competitions are the most democratic way to award public commissions, shouldn't they be open to all architects? Another questionable matter about competitions in Spain is the qualification of juries and jurors. As most design competitions are for public construction projects, a majority of the judging panel usually are politicians. This results in the fact that the more ambitious, innovative and game-changing proposals are not always the ones most valued by jurors. The wins of left parties in the 2015 municipal elections in Madrid, Barcelona and other cities in Spain meant a huge improvement in the democratization and openness in public competitions management—a promising future not only for emerging architects but for the whole architecture sector.

what happens next

Realization is the final goal in the whole process both for client and architect, yet the path from prize to realization is not necessarily a straight one. However, taking part in a competition is more than getting a commission or the possibility of realizing a building. It may well be the side effects – positive or negative – which turn out to be the most important things to come of it.

Architect

VS.

Architect?

Increasing competition among European architects, or How can something new come into the world of the architectural profession?

From an architect's perspective, everything seems clear: greater economization of the classic profession has to be prevented! By contrast, the question raised here, however, is whether greater economization of architecture would at all be possible, and if so, what it would be good for.

It is indeed common in the industry not to withhold pointed criticism from selected colleagues, but otherwise architects traditionally are far above the ballyhooing of other professions. In view of the advantage that their expert knowledge gives them over the rest of the world, more self-marketing would not make much sense at all for architects, right? Architectural competition, including classic architecture contests, therefore is an inside thing for the most part. Also, architects strongly criticize the "higher, faster, further" attitude that is rampant in our contemporary society. All the more so since competitive thinking really is new for many architects. As late as 1970, every second UK architect was engaged by the public sector, meaning they were exempted from competition. Today that rate is only 9 %.

In its study, "The Future for Architects", the Royal Institute of British Architects forecasts further dramatic changes for European architecture offices. The organization, founded in 1834, predicts upheavals that could herald the end of the office in a classical sense. Most remarkably, the British analysis says that while the demand for architecture will remain consistently high, the manner in which architects do business will change dramatically. If one believes the RIBA vision, it is not technological developments, which will dominate construction, but rather an economic revolution that is lying ahead for the architecture world. Competition among architects will increase, in Europe and globally.

The reason for this is an unbroken growth of the number of architects in the market, with a simultaneous decline of demand for their services. According to the RIBA researchers, many offices have an underdeveloped business sense. They criticize, e.g., that merely 50% of the smaller British offices work with a business plan. Moreover, the study describes a trend towards larger projects which are more strongly structured so as to bundle the risk. Most architecture practices are not dimensioned for this, which leads to the situation that projects are more frequently contracted out as a complete package and architects, with their creative interest, are increasingly losing influence. A further challenge is the internationalization of the market in Europe and beyond. An anticipated construction boom in developing and emerging countries will very strongly alter the global market. The British researchers see chances here for established and large European firms, and suggest that this development could quickly spell the end for smaller offices without a specialized profile.

But doesn't architecture live from the fact that it is not as commercial as other design professions such as graphic or product design? Irrespective of the occasional craze, one strength of architects seems to be that they take their orientation from artists rather than from business people. After all, architecture's core principles, purpose and results are universal and timeless: building analysis,

uses such as living, working, and culture; the structuring of space, scale, aesthetics, urbanity, etc.

If, however, the principles of architecture are not going to change in any revolutionary sense, how can it be that the economy of the profession is changing, and what does that mean? Will the smaller offices which make up the majority of today's market still stand a chance at all? In some countries, there is already talk of fee dumping and conditions of self-exploitation. Often, this also goes for the general conditions of the architectural competitions described in this chapter.

From an economic standpoint, architecture competitions are by no means a sign of tough competition; quite the contrary. They are vehicles painstakingly organized to bring some innovation and performance pressure to an otherwise comparatively comfortable profession. For, even if that is not apparent in an architect's everyday life, the profession is not developing quite as rapidly as one would perhaps assume. Rather slowly and steadily, in comparison to many other professions. Naturally, there are a lot of new things for architects today; not only materials and work tools, but also requirements have fundamentally changed, e.g., regarding climate protection. But if we compare the millennia-old job of the architect with other technological fields of work – the majority of other engineering professions did not even exist two hundred years ago.

Economic historian and Nobel laureate Douglass C. North distinguishes "limited access" and "open access" in determining society's economic state of development. It was only the "open access" regime, comprised of market economy, democracy, and rule of law, which, according to North, could afford education, chances for participation and self-realization to broad sections of the population. Before that, these had always been the privileges of a few. According to North, this social integration process triggered the extensive productivity boosts that were still unimaginable in pre-modern societies. The "limited access" society suffered not least from the fact that a large part of the manpower was invested in the limitation of competition. This meant that – instead of what is usual today – specialists did not productively take on competition, but kept sacrificing resources to eliminate competitors, if necessary with violence.

What economists today understand by competition thus is not much older than 200 years. Although there still are some structures and regulations in the market that remind us of earlier times, the majority of readers today have certainly arrived in the "open society". Nonetheless, we should not forget that the construction industry leads the list of the most corrupt sectors in almost all countries worldwide. Some architects still live in the "limited access" reality. They are, of course, not alone with their wish to somewhat curb competition. The trend towards market economy is certainly not irreversible. Figures on regulation in the U.S. attest to that: while in the 1950s, a license was required for less than 5% of all jobs on the American market, the share of workers who need a license for their job has meanwhile risen to around 30%.

The development of our market-oriented economies did not take place in a linear manner, but in epochs and in parallel to the technical and social quantum leaps that have occurred ever since the Industrial Revolution. From an economic history perspective, it was the nature of competition and the extent of transnational labor division which took things in the right direction. According to this interpretation, European economic cooperation and the Common Market are not the result, but rather the main precondition for the current prosperity in Europe and the relatively peaceful course of recent European history. As a consequence, running an economy in pre-modern competitive conditions not only has a monetary price (theoretically paid by the demand side). If one considers the significance of competition for innovations and the development of sustainable solutions, quality in the market suffers as well and social costs arise.

What is interesting is the comparison with other areas of society which are also organized competitively: the world of music and the arts and science. Here again the degree of innovation varies, depending on the openness and applicable rules in the respective subsystem of society. Therefore, the question cannot be how politicians, or scientists for that matter, may get along well and without competition. It is only in competitive conditions that their activities become valuable and meaningful for society. And then there are always competitors who attack power monopolies in the market and keep the actors on their toes. Thus, the question is: how high are the obstacles for outsiders to participate? Which incentives are there?

On the surface, many architects see competition mainly as a suffering process: first everyone suffers, and then at least a few can be happy. The majority, however, the defeated participants and those who were not invited at all, criticize the task, conditions and make-up of the jury and – how could it be otherwise – their decision. Sometimes the jury suffers as well. And it is only after the whole process has been concluded that positive thoughts stand a chance again (notwithstanding the many pitfalls of architectural practice that follow upon the competition proceedings and will be dealt with in the other chapters of this book).

This proves one thing: an architectural competition has more in common with an economic understanding of competition than you would think in everyday life, which means that competition that works is more than the sum of its parts. A creative discovery procedure is set in motion, which is an investment in the future, even for those who do not win the first prize. In the best case, the competition will become a societal learning process. Both types of competition need some organizational preparation, which can be labor-intensive and is not a matter of course. One basic prerequisite for either type is good rules which eventually also need to be observed. Detailed articulating of these rules is a long-lasting optimization process. Economists also are at odds about how exactly competition has to be cultivated or curbed. Particularly in Europe, much potential surely lies in nations learning from each other.

The comparison to sports suggested by

Gilbert & Jormakka (see "The willing suspension of disbelief" in this book) may be helpful here, even though many differences of course continue to exist. However, looking at what they have in common is insightful. Losers will only be in for new matches if the rules of the game are all right. The idea of awarding points according to a seniority (or juniority) principle in soccer would simply ruin the "noble game'. Applying such a rule to competition among architects would surely have the same effect. Permanent "rule breaking" is not a viable long-term option, either. An architectural professional organization therefore cannot have an interest to eliminate competitors and competition. But if the game does not really get under way, a rule adjustment or extension may indeed be an option to be jointly considered.

We are already looking back upon several thousand years of human division of labor, to which architects have always made a meaningful contribution (incidentally, in totally different economic systems and cultural spheres). In a world which is becoming smaller, we will have more competition among architects in the future. That is okay, and chances are that it will add to the results of the work. Instead of opposing competition, dealing with it constructively is more productive. This includes the making of binding, transparent and motivating rules and a working price mechanism, that is, flexible fee scales, which offer real chances instead of cementing conflicts of interest with clients. The question, then, is how to improve competition, also internationally. Perhaps what is needed is more competition for competition?

* One classic notion is that especially young architects are at a disadvantage in the market, although that is not really certain, either; after all, it might be the case that older colleagues are not so open and articulate about their economic situation.

WINNING CAN BE LOSING, AND LOSING CAN BE WINNING

Not all won competitions actually have a happy ending, and lost competitions can bring unexpected positive results. Unexpected consequences range from personal and private aspects (such as finding a wife) to professional ones (such as unintentionally becoming a school-building specialist). In the end, the result is possibly about a basic emotional approach. As one of the teams put it, it ultimately is about the desire to go on working and competing.

Where do you see the benefits that the project gave your practice?

- **79%** Acknowledgement in the profession
- **73%** Media attention
- **56%** Material for exhibitions
- **52%** New clients and commissions
- **51%** Getting the job
- **16%** Another project on the shelf

HOW MUCH INVESTMENT

We have counted an across-the-board average of
3.4 competitions done per office and year on a long-term
basis. In the year preceding the survey, however, the average office did **5.6 competitions**. The majority does less than
5 competitions per year, 21 % manage between 6 and
10 competitions per year, 8 % even more.

1,891
hours/year is the
average working
time invested for
competitions

Numbers of competitions done last year

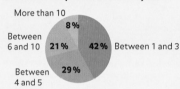

More than 10
8 %
Between
6 and 10   21 %   42 %   Between 1 and 3
Between   29 %
4 and 5

What about the return on investment?

In the end, 19% of the commissions received resulted from
competitions. But only one of ten competition entries led
to a realized project. So it takes a lot of effort to achieve a
realized project, and – of course – there is no guarantee of
success.

19 %
of the realized
commissions were
obtained through
competitions

21 %
of the fees
earned through
competitions were
less than
50,000 Euros

Commission rate

Number of buildings
realized so far thanks to
competitions
19 %
Number of
buildings realized
so far thanks to   81 %
direct commissions

Resulting fees in EUR

As a detailed analysis of the projects surveyed shows, the
average fee for a commissioned project is 309,660 Euros.
Still, the majority of the fees are below 211,000 Euros.

More than 1,000,000
Less than 10,000
7 %   15 %
Between 210,000
and 1,000,000   32 %   16 %   Between 10,000
and 50,000
15 %
15 %   Between 50,000
and 100,000
Between 100,000
and 210,000

GETTING IT DONE

The overall experience of the participating offices is that at least one third of the winning entries eventually are not realized.

Of the **100 projects** awarded a first prize which we surveyed, 39 were realized, 6 were under construction, and 33 were under way toward construction. In addition, one second prize was realized in part, and one project was realized by another office. **11 were on hold and 8 were canceled** – one of them even after construction had begun. In three cases, the competition prize actually was the (unpaid) possibility of realizing the project on the architects' own initiative (raising funding, finding a developer, etc.) on a plot provided by the municipality holding the competition.

Of 100 winning projects...

Unrealized   Contract negotiation
13%   **9%**
Canceled **10%**
On hold **10%**   **9%** In progress
36%
Realized

Overall experience

Of every 100 competition entries, 17 win a first prize. Of these, 8 are eventually built.

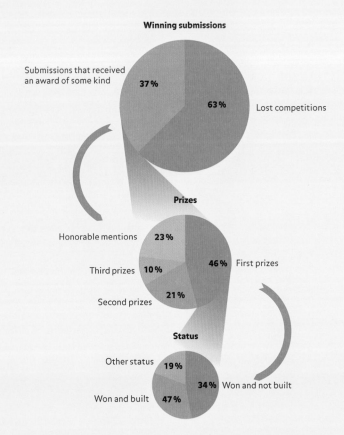

Winning submissions

Submissions that received an award of some kind   **37%**

63%   Lost competitions

Prizes

Honorable mentions   **23%**

Third prizes   **10%**   **46%**   First prizes

21%

Second prizes

Status

Other status   **19%**

34%   Won and not built

Won and built   **47%**

EXPERIENCE REPORTS
What happens next

////// More work than expected //////////////

CAN RICART SPORTS CENTER, BARCELONA, SPAIN

vora arquitectura (ES)
www.vora.cat
Sports facility/Local authority

 Ideas competition
30 participants
500 hours worked
600 Euros prize money

Status: realized
24 months to complete the project
48 months to finalize the contract
310,000 Euros worth of commissioned se

1st Prize

We did the competition just for the fun of it. When we were told that we had won, we decided to start our office in Lisbon. But the project took 2 years to start, so we had to live on virtually nothing, except for a few very small commissions. Finally, we moved to Barcelona. We gathered a very experienced team around as reassurance for the client. I think this was the key to continue with the commission. **We designed 2 complete projects, of which the second was eventually built 6 years after the competition.**

AUSTRIAN PAVILION AT THE EXPO 2008, ZARAGOZA

SOLID architecture with Michael Strauss
and Scott Ritter (AT)
www.solidarchitecture.at; www.ms-a.at
Exhibition pavilion/National authority

Two-stage open competition
30 participants
750 hours worked
0 Euros prize money

Status: realized
2 months to finalize the contract
8 months to complete the project
278,000 Euros worth of commissioned se

1st Prize

After winning a competition you will start a new from scratch if the client failed to precisely define his program and requirements. At this point, there is fresh input on the project, because this is the time when the client starts to think seriously about his requirements. So checking the plausibility of the competition brief has much influence on the time spent on specific topics during the competition phase. **The winning competition design and the built project may be quite different.**

THE RENOVATION OF THE TORRE DI PORTA NUOVA, ARSENALE DI VENEZIA

MAP studio (IT)
www.map-studio.it
Cultural facility/Local authority

 Open competition
130 participants
165 hours worked
5,000 Euros prize money

Status: realized
3.5 months to finalize the contract
26.5 months to complete the project

1st Prize

This competition was an opportunity to participate in the transformation of a much-discussed historical site, the Arsenal of Venice. The project aims to ensure the preservation and enhancement of the historic Crane Tower, combining these requirements with the needs arising from its new functions as exhibition space and cultural centre. The strategy employed to keep the old 'machine' and the new 'facility' clearly distinct was to leave all the existing walls untreated and visible, simply repairing them with reused bricks. **We made a big effort, not only from a design perspective, but also to control the entire process** as the client decided to appoint his own site supervisor.

ACADEMY OF PERFORMING ARTS, SARAJEVO, BOSNIA AND HERZEGOVINA
Archipelagos (US)
Education/Local authority

Ideas competition
52 participants
200 hours worked
12,500 Euros prize money

Status: in progress
6 months to finalize the contract

1,250 Euros worth of commissioned services

Our participation in the competition was initiated by our founder and co-owner Jonus Ademovic, primarily because of his wish to re-establish a connection to, and presence in, the region he came to New York as a war refugee from in 1995. Our ultimate goal was to participate in the post-competition show and contribute in some way to the emergence of the post-war architectural scene. Not having any pretension to winning anyway (not that we wouldn't have liked to, of course) we approached the competition project with a pure desire to produce the best possible solution for an extremely difficult site and program. We were completely overwhelmed when we received notice that we had won 1st prize. As winners (officially, the author is Jonus Ademovic) we were guaranteed authorship and at least a consulting contract in the further development of the project. About six months after the end of the competition, a public tender was announced for the construction documentation. We couldn't take part since we do not have an office in Bosnia-Herzegovina. A local company won, and we have been jointly preparing the construction documents. Given that we are not being paid for our consulting services this puts us in very strange situation. **We are legally obliged to green-light every decision (as we hold the authorship), but practically cannot work actively on the project.** We are supposed to independently negotiate the contract with the local architectural office. If we do not approve the steps in the project development because we are not happy with our contract (or rather with the fact that we do not have) we will kill the project.

Note: Despite being barely compensated for our further involvement in a project past the competition stage we participated in the supervision of the construction documents, we had no other choice, really. The construction documents were completed at the beginning of 2009 by the local architect of the record. Construction started in 2009 but and after numerous delays should be completed in 2019.

DE EENVOUD – SIMPLICITY
711 LAB – Stefan Werrer and MBA/S (DE)
http://711lab.com
Experimental housing/Public institution

Open competition
330 participants
220 hours worked
10,000 Euros prize money

Status: unrealized

Following the initial happiness of being a winner the question of what exactly we had won emerged. **There was neither a commission to obtain nor a big prize money. It turned out that, as a first step, we had to form alliances with the other winners and interested parties in the private and public sector.** By the end of 2007, all participants agreed on an urban plan. On this basis, we started the sale of the projects with an exhibition in 2008. In 2011 the overall planning became part of the pilot phase of the official certification of sustainable building projects by the DGNB (German Sustainable Building Council).

THE RUBBER HOUSE
CITYFÖRSTER –
Network for Architecture (DE)
www.cityfoerster.net
Experimental housing/Public institution

Open competition
330 participants
200 hours worked
2,000 Euros prize money

Status: realized
36 months to finalize the contract
28 months to complete the project
28,000 Euros worth of commissioned serv

'The Rubberhouse' was awarded 2nd prize in the international architectural competition 'De Eenvoud – Simplicity'. **Considering the process, the project should instead have been named 'complexity'.** Since 2006, we have travelled about twenty times to the Netherlands. After long phases of silence in which neither the initiator of the competition nor the municipality felt responsible for keeping things going, the whole project was canceled for political reasons. The site finally had become too exclusive for a settlement of experimental freak houses. Fortunately, the project was reborn in summer 2008, and we were assigned a new site to realize our design. The house was completed in autumn 2011.

GOVERNMENT DISTRICT, BUDAPEST, HUNGARY
TEAM 0708 (HU) with
Kengo Kuma Architects
Urban design/mixed-use for
public private partnership

Open competition
17 participants

75,000 Euros prize money

Status: canceled
3 months to finalize the contract

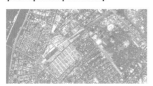

STORY IN 405 HEADLINES (EXCERPT)

2007.08.02	Monsters and Critics: **Japanese and Hungarian architects to design government quarter**
2007.08.03	Flott Invest: **Plans of the New Government's Quarter**
2007.08.04	designbuild-network.com: **New Government Buildings, Budapest, Hungary**
2007.08.17	Dexigner: **Peter Janesch and Kengo Kuma Win the Competition of Hungarian Government District**
2007.12.13	realdeal.hu: **Doubts mount over Hungarian government quarter project**
2008.01.08	Newser.com: **Hungary halts plan to build government quarter in Budapest**
2008.01.08	Budapest Sun: **Gov't quarter troubled**
2008.01.09	Euro Topics: **The misadventures of Hungary's government**
2008.01.10	Frankfurter Allgemeine Zeitung: **Budapest gegen Neubauten**
2008.01.14	Budapest Times: **Suspended gov't quarters project not to impact budget, says FinMin**
2008.01.14	Budapest Times: **Gov't quarter crumbling**
2008.01.14	Askaboutmoney.com: **Budapest – Hungary dumps new government quarter project**
2008.01.16	Budapest Sun: **Government quarter project halted**
2008.02.28	Frankfurter Allgemeine Zeitung: **Eingestürztes Luftschloss**
2008.09.12	Financial Times: Architecture: **A depressing tale of what might have been**
2008.09.25	olcim Foundation: **Regional Holcim Awards 2008 Europe**
2008.09.26	realdeal.hu: **Aborted government district project wins "sustainable construction" prize**
2008.10.08	Budapest Sun: **Janesch awarded**
...	
...	
...	

CAMPUS UNIVERSITY OF APPLIED SCIENCES, FRANKFURT/MAIN

Heribert Gies Architekten (DE)
www.gies-architekten.de
Education/Local authority

 Two-stage open competition
262 participants
1,200 hours worked
41,500 Euros prize money

Status: realized
9 months to complete the project
60 months to finalize the contract
1,300,000 Euros worth of commissioned service

We won the competition in August 2001 and started planning and building the project. From that time onwards, the office staff grew up to 20 people, and in December 2001 we won another competition for a new University of Applied Sciences in Mainz. **Since then, we have done more or less nothing but school buildings.**

TRANSFORMATION DU CHÂTEAU D'EAU, PLOUBALAY, FRANCE

espace gaïa architectures (FR)
www.espace-gaia.com
Tourism (bungee jumping platform)

 Restricted competition
3 participants
900 hours worked
10,000 Euros prize money

Status: canceled
1 month to finalize the contract

268,000 Euros worth of commissioned services

After 600 hours of hard work, the project was done. We had to wait three long weeks until the presentation. Five days later, we got a phone call from the president of the Committee: "We like your project, but you have one hour if you want to make any changes in the proposed fee." The next day, they informed us that we had been selected for the project. At that time, it was great news. A few weeks later, the project turned into a nightmare. Because of the originality of the project, it is very difficult for the main contractor to fix the construction program. It is impossible to make a budget without including a lot of options.

This uncertainty made the first phase of the project approval very difficult. The members of the Committee (elected members of the municipal councils participating in the project) could not understand the different options and the related budgets.

SSTU

[dAZ[with IDU architecture (FR / HK)
www.iduarchitecture.com

Experimental housing/Local authorities

 Invited competition
12 participants
500 hours worked
15,000 Euros prize money

Status: unrealized

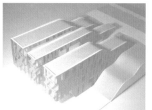

The Cook (the jury), the Thief (politics), His Wife (the project) & Her Lover (the architect),
June 2008: we are invited to participate in the international design competition for the SSTU–Southern Science and Technology University Campus, organized by the Shenzhen Planning Bureau and the Southern Science and Technology University Campus Bureau.
We can already tell that all of us have lost. September 7 is the date of the presentation in Shenzhen. 30 minutes presentation time for each team.
This is the time of the masquerade.
The competition was not anonymous; it was an invited competition, but the committee suddenly changed its mind and decided to "anonymize" the procedure. So they had a large curtain hung up to separate the architects from the jury. We had to stay on the other side of the curtain without seeing the jury and our works except in the PowerPoint presentation, speaking to a curtain …
Results: the winner is a local team and the second prize-winner is a local team as well. Now to make things worse: all the other teams are **still waiting to be paid**.

303

SPECIALIZATION THROUGH PARTICIPATION IN ARCHITECTURAL COMPETITIONS – A DEAD END

On the one hand, the architect, as an all-round specialist, should be able to responsibly plan and supervise all areas of architecture between economics and ecology. On the other hand, the increasingly complex professional profile offers various different possibilities for specialization. The widespread separation between designing architects and architects who execute and manage construction projects should, in an ideal case, lead to more efficiency. But how will the quality of the design be carried over to the execution phase under these circumstances? And will precisely that specialization not make execution and construction management a mere matter of routine in which innovation and creativity fall by the wayside?

Opinions about this may surely be divided. Can the separation of the teams which have a holistic approach to planning or cooperation of specialists in the same team be regarded as a solution to the problem? In effect, both ways of planning and execution, however fundamentally different, can produce good results. Also, it is not in the least dependent on individual office philosophy, nor on an architect's notions about which path he/she wants to take.

Running contrary to specialization are the competitive tender procedures that are currently in place in the EU or , in Germany, the so-called VOF procedures (Contracting Rules for Freelance Services) and the Guidelines for Planning Competitions, RPW 2008, or other guidelines in different countries, for example, SIA 152 (Swiss Society of Engineers and Architects) in Switzerland. The requirements imposed on participating architectural offices in competition procedures are completely inflated and, in my opinion, only serve the purpose of reducing the number of participants and singling out the so-called specialists.

Text by Heribert Gies, Darmstadt, Germany

Moreover, regulations for admissible requirements under a VOF procedure are very weak so that awarding authorities are left with many possibilities to whittle down, through obscure criteria, the number of participants to a circle of a chosen few. Selection procedures are not transparent, and quantity often comes before quality.

As a result, requirements in competition procedures – such as recent reference projects of comparable size or value – give rise to unwanted and senseless specialization. And what is more, the definitions of "comparable size" or "equal value" remain open. Reducing building typology to mere use or purpose appears to be the lowest common denominator here.

In competitions for schools buildings, for example, offices must have realized at least three schools in the past five years to be allowed to take part. Additional quantitative requirements, as were usual previously, such as turnover figures and the number of computers per office, were excluded for the sake of simplicity. This leads to the fact that whoever is going to build a schoolhouse in the coming years will most likely be able to participate, if at all, in competitions for schools only, perhaps for the rest of his/her life, and will only be able to build schools once he/she has won one competition for a school. He/she will become a so-called school building specialist. This means that he/she will not be given an opportunity to build apartment buildings, administrative buildings or even sports facilities, and free market access that it is desired and promoted by the EU is in fact impeded. Procedures that are limited to a few specialists run contrary to the goal of unrestricted market access for everyone.

Architects are thus more or less forced to compete for the same building type again and

again, which again results in lifeless routine and the loss of creativity and innovation. Why are architects not allowed to show that he/she cannot only plan and build creative and innovative schools, but can also apply his/her creativity and ideas to other building types?

Apart from the marked fall-off in the total number of competitions in the face of the VOF procedure, access to competitions is increasingly being limited, and this will have negative effects on the profession in general, as well as on young and emerging architects in particular. A radical simplification of the procedure is urgently needed. Transposing this to the awarding procedure, it is also clear that, with the way things are currently being practiced, architectural quality will be lost along the way.

Many competitions show that it is precisely young and non-specialized teams who, given a chance to compete against so-called specialists, often have the edge with innovative ideas and come out winning. Countless competitions were won by unknown architects. Open competitions and the free choice to take part in them are therefore urgently necessary – not only for young architects' offices.

Needless to say that many established offices of today were only able to become established because they won competitions in their early years. These days, the only possibility to break away from this forced specialization is actually not to participate in competitions and to acquire contracts in a different way. But imagine what the impact on society would be if only specialized couples were allowed to procreate, and only if they could furnish evidence showing that they have already procreated three times before or that they have made at least 52 attempts to procreate over the last three years …

Research on architectural competitions: a systematic review

A content analysis of articles and books about competitions from the '70s onwards

Text by Beatrice Manzoni, Milan, Italy

"From the end of the seventies the increasing use of competitions has revealed a change in the nature of the architectural debate"
Lucan, 1991

Despite their long history and the growing interest towards them, the information available on architecture competitions is relatively small and 'highly anecdotal', and studies on them have often been instrumentalist rather than truly critical. However, the role and value of competitions in the process of generating the built environment are a debated topic. Design competitions have always attracted, and still attract, architects, even, or all the more so, in times of recession. "The relationship therefore depends at least partially on something other than the economy [...] With its ritual aspects and its accompaniment of mythical beliefs, it is the open architectural competition that best illustrates the idiosyncrasies of architecture as a profession" (Larson, 1994: 470). The aim of this article is to provide a comprehensive and systematic review of the literature on architectural competitions, to evaluate the structure and the content of the existing literature, and to present some conjectures about further developments and areas where research could be intensified to produce insightful studies.

Who talks about competitions and where?

Despite their complexity and cross-disciplinary nature, competitions have been and are still preponderantly addressed as a subject of research by architecture and urban planning schools (74%), followed by arts and humanities, sociology and cultural studies (16%). 10% of the contributions of the past five years come from management, innovation and organization studies departments. Most of the research is done in the U.S. (52%). In Europe, the most active countries are the Nordic ones (22% against the 10% in the UK and the 16% in the rest of Europe). Speaking of the rest of Europe, from 2006 onwards, there has been a growing interest towards the topic in Spain, Germany, Greece and Italy (16% in total). This is a signal of a broadening interest in the subject, which is not confined any longer to those countries which have a tradition of architectural competitions.

What are the 'hottest' research themes?

Reviewing the literature, four main research topics emerge, some of which have been continually and recurrently researched over the past 35 years and therefore represent a more mature 'state of the art', while some others indicate a potential area for future research, open to a real cross-disciplinary approach.

For and against competitions

29 contributions to literature have dealt with the debate over the role and the benefits of competitions, highlighting that mixed feelings towards them still prevail, regardless of the discipline addressing the topic. Although this is one of the first and primary topics to be discussed, it never has really gone out of fashion.

As De Haan Haagsma (1988: 7) observes, while the system of tendering is not considered as controversial, "the opposite is true of competitions, which are almost always accompanied by gossip, backbiting, arguments, quarrels, reproaches and vilification". In fact competitions have been often variously addressed as "guessing games" or "carnivals" due to their intrinsic ambiguity and duality. While competitions apparently have a number of beneficial results, they also raise a number of controversies relating to the architecture world, architects and clients (Seidel, 1990).

From architecture's perspective, the competition system is recognized on the one side as a catalyst for research and experimentation (Malmberg, 2006), being central also to the educational processes developed by academies and universities and reflecting emergent architectural trends. Moreover, competitions seem in fact to bring architectural markets closer to the state of perfect competition according to economic theory. On the other side, competitions are seen as being too slow and too utopian, therefore failing to provide practicable solutions to spatial problems.

The same kind of conflicting arguments arise from the architects' point of view as well. The benefits that result from taking part in competitions are rather related to activities diversification, publicity and reputation than to actual job commissions. For young architects, competitions may be a launching pad or a curious gamble. For well-established practices, they are the way to try to extend their range of work or to introduce new clients. On the one side, there are no awards (apart from the Pritzker Prize) that can match the stamp of approval conferred by winning an important design competition. "Built or unbuilt, the projects ranked in an important competition are published, diffused, examined, discussed, and entered as credits in their authors' resumes" (Larson, 1994: 472). On the other side, the lack of dialogue with the client, the exploitation of architects' labor, and the fact that winning projects frequently end up as unbuilt projects are considered the main downsides of competitions (Nasar, 1999). Moreover, many researchers observe

that any competition is a pointless exercise and a waste of huge creative and financial resources.

From the client's point of view, competitions provide a unique opportunity to choose, not just an architect, but an architect and a design at the same time, selecting the best designer from a pool of almost all adequate aspirants in search of the superior design (e.g. Seidel 1990). The client gets a design, models, drawings and publicity and can explore possibilities of a public-private partnership before making any long-term commitments or signing an agreement. The other side of the coin is pointed to by Collier (2004) who names several examples in the history of competitions of winning designs which never saw the light of day. Most competition-winning designs that don't get built do so because the client doesn't have the money to build it, doesn't like the winning design, or because the winning design is in itself not realistic and feasible.

References marked with an asterisk ("") were quoted in the text.*

* De Haan, H., Haagsma, I. (1988), *Architects in competition. International architectural competitions of the last 200 years*, Thames and Hudson, London

* Collier, G. S. (2004), *Competing globally in architecture competitions*, Wiley Academy, London

* Larson, M. S. (1994), "Architectural Competitions as Discursive Events", in: *Theory and Society*, 23, 4, pp. 469–504

Lipstadt, H. (2000), "Theorizing the competition: the sociology of Pierre Bourdieu as a challenge to architectural history", in: *Thresholds*, 21, pp. 32–36

* Malmberg, C. (ed.) (2006), *The Politics of Design: Competitions for Public Projects*, The Policy Research Institute, Princeton University, Princeton, NJ

* Nasar, J. L. (1999), *Design by competition: making design competition work*, Cambridge University Press

* Seidel, A. D. (1990), "Design competitions receive mixed reviews", in: *Journal of Architectural and Planning Research*, 7, 2, p. 172

Tostrup, E. (1999), *Architecture and Rhetoric: Text and Design in Architectural Competitions, Oslo 1939–1996*, Papadakis, London.

Tostrup, E. (2009), "Tracing Competition Rhetoric", in: *Nordic Journal of Architectural Research*, 21, 2/3, pp. 23–36

The history of competitions

Another frequent research topic (15 publications), which deals with the history and tradition of architectural competitions, is rather descriptive and mature. All contributions (e.g. De Haan Haagsma, 1988) generally start from a common background of information relating the old history of competitions, which dates back as far as 448 BC when the senate of Athens in Greece decided to build up a war memorial on the Acropolis and invited several architects to submit proposals, and to the Italian Renaissance when, in 1418, a competition was called for the dome of the cathedral of Florence. The book by Collier (2004) is one of the most recent studies on the topic and focuses specifically on international and global competitions, comparing the history of competitions in different European and extra-EU countries. In the book edited by Malmberg (2006), the U.S. 200-year history of competitions for major government buildings is addressed, too.

Adamczyk, G. et al. (2004), "Architectural competitions and new reflexive practices", in: *ARCC-AEEA Conference "Between Research and Practice"*, Dublin

* Collier, G.S. (2004), *Competing globally in architecture competitions*, Wiley Academy, London

* De Haan, H., Haagsma, I. (1988), *Architects in competition. International architectural competitions of the last 200 years*, Thames and Hudson, London

Hossback, B., Lehmhaus, C. (2006), *[phase eins]. The architecture of Competitions 1998–2005*, DOM publishers, Berlin

Lipstadt, H. (1989), "The experimental tradition", in: *The Experimental Tradition. Essays on competitions in architecture*, The Architectural League of New York, Princeton Architectural Press, Princeton, NJ, pp. 9–19

Lipstadt, H. (2006), "The Competition in the Region's Past, the Region in the Competition's Future", in: C. Malmberg (ed.) *The Politics of Design: Competitions for Public Projects*, The Policy Research Institute, Princeton University, Princeton, NJ, pp. 7–27

* Malmberg, C. (ed.) (2006), *The Politics of Design: Competitions for Public Projects*, The Policy Research Institute, Princeton University, Princeton, NJ

* Wynne, G.G. (1981), *Winning Designs: The Competitions Renaissance*, Transaction Books, New Brunswick, NJ

Competitions systems across countries

There are also several articles and manuals that provide rules and suggestions to run and manage competitions across different countries and compare legislation on the matter (24 publications).

Some first books (e.g. Strong, 1976) are written as handbooks on competitions, providing a source of reference and information for promoters on ways and formats to organize competitions. Generally speaking, this has been the angle over years for the publications on the topic. Wynne (1981) reviews ways of running competitions in Germany, France, the Netherlands, Sweden, UK, Australia, and Japan; Alexander, Casper and Witzling (1987) suggest giving some closer examination to competition formats such as 'design-developer' competitions and to provide comparisons across countries to learn from experiences gathered under different cultural, political and professional conditions. Collier (2004) focuses more on the present global character of competitions. Other recent manuals, written by practitioners, give guidelines in point of the elements and management of the competition procedure and reflect about the never-ending debate about competitions' profitability and value for money.

* Alexander, E. R., Witzling, L. P. and Casper, D. J. (1987), "Planning and Urban Design Competitions: Organisation, Implementation and Impacts", in: *The Journal of Architectural and Planning Research*, 4,1, pp. 31–46

* Collier, G.S. (2004), *Competing globally in architecture competitions*, Wiley Academy, London

Kazemian, R. and Rönn, M. (2009), "Finnish architectural competitions: structure, criteria and judgment process", in: *Building Research & Information*, 37, 2, pp. 176–186

* Strong, J. (1976), *Participating in architectural competitions: a guide for competitors, promoters and assessors*, The Architectural Press, London

* Wynne, G.G. (1981), *Winning Designs: The Competitions Renaissance*, Transaction Books, New Brunswick, NJ

Managing competitions

The management of competitions is not a new topic. In 1990, Ollswang already pointed out the need for effective competitions management in order to guarantee positive effects. However, the management of competitions has always been studied in the twentieth century through an architecture and urban-planning lens. In our literature review, we find that competitions management is addressed 37 times, but only 6 publications have appeared in the management field. In the 1980s, management studies started looking at architecture, but rather with an interest in architectural office management in general, thus neglecting one of the most important architecture rituals and ways to get work. From a strategy and organization study's perspective, the interest towards architectural competitions is a recent but increasingly growing one.

Many studies in the 1980s and '90s adopted a more descriptive approach since there was little prior research available on the management of architectural competitions, while more recent studies characteristically try to develop a conceptual theoretical model that was sometimes missing before. Descriptive studies of competitions of the past were useful in that they provided insights into how to improve competition organization, program development and management, but sometimes failed to suggest a replicable theoretical model. Alexander, Casper and Witzling (1987) analyze, through a survey of 51 competitions and in-depth case studies, the impact of one hundred variables related to the organization, programming and evaluation of competitions on competition results. However, they focus on clients and sponsors, adopting their views to the point that competitions are considered successful whether the winning project is implemented or not. Seidel (1990) used a survey of 100 questions answered by 33 players in the competition system (sponsors, jurors, participants), similarly to what Eley (1990) did on 94 competitions from the RIBA, in order to review reasons for success or failure under different management aspects.

What is missing is the point of view of architectural practices themselves. Managing a competition implies several aspects also on the architect's side, which have not been investigated yet: how do competitions fit in with the intended – if perhaps only emergent – strategy of an architectural firm? Is it possible to define competition strategies? Are there management techniques that can to maximize success in competitions? How can collaborative design work be made successful in competitions? How do teams 'play' in competitions? In fact, architects in competitions perform a "shadow dance" (Kreiner, 2009). Recognizing the uncertainty of the process, there still is a need to find "solid knowledge and information to direct teams' design efforts". The ambition is to provide more effective strategies and architectural habits for competitions. The simulation of management strategies used by architectural practices on repeated competitions highlights that "the value of wins that are won by chance may systematically be related to competition strategies". This opens new directions for research on competitive and team-management strategies for competitions.

* Alexander, E. R., Witzling, L. P. and Casper, D. J. (1987), "Planning and Urban Design Competitions: Organisation, Implementation and Impacts", in: *The Journal of Architectural and Planning Research*, 4,1, pp. 31–46

Alexander, E. R., Casper D. J., Witzling L. P. (1990),"Competitions for Planning and Urban Design: Lessons of Experience", in: *Journal of Architectural and Planning Research*, 7, 2, pp. 142–159

Alexander, E. R., Witzling, L.P. (1990), "Planning and urban design competitions: introduction and over view", in: *Journal of Architectural and Planning Research*, 7,2, pp. 91–104

* Eley, J. (1990), "Urban design competitions: a British perspective", in: *Journal of Architectural and Planning Research*, 7,2, pp. 132–141

* Kreiner, K. (2009), "Architectural Competitions - Empirical Observations and Strategic Implications for Architectural Firms", in: *Nordic Journal of Architectural Research*, 21, 2/3, pp. 37–51

* Ollswang, J.E. (1990), "Successful competitions: planning for quality, equity and useful results", in: *Journal of Architectural and Planning Research*, 7,2, pp. 105–113

* Strong, J. (1976), *Participating in architectural competitions: A guide for competitors, promoters and assessors*, The Architectural Press, London

TOP TEN COMPETITIONS

According to Wikipedia, the most significant architectural competitions are **internationally open project competitions**, which attract a **large number of design submissions** and with the **winning design** being actually **built.** The following list was produced on the basis of these criteria.

Average number of participants
614

Design entries	Competition	Year	Location, country	Winner(s)
1557	**Grand Egyptian Museum**	2002	Giza, EG	**Heneghan Peng, Dublin, IR**
750	**Opéra Bastille**	1983	Paris, FR	**Carlos Ott, Montevideo, UY**
681	**Centre Georges Pompidou**	1971	Paris, FR	**Renzo Piano, Genoa, IT, and Richard Rogers, London, GB**
523	**Bibliotheca Alexandrina**	1989	Alexandria, EG	**Snøhetta, Oslo, NO**
516	**Kiasma Contemporary Art Museum**	1992	Helsinki, FI	**Steven Holl, New York, US / Paris, FR**
500	**Toronto City Hall**	1956	Toronto, CA	**Viljo Revell, Helsinki, FI**
471	**Parc de la Villette**	1982	Paris, FR	**Bernard Tschumi, New York, US / Paris, FR**
420	**La Grande Arche de la Défense**	1982	Paris, FR	**Johann Otto von Spreckelsen, Copenhagen, DK**
395	**Tokyo International Forum**	1987	Tokyo, JP	**Rafael Viñoly, New York, US**
329	**Parliament House**	1978	Canberra, AU	**Mitchell/Giurgola, Philadelphia, US**
296	Felix Nussbaum Museum	1995	Osnabrück, DE	Daniel Libeskind, New York, US
292	Geo Centre Møns Klint	2002	Møn Island, DK	PLH Architects, Copenhagen, DK
260	Tribune Tower	1922	Chicago, US	John Mead Howells and Raymond Hood, New York, US
244	Bibliothèque Nationale de France	1989	Paris, FR	Dominique Perrault, Paris, FR
233	Sydney Opera House	1955	Sydney, AU	Jørn Utzon, Copenhagen, DK
226	Austrian Cultural Forum	1992	New York, US	Raimund Abraham, New York, US
200	Millenium Bridge	1996	London, GB	Norman Foster, Sir Anthony Caro, and Ove Arup, London, GB
179	Royal Danish Library	1993	Copenhagen, DK	Schmidt Hammer Lassen, Aarhus, DK
177	Federation Square	1997	Melbourne, AU	Lab Architecture Studio, Melbourne, AU
165	Jewish Museum	1989	Berlin, DE	Daniel Libeskind, New York, US
117	ANZAC War Memorial	1929	Sydney, AU	Charles Bruce Dellit, Sydney, AU
98	Houses of Parliament	1835	London, GB	Charles Barry, London, GB

Source: en.wikipedia.org/wiki/Architectural_design_competition (June 2018)

epilogue

Open questions

We started this book while traveling on the **wonderland** Europe tour (2004–2006), together with 99 architectural teams. Through this traveling exhibition and associated workshops, a cross-national network and a platform for the exchange of ideas and experiences developed. The intention of the book was to facilitate and promote the exchange of experience and ideas.

Spanning more than 15 years, it has meanwhile unfolded a perspective across time. The emerging generation that we were part of has come to the forefront, making room for younger architects to move up and get started with different ideas. We are not sure if the advantages and possibilities that Europe offers to all of us are still as important for young architects, given that their idea of Europe may have changed. And yet, we hope that the next generation is going to live and fight for the European ideas the way we did and still do, and that they will continue to benefit from the broad range of possibilities of defining what the profession of the architects is, or could be, about.

Exploring the range of the profession as a potential without fixating on a one-for-all solution has, in retrospect, also been the focus and perhaps the strength of this Manual. We wanted to understand the 'how' of the profession in the context in which it is performed, including the geographic and economic dimensions. We believe that meaning is found in the occupation if ideas and possibilities that inform professional profiles and services in architecture are actually functioning in a market, where architects who provide creative design and consultancy services are able to earn a livelihood with dignity.

There is still plenty of research to be done here. In many respects, the profession continues to be stuck in an ideology of creative production that implicitly calls for, and idolizes, work around the clock and self-exploitation, with little chance for achieving an acceptable work-life-balance. This ideology, also embedded in the educational system, works for a few, but comes at a high personal price for many. It has particularly detrimental effects on women and others who are not able to give priority to the job over the need to care for others, and for themselves.

What we are trying to say is that architecture is also always about architects as people, with their personal problems and difficulties, their failures (not only their successes). And in all this, we see the need for further discussion and exchange, free from ideological constraints, for working together across all kinds of borders to create attractive conditions for this profession, and the professionals living and working in it, in order for it, and them, to make a meaningful creative contribution to a better world.

Silvia Forlati and Anne Isopp

Participating teams

00:/, GB, www.architecture00.net ●➦ +architecture, BG ○ ➦ 4B Arkitekter, NO ➦)!!(E. Bompan, G. Caliri, M. Lampugnani, B. Manzoni, M. Restuccia, IT ○ ➦ [dAZ[, FR ○ ➦ ¬parallelprojekt, DE, https://parallelprojekt.jimdo.com ○ ➦ 2012 ARCHITECTEN, NL ➦ 2A + P/A, IT, www.2ap.it ○ ➦ 2by4-architects, NL, www.2by4.nl ○ ➦ 3h architecture, HU, www.3h.hu ○ ➦ 3LHD, HR, www.3lhd.com ○ ➦ 4a architekti, CZ, www.architekti4a.cz ○ ➦ 711LAB, DE, www.711lab.com ○ ➦ **A** aaa, FR, www.urbantactics.org ●➦ a.s*, atelier de santos, PT, https://a-s-atelier-de-santos.divisare.pro ○○ ➦ A69 ARCHITEKTI, CZ, www.atelier69.cz ○ ➦ AB Head arhitektid, EEs2 ➦ ADEPT, DK, www.adeptarchitects.com ○ ➦ aether architecture, HU, www.aether.hu ○ ➦ AG Planum, HR, www.agplanum.com ○ ➦ Alicia Velazquez, NL, www.in-transition.net ○ ➦ analog, HR ○ ➦ André Campos.Joana Mendes – Arquitectos, PT, http://ajarquitectos.com ○ ➦ Andreas Angelidakis, GR, www.angelidakis.com ○ ➦ Andres Jaque Arquitectos, ES, http://andresjaque.net ○ ➦ Anorak, BE, www.anorak.be○ ➦ Antonella Mari, IT, https://antonella-mari.divisare.pro ○ ➦ Anttinen Oiva Arkkitehdit Oy, FI, www.aoa.fi ○ ➦ Arbau studio, IT, www.arbau.org ○ ➦ ARCHIPELAGOS, US ○ ➦ Architekt Clemens Kirsch, AT, www.ckirsch.at ○ ➦ Architekt Ferdinand Certov, AT ○ ➦ Architekt Michael Wallraff, AT, www.wallraff.at ○ ➦ Architetto Francesco Matucci, IT ○ ➦ Ark Arhitektura Krusec, SI, http://arhitekturakrusec.si ○ ➦ Arhitektuuri Agentuur, EE, www.arhitektuuriagentuur.ee ○ ➦ ArmaniCogulStudio, ES ○ ➦ Artgineering, NL, www.artgineering.nl ○○●● ➦ ATELIER BRÜCKNER, DE, www.atelier-brueckner.de ➦ ATELIER H-2-A, AT, www.h-2-a.com ○ ➦ ateliermob, PT, www.ateliermob.com ○ ➦ A T M O S F E R A, HR, www.atmosfera.hr ➦ Audrius Ambrasas Architects, LT, www.ambrasas.lt ○ ➦ Avatar Architettura, IT, https://avatar-architettura.divisare.pro ○ ➦ **B** b4architects, IT, www.b4architects.com ○ ➦ BARAK architekti, SK, www.barak.sk ●○ ➦ baukuh, IT, www.baukuh.it ○ ➦ Benjamin Bradnansky, SK ➦ Bernardo Rodrigues, PT ○ ➦ Berschneider+Berschneider, DE, www.berschneider.com ● ➦ BIG CPH, DK, https://big.dk ○ ➦ Birgitte Louise Hansen, NL ● ○ ➦ bk2a, DE ➦ blacklinesonwhitepaper, ZA ○ ➦ blauraum architekten, DE, www.blauraum.eu ○ ➦ bof architekten, DE, www.bof-architekten.de ○ ➦ Buerger Katsota architects, GR, www.buerger-katsota.com ○ ➦ Büro 21, AT○ ➦ Büro Popp, DE, http://buropopp.com ○ ➦ **C** Caramel, AT, www.caramel.at ○○ ➦ Casanova + Hernandez, NL, www.casanova-hernandez.com ➦ Catalin Berescu, RO ➦ ch+ architekci, PL, www.chplus.pl ○ ➦ Chris Briffa Architects, MT, www.chrisbriffa.com ○ ➦ CITYFÖRSTER. Netzwerk für Architektur, DE, www.cityfoerster.net ○ ➦ Claudio Nardi Architects, IT, www.claudionardi.it ○ ➦ Cláudio Vilarinho, PT, www.claudiovilarinho.com ○ ➦ CUARTOYMITAD ARQUITECTURA, ES, http://cuartoymitad.es ○ ➦ complizen Planungsbüro, DE, www.complizen.de ○○●● ➦ Contentismissing Studio, IT, www.contentismissing.net ○ ➦ CVDB arquitectos, PT, www.cvdbarquitectos.com ○ ➦ CZstudio, IT, www.czstudio.com ○ ➦ **D** DCm-STUDIO, US, www.dcm-studio.net (now operating as EPIPHYTE Lab, http://epiphyte-lab.com) ●○ ➦ DAAR, PS, www.decolonizing.ps ➦ dekleva gregoric arhitekti, SI, www.dekleva-gregoric.com ○○○ ➦ deltArCHI, GR, www.deltarchi.com ○○○ ➦ DEMO architects, IT/NL ○ ➦ Die Baupiloten, DE, www.baupiloten.com ➦ Dietrich | Untertrifaller Architekten, AT, www.dietrich.untertrifaller.com ○ ➦ DORELL.GHOTMEH.TANE/ARCHITECTS, FR, www.dandorell.com ○ ➦ Doris Grabner, DE, www.grabner-huber-lipp.de ○ ➦ DRAFTWORKS* architects, GR, www.papermachines.blogspot.com ○ ➦ DSDHA, GB, www.dsdha.co.uk ○ ➦ Duncan McCauley, DE, www.duncanmccauley.com ○ ➦ DUS, NL, http://houseofdus.com ○ ➦ DVA:STUDIO, RS, www.dvastudio.rs ○ ➦ **E** ecosistema urbano, ES, www.ecosistemaurbano.com ○ ➦ elastik, SI, www.elastik.net ○○○○ ➦ Encore heureux, FR, http://encoreheureux.org ●○ ➦ enota, SI, www.enota.si,1 ➦ Éric Lapierre Experience, FR, www.ericlapierre.com ○ ➦ esestudio, ES ○ ➦ espace gaïa, FR, www.espace-gaia.com ➦ EXYZT, FR, www.exyzt.org ○ ➦ eyland 07, DE, www.eyland.de ➦ **F** FABRICA, SK, www.fabrica.sk ●○ ➦ Feilden Clegg Bradley Studios, GB, www.fcbstudios.com ➦ feld72, AT, www.feld72.at ○○●● ➦ FMarchitecture, DK/ES/IT, www.francescomatucci.com ○ ➦ Force 4, DK, www.force4.dk ○ ➦ fordewind architecture, BG, www.fordewind.com ○ ➦ FoS – Fabrication of Space, SK ➦ frank, rieper, AT, www.frank-rieper.at○ ➦ franz zt gmbH, AT, www.franzundsue.at ○ ➦ FRIEDHELM KUCHE 360, DE, www.friedhelmkuche360.de ○ ➦ Friessnegg & Rainer, AT ○○ ➦ FROETSCHER LICHTENWAGNER, AT, www.froetscherlichtenwagner.at ○ ➦ fündc, ES, www.fundc.com ○ ➦ **G** G H 3, AT, www.gh3.at ○ ➦ G.studio, FR, www.gstudioarchitecture.com ○○○ ➦ GBA_Studio, IT, www.gbastudio.it ○ ➦ Guedes + DeCampos, PT, www.guedesdecampos.com ○ ➦ GUIDO CIMADOMO ARCHITECTOS, ES, www.cimadomo.com ○ ➦ **H** Heikkinen-Komonen Architects, FI, www.heikkinen-komonen.fi ○ ➦ Hempel Architekten, DE, www.district-six.de ○ ➦ heneghan peng architects, IE, www.hparc.com ●○ ➦ heri&salli, AT, www.heriundsalli.com ➦ Heribert Gies Architekt, DE, www.gies-architekten.de ○ ➦ hobby a., AT, www.hobby-a.at ○ ➦ HUB, NL, www.hub.eu ○ ➦ Hütten und Paläste, DE, www.huettenundpalaeste.de ●○ ➦ **I** ice – ideas for contemporary environments, DE, www.icehk.com ○ ➦ Interaction Design Lab, IT, www.interactiondesign-lab.com○○ ➦ IDU_architecture, HK (CN), www.iduarchitecture.com ➦ Impromptu Arquitectos, PT ○ ➦ Indrek Peil Arhitektid, EE ○ ➦ Innocad, AT, http://innocad.at ○ ➦ IVANISIN. KABASHI. ARHITEKTI, HR ○ ➦ **J** J. Pierre Pranlas – Descours Architecture, FR, www.pdaa.eu ○ ➦ Jan Magasanik, CZ ➦ jmp land.art.scape.architecture, ES ○ ➦ Joan Anguita with Xavier Vancells Arquitectura, ES ○ ➦ John Lonsdale Architect, NL, www.johnlonsdale.org ○ ➦ jomad integrative architektur, DE, www.jomad.de ➦ Josep Cargol, ES ○ ➦ Joze Peterkoc, SI ○ ➦ **K** K2A ARCHITECTURE, BE, www.k2a.be ○ ➦ Kaden Klingbeil, DE ○ ➦ K-architectures, FR, www.k-architectures.com ○ ➦ Atelier Kempe Thill, NL, www.atelierkempethill.com ● ➦ KENGO KUMA AND ASSOCIATES, JP, http://kkaa.co.jp ○ ➦ Kombinat arhitekti, SI, www.kombinat-arhitekti.si ○ ➦ ksa, SK, http://ksaarchitects.net ○ ➦ **L** lehner en gunther, NL, www.legu.nl ○○ ➦ leit-werk, GB, www.leit-werk.com ○○ ➦ Letilović/Vlahović, HR ○ ➦ LIQUIFER Systems Group, AT, www.liquifer.at ○ ➦ liverani/molteni architetti, IT, www.liverani-molteni.com ○ ➦ LÖHMANN'S, NL, www.loehmann.nl ○ ➦ LOHER/MISKOVIC/RAJCIC, HR ➦ LOOS ARCHITECTS, NL, www.loosarchitects.nl ○○ ➦ lotus Architects, IE, www.lotusarchitects.com ○ ➦ **M** M41LH2, FI ○ ➦ ma.lo architectural office, AT, www.ma-lo.eu ○ ➦ Ma0, IT, www.ma0.it ○ ➦ Maechtig Vrhunc Arhitekti, SI, www.mvarch.

com ● ○ ➥ MaP, IT, www.map-studio.it ○ ○ ➥ MAP office, CN ○ ○ ○ ➥ Mária Topolčanská, CZ ● ○ ○ ➥ Marjan Zupanc, SI ○ ➥ MBA/S, DE, www.mbas.de ➥ McCullough Mulvin Architects, IE, www.mcculloughmulvin.com ○ ➥ McDowell+Benedetti, GB ○ ➥ MDU architetti, IT, www.mduarchitetti.it ○ ○ ➥ Mert Eyiler Mimarlik,TR ○ ➥ Mérték Architectural Studio, HU ○ ➥ Metak arkitektura tailerra, ES, http://metakarkitekturatailerra.blogspot.com ○ ○ ➥ MiAS arquitectes S.L., ES, www.miasarquitectes.com ○ ➥ Michael STRAUSS, AT, www.ms-a.at ○ ➥ Miha Kajzelj, SI ○ ➥ Mimarlar Tasarim,TR, www.mimarlar.com ○ ➥ MINUSPLUS, HU, www.minusplus.hu ○ ➥ MIOC&PRLIC, HR ○ ➥ mod. Land, IT, www.modland.it ○ ➥ monochrome architects, SI, www.monochrome.si ● ○ ➥ morePlatz, NL, www.moreplatz.com ➥ morgenbau, AT ○ ➥ Mr. Fung, DE, www.mrfung.com ○ ➥ MUTOPIA, DK, http://mutopia.dk ○ ➥ NABITO ARQUITECTURA, ES ○ ➥ nan architects & landscapes, AT ➥ nbAA, PT ○ ➥ nEmoGruppo architetti, IT, www.nemogruppo.com ○ ➥ Nicolas Maurice Architect, FR ○ ➥ no w here, DE, www.nowherearchitekten.de ● ○ ○ ○ ➥ nodo17 architects, ES, www.nodo17.com ○ ➥ nonconform architektur vor ort, AT, www.nonconform.at ● ● ○ ○ ○ ○ ➥ NPS arquitectos, PT, http://npsarquitectos.com ○ ➥ nug arquitectes, ES, www.nugarch.com ○ ➥ Nuno Abrantes Arquitecto, PT, www.nunoabrantes.eu ○ ➥ **O** od-do arhitekti, SR ○ ➥ office 03, DE, www.office03.de ○ ➥ offshore, AT ○ ○ ➥ ogris+wanek architekten, AT ● ○ ○ ○ ➥ OK PLAN ARCHITECTS, CZ, www.okplan.cz ○ ➥ One Architecture, NL, www.onearchitecture.nl ○ ➥ osa – office for subversive architecture, AT/DE/GB, www.osa-online.net ● ○ ○ ○ ➥ **P** KÄPI AND SIMO PAAVILAINEN ARCHITECTS, FI ○ ➥ PALATIUM Stúdió, HU, www.palatiumstudio.hu ○ ➥ PARASITESTUDIO, RO, www.parasitestudio.com ○ ➥ Paula Santos | arquitectura, PT, http://paulasantos-arquitectura.com ○ ➥ Paulo Moreira, PT, www.paulomoreira.net ○ ➥ PEANUTZ ARCHITEKTEN, DE, www.peanutz-architekten.de ○ ➥ PEDRO BARATA CASTRO, PT ○ ➥ Pedro Campos Costa, PT, http://camposcosta.com ○ ➥ Peter Lang, IT/US, www.petertlang.net ○ ➥ PL Barman Architekten, CH, www.plbarmanarch.com ○ ➥ plusminusarchitects, SK, www.plusminusarchitects.com ○ ➥ PPAG, AT, www.ppag.at ○ ➥ **Q** querkraft architekten, AT, www.querkraft.at ○ ➥ **R** RAFAA architecture & design, CH, www.rafaa.ch ○ ➥ RAHM architekten, AT, www.rahmarchitekten.at ○ ➥ RAUM, SK ○ ➥ RICARDO DEVESA, ES, www.ricardodevesa.com ○ ➥ raumlaborberlin, DE, www.raumlabor.net ○ ➥ roberto cremascoli, edison okumura e marta rodrigues architectos, PT, www.corarquitectos.com ○ ➥ **S** schneider + schumacher, DE, www.schneider-schumacher.de ○ ➥ Santiago Cirugeda, ES, www.recetasurbanas.net ○ ➥ servo, SE/US, www.servo-stockholm.com, www.servo-la.com ● ○ ➥ SHARE architects, AT, www.share-arch.com ○ ○ ○ ○ ➥ SHIBUKAWA EDER Architects, AT, www.shibukawaeder.com ○ ➥ SKUPINA, CZ, www.skupina.org ○ ➥ smertnik kraut, AT, www.smertnikkraut.at ○ ➥ SOLID architecture, AT, www.solidarchitecture.at ➥ Spacelab/Urban Body, NL ○ ➥ spado architects, AT, www.spado.at ○ ➥ SPIN +, IT/GB ○ ○ ➥ sporaarchitects, HU, www.sporaarchitects.hu ○ ➥ sspg arquitectos, PT, www.evora.net/sspg ○ ➥ Stalker/Osservatorio Nomade, IT, www.osservatorionomade.net ● ➥ STEALTH.unlimited, NL, http://stealth.ultd.net ○ ➥ Studio Irander, SE, http://studioirander.com ○ ➥ Studio Marco Vermeulen, NL, www.marcovermeulen.nl ○ ➥ Studio Miessen,GB, www.studiomiessen.com ○ ➥ STUDIO TZ +, DE ○ ➥ STUDIO UP, HR, www.studioup.hr ○ ➥ Studio Verne, BE ➥ studioata, IT, www.studioata.com ○ ➥ STUDYO ARCHITECTs, DE, www.studyo.org ○ ➥ **T** TEAM 0708, HU ○ ➥ terrain: loenhart&mayr, DE, www.terrain.de ○ ➥ TOPOTEK 1, DE, www.topotek1.de ○ ➥ TOUCHY-FEELY, DE, www.touchy-feely.net ○ ➥ transparadiso.com ○ ➥ TREUSCH architecture, AT, www.treusch.at ○ ➥ TRI, RS ○ ➥ TRIBU architecture, CH, www.tribu-architecture.ch ● ○ ➥ TWO IN A BOX ARCHITEKTEN, AT, www.twoinabox.at ○ ➥ **U** ü.NN, DE, www.uenn.de ● ○ ➥ Urban Platform, BE, www.urbanplatform.com ○ ➥ Urbanberry, NL, www.urbanberry.com (now working as NEZU AYMO architects, NL, www.nezuaymo.com) ○ ○ ➥ **V** Vallo Sadovsky Architects, SK, www.vallosadovsky.sk ○ ➥ Valvomo Architects, FI, www.valvomo.com ○ ○ ➥ Various Architects, NO, http://variousarchitects.no ○ ➥ Veit Aschenbrenner Architekten, AT, www.vaarchitekten.com ○ ○ ➥ Lpp, BE, www.pierret-ledroit.com ○ ➥ VIZE, CZ, www.vize.com ● ○ ➥ vora arquitectura, ES, http://www.vora.cat ○ ➥ VROA architekci, PL, www.vroa.pl ○ ➥ VYSEHRAD atelier, CZ, www.vysehrad-atelier.cz ● ○ ➥ **W** WHIM architecture, NL, www.whim.nl ○ ➥ Winfried Brenne Architekten, DE, www.brenne-architekten.de ○ ➥ **X** x architekten, AT, www.xarchitekten.com ○ ➥ Xavier Vancells Arquitectura XVA, ES, www.xvarquitectura.com ○ ➥ **Y** Yannis Aesopos, GR, www.aesopos.net ○ ➥ YF architekten, AT, www.ypsilonef.com ○ ➥ **Z** ZEROarchitects, ES, www.areazero.info ○ ➥ zerozero, SK, www.zerozero.sk ○ ➥ zoka zola, US, www.zokazola.com ○ ➥ ZONE Architects, GB, www.zonearchitects.co.uk ○ ➥

● Chapter 1	○ Survey 1
○ Chapter 2	○ Survey 2
● Chapter 3	○ Survey 3
● Chapter 4	○ Survey 4
○ Chapter 5	○ Survey 5

Editors

Silvia Forlati, Vienna, AT
Architect, studied and worked internationally. Set up
SHARE architects in Vienna with Hannes Bürger and
Thomas Lettner. Aside from the architecture practice,
her activities include teaching and research.
www.share-arch.com

Anne Isopp, Vienna, AT
Architectural journalist, studied architecture at TU Graz
and TU Delft. She writes for newspapers, architectural
journals and magazines. Since 2009 she is editor-in-
chief of Zuschnitt magazine.
www.anneisopp.at
www.zuschnitt.at

Astrid Piber, Amsterdam, NL
Architect, studied in Austria, Canada and the USA, and
is now based in Amsterdam. Since 2008, she has been a
partner at UNStudio, Amsterdam and Shanghai. Besides
practicing architecture, her interests are business models within the architectural profession.

Assistant Editors

Simone Kunz, Munich, DE, and Vienna, AT
M.A. International Cultural and Business Studies, M.A.
Fine Arts. Works in the field of contemporary art.
www.simone-kunz.de

Bahanur Nasya, Vienna, AT
Head of organization of the Wonderland – platform for
european architecture. At present she is working on her
master's thesis on traditional architecture at the Vienna
University of Technology.

Marie-Terese Tomiczek, Vienna, AT,
and Panama City, PA
Architect. Graduated from the Vienna University of
Technology and has collaborated with Wonderland
since 2006. She was the editorial assistant of the
'Going Public' issue of Wonderland Magazine and
made decisive contributions to several of the
Wonderland surveys. She works in Panama now.

Martina Zuzaňáková, Vienna, AT, and Řehlovice, CZ
Cultural manager and curator. She curated several exhibitions and projects with a focus on architecture and
contemporary art. She currently works as an assistant
editor for Zuschnitt magazine (AT) and as a curator in
Cultural Center of Řehlovice (CZ).

Writers

Paul Abelsky, Moscow, RU
Studied history and architecture at Yale University
before moving to Russia in 2004. Writes about Russian
architecture and politics.

Karl Amann, Stuttgart, DE
Partner of no w here architekten
www.nowherearchitekten.de

Nishat Awan, Berlin, DE, and London, GB
Senior Lecturer of Architecture at the University of
Sheffield. Her research explores contemporary borders
and migration with a focus on modes of visual representation and forms of research that allow an ethical
engagement with places at a distance.

Gabriela Barman-Krämer, Solothurn, CH
Graduate from ETH Zurich both in Architecture and
Urban Planning. Head of urban and environmental
planning in the City of Solothurn, Switzerland.
Between 2003 and 2010, she was a research and
teaching assistant with the Chair of the History of
Urban Design, ETH Zurich.

Ulrich Beckefeld, Vienna, AT
Lives and works as an architect in Vienna. He is a
partner of osa-office for subversive architecture.
www.osa-online.net

Cătălin Berescu, Bucharest, RO
Cătălin Berescu studied at the Ion Mincu University of
Architecture and Urbanism, Bucharest. He worked as
an editor for several architectural journals, did artistic
interventions in public space and teaches about new
media and architecture as well as other theoretical
issues. His main research and intervention field is
extreme poverty housing and housing discrimination.
He is also an adobe buildings enthusiast.

Bert Bielefeld, Dortmund, DE
The principal of a planning office based in Dortmund
(bertbielefeld & partner) and also teaches at the
University of Siegen, Germany. He has done scholarly
research in the area of architectural export for many
years and authored numerous lectures and publications
in the field.
www.bertbielefeld.com

Anneke Bokern, Amsterdam, NL
After completing a Master's degree in Art History
in Berlin, she moved to Amsterdam in 2000. She has
worked as a freelance journalist since 2001, writing
about architecture and art and design for international
magazines and newspapers. She also runs architecture
tour company architour.
anneke-bokern.tilda.ws

Eva Boudewijn, Amersfoort, NL
Studied sociology of organizations and is an expert on multiparty cooperation and conflict and non-executive supervision. As an independent team coach of project and executive teams, she focuses on intertwining a business approach and the human scale as well as stimulating organizational and individual change and innovation. For many years she worked, as a business consultant and trainer, on the development of communicative, managerial, commercial and co-operating skills of architects, designers and project managers.

Roland Broekhuizen, Amersfoort, NL
Senior partner of Motion Consult, a coaching agency for team and organizational development. He focuses on communication in and interaction between team members. He facilitates (project) team building during design and construction projects. He also works as a conflict coach.
www.motionconsult.nl

Walter M. Chramosta, Vienna, AT
Architecture critic for national and international papers and professional journals, consultant for competition matters, studied architecture, structural engineering and philosophy at the Vienna University of Technology, design and realization of several industrial and residential building projects in Austria.

Mariela Cvetić, Belgrade, RS
Artist, art theorist and engineer. Associate professor at the Faculty of Architecture, Belgrade, and at the University of Arts.

Tore Dobberstein, Halle and Berlin, DE
Graduated in business administration and economic ethics and has international experience in economic development. He has worked with complizen Plaungsbüro, office for architecture, communication and urban development, since 2003. Moderation, public space, and urban culture are the topics of his teaching activities in Weimar and Vienna.
www.complizen.de

Heribert Gies, Darmstadt, DE
Graduate of TU Darmstadt and ETH Zurich. Works as an architect and Professor of Design and Building Construction at the Frankfurt University of Applied Sciences. Taught in Switzerland, the USA, and Germany.

Mark Gilbert, Vienna, AT
Architect and urbanist; he is lecturer and critic for Theory and Design, Institute for Architectural Sciences, Vienna University of Technology, and a founding member of the interdisciplinary planning firm trans_city. As a planner, he has been active both internationally and in Vienna; he has been author and editor of numerous books, studies and essays on architecture and urbanism.
www.trans-city.at

Roland Gruber, Vienna, AT
Studied architecture in Graz, Linz, Oslo, Vienna and Zurich and culture management in Salzburg. Since 2006 lecturerships at TU Vienna and the University of Art and Design Linz. Founding partner of nonconform together with Peter Nageler und Caren Ohrhallinger.
www.nonconform.at

Laurent Guidetti, Lausanne, CH
Architecture graduate from the École polytechnique fédérale(EPF) in Lausanne, Switzerland. Founded TRIBU architecture in 2000, well-known in Switzerland for its activities in urban planning, communication and political commitment. As a member of TRIBU, he authored a number of publications, taught architecture in several schools, and won many team competitions.
www.tribu-architecture.ch

Tina Gregorič, Ljubljana, SL
Architect, professor, curator and author. She founded Dekleva Gregoric Architects in 2003 together with Aljoša Dekleva. In 2014, she was appointed Professor of Architecture at the TU Vienna.
dekleva-gregoric.com

Johanna Gunther and Mathias Lehner, Amsterdam, NL
Mathias and Johanna founded LEGU Architects, a multidisciplinary design office, in 2004. LEGU works in architecture, landscape and urban planning. They teach at the Amsterdam University of Applied Science and the Amsterdam Academy of Architecture.
www.legu.nl

Gonzalo Herrero Delicado, London, GB
Gonzalo Herrero Delicado is an architect, curator and writer based in London. He currently is curator for the architecture program at the Royal Academy of Arts. His writing has been published in Domus, Abitare, Neo2, Mark, Blueprint, Arquine, A10, a.o. His current research work explores how domestic space is transformed in response to political, social and technological changes.

Hans Ibelings, Montreal/Toronto, CA
Architectural historian and critic, lecturer at the Daniels
Faculty of Architecture of the University of Toronto
and editor and publisher of the Architecture Observer.
Between 2004 and 2012 he was the editor and publisher
of A10 new European architecture, which he founded
together with Arjan Groot. He is the author of several
books, including /European Architecture since 1890/.
He has been editorial advisor to the Wonderland magazines and manual.
www.architectureobserver.eu

Laura Iloniemi, London, GB
Laura Iloniemi is a publicist representing architecture
practices in the UK, continental Europe, and the USA.
In 2004, she published her first book Is it all about
Image? How PR works in Architecture. Iloniemi has
guest-edited an issue of Architectural Design (AD)
looking at the identity and branding of architecture
practices.
www.iloniemi.co.uk

Frank Peter Jäger, Berlin, DE
Has his own PR agency, Archikontext; works as a publicist for architects and consults practices in matters of
office development and marketing. Holds continuing
education seminars for professional associations and
on his own. He also is a writer; most recent publication
Der neue Architekt, Munich, 2008.
www.archikontext.de

Kari Juhani Jormakka, Vienna, AT
Professor for Architecture Theory at the Vienna
University of Technology until his death in 2013. He has
taught at several international universities, includ-
ing Harvard Graduate School of Design, the Bauhaus
University in Weimar, Ohio State University, University
of Illinois at Chicago, and Tampere University of
Technology.

Jānis Lejnieks, Riga, LV
Architect and editor-in-chief of the magazine Latvijas
architektura, curator of exhibitions, author of books on
20th century architecture and planning, independent
nominator for the Mies van der Rohe Award, was founding director of the Latvian Museum of Architecture.

Iva Kovacic, Vienna, AT
Associate Professor and head of research group for
Integrated Planning, at the Institute of Interdisciplinary
Construction Process Management, Faculty of Civil
Engineering, TU Vienna. She promotes research-based
teaching at the Integrated Design Lab, and is a member
of Center for Geometry and Computational Design. She
is also lecturer at University Stuttgart and University
of Zagreb.

Sigrid Mannsberger-Nindl, Vienna, AT
Project manager in national and international consulting
at the interface of education and the labor market, works
for the Vienna-based 3s corporate consulting agency and
has, to date, been responsible for more than one hundred
labor market needs and acceptance analyses about study
programs as well as qualification needs analyses.
www.3s.co.at

Beatrice Manzoni, Milan, IT
She is Associate Professor of Practice of Leadership,
Organization and Human Resources at SDA Bocconi
School of Management in Milan. Her research and
professional interests relate to managing creative
professional service firms (with a focus on architectural
firms) and to fostering creativity in teams.

Stefano Nicolin, Treviso, IT
Lawyer with expertise in international and EU law.
He practices and teaches in Italy.

Michael Obrist, Vienna, AT
Member of feld72 – collective for architecture and
urban strategies, based in Vienna. Since 2018,
Professor at the TU Vienna, Department of Housing
and Design.
www.feld72.at

Triin Ojari, Tallinn, EE
Critic and architectural historian, 2000-2012 worked
as editor-in-chief of the Estonian architectural review
MAJA. Since 2013, she has been the director of Museum
of Estonian Architecture. She has written on 20th
century Estonian architecture, contemporary housing
and urban design.

Osamu Okamura, Prague, CZ
Architect, curator of Shared Cities: Creative Momentum,
correspondent of A10 new European architecture Coop,
lecturer at Architectural Institute in Prague (ARCHIP),
member of Board of Directors of the Czech Architecture
Foundation, member of the Commission for Urban
Planning, Architecture and Public Space of the District
Council for Prague's 7th district. 2013–2017 program
director of reSITE, an international festival and conference on more livable cities, 2005–2012 editor-in-chief
of architecture magazine ERA21.

Georg Pendl, Innsbruck, AT
President of the ACE (Architects' Council of Europe,
www.ace-cae.eu), former chairman of the Competitions
Workgroup of the ACE (Architects' Council of Europe,
www.ace-cae.org), former president of the Federal
Chamber of Architects and Engineers. As an architect,
he set up his own office, pendlarchitects, in 2004.
www.pendlarchitects.at

Eric Poettschacher, Berlin, DE
Started a consultancy in 1994 and developed a
omprehensive method called Money & Meaning to
tackle the specific management challenges of the
creative economy. From 2006 to 2013, he was CEO and
mastermind behind Shapeshifters, a network made to
support creative professionals with global business
opportunities. Currently, he also works as a producer
focusing on the subject of energy literacy.
www.ericpoettschacher.com
www.energiesunited.com

Paul Rajakovics, Vienna, AT
Architect and urbanist, has been a partner of
transparadiso with artist Barbara Holub (since 2005).
His text 'About poaching' (page 38) is partly based on
his doctoral dissertation as well as on transparadiso's
engagement with the programmatic expansion of the
architect's professional field and the development of
new tactics in urbanism and architecture.
www.transparadiso.com

Daria Ricchi, Florence, IT
Studied architecture in Florence, now works as an
architectural critic and historian. Currently a Phd
student at Princeton focusing on the avantgarde.
Contributor of the Giornale dell'Architettura and A10,
among other magazines. Published a monograph book
about Diller and Scofidio published by Skira (2007).

Tatjana Schneider, Sheffield, GB
She is currently head of the Institute for History and
Theory of Architecture and the City (GTAS) at the
Technical University Braunschweig in Germany. Her
work focuses on the social and political production
of space. She was a founding member of the workers'
cooperative G.L.A.S. and is a founding member of the
AGENCY research group. She has lectured and published widely, including Flexible Housing with Jeremy
Till (2007) and Spatial Agency with Till and Nishat Awan
(2011).

Mária Topolčanská, Prague, CZ
Architect, studied in Bratislava and Barcelona, based
in Prague. Her activities include architectural practice,
research, teaching, and publishing.

Peter Torniov, Sofia, BG
Architect, studied in TU Vienna, now based in Sofia. In
2003 he founded +architecture ltd in Sofia and in 2005
a branch in Bucharest, together with his partner Stefan
Petkov. In 2010, he founded bureau XII in Sofia with
Milena Filcheva.
www.b-xii.net

Alicia Velázquez, Zurich, CH
Trained as an architect, her practice encompasses art
and design, exploring through performative crafting
intimate relations between human, non-human and
immaterial bodies.
www.aliciavelazquez.com

Łukasz Wojciechowski, Wroclaw, PL
Established VROA architects together with Marta Mnich
in 2003, he has been design tutor at Wroclaw University,
in 2005 co-established the ReWritable Research Team.
www.vroa.pl

National professional organizations (EU)

AT
Bundeskammer der Architekten und Ingenieurkonsulenten
Karlsgasse 9/2, 1040 Vienna
www.arching.at

BE
Conseil National de l'Ordre des Architectes CN
Rue des Chartreux 19, bte 4, 1000 Brussels
www.ordredesArchitectes.be (FR)
www.architect.be (NL)

Fédération des Sociétés d'Architectes de Belgique FAB
Rue Ernest Allard, 21
1000 Bruxelles
www.fab-arch.be

BG
Chamber of Architects in Bulgaria CAB
6 Mihail Tenev Str., Fl.6, 1784 Sofia
www.kab.bg

Union of Architects in Bulgaria UAB
11, rue Krakra, 1504 SOFIA
http://bularch.eu

CH
Bund Schweizer Architekten Domus-Haus
Pfluggässlein 3, Postfach 907, 4001 Basel
www.bsa-fas.ch

CY
Cyprus Civil Engineers and Architects Association
24, Stasikratous St./Office 201–202, 1065 Nikosia
www.cceaa.org.cy

CZ
Czech Chamber of Architects
Josefská 34/6, 118 00 Prague 1
www.cka.cz

DE
Bundesarchitektenkammer BAK
Askanischer Platz 4, 10963 Berlin
www.bak.de

Architects' Delegation Germany-Bund
Deutscher Architekten BDA
Wilhelmine-Gemberg-Weg 6, 10179 Berlin
www.bda-architekten.de

Architects' Delegation Germany-Bund Deutscher Baumeister
Architekten und Ingenieure BDB
Willdenowstraße 6, 12203 Berlin
www.baumeister-online.de

Architects' Delegation Germany-Vereinigung
freischaffender Architekten VfA
Kurfürstenstrasse 130, 10785 Berlin
www.vfa-architekten.de

DK
Danish Architects' Association
Akademisk Arkitektforening
Abenraa 34, 1124 Copenhagen K
www.arkitektforeningen.dk

EE
Estonian Association of Architects
Põhja pst 27A, 10415 Tallinn
www.arhliit.ee

GR
Technical Chamber of Greece
Nikis 4, 10563 Athens
http://web.tee.gr

ES
Consejo Superior de los Colegios de
Arquitectos de España CSCAE
Paseo de la Castellana 12, 28046 Madrid
www.cscae.com

FI
Finnish Association of Architects
Runeberginkatu 5A, 00100 Helsinki
www.safa.fi

FR
Conseil National de l'Ordre des Architectes CNOATour
Maine Montparnasse – 33 Av. du Maine BP 154
75755 Paris Cedex 15
www.architectes.org

Syndicat d'Architecture SA
24 rue des Prairies, 75020 Paris
www.syndarch.com

Union Nationale des Syndicats Français d'Architectes UNSFA
29, Boulevard Raspail, 75007 Paris
www.unsfa.com

GB
Architects Registration Board
8 Weymouth Street, London, W1W 5BU
www.arb.org.uk

Royal Institute of British Architects
66 Portland Place, London, W1B 1AD
www.architecture.com

HR
Croatian Chamber of Architects CCA
Ulica grada Vukovara 271/II
10000 Zagreb
www.arhitekti-hka.hr

HU
Chamber of Hungarian Architects MEK
Ötpacsirta u. 2, 1088 Budapest
www.mek.hu

IE
Royal Institute of the Architects of Ireland RIAI
8 Merrion Square, Dublin 2
www.riai.ie

IT
Consiglio Nazionale degli Architetti, Pianificatori,
Paesaggisti e Conservatori
S. Maria dell'Anima 10, 00186, Rome
www.cnappc.it; www.awn.it

LT
Architects Association of Lithuania AAL
Kalvariju g. 1, 09310 Vilnius
www.architektusajunga.lt

Architects Chamber of Lithuania
Vilniaus str. 4, 01102 VILNIUS
www.architekturumai.lt

LU
Ordre des Architectes et des Ingénieurs Conseils
du Grand-Duché de Luxembourg OAI
6, Boulevard Grand-Duchesse Charlotte
1330 Luxembourg
www.oai.lu

LV
The Latvian Association of Architects LAA
Torna iela 11, 1050 Riga
www.latarh.lv

MT
Chamber of Architects & Civil Engineers of Malta
The Professional Centre
Sliema Road 127, Gzira GZR 1633
https://kamratalperiti.org

NL
Bureau Architectenregister BA
Postbus 85506, 2508 EC Den Haag
www.architectenregister.nl

Royal Institute of Dutch Architects BNA
Postbus 19606, 1000 GP Amsterdam
www.bna.nl

NO
Association of Consulting Architects in Norway ACA
Essendropsgate 3, 0368 Oslo
www.arkitektbedriftene.no

Norske Arkitekters Landforbund NAL
Josefines Gate 34, 0351 Oslo
www.arkitektur.no

PL
Krajowa Rada Izby Architektów
Ul Stawki 2A, 00-193 Warsaw
www.izbaarchitektow.pl

Association of Polish Architects SARP
ul. Foksal 2, 00-366 Warszawa
www.sarp.org.pl

PT
Ordem Dos Arquitectos OA
Travessa do Carvalho, 23, 1249-003 Lisboa
www.arquitectos.pt

RO
Architects' Chamber of Romania OAR
Str. Pictor Arthur Verona nr. 19
010312 Bucharest 1
www.oar.org.ro

SE
Architects Sweden
Storgatan 41, Box 5027, 102 41 Stockholm
www.arkitekt.se

Swedish Federation of Consulting Engineers and
Architects – STD, O Box 55545
www.std.se

SI
Chamber of Architecture and Spatial
Planning of Slovenia ZAPS
Vegova 8, 1000 Ljubljana
www.zaps.si

SK
Slovak Chamber of Architects SKA
Panská ulica 15, 811 01 Bratislava
www.komarch.sk

TR
Chamber of Architects of Turkey
Konur Sokak 4/2, 06650 Kizilay-Ankara
www.mimarlarodasi.org.tr

International organizations:

Architects' Council of Europe
29 Rue Paul Emile Janson, 1050 Brussels
www.ace-cae.eu

European Association for Architectural Education
www.eaae.be

The International Union of Architects
www.uia-architectes.org

About wonderland

wonderland – Platform for European Architecture is a network for the exchange of experience, information and knowledge for young and emerging architects, urbanists, designers, photographers, filmmakers, researchers, and many others across Europe, who deal with space and its distribution and design.

We see ourselves as both a core network, which is defined by the "active teams", and a wider, looser network that provides opportunity for exchange. Wonderland developed as a bottom-up project for and by young architects to connect with each other. The specific goal of the non-profit organisation is to facilitate transnational collaborative projects and create working opportunities beyond existing professional and cultural borders.

wonderland has developed three different formats to assist, encourage, and inspire emerging architectural professionals.

The Project Space is an on-site workshop where selected teams work on "real projects". The participative approach offers all actors, planners, developers, financers and administrators possibilities for exchange.

The discussion format Blind Date engages participants (architectural teams who have not previously known each other) with the moderator in an active in-depth conversation on a selected subject. The involvement of the audience is crucial, as they are the local experts and can provide participants with inside information.

The pop-up film festival movies in wonderland is intended to get people with no relationship to architecture also involved in the topics of space, design, urban issues, social challenges, and architecture.

wonderland members also initiate research projects. The results are shared with the public through publications, exhibitions, symposiums and the like. The organization also provides support or participates in transnational collaborations and promotes the teams' activities through digital media, exhibitions, and on-location collaboration.

wonderland is always looking to expand its network. Getting involved is easy. If you have architecture and space related expertise you can simply create your own profile on the digital platform. You can state the services and collaboration possibilities you have to offer. You can publish your content with the wide audience and followers of the network. You can participate in wonderland events throughout Europe and initiate projects with wonderland or partners and other teams of the association. For more information and membership options please check the wonderland homepage.

Bahanur Nasya, Head of Organization, www.wonderland.cx

#3 going public

#4 getting specialized

#5 making competitions

why make competitions

how to make competitions

what happens next

epilogue

This book has been made possible thanks to many people who have generously invested their time and energy in providing and editing the know-how of this manual.

*Each of the first 3 chapters were initially published as individual issues of the **Wonderland magazine**, and distributed throughout Europe as an insert in the magazine A10, New European architecture. The chief editors of the **Wonderland magazine** were Silvia Forlati, Anne Isopp, Astrid Piber. Editorial consultant was Hans Ibelings. Also involved in conceiving and producing the **Wonderland magazine** were: Ulrich Beckefeld, Tore Dobberstein, Roland Gruber, Elisabeth Leitner, Helmut Rainer-Marinello, Michael Obrist, Paul Rajakovics, Mária Topolčanská.*

The Wonderland magazines were supported by bAIK – Austrian Federal Chamber of Architects and Engineers (#1, #2, #3), City of Vienna (#1) European Commission under the Culture Programme 2000 (#1), Ordem dos Arquitectos (#3), Austrian Federal Chancellery, Arts Division (#1, #2) Sky Europe (#1, #2), Austrian Federal Ministry for Education, Arts, and Culture (#3), Representing Irish Architects (#3).

*Marie Therese Tomiczek was the editorial assistant for the third magazine. Anneke Bokern contributed to the initial conception of the fourth chapter 'Getting Specialized', and part of the ideas and materials were developed during the eponymous **Wonderland symposium 'Getting Specialized'** at the Architekturzentrum Wien in October 2008. **The symposion was supported by bAIK – Austrian Federal Chamber of Architects and Engineers and the Austrian Bundesministerium für Unterricht, Kunst und Kultur.***

*Most of the material and ideas for the fifth chapter 'Making competitions' were first collected for the **exhibition 'Deadline Today'**, and during the connected **Wonderland symposion 'Making Competitions. Within the limits, beyond the limits'** both taking place at the Architekturzentrum Wien in June 2009. The exhibition and the symposium were developed by Silvia Forlati / SHARE architects for Wonderland, in collaboration with Roland Gruber, Anne Isopp, Timea Csaba, Paul Rajakovics, Osamu Okamura, Mária Topolčanská.*

The project was developed in cooperation with bAIK – Austrian Federal Chamber for Architects and Engineers, KÉK – Hungarian Contemporary Architecture Centre , ACE – Architects' Council of Europe (special working group architectural design competitions), and EFAP – European Forum for Architectural Policies.

The idea of making a book out of the 3 magazines was proposed by Michael Obrist during the Wonderland assembly in Budapest in 2009.
The following contributions have been developed by the authors named with the coordination of the Wonderland platform as part of the project 'Underconstructions – Innovative architectural practices in Europe', financed by the European Commission under the Culture Programme (2007–2013). *'The Europan challenge for young architects', interview with Thomas Sieverts; 'Other productions of space', by Tatjana Schneider and Nishat Awan.*

The second edition was edited by Silvia Forlati and Anne Isopp, with the help of Martina Zuzaňáková in 2017 and 2018

Edited by	**wonderland** *platform for european architecture, Vienna, Austria*
	Silvia Forlati, Anne Isopp
	with Astrid Piber
Editorial consultant	*Hans Ibelings*
Editorial assistant	*Simone Kunz, Bahanur Nasya, Marie Therese Tomiczek, Martina Zuzaňáková*
Graphic Design	*Drahtzieher Design + Kommunikation, Barbara Wais, www.drahtzieher.at*
	(in collaboration with Marcus Sterz (FaceType), Corinna Wimmer,
	Stefanie Schwarzwimmer, Lena Jamkojian)
Translations	*James Roderick O'Donovan, Brian Dorsey, Jan Korbelik, Martin Thomas Pesl*
Copy-editing	*Erica Schenk, Michael Strand*
Surveys	*SHARE architects – Silvia Forlati, Hannes Bürger, Thomas Lettner with*
	Carmen Braun, Marie Therese Tomiczek, Timea Csaba, Simone Kunz

Library of Congress Control Number	*2018937571*

*Bibliographic information published by the German National Library
The German National Library lists this publication in the Deutsche
Nationalbibliografie; detailed bibliographic data are available on the
Internet at http://dnb.dnb.de.*

Acquisitions Editor	*David Marold, Vienna, Austria*
Project and Production Management	*Angela Fössl, Vienna, Austria*

© 2019 Birkhäuser Verlag GmbH, Basel	*P.O. Box 44, 4009 Basel, Switzerland*
	Part of Walter de Gruyter GmbH, Berlin/Boston
	www.birkhauser.com
	1st edition 2012: SpringerWienNewYork

Printed in Austria	*Holzhausen Druck GmbH, Wolkersdorf, Austria*

ISBN	*ISBN 978-3-0356-1552-4*
This publication is also available as an e-book	*ISBN PDF 978-3-0356-1538-8*

Supported by ⊇ Bundeskanzleramt

Arch+Ing
Federal Chamber of Architects and
Chartered Engeneering Consultants